NIKOLAI TOLSTOY

The author was born in England fifteen years after his father's escape from Russia after the Revolution. He lives with his family near Oxford.

Nikolai Tolstoy holds an MA in Modern History and is a Fellow of the Royal Society of Literature and an Honorary Associate Member of St Antony's College, Oxford. His previous books include VICTIMS OF YALTA, THE HALF-MAD LORD, STALIN'S SECRET WAR, THE TOLSTOYS and THE MINISTER AND THE MASSACRES.

sceptre

Nikolai Tolstoy

THE QUEST FOR MERLIN

First published in Great Britain in
1985 by Hamish Hamilton Ltd.

Coronet edition 1986

Sceptre edition 1988

Sceptre is an imprint of Hodder and
Stoughton Paperbacks, a division of
Hodder and Stoughton Ltd.

British Library C.I.P.

Tolstoy, Nikolai
    The quest for Merlin.
    1. Merlin – Legends – History and
criticism
    I. Title
    398'.352   PN686.M4

ISBN 0-340-42777-9

Printed and bound in Great Britain
for Hodder and Stoughton Paper-
backs, a division of Hodder and
Stoughton Ltd., Mill Road, Dunton
Green, Sevenoaks, Kent TN13 2YA
(Editorial Office: 47 Bedford
Square, London WC1B 3DP) by
Richard Clay Ltd., Bungay,
Suffolk. Photoset by Rowland
Phototypesetting Ltd., Bury St
Edmunds, Suffolk.

Contents

List of Illustrations

Acknowledgements

It would be impractical and invidious to record my gratitude to everyone who has helped me over the years in my quest. However I must single out the quite exceptionally generous advice and help received over a considerable period of time from friends and scholars (some sadly passed over to the *tír tairngiri*); these include Dr Rachel Bromwich, Professor James Carney, Mrs Nora K. Chadwick, Dr Kathleen Hughes, Professor A. O. H. Jarman, and Mr Dick Walden-Jones. Mrs Bromwich, in particular, read carefully through the first twelve chapters, making many valuable suggestions and saving me from as many solecisms. I alone, however, am responsible for any of the latter still remaining. Mrs Juliette Wood, Dr David Dumville, and Professor D. Ellis Evans kindly advised me on specific points; and I am grateful to Professor J. E. Caerwyn Williams for arranging to publish my article 'Merlinus Redivivus' in a forthcoming number of *Studia Celtica* (this will be a revised version of the paper I read in July 1983 at the Seventh International Congress of Celtic Studies.) In October 1982 at Kyung Hee University, Seoul, Professor Taegon Kim expounded to me from his unrivalled knowledge of the nature of shamanistic belief. From early days I recall with pleasure stimulating discussions with Mrs Iris Strick and her cousin Charles Richard Cammell, Charles Barrington, Michael Scott, and Richard Croft. Mr Lewis Edwards bequeathed me some precious books.

Finally I must thank my cousin Adrian Slack, who accompanied me with enthusiasm through the hills and hostelries of Dumfriesshire; and my dear wife Georgina, who patiently suffered two years and more of Merlin-mania.

He that made with his hond
Wynd and water, wode and lond;
Geve heom alle good endyng
That wolon listne this talkyng,
And y schal telle, yow byfore,
How Merlyn was geten and bore
And of his wisdoms also
And othre happes mony mo
Sum whyle byfeol in Engelonde.

(*Of Arthour and of Merlin*, c. 1260)

Preface

The Dark Ages in Britain have exerted a hold on me almost as long as I can remember. I vividly recall my first reading of the Arthurian legends in a finely illustrated children's version. We lived above an old fishing-village on the edge of the Atlantic. As I played among the rocks of the seashore, I saw gigantic figures reflected in the clouds; I paused to gaze out through sea-mists at the dark presence of Lundy on the Western horizon and I pictured a land of everlasting delights on a green hill above Bideford which I could see from my grand-parents' bedroom:

> 'Loud are birds, wet is the shore.
> Bright is the wave with its wide motion.
> That which youth believes –
> I would love to get it again,'

as the old Welsh poet sang.

However, I was fortunate in that my childhood was prolonged beyond the age which duty normally requires, and at nineteen and twenty the old enthusiasm overwhelmed me once again with all its pristine vigour. For nearly two years, after being invalided out of a brief and inglorious military career and before going up to university, I lived a happy, sort of limbo existence. During that time I taught in a cheerful, Evelyn Waugh-like school by the Thames at Pangbourne, thriving on the princely sum of £300 a year.

A pang of guilt crosses my mind as I think how little direct educational advantage my charges received at my hands. Of what use in the twentieth century are the old stories of Tristrem and Palamedes, the Questing Beast, and the deeds of Lancelot before Joyous Garde? But I had rejected the twentieth century, lock, stock and barrel; and today I still feel the same thrill whenever my eyes fall upon those inimitable opening words,

'Hit befel in the dayes of Uther Pendragon, when he was kynge of all Englond and so regned, that there was a myghty duke in Cornewaill that helde warre ageynst hym long tyme, and the duke was called the duke of Tyntagil . . .'

But eventually I found myself drawn behind the glitter and glow of the romances themselves to a mysterious hinterland glimpsed beyond the courts of kings and clangour of tournaments. It was the problem of *origins* that first fascinated and finally absorbed all my enthusiasm.

This idyll came to an end when my dear grandparents, to whom I owe more than I can say, sent me to Trinity College, Dublin. The principal sources of the Arthurian legend lay, as I now knew, deep in Britain's Celtic past, and the magnificent facilities of Trinity's library, together with the indulgent nature of my five years' leisurely course, allowed me to pursue my obsession with the minimum of interruption.

The Protestant and Ascendancy ethos which still obtained at Trinity in those days meant that Celtic studies were not accorded the status they deserved. Indeed, they only existed in the formidable shape of the late Professor David Greene, whose burly bearded form occasionally startled the impressionable daughters of Dun Laoghaire by emerging dripping naked from the sea, to all appearance the god Manannan mac Lír himself.

In my case this neglect was more than compensated for by the riches of Dublin's second-hand bookshops – above all, the dark sanctum presided over by my friend Mr Walsh at the back of Messrs Hodges, Figgis. For sums so trifling as now to appear incredible, I swiftly built up a Celtic library of books and offprints which has continued to grow ever since. My impressionable brain buzzed with questions of the language of the Picts, the antiquity of the Llywarch Hên cycle, the dates of St Patrick's mission, the geography of King Arthur's battles, and all the other assemblage of 'ye olde types' – as darling Susan Gregory, shaking her reddish-gold curls dubiously, chose to term them.

For long my enthusiasm was all for the elusive figure of the historical Arthur, but he was replaced in time by the more mysterious and challenging shade of the wizard Merlin. I see now that I was unconsciously reflecting the spirit of the times. In the 1950s religion, magic and mystery appeared to have been shuffled into the wings by the giant advances effected by the natural sciences. Since then, however, we have seen a reaction against a blind acceptance of the empirical method as the only source of knowledge. It began to be realised that the continuing illumination of dark areas had paradoxically obscured the extent to which vitally important aspects of cosmic existence remained unexplored – even perhaps inaccessible – to a narrowly rationalistic approach. Attempts to eradicate religious man as the independent factor in evolution have simply resulted in images as partial and lifeless as those of the proverbial tone-deaf man describing his impressions of a Beethoven symphony.

Initially, my quest for Merlin was motivated by a simple desire to establish whether or not there really existed an historical figure from whom the Merlin of legend derived. The first five chapters of the book are concerned with this question, which represents something of a detective story. Presuming that few readers are likely to be content with a mere assertion of opinion or superficial assumption of probability, I have been at pains to set out the evidence as fully and clearly as possible.

Two hundred years ago, Dr Johnson claimed that, 'all that is really *known* of the ancient state of Britain is contained in a few pages'. In one sense this could still be held to be true, if by 'known' is meant a generally-accepted historical chronicle of events. Modern scholars are less concerned with establishing a precariously-founded history, than in painstaking evaluation of the varied sources. Precisely how old is a given heroic elegy from the Welsh? In what circumstances and for what purpose was it written? Was it an original creation in its existing form, or does it reflect an older composition or convention?

Questions like these are being propounded by historians, philologists and archaeologists, and increasingly a broadly convincing picture is being built up of life, culture and history in fifth- and sixth-century Britain. It is one infinitely more satisfactory and solidly based than the enthusiastic narrative accounts provided by E. A. Freeman and J. R. Green in the last century, and misguidedly revived by the late John Morris in his *The Age of Arthur*.

For this reason I have attempted to explain the basis of my reasoning throughout. The ancient sources are quoted as extensively as possible, and the interpretations of modern scholars I hope fully taken into account. Only in this way can the reader judge the value of my conclusions. These are that Merlin was indeed an historical figure, living in what are now the Lowlands of

Scotland at the end of the sixth century A.D. I believe I can show
that he was an authentic prophet, most likely a druid surviving in
a pagan enclave of the North. Much of the early poetry attributed
to him in Welsh manuscripts is drawn, it seems most likely, from
an earlier body of authentic prophetic verse uttered by Merlin
himself. From this and other evidence a convincing composite
picture of the prophet can be reconstructed. Perhaps the single
most exciting (and unexpected) find was the discovery of the sacred
chalybeate spring on a mountainside in the wilderness of the former
Caledonian forest, where Merlin sought lonely refuge, bewailed
his exiled existence, and uttered those prophecies which, in embellished form, so profoundly affected the mind of mediaeval man.

In subsequent chapters I delve further into Britain's remote past
in an attempt to explain the significance of Merlin's historical
rôle as last heir of the druidic tradition. In a setting of Celtic
heathendom, Merlin's association with the bright culture-god Lug,
and the dark Lord of the Forest Cernunnos, explains much of what
is at first sight obscure in the early legend. And as we move further
back in time from the evening shadows of the Dark Age into the
night of Iron and Bronze Age Britain, it will be seen that even
there the discovery of the real Merlin casts a pallid gleam.

In the concluding chapters the investigation plunges deeper still
into the remote past, as the druidism to which Merlin stood heir
is shown to represent shamanistic cults extending back into the
palaeolithic era and beyond. In his ecstatic trance the shaman
ascends the Tree of Life to the Otherworld – a journey said finally
to have been undertaken by Merlin himself in a ritual self-sacrifice
paralleling in inexplicable fashion the deaths of the Celtic god Lug,
the Norse Odin, and even the Crucifixion of Christ.

Merlin is seen as an archetypal figure, known to anthropologists
as The Trickster. Embedded in man's unconscious mind since first
he developed the power of rational thought, he epitomises man
both in his transitional existence, part beast and part human, and
at the same time a Saviour who conveyed the vital spark of divinity
which raised man onto his feet to gaze out in awe into the void; a
being at once accorded godlike powers, and by the same token
piteously aware of his separation from divinity.

Finally, an extended epilogue attempts to place Merlin in this
cosmic setting. Is it really conceivable that the seer in his mantic
trance was able to transcend time and space, attaining unity with
the divine? It will be argued that, given the likely circumstances in
which man was created by God and attained consciousness, there

is abundant reason to believe that the subjective experience of the prophet-mystic is objectively real, and that the lonely ascent to Merlin's mountain spring, like the Stations of the Cross, represents a *rite de passage* symbolic of life itself, and its cyclical reunion with the infinite.

The story of Merlin has a strong historical basis. I argue that there was a real Merlin, of whom at one remove we catch a near-personal glimpse in an early and reliable account of a visit to one of his hieratic predecessors. The very places where he lived, fought and prophesied can be visited, little changed today in some cases after fourteen centuries.

But in addition to the Merlin of history, there is also a Merlin of myth. In popular usage the word 'myth' implies a mere fiction, possibly with an implication of deliberate untruthfulness. Here it is used throughout in the sense employed by anthropologists and historians of religion. A myth is a traditional story explanatory of archetypal truths – of the creation of the earth, of man's relationship with God, of the origins of social institutions, and so forth. Myths are revelations of man's condition, making an otherwise chaotic cosmos explicable and accessible in human terms. Frequently they account for the beginnings of things, though they are not exclusively concerned with the past.

In this sense, therefore, myth represents reality. It is possible, too, for myth and history to overlap, and for the same event to be seen in historical and mythical terms. For example, it is arguable that Jacob in the *Book of Genesis* was an historical figure, and so for that matter may have been his brother Esau. Their quarrel, too, may really have occurred, for aught we know. But the story in *Genesis* is overlaid by a myth, intended to account for the displacement of hunting communities by a nomadic pastoral culture.

Still more apposite, as I show in Chapter Eleven, is the example of the Crucifixion. Jesus died on the Cross as an atonement for man's sins, or alternatively as a divine self-sacrifice in recompense for the suffering of man. But he was also a human being, nailed to a wooden cross, 'who suffered under Pontius Pilate'. The same event was at once historical and mythical, and yet arguably in both senses 'true'. It is in this imprecise yet comprehensible sense that I employ the words 'myth' and 'mythical' throughout this book.

To return to Merlin. The story, mythical and historical, is not irrelevant to the times in which we live. Like ours, his was a time of upheaval, destruction and rebirth. Civilisation was collapsing in the face of barbarian invasions from the East. In 542–43 bubonic plague swept through all Europe as far as the British Isles, causing mortality in all likelihood proportionate to that resulting from a nuclear war. Cities were abandoned to dogs and crows, robbers infested the countryside, and ordered life everywhere appeared collapsing to its close. Educated men prognosticated and even welcomed the coming end of the world, and apocalyptic images and visions abounded. The catastrophic effect of all these destructive revolutions is graphically attested by the speed with which the British language spoken under the Romans changed to the parent form of Welsh still spoken at this day.

Amidst all this evidence of the ephemeral nature of terrestrial life, it is not surprising that people turned their thoughts to eternal truths, beside which the turmoil of war was but as the 'battle of kites and crows' – as Milton derisively termed the wars of early Britain. In the Matter of Britain it is Merlin's art which wards over the England of Uther and Arthur, and time and again he reappears as the archetypal enchanter, possessed of wisdom and power for those who seek him out. W. B. Yeats once confessed that, 'an obsession more constant than anything but my love itself was the need of mystical rites – a ritual system of evocation and mediation – to reunite the perception of the spirit, of the divine, with natural beauty'. Perhaps the time has come for a 'return to the beginnings', to the path of the perennial Master himself.

In Celtic society, poetry and prophecy fulfilled in large part an indissoluble function, and it was this mediation that the prophet exercised in the context of his cult. After complex and demanding initiatory rites, he became the inspired revealer of the divine will, as the god spoke through his medium. His prophecies were not concerned solely with expounding the future. The whole of time lay ranged beneath his view, and past, present and future passed before him as an indivisible whole. Much of the surviving prophetic material attributed to Merlin concerns the coming succession of kings in Britain. In their present form these lists appear to have been compiled retrospectively, a major purpose in doing so being to legitimise an existing royal line. Originally, however, their purpose was much deeper than a merely deceptive pragmatism of this sort might suggest.

The sacral kingship was the apex of a divinely-ordered world, the king being the earthly reflection and even incarnation of the supreme god. Thus Merlin's inspired prophecies of the ordered succession of coming kings possessed a deeply cosmic significance.

One monarch succeeds another, not as the result of hereditary chance or internecine conflict among the royal kinship, but as a crucial link in the chain which binds the natural and the supernatural, preserving balance and continuity. This cosmic balance maintained all things in harmonious equilibrium. It was known in Vedic India as *rta*, in ancient Egypt as *maat*, in Greece as *themis*, and in early Ireland as *fír flatha*. A hieroglyph representing the word *maat* symbolically depicts the primordial earth-mountain at Heliopolis, from which the world was created, and which Pharaohs ritually ascended at their accession. In the same way Merlin's royal prophecies were uttered, as will be demonstrated, from the edge of a great mountain in Dumfriesshire which formed the Sacred Centre or Navel of North Britain between the Roman Walls.

The concept of a cosmic order, expounded by the inspired prophet and symbolised by the divinely-ordained king, should not be viewed as superstition of no value to our own age. It is at our mortal peril that we abandon a subconscious wisdom acquired over thousands of generations, of whose true sources we can have but an intuitive feeling. For the central teaching of Merlin's prophecy is one which transcends history and assumes greater significance than the mere 'apprehension of historical facts'. In the words of the great Russian philosopher Nicholas Berdyaev, 'History stands still and settles in the past. Only a prophetic vision of the past can set history in motion; and only a prophetic vision of the future can bind the present and the past into a sort of interior and complete spiritual movement. Only a prophetic vision can re-animate the dead body of history and inform the lifeless static with the inner fire of spiritual movement.'

Nikolai Tolstoy
Berkshire, England, 1984.

1

The Matter of Britain

Britain's first bestseller dates from the year 1136. Breezily self-confident and enthusiastic, the author appears to have been convinced of success. He was not mistaken: public reaction was overwhelmingly favourable, and within a few years there can scarcely have been an educated person in the country who was not at least aware of the nature of the book. Even the author, however, is unlikely to have anticipated the lasting extent of his triumph, which was to fill not only his own age but that of centuries to come. Today, nearly eight hundred and fifty years later, Geoffrey of Monmouth's *History of the Kings of Britain* (*Historia Regum Britanniæ*) remains in print (in translation), and much of its story is familiar to people throughout the globe. It seems safe to hazard, too, that if the human race survives another eight centuries the story of King Arthur and his knights will ring still as fresh as it does today or did in the twelfth century.

The *Historia Regum Britanniæ* is (or purports to be) a history of the island of Britain from its first peopling about the year 1170 B.C. by the Britons, down to the tribulations of their descendants, the Welsh, after the death of King Cadwallader in Rome in 689 A.D. Writing at Oxford, Geoffrey was at pains in his introduction to disclaim direct authorship of the work, declaring himself to be merely the translator and editor of, 'a very ancient book in the British [i.e. Welsh] tongue', lent to him by the Archdeacon of Oxford. As Geoffrey pointed out, hitherto the world had known nothing, 'of those kings who lived here before the Incarnation of Christ, nor of Arthur, and many others who succeeded after the Incarnation.' True, there were oral recitations and traditions, but only now was it possible to provide a full and continuous narrative.

This indeed the *History* supplied in a manner far exceeding all expectation. The story starts with the arrival of Brutus, great-grandson of Aeneas the Trojan, at Totnes in Devonshire at the time when Eli was High Priest in Israel (c. 1170 B.C.). Brutus conquers Britain from the giants who have hitherto lived in undisputed occupation and, in fulfilment of a prophecy of the goddess Diana revealed to him in Greece, establishes a dynasty of kings with their capital at New Troy, later renamed *kaerlud* (i.e. London).

The history of Brutus' heirs is related in similar detail, successive kings founding cities, effecting conquests overseas, and providing a legal code. With the arrival of Julius Caesar the reader first reached familiar territory, but instead of the classical account of the subjugation of Britain to the Roman Empire we learn of proudly independent native kings refusing to pay the Roman tribute, and shaking off their oppressors' yoke. Thus a continuity, entirely absent in all previously accepted history, was established.

Eventually the Romans depart, and with their exit begins the most exciting section of the book. The monarchy (which seems to have been at least partially elective) is entrusted to Constantine, the legitimate heir. His son Constans is, however, treacherously assassinated at the instigation of a nobleman, Vortigern, who in turn assumes the throne. The two brothers of Constans, Aurelius Ambrosius and Uther Pendragon, flee to Brittany where they raise an army preparatory to asserting their legitimate rights. Terrified by this threat and that of a Pictish invasion in the north, Vortigern invites to Britain two Saxon mercenaries, Hengist and Horsa, with their followers. At a drunken feast Vortigern is consumed with lust for Hengist's daughter, Rowena, and marries her in return for fatal territorial concessions to her father.

But now the Saxons, having obtained a secure foothold in Britain, set about conquering the kingdom for themselves. The infatuated Vortigern flees to the recesses of Snowdonia, where he resolves to fortify an impregnable retreat. But toil as the workmen may, the foundations are no sooner erected than they are levelled overnight to the ground by some malign influence. Vortigern assembles his magicians (*magi*), and asks them what may be done to counter this misfortune. They tell him that the walls will never stand until a youth be found who never had a father; sprinkle his blood upon the stones, and all will be well. In South Wales the King's envoys find such a youth, whose name is Merlin. His mother conceived him when visited one night by an incubus, a demon inhabiting the aery space between moon and earth.

Merlin counters the magicians' claim by challenging them to reveal what lies beneath the soil on which the foundations had been laid. Baffled, they are obliged to allow him to uncover two fighting dragons in a concealed pond, of whose existence they had been unaware. At Vortigern's request, Merlin in a long prophetic speech explains the significance of this apparition, and relates it to the temporary victory of the Saxons, the subsequent resurgence of the Britons, and the history of the kings to come. Couched in allegorical and symbolic terms, the prophecy ends with the stars, winds and seas raging and dissolving in turmoil.

The first part of the prophecy speedily proves itself true, as Aurelius and Uther cross the sea with their army, hunting down and destroying Vortigern in his lair. They then turn on Hengist, who is killed likewise, and Aurelius rules as king. To honour a group of British nobles, treacherously slain at a conference by Hengist's guards, Aurelius decides to erect a great monument near Amesbury. When difficulties arise over the construction, Merlin is summoned to advise as before. He recommends an edifice of vast stones, at present in Ireland, as the only fitting memorial. Accompanying the expedition fitted out for the purpose, he employs magic arts which are alone sufficient to shift these stupendous boulders. Thus was erected the wonderful monument, 'known in the English language as Stonehenge'. Not long afterwards Aurelius is poisoned by a Saxon, but his brother Uther Pendragon utterly routs the remaining Saxons and rules as king.

Now began that marvellous chronicle which swiftly enthralled all chivalric Europe. At a triumphant feast in London, Uther fell desperately in love with Igerna, wife of Gorlois, Duke of Cornwall. His passion was so unrestrained that Gorlois took the precaution of depositing his lady in the cliff-castle of Tintagel, while he himself retired to a nearby stronghold, named Dimilioc.[1] The enraged Uther swiftly laid siege to it, but as time went by found himself unbearably frustrated by his inability to gain access to Igerna. Finally, he accepted advice to send for the resourceful Merlin. The wizard, by dint of his magical arts, transformed King Uther and himself into the likeness of Gorlois and one of his familiar henchmen. Geoffrey's admirably laconic but vivid style is well expressed in what follows:

'They then set forward on their way to Tintagel, at which they arrived in the evening twilight, and forthwith explained to the porter that the consul [Gorlois] was come; upon which the gates were opened, and the men let in. For what room for suspicion could there be, when Gorlois himself seemed to be there present?

The king therefore stayed that night with Igerna, and enjoyed his longed-for love-making, for she was deceived by his disguise, and the cunning and winning arts he employed. He told her he had left his own place besieged, purely to provide for the safety of her dear self and the stronghold she was in. Believing all he said, she denied him nothing which he desired. As a result she conceived that very night the famous Arthur, whose heroic exploits have rightly made his name renowned to all posterity.'

That same night too Gorlois was killed by Uther's men, as a result of which Uther was enabled to marry Igerna; though without revealing that he had lain with her before.

Other stories, familiar to all, tell of Arthur's upbringing at a nobleman's castle, in fulfilment of a promise made by Uther to Merlin, and of the subsequent revelation of his royal birth when he drew the sword from the stone. Geoffrey has none of this, however, and appears to imply that the marriage of Uther and Igerna followed so swiftly upon their night of illicit love that neither the Queen nor anyone else was ever aware of Uther's deception. Merlin does not feature again in the story, which goes on to tell of the wonderful court and Continental conquests of Arthur, of his death at the hands of a treacherous nephew in 542 at a battle by the River Camblan in Cornwall, and of his departure to the Island of Avallon to be cured of his wounds.

The reigns of succeeding kings are detailed, with their wars against the gathering power of the Saxons. The last real King of the Britons, Cadwallader, is advised by an angel that one day the Britons will triumph, but not yet; upon which Cadwallader retires to Rome. Thereafter the remnant of the Britons is confined to Wales and assumes the appellation 'Welsh', while the more stable and industrious Saxons under the great Athelstane inherit the kingdom. Geoffrey concludes by saying that this is as far as his book takes him, and he leaves the subsequent divergent histories of the Welsh and Saxons to other contemporary historians.

The impact of Geoffrey of Monmouth's *History* was immediate. Some two hundred mediaeval manuscript copies of the book have survived in libraries all over Europe, and it is likely that others remain to be discovered. Today it remains very readable, but to appreciate its effect on its first readers one must cast one's mind back to conditions in the twelfth century. There was nothing remotely like it, except the Bible. Like the Bible, it was a mine of dramatic stories, heroic, exciting, humorous and tragic. But over the Bible it possessed two striking advantages – the stories in the *History* were virtually all new, and they were set in the familiar towns and countryside of Plantagenet England. Geoffrey no more than any other mediaeval historian imagined the past to have been 'different', so that everyone in the saga, from Brutus to Cadwallader, spoke and acted in an utterly familiar way.

Most striking of all was the tale of Arthur, which stood on its own as a classic tragedy. To the generations of Normans whose grandfathers had conquered England from the Saxons and who now faced the uncertain course of civil war following the death of Henry I, Geoffrey's description of courtly splendour and chivalrous conduct in the days of King Arthur had a great appeal. It provided an ordered model to which they might aspire, and a heritage of which they could be proud. Within a dozen years of the book's appearance, nobles in far-off Scotland were christening their off-spring 'Arthur' and 'Merlin'.[2] There had developed a cult which continued to arouse an enthusiastic response from each succeeding generation until the close of the Middle Ages.

In the early twelfth century the previous thousand years had up to then been represented by the arid chronological entries of the *Anglo-Saxon Chronicle*, and the passing allusions of a few Roman historians. (There was of course Bede's magnificent *Ecclesiastical History of the English People*, but neither the subject-matter nor the nationality of the author were likely to appeal to the fighting nobility of King Stephen's England.) Now the gates to Britain's past had been flung open, and all was clear as daylight.

To the modern reader it may seem odd that anyone could for a moment have accepted such a tale as authentic, including as it does long conversations reported verbatim from the twelfth century before Christ, but this is to mistake the mediaeval approach to history. The chronicler's conception was essentially religious: God had ordered man's state on earth, and his prime concern was how most fruitfully to employ his brief terrestrial existence. The past was interesting as story and object-lesson, but it contained no pattern, message or discernible progress other than the continuing fulfilment of God's purpose. Above all, there was no tradition of historical criticism. In the Dark Ages the venerable Bede had weighed and declared his sources; in the early Middle Ages such a scholarly approach was almost unknown.

In any case, few even among the well-read at Stephen's court would have found any *prima facie* reason for objecting to the veracity of Geoffrey's 'most ancient book'. Direct speech and lively detail were expected of the historian; they were the stock-in-trade by which his skill was measured. Thucidides, and Tacitus had placed appropriate speeches in the mouths of their protagonists, and Geoffrey could do no less. Indeed, in his introduction he clearly implies that he could quite legitimately have 'improved' the matter of his book still further had he felt up to it. Then again, though the *History* was majestically novel, its matter was not so entirely new as to suggest total invention. The story of Brutus's colonisation of Britain (hence the name) was already known in scholarly circles, and the names and exploits of Roman emperors, Arthur, and some of the British kings were more or less familiar.[3]

There were reasons, too, why for many people there were powerful incentives for accepting the *History* as a fact. In general terms it added great lustre to a country which had for so long been ruled by a succession of great kings, and whose national history now proved to be as old and honourable as that of Rome herself. More specifically, the European conquests of Arthur and his predecessors provided powerful precedents for English kings asserting Continental territorial claims. It was significant that the heir of Henry II's great Angevin empire was christened Arthur in 1187. A contemporary register recorded that, 'Arthur, son of Geoffrey Duke of Britanny, is born, the one hoped for by the people'.[4]

The last phrase alludes to another significant factor in the popularity of Geoffrey's work. The seventh book of the *History* comprises the lengthy prophecy delivered by Merlin to Vortigern among the foundations of his Snowdonian fortress. It is an extraordinary mixture of allegorical references, amongst which it was not difficult to detect references to events occurring in the readers' own time. Most striking was a passage foretelling that:

> 'Catuli leonis in equoreos pisces transformabuntur'
> 'The lion's whelps shall be transformed into sea-fishes'

It was impossible for an early twelfth-century reader not to see here an allusion to the tragic drowning of Henry I's son in the White Ship on 25 November 1120. Then a few sentences on, came an even more ominous prognostication:

> 'Ue tibi neustria quoniam in te cerebrum leonis effundetur et dissipatis membris a natiuo solo eliminabitur;'

> 'Woe to thee, Normandy, because the lion's brain shall be poured

upon thee, and he shall be banished with shattered limbs from his native soil.'

The 'lion' was clearly Henry I, who died in Normandy on 1 December 1135.

The prophecies were read eagerly. The death of Henry I, which coincided with the publication of the *History*, ushered in a prolonged period of civil war which ended only with the accession of Henry II nearly twenty years later. It was a time of exceptional insecurity for high and low, and, given the apocalyptic view of life characteristic of the time, it is not surprising that Merlin's prophecy was seized upon as a guide to coming events. In the very year of publication, the Norman historian Ordericus Vitalis interpreted a section of the prophecy as it related to recent events, as did Suger, Abbot of St Denis, a year or so later. When Henry II invaded Ireland in 1171, contemporaries found passages among Merlin's sayings foretelling that portentous event. Merlin's appeal was not confined to the British Isles, however, and versions of the prophecy appeared and were commented upon as far afield as Castile, Italy, Holland and Iceland. Ultimately, Merlin came to be recognised as a great seer throughout Western Christendom.[5]

Geoffrey of Monmouth says that, 'Merlin, by delivering these and many other prophecies, aroused in all that were present an admiration at the ambiguity of his expressions.' Or, as a later English version put it quaintly, he 'be-gan . . . to speke so mystily . . .' Their vagueness made the prophecy an ideal quarry for men looking into an otherwise impenetrable future. There was nothing improbable in this. God had already preordained the course of human existence, and it might be that an exceptionally gifted seer had been empowered to obtain glimpses of the unfolding pattern in advance. Our own age is only marginally more sceptical, it seems. A year or so ago a reissue of the prophecies of Nostradamus aroused extraordinary enthusiasm in sophisticated France, and on another level one may detect in the historical determinism of Karl Marx a more intellectual attempt to penetrate this same mystery.

The figure of Merlin equalled that of Arthur as an object of fascination in mediaeval Europe, and, like Arthur's, Merlin's story was embellished at the hands of successive writers.

In 1155 Wace, a Jerseyman, translated Geoffrey's *History* into Anglo-Norman, the vernacular language of the English governing class. His plot followed Geoffrey's closely, as did that of the

Englishman Layamon who in turn rendered Wace's *Brut* (as the new version was called) into Middle English some time about the turn of the twelfth and thirteenth centuries. Each writer more than doubled the length of his predecessor's text, chiefly by expanding descriptive passages and conversations. This treatment is on the whole very effective, pointing up Geoffrey's 'factual' narrative in a lively and enjoyable manner. Picturesque touches abound, as well as elaborations of points neglected by Geoffrey. Thus, when the boy Merlin is led away from Carmarthen by Vortigern's guards, his foresight is taken into account:

'He guessed that he was taken away his limbs for to lose,
But in quite another manner he arranged that fate, before all would be done.'

And where Geoffrey has Merlin's mother describe the incubus who seduced her simply as, 'a person in the form of a most handsome young man,' Layamon again provides a much more sinisterly erotic image:

'This I saw in dreaming each night asleep:
This thing glided before me, and glistened with gold;
Oft it kissed me and oft it hugged me,
Oft it approached me, and oft it grew near me . . .'

Wace adds but one factual piece of information to Geoffrey's account. After describing Arthur's death, he writes that:

'Master Wace, who made this book,
Does not wish to say more of his end
Than was uttered by the prophet Merlin;
Merlin said of Arthur, as I understand it,
That there would be doubt concerning his end:
The prophet spoke truly.'

Wace seems here to have had access to independent Welsh tradition, which asserted that, 'the world's wonder a grave for Arthur'.[6]

In Geoffrey's account, Merlin disappears from the tale immediately after the conception of Arthur in Tintagel. Wace and Layamon allow him one reappearance, when he is summoned to advise Uther, but otherwise half of the familiar tale is still missing. There is as yet no mention of the infant Arthur being entrusted to foster-parents, there is no sword in the stone, no Round Table, no Grail, no counselling at Arthur's court.

All this was supplied by another writer, Robert de Boron, a Burgundian poet whose *Merlin* was written about the year 1200. De Boron had already composed a lengthy verse epic usually known as *Joseph of Arimathea* which related the history of the Grail, in the form of the chalice used by Jesus at the Last Supper. Towards the end of the poem we are told that the Grail will ultimately be borne by its guardian 'to the land in the West . . . in the vales of Avaron', an apparent reference to Avalon, believed to be the Somerset flats around Glastonbury.[7] The *Merlin* poem was a sequel, apparently designed to explain how it was that the Grail travelled from the Holy Land to Britain and to recount its subsequent history. The whole subject is replete with fascinating mystery.

De Boron's *Merlin* begins with a highly melodramatic account of Merlin's origin, detailing events before the point where Geoffrey of Monmouth takes up his tale. We find ourselves in Hell, where the devils are raging at Christ's entry and rescue of Adam, Eve and subsequent sinners. They decide to be avenged by means of a satanic counterpart to the Saviour, who will be a prophet, half human and half devil. A devil is despatched into the world, and sets to work on a wealthy man possessing three young daughters. Under diabolical influence the man and his wife commit suicide, the eldest daughter allows herself to be seduced and is buried alive on being discovered, and the second girl is abandoned into prostitution. A kindly priest, Blaise, protects the third, but is outwitted by the demon who cohabits with her as she sleeps. She confesses to the priest, who foils her seducer by blessing the coming child with the sign of the cross. Confined to a chamber in a tower, the girl gives birth to Merlin, an extraordinarily precocious child who speaks fluently when eighteen months old. Thanks to his eloquence he saves his mother from condemnation. He then repairs to the good priest Blaise who has explained to him that his demoniac paternity conferred on him full knowledge of all things past, but that his mother's piety has saved him from inheriting his father's evil. In addition, 'Our Lord has given me the capacity to know all that is to take place in the future.'

The story rather abruptly moves to Vortigern's Britain, where it merges into Geoffrey of Monmouth's account. After the prophesied death of Vortigern, Merlin becomes the counsellor of his successor, Pendragon. When Pendragon is slain in battle with the Saxons, his younger brother Uther (a separate person in de Boron's version) succeeds to the throne. Merlin arranges for the boulders of Stonehenge to be transported from Ireland, and also (a novel conception) for a Round Table for fifty knights to be established at Carduel (Carlisle). There follows the familiar story of Uther's seduction of Igerna at Tintagel, but the sequel has developments not to be found in Geoffrey's history. The infant Arthur is taken by Merlin to be brought up at the castle of a knight named Antor.

The years pass by and Uther, now elderly, is borne on a litter to his last battle. It is now necessary to find a successor to the throne, and Merlin requires all the barons of the kingdom to assemble at Logres on Christmas Day, when God will make His choice plain. There follows the familiar story of the sword in the stone, at which the youthful Arthur proves his claim. Arthur had to prove his fitness by a miraculous feat because of his illegitimacy.[8] In Geoffrey's *History* Uther and Igerna are married within hours of their first lying together, so that the child's paternity does not appear in doubt. Robert de Boron makes the wedding take place thirty days later; moreover Igerna, discovering that her visitor was not her husband who had been killed that very night, realised the baby's father could not be him, since he had been separated from her since the siege of Tintagel began.

The story ends inconclusively with the coronation of Arthur, who held the land and the kingdom in peace. Robert de Boron added another important factor in the development of the legend: he relates numerous anecdotes detailing Merlin's shape-shifting powers, which the wizard employs both as effective disguise and as a means of playing pranks on those around him. At times his appearance is ridiculous and yet awe-inspiring. Often he introduces a prophetic utterance with a sardonic laugh, as when he reveals that a priest conducting the burial of a child is in reality its father.

Merlin's character is strongly portrayed: acerbic, cunning, perceptive, waspish, Mephistophelean, he is gifted with supernatural powers. Overall, however, he is benevolent, and acts for the good of those around him and the community at large. Indeed, were it not for his skilled guidance, the kingdom would come to ruin. Robert de Boron thus established Merlin's personality in a form which altered little in the literature of succeeding centuries, and he remained a central figure throughout the vast gathering, creation and spread of Arthurian cycles and tales throughout the Middle Ages, the undisputed master of all magical arts.

It is fitting that the popular image of Merlin is that created by Sir Thomas Malory in his *Morte Darthur*, published by Caxton in 1485.

For it was in the last St Martin's summer of English chivalry, the reign of Edward IV, that Arthurian romance reached near perfection. In a measured, archaic, yet eternally fresh diction, Malory took virtually the whole cycle and fashioned it into a miraculous tapestry, a magical land. Here are the

> 'fairy damsels met in forest wide,
> knights of Logres, and of Lyonesse:
> Lancelot, and Pelleas, and Pellinore.'

And there 'Mage Merlin' appears to play the unifying rôle which creates the fellowship of the Table Round, guides it to the supreme quest of the Grail, and ultimately envelops him in tragedy. Like Arthur, he lives on in his Otherworld prison-house, close to the abodes of men yet unapproachable by them. Malory ignores Merlin's early history completely, introducing him as a well-known sorcerer whom Sir Ulfius seeks out to help Uther Pendragon gain the fair Igrayne in Tintagel.

'"Well," said Merlyn, "I knowe whome thou sekest, for thou sekest Merlyn; therefore seke no ferther, for I am he. And yf kynge Uther wille wel rewarde me and be sworne unto me to fulfille my desyre, that shall be his honour and profite more than myn, for I shalle cause hym to have alle his desyre."'

The seer's appearances are mysterious and unexplained, and he can read men's minds openly. We are told simply that:

'Therwithal Ulfius was ware where Merlyn stood at the porche of the pavelions dore, and thenne Merlyn was bounde to come to the kynge. When kyng Uther sawe hym he said he was welcome. "Syr", said Merlyn, "I know al your hert every dele."'

So it begins. Merlin arranges the impersonation which results in the birth of Arthur, and takes the baby to be brought up at the castle of Sir Ector. In improbable alliance with the 'Archebisshop of Caunterbury', he later arranges the test of the sword in the stone and tides over initial opposition to Arthur's accession to the kingship. His enemies denounce him as 'a wytche' and 'a dreme-reder', but 'with that Merlyn vanysshed aweye'. During the civil war which follows, Merlin guides Arthur's forces to victory sometimes by magic (as when he provides 'plenté of vitayle' for fifteen thousand cavalry and puts an enemy force to sleep), and at others by straightforward strategic advice on how best to lay an ambush.

All that is to come is provided or revealed by the wizard. He supplies Arthur with a wife and the magical sword Excalibur of the Lady of the Lake, arranges the Round Table, and prophesies the Quest of the Grail. But even as all sets out so fair, he warns the King of their fated ends:

> '"But ye have done a thynge late that God ys displesed with you, for ye have lyene by your syster and on hir ye have gotyn a childe that shall destroy you and all the knyghtes of youre realme . . . hit ys Goddis wylle that youre body sholde be punyssed for your fowle dedis. But I ought ever to be hevy," seyde Merlion, "for I shall dye a shameful dethe, to be putte in the erthe quycke; and ye shall dey a worshipfull dethe."'

Thereafter Merlin intervenes in the tale in his customary unexpected and unexplained manner. Robert de Boron's characterisation of the sorcerer as part magician, part prophet and part joker is preserved faithfully. A 'faytoure' ('impostor') is what his enemy King Lot calls him, and another treacherous opponent warns his collaborator to 'beware . . . of Merlion, for he knowith all thynges by the devylles craffte'. Merlin creates statues for Arthur, 'by hys subtyle crafte'; and constructs an enchanted sword for Galahad when the time comes. Time and again he warns Arthur and his knights, 'that there sholde be a grete batayle besydes Salysbiry', foretells the activities of the questing beast, and in veiled terms advises King Mark that one day Sir Tristram will be, 'takyn with his soveraigne lady' ('thou arte a boysteous man and an unlyckly, to telle of such dedis', responds the monarch). Many of Merlin's utterances are in this teasing vein, and he delights in startling people by appearing without warning, disguised 'lyke a chylde of fourteen yere of ayge', 'in a beggars aray'; and, on one memorable occasion in the snows of Sherwood Forest at Candlemas, 'all befurred in blacke shepis skynnes and a grete payre of bootis, and a boowe and arowis, in a russet gowne, and brought wylde gyese in hys honde.' Merlin loved to surprise his audience, though generally with good effect, 'so they had grete disporte at hym'.

Merlin's end came as he had foreseen. He 'felle in dotage on . . . one of the damesels of the Lady of the Lake, that hyght [was called] Nyneve'. The lady proved to be a match for the old wizard, and gradually prised out of him the secrets of his art. It was an unnerving situation for a young woman, for the old gentleman 'allwayes . . . wolde be wyth her . . . and he was assoted uppon hir, that he myght nat be from hir'. He accordingly accompanied her everywhere, even on trips to the Continent, and as he possessed skills denied to other elderly seducers she 'made hym to swere that he should never do none enchauntement uppon hir if he wolde have his wil, and so he swore.' But nature will out. The ill-matched couple returned home and, riding in the lanes of Cornwall, Nyneve realised her companion was prey to an enchantment older and more potent than he had learned from the wizard Blaise in Northumberland:

> 'And allwayes he lay aboute to have hir maydynhode, and she was ever passynge wery of hym and wolde have been delyverde of hym, for she was aferde of hym for cause he was a devyls son, and she cowde not be skyfte of hym by no meane. And so on a tyme Merlyon ded shew hir in a roche whereas was a grete wondir and wrought by enchauntement that went undir a grete stone. So by hir subtyle worchyng she made Merlyon to go undir that stone to latte hir wete [know] of the mervayles there, but she wrought so there for hym that he came never oute for all the craufte he coude do, and so she departed and leffte Merlyon.'

In this way were fulfilled Merlin's own words to King Arthur, namely 'that he scholde nat endure longe, but for all his craftes he scholde be putte into the erthe quyk [alive]'.

Malory's *Morte Darthur* was published just as the light of the Renaissance was spreading northwards from the Mediterranean, and it was only by a freak of history that Merlin and Arthur were not despatched with all the other lumber of Gothic ignorance and superstition. Caxton published the *Morte Darthur* on 31 July 1485, and it was a bare three weeks later that Richard III was killed at Bosworth. The victor was of course Henry Tudor, a prince of Welsh ancestry. It was not only the Welsh who saw in this a fulfilment of Merlin's prophecy to Arthur that a time would come when they would once again rule Britain.

Patriotic Englishmen joined their Welsh brothers in hailing the happy event as predestined from ages past, and looked to Geoffrey of Monmouth's account of Arthur's Continental conquests as precedent for a resumption of their grand-sires' stirring deeds on French soil. In the following year the King christened his newborn son, the heir of York and Lancaster, with the glorious name of Arthur. Panegyrists, poets and historians repeated and embellished the British history, and exhibited patriotic fury when an impudent

Italian historian, Polydore Virgil, wrote a few sceptical remarks questioning the historicity of King Arthur. It was in this chance way that Arthur, Merlin and even Brutus the Trojan (one could not reject him without endangering his companions) received a new lease of life at the very moment they might have been expected to end it.[9]

The development of the printing press made the stories more widely accessible. In 1510 Wynkyn de Worde published *A Lytel Tretys of the Byrth and Prophecyes of Merlin*, which ran to a second edition in 1529, and a third in 1533.

It was not long before sceptical voices were heard, but they were shouted down by the majority of respectable chroniclers. In 1586 the greatest of all early modern historians, William Camden, gently hinted in the first edition of his *Britannia* that there was precious little evidence to support the story of Brutus and much to counter it. But it was not until the seventeenth century, when the Tudors had departed to join King Arthur, that scepticism gathered momentum and swept most, if not all, of Geoffrey's long-lived *History* from the shelves of respectable scholarship. In 1675 even the University of Oxford dropped King Brutus' name from the University Almanac (a lingering loyalty entirely fitting if, as has been suggested, it was the *History of the Kings of Britain* which earned Geoffrey of Monmouth his Master's degree). But if Geoffrey of Monmouth appeared dead, he declined to lie down. Even in the twentieth century eccentric popular historians from time to time have arisen to claim that *The History of the Kings of Britain* is indeed what it claims to be – a perfectly reliable chronicle of early Britain.[10]

But if historical scholarship was the loser, literature was surely the gainer. Merlin appeared in his prophetic guise in Ariosto's *Orlando Furioso* (first published in 1532). In Spenser's *Faerie Queene* (1590), a work based on a deep understanding of the available sources, the seer Merlin plays a crucial rôle. It is he alone, to whom the past and future have opened up their secrets, who can guide Prince Arthur, the Redcrosse Knight and Arthegal forward to their destiny. Spenser saw the history, as others were to do in increasing numbers, as a magnificent source for the poet to plunder and fashion in his own way. In *The Faerie Queene* the wizard's mantic vision is delivered in a cave at Dynevor Park near Llandeilo in Carmarthenshire, still shown to visitors:

'There the wise *Merlin* whylome wont (they say)
To make his wonne, low vnderneath the ground,
In a deepe delue, farre from the view of day,
That of no liuing wight he mote be found,
When so he counseld with his sprights encompast round.

'And if thou euer happen that same way
To trauell, goe to see that dreadfull place:
It is an hideous hollow caue (they say)
Vnder a rocke that lyes a little space
From the swift *Barry*, tombling downe apace,
Emongst the woodie hilles of *Dyneuowre*:
But dare thou not, I charge, in any cace,
To enter into that same balefull Bowre,
For fear the cruell Feends should thee vnwares deuowre.'

Not all, however, were polite in their treatment of the British
wizard; some writers discovered in the incoherent, rambling prophecies attributed to Merlin matter for ridicule. Shakespeare's passing
references, for example, are disrespectful, despite the fact that the
plots for *King Lear* and *Cymbeline* derive ultimately from Geoffrey
of Monmouth's *History*. In *King Henry IV* Hotspur sneers at the
Welsh leader Glendower's boasts:

'Sometimes he angers me,
With telling me of the moldwarp and the ant,
Of the dreamer Merlin and his prophecies;
And of a dragon and a finless fish,
A clip-wing'd griffin, and a moulten raven,
A couching lion, and a ramping cat,
And such a deal of skimble-skamble stuff
As puts me from my faith.'

And in *Lear* it is the fool on the heath who declaims, with a glib
reminder of the anachronism,

'. . . when usurers tell their gold i' the field;
And bawds and whores do churches build; –
Then shall the realm of Albion
Come to great confusion.
Then comes the time, who lives to see't,
That going shall be us'd with feet.
This prophecy Merlin shall make; for I live before his time.'

This last passage is considered by some scholars to be 'an incongruous theatrical interpolation',[11] and in any case it is clear that much of the ridicule was directed against the survival of popular utterances attributed to Merlin. In 1603, for example, just two years before the conjectured date of the writing of *King Lear*, an edition of Merlin's and Thomas the Rhymer's prophecies appeared in Edinburgh. Though they included a fair proportion of gibberish, some passages are not without a certain wild magic of their own,

'When the Cragges of Tarbat is tumbled in the sey,
At the next sommer after sorrow for euer:
Besides [Bede's] bookes have I seene, and Banisters also,
Meruelous Merling and all accordes in one:
Meruelous Merling is wasted away,
With a wicked woman, woe might shee be;
For shee hath closed him in a Craige on Cornwel cost.'

In the seventeenth and eighteenth centuries 'Merlin' pamphlets and almanacs appeared in profusion. Often they were directed towards contemporary political events, such as King Charles I's exclusion from Hull in 1642, and Charles II's defeat at Worcester in 1651, and an appeal was unashamedly made to the gullible and susceptible.

More influential was the astrologer William Lilly's (1602–1682) *England's Propheticall Merline foretelling to all nations of Europe*. Like the originator of the *genre*, Lilly intended his readers to relate the allegorical allusions to contemporary events. Daniel Defoe recorded that in 1665 the Great Plague aroused a proliferation of new 'Merlin' material. Even the eminent mathematician Robert Hooke looked to Merlin's oracle for guidance during the Revolution crisis of 1688–89.[12]

It was the greatest of all pamphleteers, Jonathan Swift, who opened the eighteenth century with *A Famous Prediction of Merlin, the British Wizard. Written about a thousand years ago, and relating to the year 1709*. Naturally the treatment was wholly jocose, and the Age of Reason deposed the great wizard to the spheres of the burlesque. In 1755 was published *Merlin's . . . predictions relating to the late contest about . . . Richmond Park*, and the same year saw the tragic death of the poet Stephen Duck, formerly prophet-in-residence in a mock Merlin's Cave at neighbouring Kew. The almanacs continued well on into the nineteenth century, by now it seems solely for the benefit of newly literate shop-girls and bank-clerks.

Merlin's magic was far from exhausted, however, and it was

appropriately Scott, the Wizard of the North, who restored him to poetry. It was natural for the new generation of Romantic poets to find inspiration in the greatest of all chivalric epics, and Wordsworth wrote enthusiastically in *Artegal and Elidure* of Geoffrey's enchanted *History* and 'The sage enchanter Merlin's subtle schemes'.

But it was Tennyson who, drawing on Malory's version, first fully restored Merlin to the literary majesty from which he had been deposed for over two centuries. In *Merlin and Vivien* (1859), the Poet Laureate begins in solemn vein:

> 'A storm was coming, but the winds were still,
> And in the wild woods of Broceliande,
> Before an oak, so hollow, huge and old
> It look'd a tower of ivied masonwork,
> At Merlin's feet the wily Vivien lay.'

The story, reflecting Victorian concern with the precarious dominance of civilised values, tells of a conspiracy instigated by the corrupt King Mark of Cornwall to destroy the fellowship of the Table Round. The beautiful seductress Vivien insinuates herself into the court at Camelot, and:

> '. . . she set herself to gain
> Him, the most famous man of all those times,
> Merlin, who knew the range of all their arts,
> Had built the King his havens, ships, and halls,
> Was also Bard, and knew the starry heavens;
> The people call'd him Wizard . . .'

The old man is not immune to her wiles and, deeply troubled, leaves in a boat for Brittany. Vivien accompanies him, and in 'the wild woods of Broceliande' she works upon 'the great Enchanter of the Time' to reveal the charmed words. In an erotic passage we see Vivien:

> 'Writhed toward him, slided up his knee and sat,
> Behind his ankle twined her hollow feet
> Together, curved an arm about his neck,
> Clung like a snake . . .'

Despite this, Merlin long resists her blandishments, but ultimately all his magic arts are impotent before the wiles of a determined woman, and his surrender is described in a passage replete with remarkably frank sexual imagery.[13] A fearful storm breaks out over the forest, and Vivien

> '. . . crying out,
> "O Merlin tho' you do not love me, save,
> Yet save me!" clung to him and hugg'd him close;
> And call'd him dear protector in her fright,
> Nor yet forgot her practice in her fright,
> But wrought upon his mood and hugg'd him close.
> The pale blood of the wizard at her touch
> Took gayer colours, like an opal warm'd.
> She blamed herself for telling hearsay tales:
> She shook from fear, and for her fault she wept
> Of petulancy; she call'd him lord and liege,
> Her seer, her bard, her silver star of eve,
> Her God, her Merlin, the one passionate love
> Of her whole life; and ever overhead
> Bellow'd the tempest, and the rotten branch
> Snapt in the rushing of the river-rain
> Above them; and in change of glare and gloom
> Her eyes and neck glittering went and came;
> Till now the storm, its burst of passion spent,
> Moaning and calling out of other lands,
> Had left the ravaged woodland yet once more
> To peace; and what should not have been had been,
> For Merlin, overtalk'd and overworn,
> Had yielded, told her all the charm, and slept.'

A contemporary of Tennyson's, whose work he admired, was the eccentric Vicar of Morwenstowe, Robert Stephen Hawker. Hawker built himself a hut of driftwood high on the cliffs that look westwards along the coastline to distant Tintagel on its misty promontory. There he composed an unfinished verse-epic, *The Quest of the Sangraal*. After foretelling the doom of Imperial England, unless she devote herself anew to the higher purpose symbolised by the Grail, Merlin falls silent.

> 'He ceased: and all around was dreamy night:
> There stood Dundagel, throned; and the great sea
> Lay, a strong vassal at his master's gate,
> And, like a drunken giant, sobbed in sleep.'

Merlin introduces and concludes Thomas Hardy's *The Famous*

Tragedy of the Queen of Cornwall (1923), and in 1938, T. H. White
provided the world with a Merlyn more popular than at any period
since the fifteenth century. In *The Sword in the Stone*, Merlyn is
an eccentric, donnish figure, living both backwards and forwards
in time, who instructs the youthful Arthur in all the arts and
skills necessary for a king. The picture abounds in whimsical
anachronisms and elemental, if at times juvenile, humour, but is
still not far removed from the Merlin of tradition. White was
absorbed in Malory, his chief and perhaps only direct source, and
the eccentricities are as legitimate an expression as the awesome
magical powers. Then in the spring of 1941, when it seemed another
Dark Age was about to engulf the British Isles, the poet Charles
Richard Cammell, staying in the West Country, wrote *The Return
of Arthur*. In this poem he saw the prophecy fulfilled whereby
Arthur would return in the moment of his country's direst
need:

> 'From his dread sleep in Broceliande
> Merlin the Mage shall wake,
> And Pelleas forsake his love
> Beneath the faery lake . . .
> Flows not the wine of Camelot
> Red through the British lands?
> Feel we not Arthur in our hearts,
> And Launcelot in our hands?'

But the most striking development of the Merlin legend in the
twentieth century has been a return to the earliest sources. John
Cowper Powys, in his strange novel, *Porius: A Romance of the
Dark Ages* (1951), takes us back to an imaginative and in many
ways convincing fifth century A.D. Powys's Merlin becomes the
Myrddin Wyllt of early Welsh poetry, dressed in animal-skins and
accompanied by his familiars:

'The man's head was bare of everything but a crop of coal-black
hair, and his ears were the largest appendages of that kind that
Porius had ever seen . . . He could also make out as he bent
forward a little to catch the fellow's replies, which were still
hoarse and husky, that his eyes were unnaturally circular in
shape and so close together that when they flashed with an
interior light . . . they created the illusion that they actually
mingled with each other and became one . . .'

This is the authentic Merlin of the earliest traditions, grotesque and awe-inspiring; and the novel itself represents an astonishing *tour-de-force*, an exploration into the dark recesses of mythic thought.[14]

More recently the poet Robert Nye turned primarily to Robert de Boron's account of Merlin's demoniac parentage in his *Merlin* (1978). This starts promisingly with lascivious devils in Hell begetting the infant Merlin on a beautiful daughter of earth, but is unfortunately too much the product of its decade to resist descending into repetitive pornography.

The resilience of the old wizard is also well illustrated by his success in the contemporary medium of the cinema. How vivid is my memory of MGM's film *The Knights of the Round Table*, which I saw at the Odeon Cinema, Leicester Square, in (I think) 1954. For months the image lingered, as I wandered in a haze of youthful dreams by the Thames at Pangbourne. Happy, happy time, when Frances Hitchins, seated in our skiff, appeared to me as the Lily Maid of Astolat! A year ago (1982) John Boorman's *Excalibur* returned with considerable effect to a theatrical Dark Age, filmed among appropriately misty lakes and forests in Ireland, with Nicol Williamson as a jocular but dominating Merlin, well in the authentic literary and historical tradition.

But the Merlin most familiar to millions of people all over the world today is one known by another name. Professor J. R. R. Tolkien knew Celtic and Teutonic myth as have few other people, and there can be no doubt that the wizard Gandalf of *The Hobbit* (1937) and the trilogy which follows, is drawn from the Merlin of early legend.

Like Merlin, Gandalf is a magician of infinite wisdom and power; like Merlin, he has a sense of humour by turns impish and sarcastic; and, like Merlin, he reappears at intervals, seemingly from nowhere, intervening to rescue an imperilled cosmos. Even minor aptitudes are openly appropriated, such as Merlin's propensity for appearing in the incongruous guise of a beggar, and his capacity for launching splendid displays of pyrotechnics. Devotees of Tolkien will remember how Gandalf saved the Hobbits from wolves by the Misty Mountains with a discharge of magical multicoloured fireballs. In the thirteenth-century English poem *Of Arthour and of Merlin*, when a group of truculent barons challenged Arthur's right to the throne:

'Merlin made enchantment
And cast great damage
Into the pavilions, wild fire
That burned bright as a candle clear . . .'

The wizard's enchantments have secured him a permanent place, it seems, in the consciousness of mankind. The centuries come and go, literary fashions pass, but the magician reappears before us: shifting his shape and changing his name, now mocking, now awe-inspiring, but essentially the same character whose fame flew over all Europe eight centuries ago. Trickster, illusionist, philosopher and sorcerer, he represents an archetype to which the race turns for guidance and protection.

2

Merlin the Prophet

Encouraged by the startling success of his first book, Geoffrey eventually set to work to produce another. Second only to the fascination exerted by the towering figure of Arthur had been the spell cast by the mysterious figure of Merlin, and it was about the year 1150, some fourteen years after the appearance of the *History of the Kings of Britain*, that Geoffrey issued his *Life of Merlin* (*Vita Merlini*). In the earlier work Geoffrey introduced the stories of Merlin's birth and his relations with Vortigern and Uther as episodes in his major history. In the new work he supplied a biography of Merlin alone, in the form of 1529 lines of narrative verse, much of it of high dramatic and literary quality.

The story in outline is as follows. Merlinus was king and prophet to the Demetae, that is the men of Dyfed in south-west Wales. Together with Rodarcus, king of the Cumbri, he fought in a battle against Guennolous, king of Scocia (Scotland). Three brothers to whom Merlin was greatly attached perished in the conflict and, maddened with grief, the seer withdrew to the solitude of the forest of Caledon. His sister Ganieda, who was married to Rodarcus, persuaded him to return to court. There Merlin provided evidence of his prophetic powers by revealing to Rodarcus his queen's infidelity, though the queen employed a trick to lull her husband's suspicions. Merlin, disgusted by city life, announced his intention of returning to his wild life in the Caledonian Forest. Somewhat illogically, it was the queen who tried to dissuade him, summoning the prophet's wife Guendoloena to assist her supplications. But Merlin was adamant, urged his wife to marry another, and departed. However, when Guendoloena did remarry, he reappeared riding on a stag and accompanied by a herd of deer. In a spasm of jealousy, he killed the bridegroom and rode off again. Again a little improbably, his sister followed him back to the woods, and at his request constructed for him an elaborate circular observatory.

There he studied the stars in their courses and uttered a prophecy similar in its allegorical allusions to that delivered to Vortigern in the ruined castle by his counterpart in the *History*.

Soon afterwards, Merlin was visited by another philosopher prophet, Telgesinus, to whom he expounded much learned information on natural history and knowledge in general. After further political prophecy, Merlin explained that he had 'lived long and seen much', and gave an outline of the history of Vortigern, Uther and Arthur as set out in Geoffrey's earlier book, continuing it as far as the reigns of Arthur's two successors. After more conversation on scientific matters, and another prophetic incident, Merlin refused an appeal by the lords of his country to return home, and settled down to lead a contemplative life for the rest of his days in the forest he loved so dearly. He was joined by Telgesinus, by an inspired madman whose sanity he had restored and by his sister Ganieda, whose husband King Rodarcus had died. The story ends with a prophecy by Ganieda, which was clearly related to events taking place in England at the time of Geoffrey's composition of the poem.

The *Life of Merlin* is by any standard a remarkable composition. There are incongruities of plot and character, but the story is highly dramatic and vividly told. The delicate balance between insanity and prophetic genius in Merlin's own character is particularly lively and convincing, as are the indignation and cunning of the accused queen and the pathetic plaints of the prophet's deserted wife. There is a strong feeling for the beauties of nature, expressed in many fine passages, and the Caledonian Forest is no dramatic stage-property but a real wilderness, welcoming in summer and grim in winter. Whether or not this aspect of the poem, which is absent from the *History*, derives from older literary sources, there cannot be any doubt that Geoffrey himself possessed a mind keenly attuned to natural beauty. Take this passage, where Merlin is watching the stars from a high hill:

> 'It was night, and the horned moon was shining brightly; all the lights of the vault of heaven were glittering. The air had an extra clarity, for a bitterly cold north wind had blown away the clouds, absorbed all the mists on its drying breath and left the sky serene again.'

As it stands, of course, the poem bears many of the familiar hall-marks of Geoffrey's cavalier approach to literary materials. The dramatic conception is clearly his own, as is much of the esoteric information contained in Merlin's learned discussions with Taliesin (Telgesinus), and the historical matter on which his and Ganieda's prophecies are based. But, this said, there are weighty reasons for placing the *Vita Merlini* in quite a different category of composition from the *History* of fourteen years previously. Whereas the latter may largely be described as an historical romance, the former can be shown to derive a significant amount of its narrative and structure from sources which Geoffrey was in part at least at some pains to represent accurately. Some of this material is very archaic indeed, being as far removed from Geoffrey's lifetime as is his from our own.

The *Vita Merlini* was not designed, if one may turn again to the modern analogy, to 'cash in' on the stupendous success of Geoffrey's earliest bestseller. It was a poem for a limited number of friends. In contrast to the more than two hundred surviving early manuscripts of the *History of the Kings of Britain*, only one complete version of the *Vita Merlini* exists, together with six other extracts of varying length. The *Vita* is dedicated to Robert, Bishop of Lincoln, who was a prelate of scholarly reputation, and it was presumably to him and a chosen *coterie* of friends that the poem was read. Mediaeval standards of scholarship do not bear exaggeration; but it is reasonable to suppose that Geoffrey must have anticipated some interested questioning on the nature of his sources.

Geoffrey, we know, was an extremely skilful forger and there is no doubt that he was readily capable of concocting a story consistent with what he had already written in the *History*. In fact, however, the plot of the *Vita Merlini* is strikingly inconsistent with its predecessor, and Geoffrey was obliged to exercise considerable skill in reconciling the two.

In the *History*, Merlin prophesies to Vortigern and assists Uther to seduce Igerna. In the *Vita Merlini* he is represented as being in the prime of life about a century after these events. Vortigern flourished in the middle or early part of the fifth century, whilst the kings whose battle drove Merlin mad were historical characters living in the second half of the sixth century. Geoffrey's audience perhaps had no means of knowing this, but in Geoffrey's own scheme of things such events could only have taken place after the death of Arthur, which he dated to A.D. 542. All Geoffrey could do was explain away the inconsistency as convincingly as he could. This he did by attributing supernatural longevity to the prophet, who explains that he is as old as one of the most ancient oaks in the Caledonian Forest. As if to emphasise that the two Merlins are identical, Geoffrey has the Merlin of the *Vita Merlini* reminisce about the events he is described as experiencing in the *History*.

This fusing of two discrepant sources was sufficiently skilfully done to impress that small circle of Geoffrey's contemporaries who read the poem. To modern scholars, however, the fusion betrays the fact that Geoffrey did not invent the Merlin of the Caledonian Forest, but was obliged to take already existing material into account when composing his verses. That material was sufficiently extensive, it may also be inferred, to prevent Geoffrey's adapting it more freely. Finally, the atmosphere of a small learned circle may have been more conducive to serious antiquarian lore, whereas the earlier *History* had been intended for a wide public.

Thus, the internal evidence of the *Vita Merlini* suggests, firstly, that Geoffrey had recently gained access to stories about Merlin previously unknown to him; and, secondly, that this material was sufficiently full and specific in its outlines to prevent the great forger from blending it harmoniously with his earlier account.

Fortunately it is not necessary to rely solely on deductive analysis of this sort to show that Geoffrey of Monmouth did not invent the Merlin story, since there is evidence that much of it was already in existence well before his time.

The most valuable manuscript collections of early Welsh poetry are preserved in what their first editor termed the Four Ancient Books of Wales. These bear titles redolent of ancient mystery: *The Black Book of Carmarthen*, *The Book of Taliesin*, *The Book of Aneirin*, and *The Red Book of Hergest*. *The Black Book of Carmarthen* and *The Book of Aneirin* were probably compiled some time around the year 1250; *The Book of Taliesin* a little later, perhaps 1275; whilst the *Red Book of Hergest* was 'written with few exceptions during the last quarter of the XIVth, and the first quarter of the XVth centuries.'[1] *The Red Book* contains a great deal of prose literature, including the famous tales known as *Mabinogi* and a Welsh version of Geoffrey's *History*. Otherwise the contents of all four books comprise a wonderful collection of Welsh verse, much of it far older in origin than the manuscript in which it has chanced to be preserved. The language in which these poems are written is frequently archaic and obscure, and it is clear that on occasion the mediaeval transcriber could not understand all he copied. Small wonder that eighteenth- and nineteenth-century scholars, even those whose native tongue was Welsh, ranged in their translations into English from grotesque errors to downright gibberish. It is only during the past century that philologists and palaeographers have succeeded in evolving techniques for dating and interpreting the poetry.

Since much of it is replete with allusions to historical events and mythological tales dating from the far past, this investigation has resulted in extraordinarily exciting discoveries. The most dramatic of these is that a nucleus of the poems in the Books of Taliesin and Aneirin was composed as long ago as the sixth century A.D. This was soon after the Welsh language first came into existence as a result of linguistic changes in the British tongue spoken in this island under the Roman occupation. These ancient verses comprise therefore the oldest literature in Europe outside Latin and Greek. Apart from the complete poems, now generally accepted as the authentic work of the sixth-century poets Taliesin and Aneirin, the bulk of later poetry contains a mass of archaic allusions and possibly complete fragments of ancient poetry.

The whole *corpus*, which is to be found also in other manuscripts besides the so-called *Four Ancient Books*, is thus a wonderful mine of historical and mythological lore. Between 1888 and 1911 they were lovingly reproduced in magnificent facsimile editions by a devoted Welshman, Dr J. Gwenogvryn Evans. I obtained copies nearly thirty years ago in those havens of Celtic bibliophily – Griff's Bookshop in Cecil Court, London, and Hodges Figgis in Dawson Street, Dublin. To this day I feel a tremor of excitement when I open one of these handsomely-bound volumes; for there, written in a mysterious tongue that continues in part to baffle the clearest minds, lies half-hidden the *detritus* of the fragmented lore of the Matter of Britain.

Amongst this collection are a number of poems attributed to Myrddin, the Merlin of Geoffrey of Monmouth. They include *Yr Afallennau* ('The Appletrees'), *Yr Oianau* ('Greetings'), *Ymddiddan Myrddin a Thaliesin* ('The Dialogue of Myrddin and Taliesin'), *Cyfoesi Myrddin a Gwenddydd ei Chwaer* ('The Conversation of Myrddin and his sister Gwenddydd'), *Gwasgargerdd Fyrddin yn y Bedd* ('The Song uttered by Myrddin in the Grave'), *Y Bedwenni* ('The Birch Trees'), and *Peiryan Vaban* ('Commanding Youth'). Versions of these poems are to be found principally in the *Black Book of Carmarthen* and the *Red Book of Hergest*, but also in the *White Book of Rhydderch* and other manuscripts. In some cases variant versions have survived, often revealing considerable discrepancies, usually in the form of additional material.

It has to be said at once that none of these poems in its extant form can possibly be the work of a sixth-century bard, whether Myrddin or another. Metre, orthography and language point to a much later date. Still more telling evidence lies in the fact that several of the poems are couched in the form of prophecies clearly referring to events of the twelfth century and after. Unless we are to suppose that Myrddin possessed genuine prophetic powers and cherished a strong interest in political happenings in early Plantagenet England, it is reasonable to assume that all this material was composed at the time of the events themselves some six centuries after the time when Myrddin was held to have lived. These prophecies, which form the greater proportion of the poetry attributed to Myrddin, must accordingly be discarded as having no connection with an historical or legendary Myrddin, beyond indicating that later ages looked upon him as a great prophet.

Whether or not an older substratum of material lies beneath these rambling vaticinations and obscure exchanges rests chiefly on an appreciation of a core of narrative material found in its clearest form in the *Afallennau*:

'Sweet-apple tree which grows in a glade,
Its peculiar power hides it from the men of Rhydderch,
A crowd by its trunk, a host around it,
It would be a treasure for them, brave men in their ranks.
Now Gwenddydd loves me not and does not greet me
– I am hated by Gwasawg, the supporter of Rhydderch –
I have killed her son and her daughter.
Death has taken everyone, why does it not call me?
For after Gwenddolau no lord honours me,
Mirth delights me not, no mistress visits me,
And in the battle of Arderydd my torque was of gold,
Though today I am not treasured by one of the aspect of
    swans . . .
For ten and forty years, in the wretchedness of outlawry,
I have been wandering with madness and madmen;
After goodly possessions and pleasing minstrels
Now I suffer want with madness and madmen.
Now I sleep not, I tremble for my lord,
My sovereign Gwenddolau, and my fellow-countrymen.
After enduring wickness and grief in the Forest of Celyddon
May I be received into bliss by the Lord of Hosts.'[2]

From this it can be deduced that 'Myrddin is a madman, wandering in misery in the Caledonian Forest and endowed with the gift of prophecy. He refers bitterly to the battle of Arderydd at which he wore a golden torque but before the close of which he lost his reason and his lord Gwenddolau was slain. Now he believes he is being hunted down by the men of Rhydderch Hael, obviously the victor of Arderydd, and he complains that his sister Gwenddydd does not visit him. In one line he declares that he has been guilty of the death of the son of Gwenddydd. From other references it would appear that he hides himself from his pursuers, real or imaginery, in an apple tree, which has the power of rendering him invisible, and each stanza in the *Afallennau* poem begins with an invocation to this apple tree.'[3]

That this consistent narrative is implicit in the text may suggest either that the poetry is all that has survived of a prose saga telling the life of Myrddin,[4] or that the events (real or fictitious) of Myrddin's career were so familiar to an earlier audience that a full acquaintance with his story could safely be assumed. There is also a third possibility: namely, that the poems were in their original form the genuine effusions of Myrddin himself, who of course required no commentary on matters so personal. From what has been noted earlier concerning the prophecies this might appear improbable, but there are other considerations.

Clearly the Myrddin of Welsh poetry is to be identified with the Merlin of Geoffrey of Monmouth. It has been suggested that Geoffrey latinised the Welsh name *Merlinus* rather than the expected *Merdinus* on account of a possible confusion with the obscene French *merde*. Rhydderch, Gwenddolau, Gwenddydd and Taliesin in the Welsh poems clearly correspond to the Rodarcus, Guennolous, Ganieda and Telgesinus of Geoffrey's poem.

In both versions the seer is driven mad by the loss of persons near to him in the course of the battle in which he participated, and in which King Gwenddolau was defeated. There are discrepancies as well as similarities, but it is clear that both versions draw ultimately on the same source-material. The Welsh poems did not derive their material from Geoffrey's work, since a proportion of them can be shown from their language to date from an earlier period, and there are other indications that they are rooted in Welsh traditional literature. In the twelfth-century *Life of St Kentigern*, patron saint of Glasgow, we read of the Saint's close association with a King Rederech, who is to be identified with the Rhydderch of the Myrddin poetry. In the first chapter of the *Life*, King Rhydderch is said to have maintained at his court a madman named Laloecen, who abandoned himself to abject grief when Kentigern died, and prophesied that Rederech and one of his nobles would die in the same year.

A manuscript in the British library, MS Cotton Titus A. xix, preserves two further accounts of this Laloecen, or Lailoken as they call him. They are discrepant in minor detail, but provide fuller versions. In the first we learn that St Kentigern met a naked hairy madman in a wood, who told him that he had been driven wild during a terrible battle fought on a plain between the River Liddel and a place known as Carwannok. Hosts of warriors appeared threateningly in the sky, and an accusing voice condemned Lailoken as responsible for all the slaughter. Driven by an evil spirit, he repaired to the forest. Later, he interrupted St Kentigern's services by sitting on a nearby rock and uttering prophecies in obscure terms. Some of these, the document asserts, were copied down at the time. But as the hour of his death approached, the madman requested Kentigern to reconcile him to the Church. At the same time, he foretold his own death, which would occur, he claimed, in three distinct ways. Improbable as it seemed, the prophecy was fulfilled when the wretched man was stoned and beaten to death by some shepherds, slipped down a bank of the Tweed, was impaled on a sharp stake and simultaneously drowned.

The other version of the Lailoken story is briefer, telling of the prophet's sardonic laughter when he detects the adultery of a King Meldred's queen (a story which Geoffrey of Monmouth attributes to King Rodarcus) and a shorter account of Lailoken's threefold death.

The Lailoken story is plainly to be related to that of Merlin, despite the different name attributed to its central character. He is a prophet who goes mad after a battle in similar circumstances of distress, takes to the forest where he lives as a madman and prophet, and is connected with King Rhydderch (in the Lailoken tales implicitly, through the connection with St Kentigern). The themes of the Threefold Death and the Queen's adultery – with attendant length – also recur, though not involving the same characters. The precise reference to the battle-site given in the Lailoken story ('between Liddel and Carwannok') – a site which the anonymous author describes as, 'so well known to all citizens of this land' – indicates the same spot as the battle of Arderydd mentioned in the Welsh Myrddin poetry. Furthermore, both Lailoken tales expressly identify Lailoken with Merlin. The first begins by explaining that, 'he was known as Lailoken, and some say he was Merlyn, who was an extraordinary prophet of the British; but this is not certain'. The second version makes the same claim implicitly, since it concludes the account of Lailoken's death with the distich:

> 'Sude perfossus, lapidem perpessus, et undam;
> Merlinus triplicem fertur ississe necem.'

> 'Pierced by a stake, suffering by stone and by water,
> Merlin is said to have met a triple death.'

Finally there is a version more distantly removed, but bearing equally marked indications of close relationship. The Irish Tale of *Buile Suibhne*, 'The Frenzy of Suibhne', dates in its present form from about the year 1200, but is clearly much older in its original provenance. It tells how Suibhne, King of Dal Araidhe in Northern Ireland, went mad during the battle of Magh Rath (A.D. 642), and spent the rest of his life wandering in desolate regions throughout Ireland, living on a diet of wild cresses and water. Like Myrddin, Merlin and Lailoken, he repeatedly rails against his brutish existence. A novel aspect is introduced: at the instant of his battle-panic Suibhne literally flew up to the neighbouring trees, and thereafter regularly flies among the tree-tops. There is no mention of levitation in the British legends, but as Myrddin's apple-tree in the *Afallennau* is said to possess magic powers concealing him from Rhydderch's followers, the theme may well once have been present. Finally Suibhne meets his end by a plebeian hand (as did Lailoken), when the jealous husband of a cook, who suspects her of adultery, drives a spear through the unfortunate madman.

Thus four distinct versions of the prophet's career have survived: the *Vita Merlini* of Geoffrey of Monmouth, the Welsh 'Myrddin' poems, the Lailoken episodes, and the story of Suibhne's frenzy. That they all ultimately represent the same saga (though obviously with accretions and distortions acquired along the way) is abundantly clear and is accepted by the best authorities.[5] There also seems little reason to doubt that the nucleus of the Myrddin-Merlin story is substantially historical, and that Myrddin was one of the bards of the sixth century A.D. whose fame (and, in the cases of Taliesin and Aneirin, their works) has been handed down from earliest times.[6]

In this book it will be argued that Myrddin was a pagan druid or bard, surviving in a predominantly Christian age, and that his poetry was of an overtly heathen nature. Indeed it may be that the disappearance of his original work was no accident, but the work of censorious copyists in early times. In any case, the pagan elements in the Myrddin poetry are so archaic as to make it inconceivable that they could be concoctions of the mediaeval Christian mind.

3

The Kings of the North

Both the Welsh poems and Geoffrey of Monmouth's *Vita Merlini* connect their protagonist with two Northern kings, Gwenddolau ab Ceidio and Rhydderch Hael ('the Generous'). In the poetry Gwenddolau is represented as Myrddin's late patron, whose death at the Battle of Arderydd is so movingly lamented by the bard. For Rhydderch, on the other hand, he expresses only dread as a persecutor whose followers molest him even in the fastnesses of the Caledonian Forest. Gwenddolau and Rhydderch were undoubted historical characters, and enough is known of the age in which they lived to attempt an impression of the land and people among whom the real Merlin lived and prophesied.

In the poem *Hoianau*, preserved in *The Black Book of Carmarthen*, is the following quatrain:

'Yd welese guendolev in perthic riev.
in cynull preitev o pop eithaw.
y dan vyguerid rut nv neud araf.
Pen teernet goglet llaret mvyhaw.'

'I saw Gwenddolau in the track of the kings,
Collecting booty from every border,
Now indeed he lies under the red earth;
The chief of the kings of the North, of greatest generosity.'[1]

This has the ring of an early elegy, like the authentic sixth-century lament for Owain ab Urien in *The Book of Taliesin*, which celebrates the valour and generosity of the fallen ruler, 'whom the heavy sward covers.' At all events, it seems more likely that the quatrain represents a resetting of a genuine elegy for Gwenddolau, than that a later poet should compose an original lament in honour of a prince who had been dead for centuries, and whose family and kingdom had as long ago ceased to exist.[2]

Gwenddolau the son of Ceidio was an historical prince of

Northern Britain, who flourished in the second half of the sixth century A.D. This was a period later regarded as an Heroic Age, similar in many respects to those which existed in Homeric Greece and other semi-barbaric societies, a characteristic mark of which is the disintegration of tribal society, based on bonds of kinship, and its replacement by more personal ties between prince and follower. One effect of this transformation is the prevalence of war between related princes, probably caused by this reorganisation of the kindred. On the spiritual level it is also possible to detect in this transitional phase of society the subjection of traditional tribal and local cults in favour of universally recognised anthropomorphic gods.[3] In Northern Britain during the unsettled times following the collapse and withdrawal of Roman power, an added complication derived from the spread of Christianity, with its own exclusive outlook.

Gwenddolau's pedigree is preserved in the composite genealogical collection known as *The Lineage of the Men of the North* (*Bonedd Gwyr y Gogledd*), where he is represented as sixth in descent from Coel, the legendary Old King Cole of the nursery rhyme. As with so many sixth-century figures, references to Gwenddolau are more tantalising than informative. Once there must have existed a body of poetry extolling his deeds, of which the verse quoted above attributed to Myrrdin is the only likely survivor. Another verse from *The Black Book of Carmarthen* runs:

> 'I have been where Gwenddolau was slain.
> Son of Ceidio, patron of poets,
> When ravens were croaking above blood'

Other allusions testify to apparent pagan connections and to his death at the battle of Arderydd, whilst the *Hoianau* and *Afallennau* poems suggest that Myrddin had enjoyed his patronage – perhaps as one of the poets mentioned in the *Black Book* verse.

An early verse in *The White Book of Rhydderch* extols the poet Taliesin's powerful patron:

> 'Urien of Rheged, most generous that is,
> That has been since Adam, and that will be:
> Of broadest sword – proud in his hall –
> Of the thirteen princes of the North.'

'The North', in Welsh *Y Gogledd*, is a term referring to the region between 'the Wall (of Hadrian) and the Forth',[4] famed in Welsh tradition as the setting of the heroic age in the sixth and seventh centuries A.D. An early genealogical list divides 'the Men of the North' into sub-groups of thirteen of whom Gwenddolau ab Ceidio is one. In what appears to be a further subdivision, a memory is preserved of

> 'The three hundred swords of the tribe of Cynfarch, and the three hundred shields of the tribe of Cynnwyd, and the three hundred spears of the tribe of Coel: on whatever expedition they might go in union, they would never fail.'[5]

The area north of Hadrian's wall was never absorbed into the civil administration of the Roman province, and the tribes must have enjoyed local autonomy much as Highland clans did under the Stuart kings of Scotland. It is likely they were ruled by kings, as were the better-recorded tribes encountered by the Romans in southern Britain, and the Roman military authorities had no reason to interfere with them unless their cattle-raiding and blood feuds threatened communications with the North or the security of the Wall. This they seem to have prevented by the classic method of *divide et impera*. Favoured tribes were taken under Roman influence and patronage, and so were persuaded to overawe less dependable neighbours. Of the four great tribal groupings the Votadini and Damnonii appear to have been pro-Roman, and the Novantae and Selgovae potentially hostile.[6]

After 367 the Romans abandoned all their outposts north of Hadrian's Wall, and by 410 the Wall itself was evacuated.[7] The effect of the withdrawal of troops from Britain was devastating in the South, which became racked with internal strife, and a prey to barbarian invasions from east and west, until Arthur led his countrymen to twelve spectacular victories over the invaders. North of the great Wall (known to ensuing awestruck generations simply as *guaul*, 'The Wall'), however, the effects were much less drastic. Accustomed to self-rule, and permitted the maintenance of trained warbands (*teulu*), the great tribes were for the moment more than a match for their less civilised neighbours, Picts and Scots.

The three major tribal groups listed in early Welsh genealogical tradition may therefore well reflect direct continuity with the tribes with whom the Romans dealt. The 'three hundred swords of the tribe of Cynfarch' (three hundred was the traditional number of a Dark-Age British warband)[8], must surely refer to the army of Urien son of Cynfarch, greatest of Northern kings, whose praises were sung by Taliesin. He ruled over a kingdom known in the Dark Ages as Rheged, which, as it included Carlisle and is reflected in a placename *Dunragit* in Wigtownshire, must have covered the coastal area bordering the Solway Firth – the territory of the Novantae.[9]

The 'three hundred shields of the tribe of Coel' refers to twelve listed kings descended from Coel, including Gwenddolau ab Ceidio. There is no entirely satisfactory means of localising the patrimonies of these princes: Clydno Eidin may have come from the vale of the Eden in Cumberland[10]; Cadrawd Calchvnydd possibly ruled at Kelso[11]; and Gwenddolau ab Ceidio's stronghold was at the confluence of the rivers Esk and Liddel. We seem to have here a list of the princes of the Selgovae.

Finally, the 'three hundred spears of the tribe of Cynnwyd' very likely represent the Damnonii of Ayr and the Clyde basin, since Rhydderch of Strathclyde, Myrddin's persecutor, was great-great-grandson of 'Cinuit'.

One should not exaggerate the continuity of tribal identity from the Roman period to the early Dark Ages, in view of the paucity of the evidence and the likelihood of new principalities being carved out of old. But on the whole it is reasonable to suppose that tribal cohesion lingered in an area relatively untouched by direct Roman rule. After all, in the south, where Roman influence was enormously greater, there is plenty of evidence for survival of tribal consciousness into the sixth century. The names of Kent, Devon, Cornwall and Dyfed still preserve tribal names of the Cantii, Damnonii, Cornovii and Demetae, and post-Roman tombstones commemorate men identified as members of the Elmetian, Venedotian and Ordovician tribes.[12] Thus, in all probability the Dark Age Kingdoms of the Scottish lowlands were the successors of native tribes from the Roman period and before.

The second half of the sixth century A.D. was the apogee of the British heroic age, when the great kings of the North reigned in glory, warring with reckless gallantry against the Angles, the Picts, and each other. The fame of their deeds, the splendour of their courts and the profusion of their generosity was praised in song by the greatest of poets. The compatriots and spiritual heirs of the Men of the North, the Welsh of the Middle Ages, for centuries looked back to that time as their Golden Age. Taliesin sang of his greatest patron, Urien of Rheged:

'And until I perish in old age
In my death's sore need,
I shall not be happy
If I praise not Urien'

And Aneirin proudly proclaimed of the fallen heroes of Gododdin that:

'Three hundred men hastened forth, wearing torques, defending the land – and there was slaughter. Though they were slain they slew, and they shall be honoured till the end of the world; and of all us kinsmen who went, alas, but for one man none escaped.'

Life centred on the courts of the kings, who vied with each other for fame and glory: the courts of Urien at Cair Ligualid (Carlisle), of Mynyddawg Mwynfawr ('the wealthy') at Din Eidyn (Edinburgh), of Rhydderch Hael ('the generous') at Alclut (Dumbarton). Their strongholds, only a few of which are now identifiable with certainty, for the most part occupied strategic positions on hills and crags. As they tended to be replaced in succeeding centuries by the stone castles of mediaeval barons, there is little for the archaeologist to excavate. But other comparable sites provide a convincing picture of the physical setting for the gatherings of the Thirteen Kings of the North.

Dominating the surrounding area, the palace-fortress (*llys* or *caer*) was the focus of all the countryside. Generally they were constructed on natural eminences – hills or promontories – or occupied pre-existing Iron Age fortress sites, ringed by formidable earthen dykes. A stone-faced rampart, surmounted by a wooden (possibly machicolated) stockade comprised the major defence, whilst a wooden gatehouse controlled the most vulnerable point of entry. Within was a hive of activity and noise. Later Welsh Laws specify nine buildings pertaining to a king: the hall, chamber, kitchen, chapel, barn, kiln-house, stable, porch and privy. There was also the smithy, and the daytime bustle and noise of so compact and crowded a community must have been considerable.

With the collapse of Roman order the use of coinage had disappeared. All exchange was in kind, or in the form of tribute. In surrounding fields men whistled behind their ox-teams, and on upland pastures tended herds of sheep and cattle. The villages consisted of reed-thatched houses crowded together for security and comradeship at night, though this made the hazards of fire considerable. Of these humble folk, whose labours sustained the

princely household, we know little enough. Their lives were doubtless hard, though by no means necessarily wretched. In a contemporary British penitential a three-year fast is specified for presbyters
or deacons committing fornication or sodomy:

> 'He shall have bread without limitation and a titbit fattened
> slightly with butter on Sunday; on the other days a ration of dry
> bread and a dish enriched with a little fat, garden vegetables, a
> few eggs, British cheese, a Roman half-pint of milk in considera-
> tion of the weakness of the body in this age, also a Roman pint
> of whey or buttermilk for his thirst, and some water if he is a
> worker.'

It is possible that a monastic worker was better fed than his lay
counterpart, but as the sin for which this diet was ordained is the
most heinous in the canon it seems likely that this by no means
insubstantial diet was that considered suitable for a sixth-century
labourer. Of his state of mind we have scarcely a glimpse.

Anonymous Welsh poets sang that 'The plough is in the furrow,
the ox at work,' and 'keen the wind, cowherds in the open'.
Doubtless the hours were long, but there were recompenses accessible in all ages. 'Delightful is the top of the broom, a trysting-place
for lovers. Very yellow are the clustering branches . . .' When the
days shortened, and 'Cold and wet is the mountain, cold and grey
the ice,' then 'Usual is a day with a blazing fire in the damp of
winter,' as are 'talkative men in the tavern.'

For their betters, the king's court was the centre of attraction.
All winter long he maintained his war-band of well-armed warriors,
many of them doubtless his kinsmen. If the prince were a great
man such as Urien of Rheged, his court attracted adventurous
noblemen from other far-flung principalities. As winter drew on,
these visitors were welcomed as festive companions and harbingers
of future exploits when high summer should come.

After dusk a welcoming lantern glowed by the gatehouse. From
the lodge emerged the king's porter, who checked the new arrival's
qualifications; illustrious ancestry and skill at arms were the pass-
ports to entry. It is not difficult to picture the bustling scene around
the cluster of wooden buildings: the watchcries of the huddled
sentinels; the clangour of the smithy, his kiln's glow burning in the
murk; the harsh grinding of querns; the lowing of the cattle in the
king's barn, the baying of his hounds and growling of chained
watchdogs; and the mingled chatter, shouting and snatches of song
accompanying the activities of several hundred closely-knit men

and women living as one enormous family in the confined area of a dozen or so acres.

Amidst the rain and cold of the North there was no more cheering sight than that of 'the well-fed fire, and pine-logs blazing from dusk to dusk, the lit-up doorway for the purple clad traveller'. A king's hall was an impressive sight, frequently of a great size. At the famous hill-fort of South Cadbury in Somerset, believed to be the original of King Arthur's 'Camelot', there are traces of a building sixty-three feet long by thirty-four feet wide. At Castle Dore in Cornwall the main hall was still larger: ninety feet by forty feet, comparable in size to the halls of colleges at Oxford or Cambridge. They were constructed entirely of wood, the work of skilled carpenters, and the roof was supported by a double row of parallel pillars running down the interior. The hearth was in the centre of the hall, while guests and hosts appear to have sat along opposite sides, the pillared aisles making a natural division.

The poetry of Aneirin and Taliesin provides vivid glimpses of the scene in the smoky chamber, lit up by flaring tapers. The steward 'led us up to the bright fire and to the reclining seat covered with white fleece.' There were couches set out on which the revellers sat or reclined, and the company was resplendent in clothing 'gold and purple', with glint of jewellery and fine brooches. As none of the clothing and all too few of the artefacts have survived, the original 'Age of Arthur' is frequently popularly represented as crudely barbaric. The literary evidence provides a very different picture.

'Reclining on his cushions, Blaen used to dispense the drinking horn in his luxurious palace.'

Buffalo horns, magnificently ornamented, were the usual drinking receptacles, but there were glasses in plenty, as well as gold and silver goblets. Mead, wine and ale were the principal drinks, and we even read of a 'sparkling wine' enjoyed by sixth-century connoisseurs. As in the later mediaeval period, meat (beef, pork and mutton) formed the staple course of the banquet to which vegetables merely added variety. But there was fish, cheese, milk and honey and bread in abundance, and the existence of herb-gardens may suggest that culinary skills were more discerning than might perhaps be expected.

The meat appeared in a richly-chased cauldron, probably seething over the central hearth, from which the diners extracted choice morsels with their flesh-forks. This was a ceremony conducted with strict regard to social precedence, disregard of which could result in terrible resentment or open quarrel. Prestige and honour were indeed all-important. The purpose of all this entertainment was the cementing of links of loyalty between the prince and his military following. In return for the winter's mead, symbolising princely hospitality, the war-band solemnly vowed themselves to their lord's service in the coming campaigning season. Men publicly 'boasted', telling of the terrible devastation they would inflict on the foe, and enumerating their claims to aristocratic worth. This self-advertisement was by no means so indecorous as might appear. It was an expected ritual, designed to extol the prince by the merit of his supporters, at the same time publicly committing them to honourable actions from which there could be no retraction. This was just a return for the prince's lavish hospitality, whose generosity must bear no stigma of parsimony. 'As thou gatherest, so thou scatterest,' Urien of Rheged was reminded by Taliesin.

The oldest Welsh poetry, the laws, and the tales of the *Mabinogi* unite in stressing the courtly prerequisites of chivalrous bearing and attention to the etiquette of polite society. Just as unyielding ferocity was the greatest virtue of the warrior in battle, so mild and courteous behaviour (actually described by Aneirin as 'refined manners') at home exalted a nobility only partially conferred by illustrious ancestry. Of one hero it is recorded that he, 'was courteous and tenacious, he was grave,' and of another, 'distinguished man . . . his manners were like the sea-flood for graciousness and liberality and pleasant mead-drinking.' In particular it was regarded as a mark of gentlemanly conduct to comport oneself chivalrously before the ladies. Of a fearless chieftain named Madog, Aneirin noted approvingly that he was, 'breathless in the presence of a girl.' Grace, beauty, modesty and dignified sense of worth are the qualities frequently attributed to ladies, and in the Welsh laws they were accorded considerable independent status. Wives deserted by their husbands were awarded up to half their mutual property and were permitted to desert a husband with dowry intact, should he prove impotent – or even suffer from bad breath.

We have only glimpses of the degree of sophistication which prevailed. Professional poets, storytellers and jesters attended on the feasts. There were light-hearted games, played by both sexes and allowing opportunity for flirtation and doubtless much other amusement of which we know nothing. It is impossible even to guess at the state of knowledge among the well-educated classes at the time. Some poetry has survived, and perhaps some bardic lore, but there is no reason to suppose this was the only type of information available.[13]

The British heroic age differed in one marked respect from other counterparts. It enjoyed the heritage of Rome. Sixth-century kings in the Scottish Lowlands cannot have been wholly beyond reach of the Empire of Justinian and his successors. Wine-merchants sailed from Gaul, Africa and further east in the Mediterranean to sell wares to the free-spending princes of North Britain.[14] Above all there was the Christian Church, which ensured the daily usage of the Latin language from Tintagel to Iona, and whose ecclesiastics travelled widely in Britain and on the Continent. A particularly relevant example is that of St Kentigern, who returned from being a bishop in Gaul to take up the episcopate of Glasgow in the time of King Rhydderch, Myrddin's Christian persecutor.[15]

The Empire which had administered Britain for nearly four centuries did not live on only in her memorials: a road-system travelling from the Clyde to the Channel, crumbling remains of cities and fortresses and, above all, the great Wall, twelve feet high and stretching from sea to sea.

The evidence suggests that there also survived a 'Roman' attitude or public opinion alongside the native Celtic. This centred on the Church, but was not necessarily exclusive. The one undoubted contemporary writer of sixth-century Britain was Gildas, an ecclesiastic who, some time before the year 550, wrote an excoriating denunciation of what he took to be the parlous state of his country's affairs. Most of his strictures were directed at his fellow-clergymen's back-slidings, but he did not spare the leading laity.

In particular he denounced five kings, who were the major rulers of south-western and western Britain from the Channel to North Wales. Gildas's general charges are that they engage in plundering and civil war, practise polygamy, and maintain bands of robbers who dine at their tables:

'Alms they give profusely, but over against this they heap up a huge mountain of crimes . . . Despising the innocent and lowly, they to their utmost extol to the stars the bloody-minded, the proud, the murderous men, their own companions . . .'

In fact what we have here is not a description of unusual tyranny, but simply a hostile version of the society described earlier where kings, permitted concubinage under native law[16], extended lavish hospitality to their war-bands over the winter as a prelude to raiding their neighbours in the summer.

Gildas's viewpoint is explicitly Christian and Roman in outlook: the Britons, in their wars with the Saxons, are repeatedly termed *cives*, 'citizens'. The concept of *Romanitas* is so ingrained in his consciousness that he takes it for granted.[17] Maelgwn of Gwynedd (North Wales), the greatest of the kings, is described as neglecting 'the praises of God in the tuneful voice of Christ's followers' for 'thine own praises,' sung by 'the rascally crew yelling forth like Bacchanalian revellers, full of lies and foaming phlegm, so as to besmear everyone near them.' The reference is clearly to the King's household bards, and the songs customarily composed in his honour. When Maelgwn engaged in a bigamous marriage, it was these flatterers who 'asserted at the tops of their voices . . . that it was a legitimate marriage . . . but our tongues say, in desecrated wedlock.' Clearly there were two bodies of opinion in the mid-sixth century. There was the view of the Church and of 'Roman' society, to which Gildas appealed, and there was the older native law and custom, upheld equally vociferously by such men as the courtiers of Maelgwn.[18]

Gildas makes it clear, however, that for all their backslidings neither Maelgwn nor his co-princes were pagans. Maelgwn himself had taken vows and entered a monastery for a time. A close study of Gildas's language suggests he was accustomed to speak his native tongue (Welsh) but wrote fluently enough in Latin. The implication seems clear that there was an educated public opinion in sixth-century Britain which understood Latin[19] and possessed a civilised, 'Roman', outlook. It clearly included the erring princes. Gildas hoped and perhaps expected that his libel would shame the five rulers into more decorous ways. On one level they considered themselves cultured citizens of that greater world beyond the Channel, calling themselves, 'magistrate' and 'citizen', and dating events by the current Roman consulship.[20] On another they conducted their lives in accordance with the unchanging structure of Celtic society, maintaining at their table the 'parasites' described by Posidonius in the second century B.C., rewarding their bards' encomiums, and preparing the next foray against an equally truculent neighbour.

A comparison may be made with the Highland Chiefs before 1745. Among the clans the old Gaelic society had survived almost unchanged over the centuries. Each chief had his household bard, who 'celebrates in *Irish* verse the Original of the Tribe, the famous warlike Actions of the successive Heads, and sings his own Lyricks as an Opiate to the Chief . . .' It was a way of life little different from that of Urien Rheged or Rhydderch Hael in the Dark-Age North. Yet these chiefs could at the same time be polished eighteenth-century gentlemen like Lochiel, Clanranald, and Keppoch, who sent their sons to university and surprised unwary Englishmen 'with their good Sense and polite Behaviour.' At home among his Fraser clansmen, for example, the notorious Lord Lovat continued a patriarchal, uninhibitedly violent way of life as did few other chiefs. Indeed, his private violence and public crimes paralleled remarkably the career Gildas ascribed to Maelgwn. Yet the same man, when at the court of Louis XIV

'dress'd fashionably and agreeably; his Language was courtly, his Behaviour polite, his Wit brilliant, and his whole Carriage graceful and manly. Thus qualified, we may easily imagine that he made no mean Figure at the *French* Levees'.[21]

The most influential and conservative element of Celtic society was that of the bards. That they existed in the Roman and pre-Roman eras is attested by Classical writers, and their influence over kings and courts was profound. Just as their praises recorded in verse assured a prince of current fame and posthumous glory, so their biting satires could destroy the reputation of the greatest of kings. In the Welsh tale of *Pwyll, Prince of Dyfed* the hero offends Arawn, King of the Otherworld, who threatens to have him 'satirised to the value of a hundred stags'. This was no mean threat, as it was believed that the most biting pasquinades could raise blisters on a man's body.[22]

When the bard declaimed, he was a man inspired by his *awen*, a heavenly inspiration which raised the poet above his ordinary self to a kind of elation or ecstasy. In this ecstasy, which took on the form of a trance, the bard frequently moved beyond considerations of the present and foretold the future of his people with tremendous authority, fervour and conviction.[23]

Every king normally maintained his own household bard, whose duties in some respects were not dissimilar to those of the English Poet Laureate. The Welsh Laws specify:

'When the king wishes to listen to songs, let the chief poet sing two songs to him in the upper hall, one of God and another of the kings . . . When the queen wishes to hear a song in her chamber, let the bard of the bodyguard sing to her three skilful songs in a quiet voice, so as not to upset the hall.'

Their singing was frequently accompanied by a harp, often of great value.[24] There were bards, too, who travelled from one king's court to another. A very great poet would be much in demand, with kings vying for his services. Equally the bard might miscalculate, and sue for reconciliation with a monarch he had rashly deserted. Taliesin's surviving poems principally extol Urien of Rheged and his son Owain, but others believed to be authentic are panegyrics on Cynan of Powys, whose court lay by the Severn, possibly on the site of Shrewsbury, and Gwallawg of Elmet in Yorkshire. This or another 'desertion' probably inspired the poem *Dadolwch Uryen, Eulogy of Urien*, in which Taliesin eloquently pleads to be received at the court of Rheged:

> 'There was none I loved better before I knew him;
> Now that I see how much I obtain,
> I will no more forswear him than the most high God.'[25]

However it no more paid a powerful prince to refuse a great poet than it did for the bard to neglect his patron. As Taliesin's words hint none too subtly, the rewards could be prodigious. From Cynan Garwyn at Pengwern, Taliesin received a hundred racehorses with rich accoutrements, a hundred purple cloaks, a hundred bracelets, fifty brooches, and a magnificent sword. His return to Urien was rewarded by, 'mead out of horns and good things without stint', 'and gold and gifts unnumbered.' Another poem from *The Book of Taliesin* specifies *largesse* of horses, cattle, wine, oil and serfs.

We may picture these proud artists, accompanied by a troop of servants, inferior entertainers, guards and packhorses, moving in stately array across the countryside. They are seeking out the court of a great king, who had plundered and laid low his foes during a busy summer's campaigning. August is perhaps the month when

> 'the bees are merry, the hive is full.'

For warfare and other diversions must be set aside in order to gather in the harvest:

> 'the work of the sickle is better than that of the bow;
> the rick is more frequent than the playing-field.'

Soon it will be winter, and then rain and snow will block the passes and fords.

At the courts of Cair Ligualid, Arderydd, Alclut and Din Eidyn there is acclamation and excitement. Nights will soon draw in, and until spring appears the harp of Taliesin will set the warriors of Llwyfenydd glancing to where their weapons hang from the wall, and the smoky rafters of Gwenddolau's hall will echo to the wild strains of Myrddin's prophetic muse. Beyond the ramparts lies the sodden stillness of the forest:

'Dry is the wind, wet the path, brawling the water-course,
cold the groves, thin the stag;
flood in the river . . .
Storm in the mountain, the rivers in turmoil,
flood wets the level of the villages;
the world is an ocean to look upon . . .
The bent deer makes for the end of the sheltered coombe;
The ice breaks, the lands are bare . . .
Very noisy is the loud-shouting wind,
Scarcely in truth can one stand outside.'[26]

But inside the hall there is warmth and laughter, comradeship, poetry and song. As rain clouds sweep in from the Sea of Rheged, and the wind howls across the snowy heights of the Coed Celyddon, Myrddin moves to his place at the end of the couch. Servants heap huge logs onto the blazing hearth, and a smell of seething pork arises from the cauldron. Let the rain drench down on shingled roof and stout timbered walls; mead is in the horn and hearts are high!

4

The Battle of Arderydd

The long, dark winter, with its feasting, boasting and scheming, was over:

> 'The beginning of summer, fairest season;
> noisy are the birds, green the woods,
> the ploughshare in the furrow, the ox at work,
> green the sea, the lands are many-coloured.'

On the first day of May families assemble outside lowland townships to begin driving sheep and cattle up the slopes towards summer steadings. In the skirts of the forest swineherds cry to their dogs as great herds of lean, bristled pigs shift from glade to glade; flocks of gulls leave the Sea of Rheged to follow the plough: men are at work in fields and courtyards, repairing hives and fences, restoring fishing-weirs carried away by the floods of February, and exercising hounds and hawks.[1]

It is a bright show in a vast landscape which has still yielded only its fringes to man. Beyond the cultivated vales, the close-cropped shoulders of the hills, and the hairline linkings of Roman road and ancestral ridgeway, lies the dark, impenetrable forest, covering the whole inland region of *Y Gogledd*, on whose fringes spread the domains of the Thirteen Kings of the North. Over gaunt regions of bog the curlew's call alone breaks the silence, while upland mountain and forest remain the unchallenged haunt of roedeer, wild boar, wolf, fox and beaver. There, too, are known to be still more terrifying beings, the *addanc* of the lake, pale *gwyllon* glimpsed flitting in the impenetrable brake, witches with their bloodstained tridents, and tracts of burned and broken bracken where some huge, destructive being has newly dragged its scaly body.

Swords and spears which had glinted idly in the firelight were taken down from palace walls, their shafts and hangings tried and their edges honed anew. Furnaces glowed and anvils rang in preparation for redder work and fiercer blows on summer battlefields. Solemn vows at winter feasts were now to be tested. For with springtime came warfare, 'Once each year the king is to have a gathering of his host from his country to a border country', ordained the tribal law. It was for this that men of gentle blood (*boneddig*) were bred, and this alone that ensured them glory in this life and deathless fame after their passing. They went to battle 'inciting each other with laughter . . . eager for fight.' From now until harvest time the campaigning season was open. Reckless courage and unyielding ferocity were the characteristics most highly cherished by the warriors and praised by the bards.

On the appointed day the king summoned his war-band, which approximated to the three hundred fixed by ancient tradition. When the trysting horn sounded, no warrior could delay his departure, 'even for that one day.'[2] At the appointed place they made a gallant showing, each high-born cavalier proudly mounted ('there were swift thick-maned horses under the thigh of the handsome youth'), his mail-coat and javelins glinting bright among blue, plaided and crimson cloaks, and gaudy pennons. The sun shone on whitened shields bearing gorgeous gold and brazen devices. Behind the élite of noble cavalry marched a disciplined throng of spearmen, and behind them trundled a train of wagons bearing the chieftains' tents (of which we catch a fleeting reference in the sixth-century poem *Gododdin*) and other impedimenta of war.

Discipline and tactics ranked high as martial qualities, though the self-sacrificing heroism of the leaders stood infinitely higher. A wider strategy can be glimpsed, but there was a marked traditional, almost ritual, element in warfare. Challenges and counter-challenges were issued and defied, hostages claimed or exchanged, and single combat offered by accepted champions. There were rituals, too, of defeat and surrender. Caesar tells how beaten Gauls sent forward naked women, an archaic propitiatory gesture recurring in the *Life of St David*; and one of the authentic poems of Taliesin provides a fleeting glimpse of beaten Saxons standing on a river's edge, pale-faced, with their arms crossed over their breasts in token of surrender.[3]

Of the numerous battles recorded from the early Dark Ages in Britain, two were pre-eminent in tradition for their significance, dramatic qualities and exceptional ferocity. These were the battles of Camlann and Arderydd, the latter of which is recorded laconically in the earliest annalistic source as, 'Bellum armterid'. The annal does not employ A.D. dating, but the year is generally calculated as 573 A.D. This brief entry is amplified in another version of the annals inscribed on the flyleaves of a copy of Domesday Book in the Public Records Office.

'Bellum erderit inter filios elifer et Guendoleu filium Keidiau; in quo bello Guendoleu cecidit: merlinus insanus effectus est.'[4]

'The Battle of Arderydd between the sons of Elifer and Gwenddolau the son of Ceidio; in which battle Gwenddolau fell; Merlin became mad.'

This is an allusion to the crucial episode implicit in the Welsh Myrddin poetry, where Myrddin bewails his fallen lord Gwenddolau. There is no means of telling how authoritative the annal entry is,[5] but it effectively summarises the traditional account. Other traditional stories connected with the Battle of Arderydd are preserved in the Welsh triads, mnemonic lists of tales for the most part no longer extant. The first refers to the 'War-Band of Gwenddolau son of Ceidiaw at Arderydd, who continued the battle for a fortnight and a month after their lord was slain,' an account suggestive of the battle's exceptional ferocity. Another tells of 'the Retinue of Dreon the Brave at the Dyke of Arderydd'. A third has a seemingly burlesque character, though as will be seen it could bear a more mythic interpretation:

'Corvan, horse of the sons of Eliffer, bore the second Horse-Burden: he carried on his back Gwrgi and Peredur and Dunawd the Stout and Cynfelyn the Leprous, to look upon the battle-fog of Gwenddolau in Arderydd. And no one overtook him but Dinogad son of Cynan Garwyn, riding upon Swift Roan, and he won censure and dishonour from then till this day.'

Finally, a fourth triad terms Arderydd one of the 'Three Futile Battles of the Island of Britain', because it 'was brought about by the cause of the lark's nest.'

For over a century, brave attempts have been made to reconstruct this political background to the campaign of Arderydd from these allusions.[6] It has been suggested that the principal motivation for this battle was religious or, as is generally the case, religio-political. On the one hand there were Christian kingdoms, heirs perhaps to a lingering tradition of Rome, whilst on the other a half paganism fostered by the bards, who recalled the old traditions of the race before they had been Christianised under the Roman dominion. There was thus a Christian and what may be called a Pagan party. The respective leaders of the two parties would have been Rhydderch of Strathclyde and Gwenddolau the son of Ceidio.[7] There is in fact no direct evidence that Rhydderch participated in the battle. But as the Myrddin poems represent the seer as fugitive bard of the dead Gwenddolau, and Rhydderch his principal persecutor, it is certainly a likely implication that it was Rhydderch who emerged triumphant in the North after Arderydd, whether or not he actually participated.

There is no doubt that Rhydderch was a powerful king ruling at Strathclyde towards the end of the sixth century, and that he was a champion of Christianity. He appears in the genealogies of the Men of the North, and is listed in an early and credible record as one of those kings who fought against the heathen Angles in Northumbria. Still earlier is the account provided by Adomnan, seventh-century biographer of St Columba, who refers to the Saint's contacts with

'Rodercus filius Tothail qui in petra Cloithe regnavit'

'Rhydderch son of Tudwal who reigned at Dumbarton'[8]

The mediaeval *Life of St Kentigern*, apostle of Strathclyde and founder of the bishopric of Glasgow, stresses the close relationship between Kentigern and his patron King Rhydderch. The Saint was at first persecuted by a pagan King Morken and obliged to depart abroad, but later returned at the invitation of Rhydderch to establish or re-establish the Faith in Strathclyde. Much of the *Life of St Kentigern* is as unreliable as any other piece of mediaeval hagiography, but it seems reasonable to accept as factual an outline which accords well with more reliable sources.

That Rhydderch was a Christian and patron of Christianity is of course what is to be expected of a sixth-century king. There is one seemingly archaic reference, however, which appears to make him a Christian *par excellence*, one contrasted by indication with heathen contemporaries. A verse in *The Black Book of Carmarthen* refers to him as 'ritech hael ruyfadur fit': 'Rhydderch the Generous, defender of the faith.' Such an epithet could surely have no meaning except in an age when the faith required defence.[9]

There is in fact a considerable body of evidence which indicates that Celtic paganism in the second half of the sixth-century was still a force to be reckoned with. Whilst no one would doubt that pagan superstitions and practice lingered among the folk throughout the Dark Ages (and indeed long after), it is generally accepted that Celtic Britain by the year 550 was a Christian country. There is abundant evidence – archaeological, epigraphical and literary – that this is broadly speaking true. Most significant of all appears the testimony of Gildas, the only contemporary writer. He is a Christian, writing for a Christian public, who denounces in fearless terms five great kings ruling from Land's End to the River Dee. His purpose is to excoriate their wickedness and backslidings, but it is significant that nowhere is there a hint of paganism among their elaborately listed sins. This might suggest then, that paganism was no longer a faith overtly practised.[10]

There is however one passage in Gildas, hitherto overlooked, which suggests that paganism was alive and kicking in his day, and that it was more by default than active virtue that the kings restrained themselves from reverting to worship in the older religion.

Denouncing the hypocrisy of kings who fulfil all the ritual demands of Christianity while flagrantly flouting God's strictest precepts, Gildas asserts that the refusal to obey God's commands is in itself 'the crime of idolatry', going on to assure his readers:

> non sibi scelerati isti, dum nongentium diis perspicue litant, subplaudent, siquidem conculcantes porcorum more pretiosissimas Christi margaritas, idolatrae.'

> 'Let not those wicked ones [the kings of Britain] applaud themselves because they do not *publicly* sacrifice to the gods of the heathens, since by treading under foot like swine the most precious pearls of Christ, they are idolaters.'

This is surely no allusion to a long-dead paganism, vanished in a previous generation, but to rites whose clutches the princes are evading only by the skin of their teeth.

Clearly the allusion, to apply at all, must be to people in an equivalent position to the five princes: presumably British kings elsewhere. But where could such pagan kings have reigned, and why if they existed did Gildas not include them in his polemic? The kings who aroused Gildas's ire ruled all that part of Britain south of the Pennines which had not fallen into the hands of the Anglo-Saxons. North of that area was the region held by the Thirteen Kings of The North, the *Gwyr y Gogledd*. Their territory extended as far as the River Forth, beyond which were the Pictish kingdoms. At the time when Gildas wrote, the predecessors of

Rhydderch Hael and Urien Rheged flourished in the North. Why were they omitted from his catalogue?

The answer may be that he thought them beyond the pale of civilised decencies, people no more capable of polished Christian behaviour than contemporary Pictish, Irish or Saxon kings whom Gildas likewise ignores. For the *Britannia* of which Gildas writes does not signify the whole British isle, but only a portion of it, inclusive of Wales and the West Country.[11] It is Britain in this restricted sense which is inhabited by 'citizens' (*cives*) and with which Gildas is concerned. To Gildas and his fellow 'citizens', it seemed that the Britons of the North were still semi-barbarians. Early Welsh tradition speaks of war between Western and Northern Britons later in the century, and the great forest north of Hadrian's Wall was believed to be populated by wandering shades. About the very time that Gildas was writing, the Byzantine historian Procopius described Britain as an island divided by a Wall. On one side of it (the south) lay a fertile, prosperous region inhabited by Britons, Angles and Friesians; while on the other there was a savage landscape whose atmosphere was too tainted for humans, peopled in consequence only by wild beasts and serpents. He added that the people (presumably of the inhabited south) preserved a fable that the land beyond the Wall was the abode of departed spirits. The source of this bizarre account was doubtless travellers' tales, but serves to confirm the ill repute with which the district between the Roman Walls was regarded by the Britons dwelling to the south.[12]

It was these Britons of the North, still semi-barbarian and semi-pagan whom Gildas could not consider on a par even with the most dissolute of kings in southern Britain. It would be an impertinence for the Christian heirs of Rome to use barbarian clansmen as a yardstick by which to measure their own tarnished virtue.

The evidence of Gildas, the only contemporary historian, is of unique importance and bears out other indications of pagan survival north of the Wall. Naturally the position is not black-and-white. There had been Christian communities in the North since the fifth century, and some of the names in the royal genealogies suggest that Christianity had reached the courts of kings favourably inclined to Rome.[13] By the end of the sixth century all the kings appear to have been at least outwardly Christian, but as might be expected, paganism was by no means extinct.

The greatest of the kings of the North in the generation following Gildas was that Urien of Rheged before whom Taliesin sang. In one of his poems the bard specifically terms Urien 'the lord of Christendom'. But a triad which refers to Urien as one of the 'three Bull-protectors of the Island of Britain' is seen as conferring a strongly pagan attribute to him. A later elegy, in *The Red Book of Hergest*, bearing strong internal indications of being based on authentic material, expresses an anonymous bard's lamentation over the death of Urien.[14] He is back at the King's fortress, now deserted and overgrown with nettles. He bears with him a grisly relic; the head of the dead monarch, its 'mouth spattered with foaming blood'. Critics have long been puzzled by the significance of this act,[15] but perhaps the bard is represented as fulfilling a traditional pagan Celtic ritual, whereby the head of a slain prince was brought home for burial. As one example among many, one may instance the end of a pagan Irish King who died about the same time as Urien;

'569 – King Dermot was slaine by Hugh Duff mcSwyne at Rathbeg, whose body was entred [interred] in Conrie & head brought to Clonvicnose, as he requested himselfe.'[16]

Urien's son Owain is connected in an early poem with the Celtic god Mabon, whose name is commemorated at Lochmaben and the Clochmabenstane in Dumfriesshire (the heart of Rheged), and in later sources is also credited with pagan attributes.[17] And in the following generation, Urien's grandson Ceneu is described as 'Ceneu of the Red Neck, who had a serpent about his neck for a year.' This can only refer to the widespread practice whereby seers wore snakes (traditionally purveyors of supernatural wisdom) round their necks.[18]

There need be nothing surprising, therefore, in the idea of a vigorous paganism flourishing in sixth-century Northern Britain, and tradition has preserved dark memories of the heathen outlook of Myrddin's patron, King Gwenddolau. Like Urien, he was one of the 'three Bull-protectors of Britain'.[19] But much more overtly pagan in its implication is the sinister reference contained in another triad to 'the Two Birds of Gwenddolau. And they had a yoke of gold on them. Two corpses of the Cymry [Britons] they ate for their dinner, and two for their supper.' This curious account strongly suggests a cult of malevolent otherworld birds. Pairs of birds, linked by gold or silver chains (and usually transmogrified humans) occur in Irish literature.[20] There also appears to be more than a hint of human sacrifice. A cousin and contemporary of Gwenddolau was Gwallawg son of Lleenawg, and a mysterious set of verses in *The Black Book of Carmarthen* refers to a bird, clearly supernatural, which disfigured him[21]:

> 'Cursed be the white goose
> Which tore the eye from the head
> Of Gwallawg ab Lleenawg, the chieftain.'

The goose possessed divine attributes for the Celts; the raven, scavenger of the battle-field, was known to the Norsemen as the 'corpse-goose'; and a Pictish carving at Aberlemno in Angus represents some such predatory fowl pecking at the face of a falling warrior. Could it have been believed that Gwallawg, like Odin, sacrificed his eye in exchange for divine knowledge?[22]

Yet another triad credits Gwenddolau with a magical chessboard:

> 'if the pieces were set, they would play by themselves. The board was of gold and the men of silver.'

A similar magical board is described in the romance of *Peredur*, and it seems likely it bore a ritual significance.

It would seem, then, that paganism was openly practised in the North in the second half of the sixth century,[23] and that stories circulating in later centuries remembered Gwenddolau in particular as a figure associated with heathen practices. There is thus some reason for believing that the battle of Arderydd was fought between a pagan prince and his Christian adversaries.

The site of the battle was identified long ago by the historian W. F. Skene in an address to the Society of Antiquaries of Scotland on 15 February 1865. It must indeed have been an exciting occasion.

He began by citing the numerous references in the triads to the battle, which prove its great importance in Welsh tradition. Next he supplied translations of some of the Myrddin poems, which allude to the death of Gwenddolau at Arderydd, and the lamentations of his fugitive supporter Myrddin in the Caledonian Forest. He concluded his historical summary by claiming that:

> 'We can see that, concealed under these extravagant fables, are the outlines of one of those great historical struggles which altered the fate of a country.'

Skene continued:

> '"Where then was this battle fought? We ought, in the first place, to look for it in one of the great passes into the country; and a

curious passage in Fordun first gave me a clue to the probable situation."'

The passage was one referring to the battle from which Merlin fled, 'which was in the field between Liddel and Carwanolow'.

The Liddel is of course a well-known river flowing into the Esk north of Carlisle and in a twelfth-century survey of the Barony of Liddel, Skene found the names *Arthuret* and *Carwindlaw*. *Arthuret* he identified with Arderydd; and *Carwindlaw* was not only clearly one with the chronicler's Carwanolow, but must also be a 'corruption of Caerwenddolew, the caer or city of Gwenddolau, and thus the topography supports the tradition.'

Naturally the enthusiastic antiquary could not wait to follow up his discovery. Taking the train from Edinburgh, he eventually

'. . . emerged into Liddesdale, along which we rattled, sweeping past what proved afterwards to be the site in question, and past the junction of the Liddel with the Esk, till we came to Longtown, where I stopped, resolving to make it the point from which I should search for the site. Longtown, the first stage on the great north road from Carlisle to Edinburgh and Glasgow, and formerly a bustling little coaching town, was now deserted and quiet, like a city of the dead; and I found the great coaching inn shut up, and an old mail-coach guard living with his wife and family in a corner of the deserted house. Though the sign of the Graham Arms was still hung, the landlady was so astonished at the sight of a traveller actually proposing to stay there for a day, that she hardly knew how to receive me. I found, however, that they kept an old dog-cart and a horse or two, which they hired occasionally; and, fortunately, the old retired guard was a native of the district, and knew the localities well. The poor people soon became reconciled to their unexpected guest, and did everything in their power to make me comfortable, and to assist me in visiting the localities in the neighbourhood.'

Skene lost no time, firstly, in setting off on foot to explore the Arthuret Knowes, a couple of small hills a mile from Longtown. Noting that the top of the highest, which overhung the river Esk, was fortified by a small earthen rampart, enclosing a space nearly square, and measuring about sixteen yards square, he turned back to the Graham Arms. *Arderydd* was now discovered, but what of *Carwindlaw*? Enquiring of the old guard, he was informed that there was nearby a stream called Carwinelow flowing into the Esk about three miles to the north. Skene eagerly pressed to be driven there, and minutes later they were trotting up the road leading past the fine mansion of the Grahams, romantic setting for Scott's poem *Young Lochinvar*. Shortly afterwards the trap crossed a bridge over the Carwinelow, passing below a wooded ridge on the left on which stood the farms of Lower and Upper Moat. Just to their north at the end of the ridge, his guide informed Skene, was a 'Roman Camp'. With a gathering sense of excitement, the antiquary clambered up the steep slope until he reached the crest of what proved to be a gigantic earthen rampart. He found himself looking down into the inner enclosure, now overgrown with trees, of what had clearly once been an impregnable stronghold. The ramparts, rising some thirty feet from the field, enclosed 'a small inner citadel measuring thirteen yards by nine', and also a well in the enclosure. Most impressive of all was the prospect on the far side, where the northern defence of the fortress was formed by a precipitous bank dropping sheer down to the Liddel, just above the point where it flows into the Esk.

Skene scrambled about the banks and ramparts in a state of brimming enthusiasm. Dismissing any idea of the construction's being Roman, to which people popular tradition ascribed virtually all monuments of this type, he knew that at last he was on the very ground where paganism made its last fiery stand, and where Merlin saw the ghastly vision in the sky which drove him to his lifelong exile in the forest. Skene continued:

'I am sorry that I am not a draughtsman, and cannot lay before you a plan or sketch of this magnificent fort. It is obviously a native strength, and would well repay a visit. The view from it is magnificent. Standing on the highest point and looking north, the river Liddel and the railway winds at the base of the rock under your feet. Looking north-east, the beautifully wooded vale of the Esk opens out before you, up which the eye carries you almost as far as Langholm, and the bare and pastoral valley of Liddesdale extends to the north-west. In the horizon, the top of Birrenswork hill, notable for its Roman camps, is most prominent. On the west the Solway Firth stretches before you; and looking south, the eye rests upon the Arthuret Knowes, and beyond them the chain of the Cumberland hills bounds the horizon.'

The old farmer of Upper Moat Farm, who had joined him, told Skene:

'that the tradition of the country was that a great battle was fought here between the Romans, and the Picts who held the camp, in which the Romans were victorious; that the camp was defended by three hundred men, who surrendered it, and were all put to the sword and buried in the orchard of the Upper Moat, at a place which he showed me.'[24]

Today, apart from the natural decay and regrowth of vegetation, the site remains unchanged since Skene's time. In fact it has become still more remote with the passing of the railway, and a pleasant way of approaching the Moat is to park one's car by the former Scotch Dyke railway station and walk along the disused railway track across the bridge over the Esk. Today rabbits frolic among the bushes where once Skene's train passed by, and a path ascending to the right leads to the summit of the camp. The whole site is littered with large blocks of dressed red stone, relics of a mediaeval stronghold once occupying the strategic site. A couple of picturesque cottages, now deserted, were at one time constructed from the debris, and snuggle in their hollows, mantled over with ivy. I felt an inclination to purchase one from the farmer, refurbish it, and equip it as a refuge in which to reflect and write on

> 'old, unhappy, far-off things,
> And battles long ago.'

However, my cousin who accompanied me was before long anxious to return to the Graham Arms in Longtown.

Skene's identification has been borne out by modern scholarship,[25] and it is worth pausing a moment to speculate on its implications. The stories recalled by the farmer could well rest on authentic local tradition. In the Middle Ages the battle at which Merlin lost his reason was referred to as one, 'so well known to all citizens of this land,' which implies the existence of popular tales in the countryside. Skene himself was justly impressed by the farmer's reference to the three hundred men who defended the Moat, since a triad refers to three hundred men of Dreon ab Nudd who were present at the battle. Interesting, too, was the old man's belief that it was the Picts who held the camp and the Romans who stormed it. It is possible that early tradition would have remembered the heathen Gwenddolau (who probably came from the mountains to the north) as 'a Pict', and his Christian adversaries from the south as 'Romans'.

Perhaps one may speculate a little. It is likely that Gwenddolau was a prince of the tribe formerly known to the Romans as Selgovae, who occupied the hill country forming the watershed between the Clyde and the Tweed, and further south as far as Annandale, Nithsdale, Eskdale and the Cheviots. Arguing primarily from the archaeological record, most authorities have concluded that the Selgovae remained consistently hostile to Roman administration and culture, continually seizing opportunity for revolt. The name Selgovae is a tribal one meaning 'the hunters', and this too may be significant in view of the fact that the locality in which Arthuret is situated was the centre of a major cult of the Horned God, Lord of the Stags. A carved ram-horned head has been found at Netherby, with squared features, narrowed eyes, and drawn-back lips; no doubt some local deity, the warrior-protector of the tribe.[26] Myrddin, as will be seen, was closely connected with a stag-cult, and afterwards sought refuge by the mountain of *Hart* Fell in the very centre of the tribal territory of the Selgovae.

The Moat of Liddel occupies a natural strongpoint comparable to Dumbarton and Edinburgh, both of which were Dark-Age tribal capitals. Its strategic position was unique, dominating as it did the only point of access between Cumbria and the Scottish Lowlands. The Roman road crossed the Esk a few miles below, while a branch road extended to the fort at Netherby (*Castra Exploratorum*). Less than a mile north of the ford the prominent glacial ridge of Arthuret Knowes rises from the edge of the flood-plain of the river and affords by far the best view in the neighbourhood. No force could pass northwards from Carlisle without being vulnerable to attack from Gwenddolau at Arderydd, and it is easy to see how it could be central to any major crisis in the north.

If the High Moat farmer's account represented authentic tradition, then something on the following lines may have occurred. Early mediaeval tradition placed the battle 'in the field between Liddel and Carwhinley.' As this involves a distance of no more than half a mile, the site is pinpointed pretty exactly.

Next one may consider the reference in a triad to the 'Retinue (*gosgordd*) of Dreon the Brave at the Dyke (*rotwyd*) of Arderydd.' It is not clear on whose side this Dreon fought; he may have been a nephew of Gwenddolau. *Rotwyd* confusingly could signify 'either a ford or an earthen dyke', or frequently a 'dyke above a ford'. Can this line of defence be identified? It seems unlikely that Gwenddolau was being attacked from the north across the Liddel, involving as it would a direct assault across the river against the precipitous cliff. Moreover, the Esk and Liddel valleys very likely formed part of Gwenddolau's own territory, whilst the evidence suggests that his enemies came from the south.[27] In that case it would be likely that Dreon was defending (or attacking) the ridge to the south overlooking the Carwhinley rivulet. A caption to the triad suggests that Dreon's dogged stand was made at a tactical *point d'appui*, as the word *adwy* means 'gap' or 'breach'.

Another triad refers to the 'Retinue of Gwenddolau son of Ceidiaw at Arderydd, who continued the battle for a fortnight and a month after their lord was slain.' It was probably this act of heroism as much as any other that marked out the battle as wholly exceptional, since it was extremely rare in heroic warfare of the period for combat to continue after a king's death.[28] However, there may have been peculiar circumstances. The early mediaeval tradition placed the battle-site of Arderydd in the field below the fort. At the same time the farmer's story located the struggle in the camp itself, where the three hundred defenders were slaughtered and afterwards buried in the ground of the Upper Moat farm orchard. As has been noted, there may have been something in the farmer's story, and in any case it is hard to see why the victors of a battle in the field below should have buried their foes on top of the ridge. An explanation could be that Gwenddolau fell in battle on the open ground, whereupon his bodyguard shut themselves up in the great fortress to hold out as long as they could. Once overcome, they were buried just outside the rampart.

Visitors to the spot, therefore, may indulge themselves with a picture something along the following lines. Up the Roman highway from Carlisle ride the cavalry of Peredur and Gwrgi, brothers from far-off York; there too flies the pennon of Dunawd the Stout, and beside them paces the tortured frame of Cynfelyn the Leprous. Behind on the dusty causeway tramp columns of lowly foot-soldiers; among their serried spears can be glimpsed crucifixes and reliquaries. Now they pass the deserted walls of the Roman fort at Netherby on their left, while ahead loom the ramparts of the pagan stronghold. As the army winds down to the ford of the Carwhinley there is a glitter of steel from the slope beyond. Horns sound out a challenge, as Dreon son of Nudd shouts defiantly down to the Christian host.

As Peredur and Dunawd marshal the phalanxes, many an eye glances expectantly back along the highway. Every man will be needed, yet where is Dinogad from distant Powys, who had sworn to be with them? Now a great shout is given, the horsemen gallop through shallow water, flinging their javelins at Dreon's men. After a ferocious conflict Dreon falls, and the Christians fan out onto the open grassy level, where Gwenddolau has drawn up his main force. Above them towers the dyke encircling the fortress, and along the rim against the skyline is glimpsed a grimmer protection: a ring of stakes, surmounted by skulls. And who is that, squatting on the slope and dressed in deerskins, a tame wolf crouched by his side, who inspires Gwenddolau's men with wild songs extolling ancestral valour? By nightfall Gwenddolau lies among the slain, a dark raven on his white breast, while the survivors of his bodyguard have withdrawn inside the fortress:

'It is a bad place we are in: we hear trumpets and outcry!'

'What is to be done?'

'We have no counsel but to close the caer upon us, and hold it as best we can.'

The stockade and gate are stout, the ramparts precipitous, and there are desperate, valiant men within. Again and again Peredur orders the assault, to recoil in bloody confusion.

Now the triad which tells of the ride of the sons of Eliffer to the Battle of Arderydd refers to, 'the battle-fog of Gwenddolau at Arderydd.' In the triad in question Peredur and his companions travel on what is clearly a magical horse[29], and it is into this context that the *mygedorth* of Gwenddolau surely falls. One of the powers most consistently credited to the Druids in Celtic Britain and Ireland was that of raising fogs and storms to serve their own ends. Examples of this belief abound in the early sources. The Druid of Mac Tail conjured up a mist in which to conceal himself from St Senan, and in the tale of *The Fight of Castle Knoc* the Druid Tadg raised a fog around Cnucha that prevented the champion Cumhail from finding his magical weapons. The Druids of the *Túatha Dé Danann* raised tempest and fog to disperse the Milesian fleet; this was successful until the Milesian Druids in their turn exerted their powers to allay the storm. The Irish hero Cú Chullain defeated a giant whose territory was covered by a dark mist. According to hagiographers, some of the British saints demonstrated their superior power over that of pagan adversaries by similarly confounding them with an enchanted mist.[30] In the romance of *Geraint the son of Erbin* there is a description of what is clearly a pagan sanctuary. It is surrounded by a hedge of mist (*y cae ny6l*) reaching high into the sky, from which protruded numerous stakes impaling human heads.

These magical fogs were held to have been in frequent use when influencing the course of battles. Thus a strange battle-mist concealed the army of Ulster in the *Taín Bó Cúailnge*, and Druids protected the Dessi tribe by sending smoke from a fire of rowan over the whole of Ossory. Most of these episodes relate to the mythological period, but a significant example is attributed to a battle fought within a dozen years of Arderydd. The battle of Cuil Dremne in Ireland was fought between a group of Christian kings and the pagan Diarmaid mac Cerbaill in the year 561. The Druid Fraechan's incantation raised a mist which was not dispelled until St Columba uttered a counter-charm:

> 'Oh God!
> Why dost thou not ward off the mist,
> That we might reckon the number
> Of the host which has taken judgement from us . . .
> My druid – he will not refuse me – is
> The Son of God; with us He will act.'

A few years later, when St Columba visited the King of the Picts at his fortress near Inverness, he was threatened by a Druid named Broichan with the same malevolent charm, 'I have power to raise an adverse wind against you, and to bring up a mist of darkness.' But once again the Saint's prayers proved the superior strength of Christ.[31]

'The battle-fog of Gwenddolau,' therefore must surely refer to one of these druidical fogs, raised to confuse and terrify an enemy, which suggests that the battle at Arderydd was indeed fought between Pagan and Christian. But even more striking evidence lies in the character and career of Gwenddolau's bard Myrddin, to be examined in the next chapter.

5

The Mountain Seer

One version of the old Welsh annals states that Gwenddolau was slain in the Battle of Arderydd, 'and Merlin was driven mad.' According to the Welsh Myrddin poetry he appears to have taken part in the fighting ('in the battle of Arderydd my torque was of gold') and laments the fact that he has killed his nephew and niece – in the battle, he seems to imply. In Geoffrey of Monmouth's *Vita Merlini* it is the loss of those dear to him which drives him to madness and exile. These accounts appear to have omitted an original aspect found in the Lailoken fragment. There the prophet suddenly hears an accusing voice from the sky and, looking up, sees

> 'numberless warlike battalions in the heavens like flashing lightning, holding in their hands fiery lances of glittering spears which they brandished furiously at me.'

In the parallel Irish tale of Suibhne, the hero at the height of the battle is driven distracted by a horribly chaotic vision in the skies:

> 'His fingers were palsied, his feet trembled, his heart beat quick, his senses were overcome, his sight was distorted, his weapons fell naked from his hands, so that . . . he went, like any bird of the air, in madness and imbecility.'

This tradition also envisaged him as seeing ghostly armies battling in the heavens above; a theme widely recorded in folktale and even by credible eyewitnesses.[1] It is just conceivable that the apparition was a manifestation of some unusual celestial phenomenon. In April 574 an exceptionally bright comet was visible in Northern Europe, which one observer likened to a 'blazing fire.'[2]

After this, all the versions concur, Merlin (it is convenient where applicable to refer to the composite figure in this way) became 'mad' and distanced himself from human society. In Geoffrey of Monmouth's pleasantly-phrased account:

> 'Then, when the air was full with these repeated loud complainings, a strange madness came upon him. He crept away and fled to the woods, unwilling that any should see his going. Into the forest he went, glad to lie hidden beneath the ash trees. He watched the wild creatures grazing on the pasture of the glades. Sometimes he would follow them, sometimes pass them in his course. He made use of the roots of plants and of grasses, of fruits from trees and of the blackberries in the thicket. He became a man of the woods, as if dedicated to the woods. So for a whole summer he stayed hidden in the woods, discovered by none, forgetful of himself and of his own, lurking like a wild thing.'

With the onset of winter, however, his condition became wretched. The natural fruits of glade and forest were gone, and wild swine grubbed up the roots on which he had become dependent. His only companion was a tame wolf, weakened also by hunger and age. Merlin raised his voice in lamentation at their pitiable plight, a complaint which forms the underlying theme of the Welsh poetry:

> 'Little does Rhydderch Hael know tonight in his feast what sleeplessness I suffered last night. Snow up to my hips among the forest wolves, icicles in my hair, spent is my splendour.'

We are not told how he overcame this sorry plight, but eventually he discovered for himself a refuge in one of the remotest recesses of the wilderness of the Forest of Calidon;

> 'There was a spring on the very top of a certain mountain, surrounded on all sides by hazels and dense thorns. Merlin had settled there, and from that place he could watch the whole woodland and the running and gamboling of the creatures of the wild.'

A messenger from King Rhydderch, who eventually tracked him down, 'saw the spring and Merlin sitting on the grass beyond it, complaining . . .' The messenger managed to soothe the prophet by strumming gently on his guitar (*cithara*), and induced him to repair to the court of King Rhydderch.

Once at court, however, Merlin felt his former frenzy grip him again and, spurning the luxuries proffered him by Rhydderch, longed to be off:

'I put above these things the woodland and spreading oaks of Calidon, the high hills, the green meadows at their foot – those are for me, not these things. Take back such goods, King Rodarch. My nut-rich forest of Calidon shall have me: I desire it above all else.'

Rhydderch employed force to restrain him for a while, but eventually the chafing prophet returned to his beloved wilderness.

Is it possible to identify Merlin's sylvan retreat? Geoffrey of Monmouth is categorical in ascribing to him a particular and permanent spot he frequented, and the Welsh *Afallennau* poetry pictures him clearly as localised in a specific refuge. On the face of it, any hope of tracing Merlin's hiding-place, some fifteen hundred years after his death, must appear quite illusory. It proved a hard task, after all, even in the prophet's lifetime! For many years I resigned myself to accepting such a realistic view, though it must be admitted with some disappointment. It would after all be one of the holiest places in Britain: the very spring beside which Merlin stood at the dividing-point of Time: gazing sorrowfully back at the unfolded centuries past, and prophetically to ages yet to come. Merlin's is the figure glimpsed at the heart of the Matter of Britain, and how dearly would one love to sit where he sat, gazing at the wild creatures of the woodland, and looking upwards at the starry mysteries he sought to penetrate!

Latterly, however, clues unexpectedly revealed themselves, a picture began to emerge, and eventually one magical April day I found myself stooping to drink from that enchanted spring by which the wizard uttered his wild mantic strains. As there may be those who wish to follow the same path, I will explain how I arrived there.

Geoffrey, as has been seen, described Merlin's flight to 'the dense-wooded valleys of the Forest of Calidon', and the Welsh poems likewise represent him as reciting 'in the wood of Celyddon'. Both the Welsh verse and Geoffrey's poem clearly envisage a real forest within reach of both Arderydd and the court of Rhydderch at Alclut (Dumbarton). Embedded in the story of Suibhne Geilt, Merlin's Irish equivalent, is a story of a British madman whose tale so closely parallels that of Merlin, that scholars are agreed it must be another early version. There, too, we learn that the Wild Man's forest is within striking distance of Dumbarton.[3]

It seems certain that there was in the early Dark Ages a place

known as 'the Wood of Celyddon' which was an identifiable location within 'British' Britain, south of the river Forth. The early
mediaeval compilation *Historia Brittonum* includes a famous
battle-list of Arthur's victories, set down in its existing form not
later than the middle of the eighth century. As it contains indications of rhyme and is paralleled by other, authentic lists included
in early elegies (some of the sixth century), scholars consider it to
be based on a fragment of heroic verse. The seventh battle was
fought 'in the wood of Calidon, that is Cat Coit Celidon', from
which it is reasonable to suppose that a Wood of Calidon was in the
early Dark Ages an identifiable location of restricted application.[4]

This probability is borne out by a statement by the mediaeval
Scottish chronicler, Hector Boece, who makes it clear that there
were *two* forests known as Calidon. In the sixteenth-century translation by John Bellenden, we read that:

'In Strivelingschire is the toun of Striveling [Stirling] . . . At this
toun began the gret wod of Calidon. This wod of Calidon ran
fra Striveling throw Menteith and Stratherne to Atholl and
Lochquhabir; as Ptolome writtis, in his first table.'

This is an admitted piece of antiquarian lore, and the past tense
of the verb implies the name had long passed out of current usage.
But in another passage the same author notes that, 'The watter of
Clyde . . . rises out of the samin montane within the wod of
Calidone, fra quhilk risis Annand . . .'[5]

It is this second Wood of Calidon that suits Myrddin's *Coed
Celyddon* nicely. It is midway between Arderydd and Rhydderch's
fortress at Alclut, and is in the heartland of the tribal territory of the
anti-Roman, pagan Selgovae, far from the reach of the emerging
Christian kingdoms of *Y Gogledd*.[6]

Confirmation of this is provided by another interesting source.
The Arthurian romance *Fergus*, which was composed by Guillaume
le Clerc before the year 1225, tells the story of a youth of humble
origin who is knighted by King Arthur at Carlisle. At court Fergus
was teased by Sir Kay, who enquired sarcastically whether he
would undertake the adventure of 'the Nouquetran', defeating a
Black Knight who lives 'where Merlin dwelt many a year.' Fergus at
once took up the challenge, swearing by 'St Mangon' (St Kentigern,
who features so strongly in the Lailoken story), and sets out. What
follows must be of exceptional interest with regard to the Merlin
story, in view of the fact that critics agree that the author of Fergus'
'Scottish geography is remarkably accurate . . . In the whole range

of Arthurian romance there is no instance of a more detailed, more realistic geographical setting.'[7]

Leaving Carlisle, Fergus arrives that evening at a strong castle above a swift and navigable stream, called Liddel. This, of course, is the Moat of Liddel, the site of the Battle of Arderydd. After entertainment there, Fergus sets off on his quest. He passes over a vast plain with mountains on either side, until at last he arrives before a great mountain which seems to touch the clouds and bear up the sky:

> 'Not a beast could climb it, unless it had wings. There was just one way up, made by a giant who lived in the forest. Fergus knew it at once. He tied his horse to the great olive-tree where people were in the habit of tethering their horses, for no horse could climb the hill. Then he went up with drawn sword. Often he slipped and fell on his knees, and only saved himself by clutching the bushes. So he climbed into the Noquetran. He was aching all over when he reached the top, but he looked round him over the wide forest, as far as the Irish Sea, and saw England and Cornwall. A marble chapel with ivory gates was guarded by a hideous villein, which proved to be an automaton. The lion was within, and turned out to be carved from ivory. Fergus secured the wimple and the horn, which he blew three times. Then he hurried down the hill, just in time to hear a noise like a hunt approaching, which scared all the deer. This was caused by the Black Knight. Fergus overcame him, and sent him to King Arthur while he went back to Liddel.'[8]

Here, apparently, are fairly precise instructions on how to track down Merlin's refuge, could we but relate them to actual topographical features. The identification provided in *Fergus* is worthy of some credence. It is interesting that Fergus bases his quest at the Moat of Liddel before riding on to the site of Merlin's refuge. It is as if he were consciously retracing the path of Merlin's flight after the battle of Arderydd, and this may well be what the author envisaged him doing. It is known that in the twelfth century, not long before the composition of *Fergus*, there was widespread popular knowledge of the Merlin legend in the Scottish Lowlands. In particular, traditions of the battle of Arderydd, and its siting at the Moat of Liddel, were described as 'so well known to all citizens of this land.'

The Moat of Liddel seems to have been a favourite setting for northern Arthurian adventures.[9] As an accurate tradition was

Gulad Myrtin: ẏ Goglet

Merlin's Land: the North

Can ẏſ mi mẏrtin guẏdi · talieſſin ·
bithaud · kẏffrediẏ · vẏ darogan ·

N

0   50 Miles

RHEGED *Dark-age kingdom*
          Roman road

PICTS

*Sea of
Iodeo*

R. Forth

SCOTS

Alclut

R. Clyde

STRATCLUT

Din Eitin

GUOTODIN

R. Tweed

COED

▲ Hart Fell

CELYDDON

LOCHMABEN

HODDOM

Annan

Arderydd
✕ 573

GUAUL

Cair Ligualid

R H E G E D

Manau

M. Verity

preserved in the twelfth century of the battle of Arderydd and its
site, so also may there have been a traditional identification of
Merlin's forest sanctuary. *Fergus* is believed to have been written
to commemorate the wedding of Alan of Galloway, chief of one
of the most powerful of the Anglo-Norman border families, to the
niece of the King of Scots in 1209. Its setting was both Arthurian
and contemporary, introducing familiar themes and places. At the
court of Carlisle there may well have been dashing young knights
who were not content to listen to hair-raising tales of expeditions
to Merlin's fountain, but who donned armour and followed the
same route in hope of encountering like adventure.[10]

At any rate, the author of *Fergus* set his adventure in a real
landscape. When his hero left Liddel Moat, he is described as
passing through a great plain bounded by mountains. Of the routes
open to him, neither Eskdale nor Liddesdale seems appropriate.
Both are narrow valleys, terminating within a few miles among the
hills. Neither is checked before anything remotely approaching the
towering 'Black Mountain' of Fergus. As Fergus may be presumed
to have continued his journey away from Carlisle (that is, in the
general direction of the North), the next alternative would be the
long strath of Annandale, which was traversed by a Roman road
still in use in the thirteenth-century, fording the Esk a mile or so
below the Moat of Liddel. Moving in a north-westerly direction
from the Esk crossing, the traveller passes across a fertile plain by
the Solway Firth. Past Lockerbie, hills appear to the east and then
to the west, bounding the horizon at some distance on either side.
The ground rises as the road continues northwards and the hills
close in, until a couple of miles south of Moffat the River Annan
divides at a confluence, where the Evan, Annan and Moffat waters
meet. It is at this point that the valley appears blocked to the north
by a ponderous mass of mountain skirted by the Moffat and the
Annan, rising ever higher, shoulder upon shoulder, combes and
rocky ghylls intersecting, until it culminates in the solemn height
of Hart Fell (2652 feet above sea level).

This, surely, is the 'Black Mountain' of *Fergus*, and a climb to
the summit at once brings to mind the astonishing prospect which
so clearly excited its author's imagination. Ettrick Forest can be
seen stretching away on all sides, ridge after ridge to distant
perspectives. That is not all. Fergus saw beyond the woods the
Irish Sea, England and Cornwall. Cornwall is clearly an exaggeration, but the rest is true enough. In the mid-nineteenth century it
was noted that:

'*Hartfell* may be ascended nearly all the way on horseback; and from its green flat summit may be seen in fine weather, the Cheviots in Northumberland, Skiddaw, and other mountains of Cumberland; Corsoncone in Nithsdale, Blacklarg in Ayrshire, and, at sunset, also Benlomond in Stirlingshire.'[11]

Hart Fell accords perfectly with the location and the description of Merlin's refuge in *Fergus*. The concept of his dwelling on a mountain overtopping the forests appears too in Geoffrey of Monmouth's *Vita Merlini*. There he is said to dwell by a spring:

'on the very top of a certain mountain, surrounded on all sides by hazels and dense thorns. Merlin had settled there, and from that place he could watch the whole woodland' –

specified a few lines earlier as the 'Forest of Calidon'.

In *Fergus* and the *Vita Merlini* the exceptional panoramic view afforded by the mountain towering above surrounding forest appears simply as a picturesque delight. In earlier times, however, it would also have borne ritual significance. In her extensive survey of locations in Ireland where the pagan feast of Lughnasa (it will be shown later what a close connection lies between Merlin and the god Lug) was celebrated, Máire MacNeill was drawn to the conclusion that:

'all of them command extensive views and this seems to have been an important factor in the original selection. When any of these summits is spoken of in the neighbourhood the number of counties to be seen from it is usually mentioned . . . the emphasis on the wide prospect may fairly be deemed to be ancient and the naming of the counties a substitution for a roll of older regional names. The prominent landmarks to be seen, the distant hills, rivers, lakes, ocean and islands are, of course, also mentioned. The importance of the wide view, it may be assumed, lay not in its variety or beauty. Each of the assembly heights which the writer has had the opportunity of visiting commanded sweeping views of the countryside. It was the hill's view over the farmlands which made it a fitting site for the celebration of Lughnasa.'

Miss MacNeill found herself deeply affected both by the natural majesty of the locations, and a deep-rooted sense of the significant rôle they had played in her ancestors' most sublime experience.[12]

In the old Welsh tale of *Culhwch and Olwen*, Arthur's knights

Cai and Bedwyr (Bedivere) are represented as seated on a beacon cairn on the top of Plinlimmon mountain 'in the strongest wind the world had ever seen'; while in the *Life of St Cadog* Arthur himself joins them on another summit to play dice. The reference is probably to some ritual game, such as the magical chessboards (*gwyddbwyll*) of Gwenddolau mentioned in an earlier chapter. As for Plinlimmon, it seems likely that it was regarded as a mountain of a peculiarly sacred character since, as local opinion recorded, from 'grey Plinlimmon's breast' flowed three important rivers, Severn, Wye and Rheidol.[13]

All in all, therefore, there are strong reasons for believing Hart Fell to be the Black Mountain ascended by Fergus in the romance, and formerly the haunt of Merlin. The mountain is the apex of the group of hills from which the rivers Annan and Clyde rise, and which Boece declared to be within 'the wod of Calidone'. It lies too in the very nodal point of the tribal region of the Selgovae, whose ruler, it was suggested earlier, may have been Merlin's patron Gwenddolau.

Boece's reference to the Caledonian Wood notes in passing that the Annan and Clyde rise from a mountain in its midst. He might have added, as did other early chroniclers, that the Tweed also has its origins in the same spot. Such a phenomenon would have been regarded with awe in early times, and an Irish parallel is strikingly significant in its implications. It was believed in Ireland that the Boyne and the Shannon arose out of an Otherworld Well, known as the well of Segais. Hazels grew by this well (compare the hazels which Geoffrey places by Merlin's spring), and those fortunate enough to find nuts 'obtained the seer's gift and became accomplished *filid*.'[14]

It is also worth noting at this stage the appearance before Fergus of the Black Knight with his ghostly hunt. The Knight is clearly a personification of the Horned God, Lord of the Animals, with his Wild Hunt, with whom the whole Merlin saga appears to be bound up. The name *Hart* Fell could perhaps allude to some such conception. As the name suggests, it was a mountain famed for its abundance of fine harts, the last of which is said to have been killed (alas) in 1754. Of course deer must have abounded throughout the forest, but on a magnificent height like Hart Fell, soaring above the line of afforestation, stags may have appeared particularly striking to travellers on the Roman road below.

*

According to Geoffrey of Monmouth, Merlin lived by a spring, 'surrounded on all sides by hazels and dense thorns.' A messenger from King Rhydderch, who 'searched the deepest valleys . . . crossed high mountains . . . penetrated the most secluded places,' eventually 'saw the spring and Merlin sitting on the grass beyond it . . .' Later he discovers a new spring with curative powers, and discourses at length on the subject of healing wells. Though none of the details of Geoffrey's account is acceptable unless corroborated, it seems likely that Merlin was indeed associated with a sacred spring. When his legend migrated in the early mediaeval period across the Channel to Brittany, the Forest of Brocéliande was substituted for that of Caledon, and a famous sacred spring at Barenton was attributed a particular connection with Merlin.[15] Sacred springs and wells played an important rôle in Celtic heathenism and analogy with cults in other societies suggests they were frequently centred on an oracle, whose prophetic power derived from drinking the sacred waters.[16]

There must have been many such springs with similar attributes, but two early Arthurian poems, the lay of *Desiré* and Chrétien de Troyes' *Yvain: Le Chevalier au Lion* recount stories so similar to the episode in *Fergus* as to suggest a common source. The heroes set out from Carlisle to visit a castle, similar to that of Liddel in *Fergus*. They then ride to a fairy fountain (near 'Calatir' in *Desiré*), beneath a magical tree, guarded by a hostile being, and attended by a beautiful maiden, generally regarded as a 'water-fay'. All this is in Lothian, a geographical term in the romances indicating the Scottish Lowlands (Fergus's hostess at the Moat of Liddel is the 'Dame de Lodien'). This suggests popular knowledge of a celebrated 'fountain in the land of Lothian, haunted by fays', which in *Fergus* was held to be the spot 'where Merlin dwelt many a year.'[17]

The beautiful damsel with whom the knight enjoys sexual relations is an element absent from the *Vita Merlini*. However, the Welsh poem *Afallennau* contains lines which appear to include the magical tree and wanton water-sprite:

'Sweet-apple tree which grows on a river-bank. A steward [one of Rhydderch's officers?] drawing near will not be able to obtain its fine fruit. While I was in my right mind I used to have at its foot a fair wanton maiden, one slender and regal.'

There are two candidates for the sacred spring of Lothian near Hart Fell. Four miles south of the summit is the well-known sulphureous spring at Moffat Well; whilst much nearer on the western approaches is Hartfell Spa, a chalybeate spring emerging from the hillside by the stream now known as Spa Well Burn. Both waters have curative qualities, which attracted enough valetudinarian visitors for a small spa to establish itself at the beginning of the eighteenth century. This pleasant little town of Moffat was attended by a youthful James Boswell in 1752, whose health the waters restored remarkably swiftly.[18]

Of the two springs, Hartfell Spa appears on the face of it the more likely candidate for the magic fountain. The sulphur spring at Moffat Well is not on the mountain, being only a short walk from the outskirts of Moffat. Hartfell Spa on the other hand is on the upper slopes of Hart Fell, lying directly in the path of anyone ascending by the shortest route from the Roman road passing to the west. The likelihood that this was indeed Merlin's spring receives some confirmation from a passage in Geoffrey of Monmouth's *History of the Kings of Britain*. When Ambrosius was baffled by the problem of erecting a suitable memorial to his nobles treacherously slain by the Saxons, he was advised to send for Merlin, the prophet of Vortigern. It was no easy matter to discover him, but eventually, 'after passing through various provinces, they found him in the country of the Gewisse, at the Fountain of Galabes where he was wont to spend his solitary existence.' What region Geoffrey intended by Gewisse is unclear, and in any case it seems that all he intended was merely to indicate that Galabes was somewhere in the territory of Merlin's master Vortigern, whom he terms elsewhere 'consul of the Gewisse.' There is however some reason for believing that Geoffrey's 'Gewisse' stands for a region in Northern Britain.[19] Where then was Galabes? It would be uncharacteristic of Geoffrey to have invented a name when he might have made use of an existing one[20], and the context suggests that he had heard Merlin connected with a place of that name, but had no idea where it was.

Could Geoffrey's source have referred to a *fons calabeatus*, 'a chalybeate spring', the initial *c* being altered to *g* by mutation or common orthographical error? There are of course chalybeate wells all over the country, but Geoffrey's only other reference to Galabes contains a hint that he had heard of the celebrated Fountain of Lothian. In the prophecy which he attributes to Merlin, there is reference to 'a detestable bird' which 'will go to the valley of Galabes (*vallem galabes*) and shall raise it up to be a high mountain.' For what it is worth, this might just be an indication that Geoffrey envisaged the Fountain of Galabes to be in a valley set on the side of a lofty mountain. But more to the point is the fact that the place-name in the immediately preceding passage refers to a heron flying 'out of the wood of Calaterium' (*ex calaterio nemore*). For it was near Calatir that the lay of *Desiré* placed the sacred Fountain of Lothian!

Finally, it may be noted that the rocky gully in which the Hartfell Spa spring rises is gouged out of the flank of a mountain forming the south-western spur of Hart Fell, known as Arthur's Seat. Numerous hills and mountains up and down the land are named after the great British hero, and local legends frequently explain the association by envisaging the mountain as hollow, the interior being an Otherworld presided over by Arthur and his companions. A natural corollary of this conception was that wells or springs on the height flowed out of the Otherworld beneath, and were hence regarded as sacred.[21] Thus there is every likelihood that Hartfell Spa (which in any case possessed healing qualities) was in early times held to be one of these sacred wells.

Having assembled all this evidence, I decided to explore the spots I had identified. Together with my cousin Adrian Slack, botanist and fellow lover of Scotland, I drove northwards in April to Carlisle. Like Fergus in the thirteenth-century romance, our expedition began from the one-time Roman and Dark-Age fortress.

Resolved to follow in the steps of Merlin himself, we travelled first to the Moat of Liddel, scene of the disastrous battle of Arderydd. On the way we walked down to the edge of the Solway at Gretna to gaze on the slumbering form of the Clochmabenstane. Once the great boulder, stranded by the retreating icecap, was the focus of forgotten *ludi*, when Selgovae tribesmen re-enacted the sacred drama of their god Mabon; and perhaps Merlin himself poured libations on the stone and presided over the mystery. Now all is quiet and reflective, but the magic is still there where the Solway stretches to the east, and distant Skiddaw with her sisters reflect sunlight from their snowy summits.

Back over the Border in Longtown, we followed the tracks of Pennant and Skene to the Moat of Liddel. There too the scene is unchanging. The huge earthworks are overgrown with trees and brambles, and everywhere lie massive tumbled stone blocks, relics of a mediaeval castle built on the site of Gwenddolau's proud fortress. Just beyond is the orchard of High Moat, where lie the bodies of the heathen king and his gallant three hundred, safe it is to be hoped from the prying noses of violators of ancestral resting-places.

After a night in 'merry Carlisle' with hospitable friends, we drove north to Moffat. As we approached on the high-road from Lockerbie, I saw the view which so impressed the knight Fergus. The broad valley up which we had driven was firmly blocked to the north by the sombre pile of Hart Fell, and soon I would be treading the very spot I had visited so often in imagination! Four miles north of Moffat we pulled up at the spot marked on the map as Russell's Brae, and set off on the last leg of the journey.

Our course was along the bank of the tumbling Auchencat Burn, until we began to clamber above the steep gully it had carved out for itself. Ahead lay the mountain, though the summit was concealed behind the broad snow-covered shoulder of Arthur's Seat. Mountains were closing in from the north, and behind us on the left we turned occasionally to look at the darkened entrance of the Devil's Beef Tub, with its great shadowy cliffs sinister against the brightly sunlit upper air. Soon we saw ahead what my map told me was our goal: a steep, dark gully gashed out of the lower slope of Arthur's Seat, where the Hartfell Spa (what exactly would it prove to be?) nestled.

My heart beating fast, I scrambled ahead into the mouth of the cleft and up among huge scattered boulders which once a giant force had torn up from the smooth mountain side. Round a final boulder – and there it was! Just on the other side of the trickling, rocky burn was a small stone grotto set into the steep hillside. I scrambled inside and drank from the rust-coloured water of the spring flowing strongly up from the ground below. The age of the original structure must be difficult to determine, as there are clear indications of a radical rebuilding at some time. But in its present form the establishment is clear enough, since the capstone above bears the date 1752 and the device and motto of the Duke of Queensberry, a local grandee and patron of the Moffat Spa. A piece of broken chain attached to a rock by the spring head allowed me to indulge a romantic fancy, as I recalled the episode in Chrétien's *Yvain*, when the Knight Calogrant visited the fairy fountain of Lothian and found that:

> 'a basin of iron hangs from it
> By a chain long enough
> To reach the spring.'

Emerging again into the sunlight, I found it not difficult to picture things as they must once have been. I saw the wild-eyed seer, clad in his mantle of feathers, seated on one of the rocks by the stream tumbling past in its stony channel. There is no other noise, except for an occasional lark high above the bare mountainside without. But there was a time when the solitude was broken by the prophet's mantic outpourings, when the inspired ecstasy came upon him. As the spring gushed up from its hidden world of chthonic secrets, so the Otherworld found a momentary channel through the disembodied *awen* of the seer. The cloak of time and space is torn, and a listening circle of initiates finds among the snatched verses a glimpse of the infinite lying beyond the grasp of conscious humanity, where the illusion of time is no more, and past, present, and future, man and spirit, are fused into one.

Reluctantly we drew ourselves away from this remarkable spot, the remote focus of a conjunction of forces where, in Blake's words:

'Man looks out in tree and herb and fish and beast
Collecting up the scattered portion of his immortal body
Into the Elemental forms of every thing that grows.
He tries the sullen north wind riding on its angry furrows,
The sultry South when the sun rises and the angry east
When the sun sets; when the clods harden and the cattle stand
Drooping and the birds hide in their silent nests, he stores his
        thoughts
As in a store house in his memory; he regulates the forms
Of all beneath and all above and in the gentle West
Reposes where the Sun's heat dwells; he rises to the Sun
And the Planets of the Night and to the stars that gild
The Zodiac and the stars that sullen stand to north and south.
He touches the remotest pole and in the Center weeps
That Man should labour and sorrow and learn and forget and
        return
To the dark valley whence he came to begin his labours anew.
In pain he sighs, in pain he labours in his universe,
Screaming in birds over the deep and howling in the
        Wolf . . .'[22]

6

The Last of the Druids?

Very likely the chalybeate spring on Hart Fell bore a sacred
character before Merlin took up residence beside it. It was in many
ways an ideal spot. Apart from the sacral implications of the lofty
mountain dominating all of the North and source of its major
rivers, there was the Roman road which passed immediately below.
He must presumably have had visitors and followers, or else how
was his poetry preserved for posterity? At the same time the
mountain was in the very heart of the Caledonian Forest, into
which the seer could withdraw should danger menace him from
Christian kings at Dumbarton or Carlisle. Possibly the best protection was the Forest itself, the lowering Black Mountain, and
the rock-strewn defile in which the wizard had concealed himself.[1]

I have suggested that Merlin and his patron Gwenddolau were
pagans, suffering at the hands of a newly-triumphant Christianity.
There is much evidence embedded in the variant tales of Merlin
which, if carefully evaluated, indicate in what that paganism consisted. It is a subject of very great interest, not simply for the legend
of Merlin alone, but for what it reveals of the scantily-documented
religious beliefs of the pre-Christian inhabitants of Britain.

There are some curious aspects of the Welsh *Myrddin* poetry
which invite investigation. What, for example, is the significance of
the 'sweet-apple tree' with its implicit magical virtues ('its peculiar
power hides me from the men of Rhydderch'), addressed by
Myrddin in the poem *Afallennau*? Magical apples and apple-trees
form a recurring theme in early Celtic literature, and in certain
localities there existed sacred groves and individual trees. In particular, enchanted apple-trees were associated with fairyland and
the Otherworld. The fairy woman who told Bran of its delights
bore one of their branches, and apples and roast-pork formed two
of the major delights of the Otherworld.[2] When King Arthur fell

at the battle of Camlann he was borne away to the Island of Apples (*insula pomorum*), later localised at Glastonbury, but in fact that Happy Isle which, 'produces crops in abundance and grapes without help; and apple trees spring up from the short grass in its woods'. There Arthur will rest until cured of his wounds.[3]

The mythic significance of the apple is not confined to Celtic countries. Everyone recalls the tree in the Garden of Eden which imparted knowledge of good and evil to those who tasted of its fruit, though the tree which stood next to it providing the gift of immortality is often overlooked. The Greeks had their Golden Apples of the Hesperides, which 'were presented by Earth to Zeus after his marriage with Hera, and guarded by an immortal dragon with a hundred heads', and which were visited by men passing to the Happy Otherworld.

It is clear that in general the apple was regarded as a fruit closely associated with the Otherworld, and that sacred apples conferred the gift of immortality.[4] A belief in their sacred character features strongly in mediaeval mysticism and folk-belief. In Wales, apples play an important rôle in games with a divinatory purpose, a power presumably conferred on the eater by their Otherworld connections. We should envisage Myrddin, therefore, uttering prophecies below a magical apple-tree, prophecies which were perhaps induced through the magical power of its fruit. Perhaps, too, the power which he claimed it had of concealing him from those around, signified a temporary departure of the soul from the body during his mantic trance. The significance of the apple-tree among the Celts is widely documented[5] and it is the more odd to find distinguished Celtic scholars apparently overlooking the fact in the context of Myrddin's tree.[6]

Odder still is the apparent lack of interest in the invocations to the 'little pig' in the *Hoianau* poetry. 'Oh, little pig!' starts each verse, followed apparently inconsequentially with lamentations over Myrddin's wretched life in the forest, and prophecies of future wars and rumours of wars.

It may be noted firstly that pigs wild and domestic played a very important rôle in the lives of the Celtic peoples. The boar was clearly the cult animal *par excellence* of the Celts, and pork their favourite food. Joints of pork were placed in the graves of the Marnian tribe, the Parisii of East Yorkshire, doubtless because 'the Celtic chief was to take with him on his journey the favourite food of the Celt.' The robbers who kidnapped St Patrick are said to have sacrificed part of the meat of pigs they had caught 'to their idols' for which reason the Saint declined to join the meal in spite of his hunger.

Pigs were credited with what to us may appear surprising qualities. They frequently acted as guides indicating where churches and other settlements should be established. The town of Glastonbury, for instance, was said to owe its site to the choice of a wandering herd of swine, and St Dubricius employed a similar method of surveying the site of his church by the Wye. Some of these stories are clearly legendary, but others may be based on actual incidents. When the Bechuanas of South Africa were about to found a new township, for instance, they allowed a blinded bullock to wander for four days and began building at the point it had then reached. Still more impressive were massive man-made features of the countryside whose origins were forgotten in time, and eventually became likewise credited to divine pigs of gigantic proportions. In Northern Ireland there is a great defensive fortification known as the Black Pig's Dyke, and the Wall of Antoninus was also named by the Irish *clad na muice*, 'swine's dyke'. Possibly it was believed that such earthworks had been ploughed up by the powerful snouts and tusks of semi-divine swine, such as the boar Twrch Trwyth hunted by Arthur and his nobles in the story of *Culhwch and Olwen*, or the magic pig slain by Diarmaid in a well-known Irish tale.

Above all, pigs were believed to come from the Otherworld, and 'were certain guides to the Otherworld'. Two lords of the Otherworld were divine swineherds and the heathen Celts sacrificed pigs, presumably in the belief that they returned to the Otherworld. In Ireland, Cian, father of the god Lug, when pursued by his enemies struck himself with a 'druidical wand' and transformed himself into a pig. Transfixed by a spear, he turned back into his own shape and was stoned to death.[7] These pig sacrifices were not confined to the Celts. In Greece, initiates at the Eleusinian Mysteries had on their second day to sacrifice a pig, for the blood of the pig was considered a very potent agent of purification with the power to absorb the impure spirit inhabiting human beings. In the same way Christ compelled devils possessing the Gadarene to enter the herd of swine (Mark 5, 1–16), and a Finnish folk-tale tells of the ritual killing of a divine pig 'with a golden club, a copper hammer, a silver mallet'.[8]

In early Ireland, a seer was said to chew a piece of the flesh of a pig which he had sacrificed to the appropriate gods. Through its sacrifice the animal became in a sense deified, and so the seer, by chewing some of the animal's flesh and wrapping himself in its hide, was believed to be able to acquire some of the knowledge possessed by the deity, which was imparted to him when he fell into a trance.[9] Could the *Hoianau* verses be the debris of an incantatory address to Merlin's pig before it was sacrificed in this way?

In addition to his pig, Myrddin in the *Hoianau* is said to live among the forest wolves, and in the *Vita Merlini* Merlin addressed an aged wolf as his companion.[10] Analogy suggests there may once have been a companion set of verses to the *Hoianau* in which Myrddin was made to utter other prophecies to a wolf. Wolves, like pigs, were objects of a devotional cult among the Celts, being seen as companions of a god. Several Celtic saints are said to have tamed wolves, a feat probably intended to indicate that they possessed powers fully as strong as those of their heathen rivals.[11]

The apple-tree, the pig, and the wolf all appear in connection with the legendary Merlin, and all have pagan connotations. There remains an even more significant associate, the stag. There existed among the early Celts an important and widespread cult of a stag-god. He is represented in iconography as a god in human form, bearing a stag's ears and antlers. An inscription from Paris names one such figure 'Cernunnos'; that is, 'the Horned One'. It is not known whether this was a name by which the god was widely or merely locally known, or even whether it was a kind of epithet. What is certain, however, is that his worship formed an integral part of Celtic mythology.

The horned god appears to have been worshipped with particular intensity around the mouth of the Solway and further inland. His peculiar attribute is a supernatural control over and affinity with the beasts of the forest. In particular he held power pre-eminently over stags, and also over boars and wolves. Thus, on the famous Gundestrup Cauldron in the National Museum at Copenhagen, the god is seen seated with his branching antlers, surrounded by wild beasts, prominent among which are a fine stag and a wolf; whilst on a cross-shaft at Clonmacnois he is portrayed grasping two wolves by their tails. The god was clearly envisaged by his devotees as a denizen of the forest, possessing supernatural control over the wild beasts, and himself displaying many of the characteristics of his favourite companion, the stag.[12]

It will at once be apparent that the Merlin of the legend (Myrddin, Lailoken, Suibhne) bears in many respects a strong resem-

blance to Cernunnos. Like Cernunnos, he lives alone in the wild
woods. Like Cernunnos, his favourite companions are the pig and
the wolf. And, most important of all, he is like Cernunnos in his
remarkable association with the stag.

This animal does not occur in the Welsh poems, which in any
case only allude in passing to the circumstances of their hero's life.
But in the *Vita Merlini* stags play a most striking rôle. Thus, when
enraged because his wife Guendoloena was about to wed another,
Merlin assembled a herd of deer and, mounted on a stag, he rode
to the wedding, together with the herd.

> 'Guendoloena came quickly, all smiles, and was astonished to
> see a man riding a stag and it obeying him, astonished that so
> many animals of the wild could be brought together and that he
> alone was driving them before him like a shepherd accustomed
> to taking his sheep to pasture. The bridegroom was standing at
> a high window, looking in amazement at the rider on his seat;
> and he broke into a laugh. When the prophet [Merlin] saw him
> and realised who he was, he promptly wrenched off the horns
> of the stag he rode. He whirled the horns round and threw them
> at the bridegroom. He crushed the bridegroom's head right in,
> knocking him lifeless, and drove his spirit to the winds.'

Merlin then flew back to the forest, still mounted on what must
be presumed to be his mutilated stag. The servants rushed forth
and flew in pursuit of the escaping assassin. Merlin was ahead, and
galloping at such a pace he would have escaped but for a river he
suddenly found flowing across his path. His stag tried to ford the
torrent, but in mid-stream the prophet slipped off its back and was
borne to the bank where his pursuers seized him, and carried him
back bound to his sister.

There are a number of points in this narrative worth consideration. Firstly, of course, there is Merlin's amazing power, here taken
for granted, over the wild deer. They are his servants, and obey
him as such. This is the important point and one in which the
prophet obviously closely resembles the pagan god. Two lesser
aspects should be noted in addition. Given that Merlin possesses
this remarkable art of controlling the wild beasts, the episode in
which he tears off his mount's antlers and hurls them at his rival
strikes one as being at once unpleasant and ridiculous. How could
Merlin perform such a feat, and how did the stag bear him off
again, apparently quite unconcerned? The answer, I suspect, is
that *it was his own antlered helm which Merlin flung at the mocker.*

If in an earlier source Merlin was implicitly credited with antlers, a misunderstanding could at some stage have arisen in the most natural way by a simple misapplication of the possessive pronoun, 'Merlin wrenched off his horns . . . and threw them at the bridegroom.' Whose horns? The answer would have appeared self-evident.

The other interesting point is the way in which Merlin is captured through being unable to cross a river. It is well-known that malign beings are held to be incapable of passing running water. In Burns' famous poem, Tam O'Shanter escaped the witches whose dance he had disturbed by putting a river between him and his pursuers:

> 'Now do thy speedy utmost, Meg,
> And win the key-stane of the brig;
> There at them thy tail may toss,
> A running stream they dare na cross.'

This belief is found everywhere in folklore tradition, and is very ancient. Pliny tells how the Druids believed that, when pursued by magical snakes, one should flee on horseback until past the safety of some stream. The belief probably arose from the conception of flowing water as a purifying agent. The rivers Glen in Lincolnshire and Northumberland derive their name from a British root *glanos* (meaning 'clean, holy, beautiful').[13] The episode in the *Vita Merlini* would seem to reflect a time when Merlin, in Christian eyes at least, was regarded as a type of demon.

Suibhne Geilt, like his counterpart Merlin, is clearly a Lord of the Stags. He too rides upon a fawn; possesses a herd of stags which he uses for his plough-teams, and upon whose antlers he rides; and races with the red stags over the fields. The harnessing of stags to the plough was a feature of Celtic paganism which was appropriated by the early Christian Church. A number of saints in early Britain and Ireland were credited with this power to domesticate stags, once again illustrating the Church's policy of appropriating cherished pagan beliefs to its own ends.[14]

Merlin and Suibhne are explicitly described as possessing remarkable domination over the otherwise wild stags of mountain and forest. They also possess another, implicit attribute which is of great significance and interest. Both were clearly possessed of such marked cervine characteristics as to become virtually deer themselves. In his woodland life Merlin is specifically said to live an animal existence (*rituque ferino vivebat*) as one of the herd (*cum grege siluestri*). He lives on 'roots, grasses, wild fruit and berries', or nuts and acorns. It is emphasised that the diet is vegetarian, since when winter comes and the trees are bare he goes hungry. This vegetarianism is inflicted on him by his nature, not by choice. Merlin suggests to his companion the old wolf, who is equally hungry, that he should hunt down wild goats and other prey. He himself presumably cannot adopt the same resource, despite the fact that he is represented as able to outrun the woodland creatures. Nor is his diet simply that of a forest hermit: when the fruitful season is over he subsists entirely as a deer, 'existing on frozen moss in the snow, in the rain, in the angry blast'.[15] And whereas most hermits and Wild Men in Irish nature poetry eat fish and wild animals, Suibhne Geilt is remarkable in keeping to vegetables and fruit alone.[16]

Behind the Merlin of Geoffrey of Monmouth's *Vita Merlini* one may detect a figure conceived as living in the remotest part of the Caledonian Forest, who ruled over the wild deer, wore an antlered helm, and possessed a stag's nature with a human (or rather superhuman) intellect. Recalling his other attributes, he was connected with a sacred apple-tree and accompanied by a pig and a wolf. It is hardly possible to have a clearer representation of the Celtic horned god, sometimes known as Cernunnos. Geoffrey of Monmouth could not have concocted such a figure, of whom traces in any case appear in other mediaeval versions of the Merlin legend.[17]

Long after piecing together this reconstruction of the original Merlin-figure lying behind the Welsh verses and Geoffrey of Monmouth's poem, I came across striking confirmation of the existence of such a conception in Celtic tradition. In an Irish legend, the prophet-historian Tuan mac Cairill invites St Finnen of Moville to his hermitage, and relates to him his story. Tuan, it appears, was the sole survivor of a terrible mortality which came upon the people of Ireland in a former age. One man survived, and that was Tuan. What follows in his tale is virtually my reconstruction of the Merlin legend.

'"For a slaughter is not usual without some one to come out of it to tell the tale. That man am I," said he. "Then I was from hill to hill, and from cliff to cliff, guarding myself from wolves, during which Ireland was empty. At last old age came upon me, and I was in cliffs and in wastes, and was unable to move about, and I had special caves for myself. Then Nemed, son of Agnoman, my father's brother, invaded Ireland, and I saw them from the cliffs and kept avoiding them, and I hairy, clawed, withered, grey, naked, wretched, miserable. Then, as I was asleep one night, I saw myself passing into the shape of a stag. In that shape I was, and I young and glad of heart."'

Tuan prophesied coming events, ending with the verse:

'"Then there grew upon my head
Two antlers with three score points,
So that I am rough and grey in shape
After my age has changed from feebleness."

"After this, from the time that I was in the shape of a stag, I was the leader of the herds of Ireland, and wherever I went there was a large herd of stags about me . . . Then at last old age came upon me, and I fled from men and wolves. Once as I was in front of my cave – I still remember it – I knew that I was passing from one shape into another. Then I passed into the shape of a wild boar . . . In that shape, he said, I was then truly, and I young and glad of mind."'

After further shape-changes (always preceded by a three days' fast) Tuan became once more a man:

'I also remember when speech came to me, as it comes to any man, and I knew all that was being done in Ireland, and I was a seer.'[18]

The triumph of Christianity in Britain spelt defeat for the native Lord of the Beasts, but not his destruction. His power was still felt in the depths of forests and wild mountain uplands, and his figure survived beneath thin disguise in Celtic folklore and literature. His horns caused him to be identified with the Devil, to whom he was in any case appropriated as a prime object of Christian hostility. In eighteenth-century Wales he was still a figure to conjure with:

'Is it any wonder that the devil should sit cross-legged in Ogo Maen Cymwd to guard the treasures there?'

The cross-legged posture recalls the Cernunnos figure who appears on the Gundestrup cauldron.[19]

We encounter him again in the romance of Owain, when the knight is witness to his power over natural creation:

'. . . you must go on until you come to a large sheltered glade with a mound in the centre. And you will see an exceedingly tall Black Man on top of the mound. He is as large as two ordinary men; he has but one foot, and one eye in the middle of his forehead. And he has a club of iron, and certainly there are no two men in the world who could bear that club. And he is no handsome man, but on the contrary exceedingly ugly; and he is the ranger of the wood. And you will see a thousand wild animals grazing around him.'

When Owain reached him, he found the Black Man's powers had been considerably underrated. Owain

'asked him what power he had over those animals. "I will show you, mannikin," said he. And he took his club in his hand, and with it he struck a stag a great blow, causing it to roar loudly; and at his belling animals came together as great in number as the stars in the sky, so that it was difficult for me to find room in the glade to stand among them . . . And he looked at them and ordered them to go and feed. And they bowed their heads, and did him homage as their Lord.'

There is no disputing the similarity to Merlin, who in a thirteenth-century lay is discovered living in the forests of North Britain. His seekers:

'found a huge gathering of wild animals and a very ugly and very hideous man who guarded those beasts',

that is, Merlin.

The Horned God appears elsewhere as leader of the Wild Hunt, an aspect which again is faithfully reflected in the Merlin legend. The first sighting to be recorded in Britain appears under the year 1127 in the *Anglo-Saxon Chronicle*, occurring at Peterborough. As the entries at this stage are written by a contemporary native of the town, the account is of great interest. A ghostly hunt was seen and heard by many terrified inhabitants:

'these hunters were black, and huge and ugly, and they rode on black horses and deer. They were seen in the very deer-park of the town of Peterborough, and in all the woods from the same town to Stamford; and the monks heard the blasts of the horns which they blew in the night. In the night trustworthy people watched them and said there were about twenty or thirty horn-blowers.'

The Wild Hunt, sometimes careering through forest glades like possessed humans, at others coursing overhead in a streaked and bloodshot sky, was a horrifying occurrence all over Britain and Europe. Sometimes the riders, at others their steeds, were seen to be headless. The yelping of spectral hounds and howling of airborne horns on a night of storm and terror was a sure sign that death would follow in the family. For the huntsmen were known to be the souls of unbaptised (that is, pagan) corpses, forever condemned to pursue a ghostly hart across night sky and midnight forest.

Among the Teutonic nations the leader of the Wild Hunt was commonly held to be the god Odin (Woden), and a fourteenth-century source refers to the troop of dead souls as *Wutanes her*, 'Woden's host'. These were frequently said to be the spirits of the hanged, over whom Odin exercised a particular protection, or of men slain in battle. But the name of Odin was but one of many given to the god who presided over the frantic spirits of the dead[20], and the god is clearly older than his name. Odin is represented as having but one eye, a feature shared with the Celtic Lord of the forest encountered in the Welsh romance of Owain.

The most celebrated manifestation of the Wild Huntsman in Britain is localised in Windsor Great Park, familiar to playgoers from the references in Shakespeare's *Merry Wives of Windsor*:

'There is an old tale goes, that Herne the hunter,
Sometimes a keeper here in Windsor Forest,
Doth all the winter time, at still midnight,
Walk round about an oak, with great ragg'd horns . . .
You have heard of such a spirit; and well you know,
The superstitious idle-headed eld
Received, and did deliver to our age,
This tale of Herne the Hunter for a truth.'

And in Harrison Ainsworth's historical novel *Windsor Castle* (1843), Herne is encountered again, clad in deer-skins and antlered helm, following the hart with his satanic companions and hounds through the moonlit avenues of the Great Park. A friend of mine, the poet Charles Richard Cammell, told me that when a boy at Eton before the Great War, he frequently talked with an old keeper who had seen Herne plunge by on his endless chase.

In the Celtic West the rôle of the 'huntsman who fetches to his abode the souls of the deceased' was fulfilled by Gwyn ab Nudd, 'a god of the dead and king of the other world, who fetches the fallen to his own realm'. He was frequently accompanied by the Hounds of Hell (*cwn Wyhir*), whose terrifying passage across the sky betokened a coming death.[21]

There is clearly a close parallel between the figure of the Wild Huntsman, and that of Merlin. The legend of the Wild Hunt is bound up with that of spectral hosts warring in the sky, both being facets of the belief in a troop of departed souls.[22] It will be recalled that Merlin (in the Lailoken version) saw a ghostly army assembled in the sky above him, that he lamented (in the Myrddin poetry) his life in the Forest of Caledon, accompanied only by *gwyllon*, 'shades, spirits', and that he galloped through the forest after the deer, wearing an antlered helm.[23]

There can therefore be little doubt that Merlin was once regarded as a Wild Huntsman, who supervised troops of departed souls in the depths of the Caledonian Forest. In the romance of *Fergus*, it will be recalled, the knight Fergus travelled to a mountain (identified with Hart Fell) 'where Merlin dwelt many a year'. After ascending the summit and gazing on the stupendous view, he hurried down the hill, just in time to hear a noise like a hunt approaching, which scared all the deer. This indicates that the belief, or a tradition of it, survived locally at least to the beginning of the thirteenth-century. It is fascinating to think that we may also possess a *contemporary* allusion. For the sixth-century Byzantine historian Procopius related, doubtless on the basis of travellers' tales, that it was to the region north of Hadrian's Wall that the spirits of the dead departed! And it was the same region which was populated by a tribe, the Selgovae, whose name epitomised the Horned God and his ghostly riders, 'the Hunters'.

The evidence really speaks for itself, and may be briefly summarised as follows. Merlin personified the horned deity who watched over men and beasts, and received the souls of the departed into his habitation in the sky. He wore an antlered helm (possibly deerskins as well), and in some degree acted out the part of the stag itself.[24] His station was by a sacred spring on the edge of a mountain in the centre of the Caledonian Forest, from whose summit he could look down upon the world spread out below. A sacred apple tree or orchard grew nearby, and the recluse was believed to be attended by animal familiars in the form of a pig and a wolf. The whole area of the mountain was regarded with awe and fear (as the *Roman de Fergus* testified more than six centuries later), but despite its remote situation overlooked a major highway much frequented by travellers.

It is scarcely conceivable that such a figure could have resulted from later literary invention in the Christian Middle Ages. To do so would have required prophetic powers as great as those of

Merlin himself, since the forgers would have had to obtain access to the fruits of modern Celtic studies. On the contrary, the authors of most of the extant versions appear to have been quite unaware that there was anything pagan at all about their hero. Only in the Welsh verses may one perhaps detect a one-time consciousness that the poetry was not altogether respectable fare for a Christian community. Incongruous interpolations invoke the name of Christ, so that the Welsh poems most replete with heathen lore often begin and end with a tribute to Christianity.[25]

The memory of Merlin did not perish. His character was too marked and his fame too wide for extinction. In an age governed by auguries men could not neglect the insights of a prophet who, even if his gifts did derive from his horned master the Devil, was so clearly able to penetrate the seemingly impenetrable veil of the future. Perhaps there was much, too, that was attractive and inspiring in his personality. All the accounts suggest a tragic, tortured figure, doomed by fate to tribulations on account of convictions and circumstances beyond his control. It may be that even the Church regarded him with grudging respect. One of the Lailoken fragments tells how he came in from the wilderness to Glasgow and, perching on the Rock of Molendinar, interrupted the prayers of St Kentigern and his clerics with wild prophecies. 'For he predicted much of the future there, as if he were a prophet.' The monks found the prophecies obscure and even unintelligible, 'but they remembered some apparently idle remarks and committed them to writing.'

These hints of a grudging co-operation might suggest an attitude of mutual respect, despite the irreconcilable hostility of the old and new faiths. Both Saint and Seer were known by sobriquets believed to be of virtually identical meaning, *Munghu* and *Llallogan*: 'dear friend'. The author of the *Life of Saint Kentigern* was clearly at pains to establish the fact that his hero possessed all the impressive powers credited to his heathen rival. Kentigern, 'by the mighty power of his word', was able to tame the wild deer and compel them to serve him; Kentigern had a wolf and a wild boar who succumbed to his enchantments and became his pious servitors; and, most wonderful of all, Kentigern, delivered

'a prophecy concerning the Britons and Angles so accurate, that all England was able to uphold a faith so demonstrably true.'

If it were not possible to eradicate popular memory of the

Caledonian prophet, what could be done was to suggest that his Christian counterpart, St Kentigern, possessed equal or superior magical powers, and that Merlin in any case had by the end acquired a certain odour of sanctity.

The setting of the cult and its practitioner have become reasonably clear, but what was its function and purpose?

From the earliest times interest focused almost exclusively on Merlin's reputation as a prophet. The poem *Gododdin*, whose reference (if not an interpolation) may be contemporary with Myrddin himself, refers simply to his *awen*, or prophetic-poetic inspiration. But in the tenth-century poem *Armes Prydein* a section begins 'Myrddin prophesies', and goes on to foretell the downfall of the English at the hands of the Welsh and their allies. The poem *Ymddiddan Myrddin a Thaliesin*, dating in its present form from about the year 1050, has Myrddin declare himself a famous prophet. In the following century Giraldus Cambrensis, Geoffrey of Monmouth and the Lailoken fragments all stressed his prophetic powers, which Welsh tradition continued to commemorate throughout the Middle Ages and after.

Fragments of what purported to be the prophecies themselves were recorded in popular tradition and in manuscript versions of the texts. Many more must have existed than have survived. In Henry II's reign Giraldus Cambrensis describes an old manuscript collection of the prophecies he had seen at Nevin in Caernarvonshire, and alludes to the story of Myrddin's vision and flight at Arderydd in a form which conflates elements now surviving only in their separate aspects.[26]

The poetry attributed to Myrddin in Welsh manuscripts consists almost entirely of prophecies, with some details of his unhappy life in the Caledonian Forest interposed. The prophecies tend to follow a similar pattern. In the early centuries following the sixth, successive kings are referred to by name, though not always in an accurate context. But as the theme approaches what is clearly the real period of composition, the references become obscure, veiled and cryptic. Current issues are obviously intended to be recognised. This obscurity may be due in part to the author's need not to be too specific lest he be proved wrong, and also to his finding similar imagery in the sources on which he was modelling his freshly 'edited' prophecies. Again, some of the prophecies may be genuine prophecy not referring to any particular event. However, there are unmistakeable allusions to events occurring at least as late as the twelfth century. These include Henry I's expedition against Gruffudd ap Cynan in 1114, Henry II's quarrels with his sons and with Beckett, the invasion of Ireland in 1171, and so forth. Much of the verse breathes forth the most intense hatred of the English invader, and was without doubt composed about the time of the events referred to, with the not unsuccessful purpose of arousing the Welsh to determined resistance.[27]

There can be no possibility, therefore, of such poetry being a composition by the sixth-century Myrddin. Equally many distinguished critics have felt that the nucleus of the Myrddin poetry is much older than the bulk of prophetic verse for which it provides the setting, and with varying degrees of caution have envisaged the possibility of its being as old as the time of the authentic Myrddin, the sixth century. For every forger has to imitate an original, and a tenth-century bard could achieve nothing by citing Myrddin as an authority unless he had already been long established as a prophet.[28] Giraldus Cambrensis asserts it as a well-known fact that in his time (the late twelfth century) the poets, 'added many prophecies of their own to the genuine ones.' Among surviving manuscripts some versions of Myrddin's prophecies contain verses additional to those in others, proving that the prophecies were indeed extended as required.[29]

Altogether, it would be as anachronistic to suppose that a later fabulist could have concocted a Myrddin perfectly suited to a context of Celtic paganism, as that a sixth-century Myrddin could really have uttered the twelfth-century prophecies attributed to him.

It is at least certain that prophecies concerning the deaths of kings were in demand as early as the sixth century. In Adomnan's *Life of St Columba* occurs an episode in which King Rhydderch of Strathclyde sends a messenger to Iona enquiring 'whether he should be slain by enemies, or not'. Columba replied correctly that, 'he shall die on his own feather pillow, in his own house.' A Christian king had to discover the future through a saint. A pagan king like Gwenddolau might be expected to look for similar information to a seer from an older native tradition.

What precisely was that tradition? An enormous amount of speculative nonsense continues to be written on the subject of druidism, but it seems possible that Merlin was a druid, or at any rate fulfilled some druidical functions. The implication seems to be present in the earliest reference to his prophetic powers, the poem *Armes Prydein*, composed about the year 930. This prophecy of the coming expulsion of the English begins one section with the words, 'Merlin foretells' (*dysgogan Myrdin*), and another with the 'druids foretell' (*dysgogan derwydon*), which suggests at the least that their rôles were similar, if not identical.[30]

This and the later Welsh verses attributed to Myrddin suggest too that the subject-matter of his prophecies was the rise and fall of kings and dynasties, and the fortunes of the Cymry in their struggle with the English. Some verses referring to sixth-century kings contemporary with Myrddin could possibly reflect the subject-matter of real prophecies made in his lifetime, the originals on which the later concoctions were based.[31]

It is probable that the prophetic poems in their present state form the palimpsest to an earlier stratum which was replaced when its relevance had passed away. But is it plausible to argue, as I have done, that the originals could date from so early a period as the sixth century, that is, from the time of Myrddin himself? As the only proof of such an assertion would be the authentic prophecies themselves, it is necessary to proceed by way of analogy and a balance of probabilities.

We have seen that there is no good reason for rejecting the belief, traceable far back into the Dark Ages, that Myrddin was an historical figure, famed for his prophetic powers, who lived in the sixth century. We possess a body of poetry attributed to him, though clearly assembled many centuries later. But the poetry is palpably written on differing levels. There are 'prophecies' relating to the struggles of the Welsh against the aggressive policy of the kings of England in the century or so following the Norman conquest. There is at the same time the saga of the suffering exile Myrddin, relating emphatically to persons and events of the sixth century. In particular there is the quatrain lamenting the death of Gwenddolau, which looks very much as if it reflects a contemporary elegy.

The tenth-century poem *Armes Prydein* contains the claim that 'Myrddin prophesies' the coming victory of the Cymry with which the poem deals, suggesting that listeners would recognise him as the likely author of such a prophecy; that is, that prophecies in the same vein attributed to Myrddin were well-known at the latest in the time of Alfred the Great.

As so often, a parallel may be found in Celtic Ireland. Two early Irish poems, *Baile in Scáil* ('The Champion's Ecstasy') and *Baile Chuind* ('Conn's Ecstasy') comprise prophecies composed in the ninth and seventh centuries respectively. The succession of kings who will rule over Tara is set out in a manner strikingly reminiscent of the treatment in the *Cyfoesi Myrddin*, and is probably connected with some ritual occurring at the inauguration of a High King.[32] A century earlier still brings us to the very year after the battle of Arderydd, when St Columba ordained Aedan mac Gabran king of Scottish Dalriada:

> 'And among the words of the ordination he prophesied future things of Aidan's sons, and grandsons, and great-grandsons,'

relates Columba's biographer Adomnan. This looks very like the familiar Christian policy of adopting a valued pagan practice – in this case one whose absence might have placed the monarch's legitimacy in doubt.

Looking back to a still earlier period, we find classical authors attributing the composition of prophecies of this type to the druids. The Aeduan druid Diviciacus told Cicero he could prophesy 'sometimes by means of augury and sometimes by means of conjecture'. Tacitus tells how the Gauls were invited to revolt by their druids, who declared that a recent fire in the Capitol was a portent of the coming triumph of the nations living north of the Alps. This appears to anticipate similar verse urging the Welsh to victory over the English, whilst another example anticipates the sort of regnal succession found in the *Cyfoesi Myrddin*. The Emperor Aurelian (A.D. 270–75) consulted a druidess, who told him of the glorious future awaiting his descendants. His successor Diocletian was told by a Gaulish druidess that, 'When you have killed The Boar, you will indeed be Emperor', a prophecy fulfilled when he slew the Prefect Arrius, nicknamed The Boar.[33] Merlin frequently employs such symbolism, prophesying in the *Vita Merlini* that, 'Dumbarton will fall, with no king to rebuild it for an age, until the Scot is defeated by a boar', etc.

The reports of Greek and Roman writers are confirmed by native tradition. In early Ireland, prophecy is the druidic gift *par excellence*, and in more scantily-documented Britain, prophecies are allotted to *magi*, who are probably to be identified with druids.[34] Certainly in early Welsh poetry appeal was made to prophecies of the druids, as if their efficacy were a matter of common knowledge.[35]

The Roman authorities are said to have adopted stringent measures against druidism in the first century A.D., but there is ample evidence for its survival into subsequent centuries. In thoroughly Romanised Gaul there is evidence of 'a revival of druidism in the fourth century', and paganism which doubtless had some druidic content survived long after that.[36] In Ireland beyond the reach of Rome, the power of the druids lasted unchallenged until the advent of Christianity in the fifth century. But long after that, until at least the eighth century, the Christian Church was obliged to war fiercely against a still resilient druidism. It is denounced as a sin for which there can be no remission in the Old-Irish Table of Commutations, compiled at Tallaght in the eighth century; while an early poem once attributed to St Patrick invoked divine protection

'Against spells of women and smiths and druids.'[37]

Irish druids were not confined to Ireland. All along the western seaboard of Britain were Irish colonies, established during the declining days of the Roman Empire and only reabsorbed into British culture in the fifth and sixth centuries. They doubtless brought their druids with them, and an inscription *c.* 500 on the Isle of Man appears to commemorate the 'son of a druid'.[38] To the north of the Britons of Strathclyde lay the territory of the Picts, whose King Bruide (a contemporary of Rhydderch and Gwenddolau) maintained a druid (mentioned by Adomnan) at his court near Inverness.[39]

All in all, therefore, the evidence indicates that the survival of druidism in Highland Britain, a region largely untouched by Roman civilisation, is intrinsically likely in the early Dark-Age period. The poem *Armes Prydein* alternates the authority for its prophecy between Myrddin and the druids, and may it not fairly be asked whether Merlin himself was a surviving druid? What has been conjectured of his refuge in the Caledonian Forest certainly accords with druidic practice. Roman writers describe them as 'meeting in secret either in a cave or in secluded groves', and declare that, 'the innermost groves of far-off forests are your abodes.'[40] It has been suggested that they sought out these remote woodland haunts only as a result of Roman persecution or disapproval, but such circumstances would in any case apply to Myrddin's condition after the battle of Arderydd. Perhaps the most that can be said is that if Merlin was not a druid, his inspiration was very much in the druidic tradition.[41]

7

The Divine Kingship

It was seen in the last chapter that the saga of Merlin is replete with allusions to early Celtic pagan practices and beliefs, to an extent which precludes invention of the story in the later mediaeval period. The pagan element, indeed, is merely implicit, and its implications were clearly not understood by the redactors of the poems in their recorded form. Merlin invokes sacred apple-trees, and has as familiars a pig and a wolf. He is identified in an early poem with the druids, and his prophecies are cast in the form attributed to the historical druids. He becomes 'mad' or inspired as a prelude to prophesying, precisely in the manner of Welsh bards who were themselves heirs to the druidic tradition.

After the downfall of his patron Gwenddolau at the battle of Arderydd, Merlin is described as retiring to the forest, where he took on the characteristics of the Lord of the Forest and the Beasts, personifying a stag and leading the Wild Hunt of departed souls. The fanciful account by the sixth-century Byzantine historian Procopius, together with references in the Welsh poetry, indicates the region north of Hadrian's Wall as the refuge of departed spirits, and this is where Merlin's Forest of Celyddon is located in early tradition.

This is one aspect of Merlin's nature. He represents the divine ruler of nature and the wild, an elemental, chthonic being of very ancient origin. This Merlin has much about him which is dark, alien and terrifying; the horned leader of a disembodied troop of spirits whom Christian mythology came to identify with the Devil. Merlin's transformation into this wild being is said to have come about after the triumph of the Christian cause at Arderydd.

Before that, however, there had been a time when he was honoured by King Gwenddolau, wore a torque of gold, and enjoyed 'goodly possessions and pleasing minstrels'. His rôle must have been very different at the court of the pagan sovereign, and one important aspect of that rôle is clearly indicated in the old poetry. When Merlin foretold the succession of coming kings he was not simply satisfying the curiosity of those who wished to penetrate the veil of the future, but sanctifying the monarch and his heirs according to pre-ordained ritual. This ritual was sanctioned by the brightest god in the Celtic pantheon, a god whom Merlin seemingly invoked and personified.

Among the pagan Celts on the Continent and the British Isles the god most widely worshipped and who approximated most nearly to a pre-eminent deity was Lug. He is found throughout the Celtic homelands, in place-names, inscriptions and legends. The city of Lyon in France was his, for its Roman name *Lugudunum* means simply 'fortress of Lug'. Laon is another French town whose name is of similar derivation, as is Leiden in Holland and, far to the east, Leignitz in Silesia. In Britain he is found in the North at Carlisle, *Luguvalium*, a name meaning 'strong in Lugus'. Numerous inscriptions in Spain testify to the strength of his cult in the most westerly of Celtic domains.

It is well known that the Celtic pantheon differed greatly from those of the Greeks and Romans. There was no Celtic Olympus, and no clearly-defined hierarchy of gods, each with his own marked skills, characteristics and particular sphere of competence. Local variations abounded, the gods lived hard by the abodes of men, and their attributes and adventures appear confusingly intermingled – at least, in the form in which they had been handed down to us. Nevertheless there are consistencies about the figure of Lug which suggest strongly the existence of a widely-accepted, recognisable myth.

The Romans, who appreciated order above all things, liked to equate foreign gods neatly with their own: a practice causing endless confusion to later students of comparative religion. But when Julius Caesar reported that the most widely-worshipped god in Gaul was Mercury, an identification with the native Lug seems certain enough. Memorials and inscriptions to a Gaulish Mercury survive in profusion, and when Caesar goes on to say that the Gauls 'declare him the inventor of all arts,' we find an exact parallel with the epithet of the Irish Lug: *samildánach*, 'skilled in the arts.'

A famous Irish tale describes Lug's entry to a gathering of gods. When challenged as to his qualification to join the company, he replies that he is a wright. But there is a wright already present; to which Lug announces that he is also a smith. To successive challenges, he lists himself confidently as champion, harper, poet, magician, doctor, craftsman, and so on. Representatives of all these skills are present too, but what there is not is one who combines all in one person. Lug is admitted in triumph. Later in the same story he is described as inventor of the game of *fidchell*, a boardgame with ritual connotation. Myrddin's patron Gwenddolau was said to have possessed such a magical board.[1]

The name 'Lug' derives from a Celtic root meaning 'light', and the god was conceived as bright, youthful and glorious above all the other gods. Approaching with his Otherworld Host, he is described in these glowing terms:

'One young man came in the front of that army, high in command over the rest; and like to the setting sun was the splendour of his countenance and his forehead; and they were not able to look in his face from the greatness of its splendour.'

The glory of his appearance was like that of the sun itself, as the words of a character in the tale from which this quotation is drawn suggest:

'Then arose Breas, the son of Balor, and he said: "It is a wonder to me that the sun should rise in the west today, and in the east every other day." "It were better that it were so," said the druids. "What else is it?" said he. "The radiance of the face of Lug of the Long Arm," said they.'

Lug is then the divine exemplar of all that is most admirable and godlike in humanity: of ethereal beauty in form and thought, of the near-divine achievements of arts and skills, and of the overthrow of evil forces threatening humanity. At the same time as he presides over the community of gods in the Otherworld, he incarnates the parallel hierarchical source of authority on earth, the sacral kingship. He is not *per se* a sun-god, but as the passage quoted earlier suggests, the sun reflects his transcendent beauty and glory.[2]

There are several remarkable parallels between the god Lug and the prophet Merlin. We know that the High Kingship of Ireland was legitimised in myth by the appearance of Lug, who revealed to Conn in prophetic verses the succession of coming kings – verses strikingly similar to those of the Welsh poem *Cyfoesi Myrddin*, in which Merlin foretells the succession of kings after Rhydderch. This and a similar poem represent Merlin as uttering his prophecies 'in his grave' (*yn y vedd*), where he is figuratively or in reality envisaged as speaking from an Otherworld where he dwells with 'mountain ghosts' (*wylyon mynyd*), that is, the refuge of the dead in the Forest north of Hadrian's Wall.[3]

There are other marked resemblances between the two figures[4], the most striking of which is the manner of their death. However, all will be made much clearer if I state my conclusion in advance, and then examine each relevant aspect in turn. I believe that the undoubted parallels stem from the fact that Merlin re-enacted on earth important aspects of the myth of Lug. This in turn suggests that he was a priestly or other representative of the god, who uttered prophecies in his name or under his inspiration, and who in important rituals acted out the benefactions and ultimate sacrifice of his divine counterpart.

Rituals associated with Lug are best documented from Ireland, where the written and oral traditions of Celtic heathendom are so much more fully recorded than in Britain. The festival of Lug (*Lughnasa*) was essentially a harvest festival, and the assemblage of the people took place at selected holy spots. These were generally associated with sacred wells, and sited on mountains or by lakes carrying dramatic views of the surrounding countryside. They were also frequently connected with megalithic monuments and other standing stones. In earlier times the festival must have involved the divine king, for it was on his physical health and fitness to rule that the fruits of nature closely depended.

Although only scanty traces of a similar festival are recorded in Britain there is, however, a specific example which appears to show beyond doubt that the Festival of Lughnasa was celebrated in Britain as an overtly pagan mystery in the same century that Merlin flourished.

The sixth century A.D. is famous as the Age of the Saints, a time when on both sides of the Irish Sea the great pioneers of the Celtic Church flourished – St David, St Cadog, St Teilo and many others, who are familiar today chiefly from innumerable commemorative names of towns, villages and church dedications. Little now is known about them that can be relied upon as historical fact. Their *Lives* were for the most part compiled centuries later, and contain such an admixture of folklore, 'learned' speculation, floating miracle-tales and the like that small reliance can be placed upon them as factual biographies, though we may be certain that a core of truth lies somewhere at the back of them.

There is however one striking exception to this collection of what really amount to historical novels rather than sober biographies.

St Samson was a Welsh bishop who founded the abbey-bishopric of Dol in Brittany and who is also remembered in dedications of Cornish churches at Golant and Southill. His existence is verifiable, since he is recorded as attending the Council of Paris about the year 560.[5]

An early *Life* of the Saint has survived, the *Vita Sancti Samsonis*, which is of exceptional interest since it can be shown to be very old and to be based upon information deriving from people who had been intimate with Samson himself. In his preface, the anonymous author (a monk of Dol) explains that his account drew, firstly, upon a still earlier *Life* compiled by a cousin of St Samson, part of which was based on stories told by the Saint's mother: and secondly, on oral traditions gathered by the biographer himself during visits to Wales and Cornwall. As there are strong reasons for believing that the existing *Life* was composed around the years 610–615 (possibly re-edited in the ninth century), these traditions presumably derived at first or second hand from those who knew the Saint.[6]

One episode in the *Life of Saint Samson* is particularly exciting. It tells of the Saint's journey across Cornwall in his passage from Wales to Brittany, and in view of its significance I provide the text as far as possible in the biographer's own words:

'Now on a certain day, as he was passing through a certain district which they call Tricuria, he heard on his left hand men worshipping at a certain temple (*phanum*) after the manner of the Bacchantes, through a dramatic representation (*per imaginariam ludum*). Then he, signing to his brethren that they should stand still and keep silent, himself descended from his chariot, stood upon the ground and, earnestly looking towards those who were worshipping an idol (*idolum*), saw before them an abominable image (*simulacrum*) standing on top of a hill. I [the author] myself have been on that hill and have with my own hand reverently traced the cross which St. Samson with his own hand carved by means of an iron tool upon the standing stone there. When St. Samson saw this image, he hastened to them (taking two of his brethren) and gently remonstrated with them for forsaking the one God who made all things to worship an idol. All this while their chieftain (*comes*) Guedianus was standing before them. They began to excuse themselves by saying there was no harm in observing the magical rites of their ancestors in a play. Some were angry, some scoffed, while the politer among them urged him to go away. But suddenly the power of God was openly displayed when a certain boy engaged in horse-racing was thrown to the ground from a swift horse and, twisting his neck as he fell headlong, lay like a corpse.'

St Samson restored the youth to life, in return for which Guedianus and his followers agreed to be baptised and destroyed their idol. Afterwards Guedianus pleaded with St Samson to assist them by destroying a maleficent serpent, which was laying waste the countryside. The Saint crossed the river and mastered the beast in its 'horrible cave' by lassoing it with his linen girdle. To quench his thirst he arranged for a miraculous spring to discharge itself in the form of a shower from the cavern roof. He then proceeded on his way and crossed the Channel.

Confirmation that this story in its original form derived from a contemporary or near-contemporary account is provided by a very early form of the name of the chieftain Guedianus found in some manuscripts of the *Life*, indicating a date no later than the seventh century for the story to have been set down. The name *Tricuria* (later Trigg, a district in northern Cornwall) is likewise very archaic.[7] There is every reason therefore to believe the account authentic.

The episode has been frequently discussed by historians, none of whom however appears to have noticed that the detailed description is clearly that of the Festival of Lughnasa. The parallels are too marked to be ignored:

1. The Festival of Lughnasa took place on 1st August.
   The date of Samson's journey in Cornwall is not given, but it was clearly in high summer. He had celebrated Easter in Wales and conducted a considerable amount of business before embarking on his voyage across the Severn Sea.
2. Showers were expected at Lughnasa.[8]
   St Samson when thirsty induced a miraculous shower to fall from the roof of his cave.
3. A myth attached to the Festival of Lughnasa tells of the death of a youth on the hill. Often described as a charioteer or huntsman, a version tells of his resuscitation by St Patrick.[9]
   A youth fell from his horse and broke his neck during the ceremony witnessed by St Samson, and the Saint revived him.
4. Horse-races took place at Lughnasa Festivals, both in mythology and fact.[10]

The youth resuscitated by St Samson was engaged in horse-racing.

5. Evidence suggests that at Lughnasa 'there was a custom of bringing a stone head from a nearby sanctuary and placing it on top of the hill for the duration of the festival.'[11]

St Samson saw 'an abominable image standing on top of a hill.'

6. In a legend associated with the Festival of Lughnasa, St Patrick or another hero overcomes a destructive serpent and confines it to a subterranean cavern.[12]

St Samson at the request of Guedianus killed a serpent in a cave.

Thus it is clear that in St Samson's encounter with Guedianus and his fellow-worshippers we have a factual account of the celebration of the Feast of the God Lug. Particularly interesting is the suggestion that the celebration was enacted in the form of a play (*ludus*), by which it seems likely that a ritual enactment of the myth of the god is intended. (Does the reference to 'Bacchantes' imply that the celebrants were in a state of ecstasy?) About this very time Gildas denounced corrupt priests who showed no interest in godly writings, preferring 'plays, and unfit tales of men of the world.' That these were not merely frivolous but (from a Christian point of view) dangerous, is implied by his next words:

'as if what reveal the way of death were the way of life.'

Both tales and plays were presumably pagan.[13]

The story of St Samson's encounter with the heathen worshippers is fascinating both for its unique glimpse of a paganism still flourishing openly in Christian Britain at so late a date, and also for its unselfconscious revelation of the nature of the encounter between the two creeds. The argument was conducted on a basis of tolerance and discussion, the pagans wistfully clinging to the ancient rites of their ancestors, and the Saint urging the inescapable claim of the risen Christ.

One further point deserves attention with regard to Samson's intervention at a Cornish celebration of Lughnasa. It is surely not coincidental that as late as the nineteenth century a popular assembly bearing marked traces of the pagan festival continued to be celebrated on the first Sunday of August at Morvah, near Land's End. During the festivities folktales were repeated bearing strong marks of watered-down myth. Important motifs were the arrival

of a gallant giant, 'Jack the Tinkard', 'master of skills and ingenuity', who delivered the locality from the oppression of a grim
rival, ascended a hill called Bosprenis Croft, and did 'there perform
some magical rites which were either never known, or they have
been forgotten.' The coincidence of date, of elements of the myth,
and other factors make it clear that the nineteenth-century Morvah
Fair was originally a Lughnasa Festival.[14]

It is of course possible that there was more than one local
celebration of Lug's Feast at harvest-time in Dark Age Cornwall.
At the same time there are indications that it may have been the
predecessor of Morvah Fair that St Samson interrupted on a
summer's day in the mid-sixth century. The chieftain of the region,
who presided at the festivities, is named as Guedianus. The Cornish
place-name Gwithian preserves the same name, but as that village
lies in the extreme south-west of the peninsula it has been dis-
sociated from the story. For Trigg (*Tricuria*), where Samson was
said to have been travelling when he 'heard' the worshippers, lies
well to the north-east.

But there is in fact no reason to suppose that the pagan festival
was in the region of Trigg. St Samson's *Life* related that 'he heard
on his left hand men worshipping', and at once intervened. But
the words 'on his left hand' are a mistranslation of the original
Latin, *in parte sinistra*. *Sinistra* normally means 'left', but in translations from Old Welsh it regularly signifies 'the north'.[15] The
correct meaning of the sentence must therefore be that Samson
'heard that in the northern part men were worshipping at a temple',
and at once resolved to intervene. The temple may have been some
way off from Trigg, and not in it as commentators have hitherto
united in asserting.

Gwithian is not north of Trigg, but it does lie on the north coast,
which could be the meaning intended. More significant may be the
fact that Gwithian is a mere dozen miles from Morvah, scene of
the great Lughnasa festival surviving into the last century. It would
be interesting to know whether there exists still a stone on Bosprenis Croft corresponding to the 'idol' on which St Samson en-
graved his cross.

The well-known Welsh mediaeval tale of *Geraint the son of Erbin*,
can also be shown to rest ultimately on genuine pagan practice. In
it, the hero out riding is warned by a mysterious 'Little King' to
avoid one of two routes he is approaching. 'Below us,' warned the
Little King, 'is a hedge of mist, within which are enchanted games,

and no one who enters there ever returns.' But Geraint resolutely entered upon the exploit. On arrival he encountered a daunting sight. The hedge of mist obscured everything within, but around its hazy perimeter was set a line of tall stakes, upon each of which was impaled a man's head. Geraint was told that it was not permitted for a companion to enter with him, and he pressed boldly forward.

Within the encircling mist with its grisly adornment lay a large orchard, in which stood a tent with an apple-tree before it, on a branch of which hung a huge horn. Geraint entered the tent, where he found a maiden seated on a throne opposite an empty chair. He sat down, defying a warning from the damsel that the rightful occupant would resent the intrusion. At that moment there came a gathering din from without, and Geraint emerged to find a mounted knight, who threatened him with punishment for his insolence. The pair fought, breaking three successive spears. Then Geraint rushed upon his adversary and overcame him. 'Spare me,' cried the Stranger, 'and you may have your will!' 'My will,' replied Geraint, 'is that this game shall continue no more here, nor the hedge of mist, nor the magic, nor the enchantment.' Then the Stranger bade him blow the horn; which done, all vanished as Geraint demanded.

To crown his Christian hero's exploits, the story-teller (*cyfarwydd*) has him enter what is clearly a pagan sanctuary and put an end to the impious rite whose mystery had previously held the countryside in awe and fear. Its terrors were increased, it seems, by drawing on whatever tradition had preserved in early mediaeval Wales of pre-Christian cultic practice. One sinister detail was omitted, however, which can be restored from the French version of the tale by Chrétien de Troyes, *Erec*. If the visitor failed in his challenge, his head would be added to those on the stakes in the enchanted hedge of mist. In *Geraint the son of Erbin* it is mentioned that two of the stakes bore no heads. The author fails to explain the point of this, the implication being that the original source had indeed specified the penalty for failure.[16]

I have suggested that the ritual St Samson encountered in Cornwall in the sixth century was a British version of the Irish Festival of Lughnasa, when the god Lug brought fertility to the land and prosperity to the kingdom. The story of *Geraint* was composed some six centuries later, and rests on a quite different basis of authority. Nevertheless it too has its roots in a pagan past, though in its existing form long degenerated into folktale.

The Irish account of the *Baile in Scáil* ('the Phantom's Frenzy')
has already been mentioned as containing a parallel to the prophetic
verses ascribed to Merlin in Welsh poetry. It is introduced by a
prose story, explaining how King Conn of the Hundred Fights
came to receive the prophecy. One day Conn rose as was his
custom at dawn and, accompanied by three druids and three poets,
went up onto the hill of Tara to fend off the menace of those
Otherworld beings whose malign influence was perpetually threatening the stability of Ireland.

As they moved on their way he happened to tread on a stone,
which gave out a fearful scream, heard in all the countryside
around. In answer to the King's query, the druids explained that
this was the sacred stone *Fal*, the number of whose screams portended the number of kings to rule over Tara. It was to be set up
at Tailtiu, now Teltown in County Meath, where annual games
would take place on whose continuance the Sovereignty of the
Kingdom would depend. (It was at Teltown that the greatest
Festival of Lughnasa was held from earliest recorded times until
the late eighteenth century.)[17]

At this moment Conn and his companions were suddenly envel-
oped in an enchanted mist, and heard the thunder of a horse's
hooves beyond. The unknown horseman flung three spears at the
King, but then desisted on the druid's announcing his identity. The
horseman approached and led the King up to a splendid house
with a golden tree at its door. Inside the house they found a maiden
wearing a crown, before whom were set a silver vat of 'red drink'
with a golden can and a golden goblet by. The Phantom himself
was seated on a throne, and it could be seen that his form and
features were glorious far beyond the sons of men.

It can have been no surprise, then, when he revealed himself to
be the god Lug, come to recount to Conn the names of his
successors to the High Kingship of Tara. The maiden was a
personification of the Sovereignty they would incarnate. Success-
ively she enquired to whom the red drink should be given, and the
god replied with the name of each king in turn, together with a
brief summary of his portended exploits. The prophecy, which is
so similar to those of Merlin, follows.[18]

The resemblances to the adventure of Geraint are obvious and
striking: the enchanted hedge of mist, the noise of the approaching
horseman, the three spear-stokes, the magical tree at the entrance,
and the waiting maiden. It is the drink conferring Sovereignty
which forms the central function in the *Baile in Scáil*, and in the

Geraint version scholars have shown that the horn hanging on the apple-branch whose blast disperses the whole enchanted scene was originally a *drinking*-horn.[19] Some of these features appear too in the romance of *Fergus*, when the knight approaches the mountain where Merlin dwelt for many a year.

The significance of the episode in *Baile in Scáil* has long been accepted by Celtic scholars as a symbolic marriage of the king on his accession to the land itself, which was conceived of as the goddess Ériu (Eire). A ritual wedding-feast (*banais rígi*, 'wedding-feast of kingship') formed part of the ceremonies at the inauguration of an Irish king.[20]

As the symbolic marriage of the king with his country took place in historical fact, it may be that the events recounted in the *Baile in Scáil* reflect elements of a coronation ritual, or rather a myth explanatory of the ritual. When the prose introduction states that the gold and silver vessels of the maiden Sovereignty were 'left with Conn' after the mantic session, we may suspect that the reference was explanatory of the origin of real vessels preserved at Tara time out of mind for use at successive inaugurative 'nuptials'.

It is essential to remember that in early Ireland, as elsewhere, the king was no mere political chieftain or symbol of authority. He represented, or rather personified, the cosmic order on earth. On his fitness to rule, his truthfulness, honour, courage and splendour, depended the welfare and fruitfulness of the country. By these personal qualities of sacral authority, together with the performance of ritual essential to preserve the harmony of earth and heaven, man and nature, the king sustained his people's prosperity and welfare. Should he fail in any of the necessary qualities, even to the extent of possessing some serious physical blemish, then the pivot would loosen and the forces of disorder unleash their baleful powers over the land. Crops would fail, plagues spread abroad and enemies violate the frontiers.

The concept of divine kingship is simply a reflection of the greater order without. In early society men held to a belief, not dissimilar to the Platonic ideal, that every piece of creation is but a feeble representation of a divine counterpart, whose perfection is the essence of its imperfect earthly version. But all these spiritually perfect Otherworld beings are in their turn the younger brothers of one Supreme Being as the essence and origin of all that exists. The king is to the microcosmic kingdom as the High God is to the macrocosmic universe, and their rôles are indissolubly linked.[21] In the *Baile in Scáil* the god Lug was clearly envisaged as the High

God who presided over the marriage of the King with the goddess personifying the Sovereignty of Ireland. Lug was the divine proto-type of human kingship, and the king on accession was seen as his earthly incarnation.[22]

What of the prophetic list of Conn's successors? It has already been shown how St Columba foretold the coming succession of kings at the coronation of Aedan mac Gabran in A.D. 574, which may indicate that such a prophecy formed an expected part of the coronation ritual. The succession was in this way shown to corre-spond to a preordained divine order. Perhaps the prophecy was partly based on a shrewd appreciation of the likely inheritance, being subsequently regarded as possessing such binding force as effectively to control the succession. However, we can hardly believe that Conn's fifty-three successors followed in order quite so obediently, and an explanatory suggestion may be made. In very early times a druid expounded genuinely mantic verses, setting out the succession of the king's heirs. As time went by, errors must inevitably have been committed and detected, until a sensible adjustment came into being. It was now a retrospective prophecy that was recited at a king's inauguration, in which a list or genealogy of his predecessors was set out from the foundation of the dynasty, being placed in the mouth of an early druid or other seer. One must avoid here anachronistic concepts of forgery or deception. Since the succession of kings was known to be preordained by the god Lug, a druid who obtained access to the god's thought must also have known the coming course of events, and it would be believed that the prophecy attributed to him was undoubtedly what he would have said.

With the establishment of Christianity, the rôle of the bards was greatly reduced. The final stage was the discarding of the prophetic element altogether, and the substitution of a simple recital of the king's genealogy. Thus, when Alexander III of Scotland was crowned at Scone in 1249, 'a Highland sennachy advanced, and, kneeling before the fatal stone, hailed him as the "Ri Alban", and repeated his pedigree according to Highland tradition through a long line of Gaelic kings, partly real and partly mythic, till he reached Gaithel Glass, the "eponymus" of the race.' And when the Macdonald chiefs were crowned Lords of the Isles on an island in Loch Finlagan in Islay, we are told on good authority that 'the Orator rehearsed a Catalogue of his ancestors, &c.'[23]

The earliest Irish prophetic king-list is the *Baile Chuind*, whose latest monarch is Fínsnechta Fledach (675–695). He indeed is followed by 'four unidentifiable names', from which it might be conjectured that the poem was recited at this king's inauguration, the succeeding obscurely identified names being those whom it was believed would succeed him. A king's immediate heir appears to have been chosen at about the same time as his own election, and as his successors were selected from among a small group of agnate relatives, the chief druid (who played a leading role in inaugurating the king) may not have found it difficult to divine the order of the coming succession.[24]

The similarity between these Irish prophetic poems and those of Merlin has already been remarked, a parallel which can hardly be due to accident. In both cases a prophet or prophetic god foretells the succession of a long line of kings, in response to the interrogation of a woman, which is repeated on each occasion. In the poem *Cyfoesi Myrddin* it is his sister Gwenddydd who enquires the names of successive monarchs, and Myrddin who supplies the answers. It seems likely, therefore, that these poems in their original form once played a similar rôle to their Irish counterparts, and were recited at the inauguration of British kings as a legitimisation of the predestined heir.[25]

That Merlin was seen as concerned with the divine kingship is also shown by an archaic conception referred to in the poem *Hoianau*:

> 'To us will be years and long days
> With false kings and withering fruit-crops.'

This is an allusion to the belief, already mentioned, that when a king fails to fulfil his righteous rôle (in Irish, *fír flathemon*) the country will be plagued by famine and blight.

The parallels suggest that, at the inauguration of a king, Merlin personified the god Lug (in British, *Lleu*). We have of course come full circle, since as everyone knows it was 'by the advys of Merlyn' and 'by Merlyns provydence' that the youthful Arthur was elected King of Britain – his election being secured by a magical sign involving an enchanted weapon. Before that Merlin had prophesied the boy's accession before the dying Uther Pendragon. Then again one may compare evidence adduced in a previous chapter indicating that Merlin's prophetic character was strongly within the druidic tradition, with the convincing contention that it was the chief druid's office to preside over coronation ritual in Ireland.[26]

There is every reason, therefore, for believing that authentic tradition lies behind Merlin's rôle as it is represented in the early Arthurian cycle. Possibly in name and certainly in function he was the Chief Druid, who presided over rituals necessary to preserve the harmony of the natural order, of which the divine king was the corner-stone. Through him the high god Lug spoke, wedding the high king to the land, and investing him with sacred symbols of office. The unchanging ceremony linked the king with his predecessors back to the dawn of time when the divine monarchy was first established, while the prophetic declaration of the order of kings to come assured security for the future. Thus all factors, divine and human, were locked into a converging harmony that defied the shadowy forces of disorder.

8

The Fighting Dragons and the Fatherless Child

We have come a long way from the Merlin first encountered in the pages of Geoffrey of Monmouth's *Historia Regum Britanniæ*. There, it will be recalled, he appeared as the Wonderful Child who expounded to Vortigern the mystery of the Fighting Dragons. Subsequently he helped Uther Pendragon to establish the kingdom, brought the Giant's Dance from Ireland and set it up on Salisbury Plain at the site later known as Stonehenge, and finally presided over the raising of Arthur to the throne.

The Merlin of history, however, is now shown to be that Myrddin Wyllt, 'the Wild', whose story was discovered by Geoffrey only after his *Historia* was completed. The real Merlin, it seems, lived a century later than the time of Vortigern and Ambrosius, and the scene of his prophesying was no king's court in fertile Southern Britain but the savage wilderness of the Coed Celyddon beyond Hadrian's Wall. Must one then dismiss the Merlin of the *Historia* as a mere phantom, a figure conjured up by Geoffrey's fertile imagination, whom later even he had ruefully to concede lived in another age and environment?

Clearly Merlin could not have attended the courts of Vortigern and Arthur unless he really enjoyed a life-span beyond that of ordinary men. Nevertheless, two stories from Geoffrey's *Historia* serve to throw considerable further light upon his sources. These are Merlin's revelation of the Two Fighting Dragons to Vortigern, and the erection of Stonehenge. It will be seen that Geoffrey seems to have picked up garbled versions of traditions extending back to the fifth century A.D. and well beyond.

Of all the tantalising records which throw some dimly-reflected light on the Dark Ages, none has aroused more continuing interest and dissection than the little collection known as 'The History of the Britons' (*Historia Brittonum*). Formerly ascribed to an elusive 'Nennius', it is now regarded as a compilation put together by an unknown author in the year 829–30.[1] Despite its title, it is not a history but a thinly edited collection of disparate writings on early British history. It is undoubtedly one of the most fascinating records of all time, one which anyone seriously interested in the beginnings of British history will find himself poring over again and again.

It is fortunate indeed that, unlike his mendacious successor Geoffrey of Monmouth, the author made so relatively small an attempt to blend his sources together into a harmonious whole, and simply lumped them together much (it may be presumed) as he found them. The materials appear to derive from the collection of a royal library of the ninth century, as on the whole they relate to matters interesting more to a court than to the Church.

The collection begins with a 'learned' history of the world, developing into the origin-legends of Britain and Ireland. From this, which was based on second-hand research, the *Historia Brittonum* moves abruptly to the story of the accession of King Vortigern, his employment of Hengist and the Saxon mercenaries, his quarrel with St Germanus, and his flight and ultimate downfall. These vividly-told stories are followed by an account of St Patrick's mission to the Irish, and the famous reference to the leadership of Arthur with its list of his battles over the Saxons. The remainder of the 'History' is taken up with the affairs of the North, *Y Gogledd*, with genealogies of Northumbrian kings followed by cryptic notices of Northern affairs, British and Anglian, in the sixth and seventh centuries.

Though certainly a hotch-potch miscellany, the *Historia Brittonum* represents a clumsy attempt to write a history of Britain from the earliest time up to the seventh century. What would one not give for an hour by the side of the redactor, as he browsed through King Merfyn's library! For there perhaps was the original text of the Old Welsh poem from which the *Arthuriana* was extracted, and on another page an early version of Myrddin's *Cyfoesi*, later updated to prophesy the accession of Merfyn's great-grandson, Hywel the Good. What certainly was there, as an original or a copy, as our author tells us, was a book entitled *Liber Beati Germani* ('The Book of the Blessed Germanus'). It was this that told of the crimes and fate of King Vortigern, with which we are here concerned.

The outline of the story is as follows. The first four sections describe

St Germanus' deposition of a tyrant (apparently heathen) king of Powys, and his replacement by a faithful believer. Next comes Vortigern's invitation to Hengist and his Saxon warriors, who defeated barbarian invaders in the North but then showed little inclination to desert their comfortable berth in Britain. When Vortigern urged Hengist to return home, the Saxon leader arranged a banquet at which his beautiful daughter plied the King with drink until he became inflamed with lust. Desperate to obtain the girl, he was persuaded to trade the kingdom of Kent for her. Hengist, now Vortigern's father-in-law, wasted no time in infiltrating yet more of his countrymen into Britain.

An odd little story follows, with strong pagan connotations, of Vortigern's incest with his daughter. Germanus and 'the Council of the Britons' condemned him for the crime, and he prepared to take flight. Consulting with his *magi* (druids), he was told to go to the uttermost bounds of his kingdom and find a fortified citadel in which he could defend himself from the Saxons, who were planning to kill him by cunning and seize his kingdom. Accompanied by his druids, Vortigern travelled to Snowdonia in North Wales, where they found a place among the mountains suitable for the building of an impregnable stronghold. The words of the druids seem to imply that the site possessed magical as well as strategic advantages: 'make the fortress in this place, for it will be most safe from barbarian nations forever.'

Vortigern accordingly collected masons and carpenters, who assembled their materials. That night stones and timber vanished mysteriously, and on two successive nights the same thing occurred. The baffled King summoned his druids to ask their advice. The reply was emphatic: 'Unless you find a fatherless child and he be killed and his blood sprinkled on the fortress, it will never be built.'

Immediately Vortigern despatched messengers throughout Britain to discover the child without a father. Eventually they came to a place called 'campus Elleti' in the region of Glywysing (a kingdom in South Wales). There they saw two boys playing ball and quarrelling. 'Oh fellow without a father', finally burst out one, 'no good will come of you!' Greatly intrigued, the messengers sought out the lad's mother, who confirmed that he was her son, but that she was beyond question a virgin. The boy was at once borne off to King Vortigern, and a meeting was arranged at which he was to be ceremoniously sacrificed.

On learning that it was the druids who had given Vortigern this idea, the boy asked for them to be summoned. When they had gathered, he asked whether they knew what lay beneath the pavement before them. When they confessed their ignorance, he instructed them to dig, the while explaining what would be found. Exactly corresponding to his account, they excavated, firstly, an underground pool. In the pool were two vases, in which (they appear to have been placed end to end) was a folded tent (*tentorium*).

'What is in the tent?' demanded the boy. Again the druids were silent, and when the tent was unfolded two snakes (*vermes*) were found sleeping within. One was red and one white, and they began to fight within (or upon) the tent. At first the red snake was beaten almost to the tent's margin, but after a stiff struggle it recovered and drove its white opponent out of the tent. There was a pursuit across the pool, and the tent vanished.

'Now,' declared the boy triumphantly to the wondering druids; 'what does all this mean?' And on their confessing their bafflement, he explained. The tent represented Vortigern's kingdom, and the snakes two dragons. The red dragon (still of course the emblem of Wales) stood for the Britons, and the white for the Saxons. So far the latter had been victorious, and would conquer the land almost from sea to sea. But eventually the Britons would reassert themselves and repel the invader back to his homeland.

'But you,' concluded the prophetic youth, 'must depart from this fortress which you cannot build, and go round many provinces until you find a safe stronghold, and remain there.'

'What are you called?' enquired the curious King. The boy replied, 'I am called Ambrosius' – that is, he was seen to be Embreis Guletic.

'And what is your ancestry?' went on Vortigern.

'My father is one of the consuls of the Roman race,' replied the (fatherless) boy, who retained the fortress for himself while Vortigern and his druids departed northwards.

An interlude next relates victories gained by Vortigern's son in Kent, resulting in the expulsion of the Saxons from the island. But they are soon back, and Vortigern (who appears in control of the country once more) feels obliged to come to terms with them. When Hengist extended peace feelers, Vortigern and his Council (*consilium*) agreed to negotiations. Delegates from both sides were to meet at an agreed spot to discuss terms; no arms were to be borne by either party. But the deceitful Hengist arranged for his men to carry concealed knives in their boots. At a prearranged signal (Hengist's watchword is given in the original Anglo-Saxon), the knives flashed out and Vortigern only saved his own life by ceding Essex and Sussex to his captors.

Once again Germanus unexpectedly reappears to hound the wretched King about the country. Eventually he calls down a miraculous fire from heaven which burns up Vortigern and all his companions. Thus the *Book of the Blessed Germanus*, but the anonymous editor adds variant versions of the feckless monarch's death.

The *Book of the Blessed Germanus* must itself have contained a number of conflated traditions. It includes some obvious contradictions, of which the most glaring is the revelation of the Fatherless Boy's father! The sources of the *Book*, part historical and part legendary, have not survived. But the central motifs are clear enough; the Collapsing Castle, the finding of the Fatherless Boy, and the prophetic interpretation of the Fighting Dragons. Fortunately the latter appear in a Welsh tale, which enables valuable comparisons to be made. This is the story of *The Contention of Lludd and Llevelys* (*Kyfranc Llud a Llevelis*), found in *The White Book of Rhydderch* and *The Red Book of Hergest*.

Lludd, King of Britain, finds his country plagued by mysterious oppressions. Upon enquiry he is told that one of them is caused by the hidden contest of two dragons. One of them is 'your dragon' (*i.e.* representative of the Isle of Britain), who is fighting with a foreign dragon seeking to overthrow him; this is causing him to utter a horrible scream every May-day eve, heard the length and breadth of the Island. Lludd is told how to discover the dragons: he must cause the Island to be measured in length and breadth so as to discover its precise centre. At that point he must dig a trench, place a vatful of mead in it, and cover the vat with a piece of brocaded silk. Then, if he watches, he will witness the dragons' fight. First they appear as horrible animals, then they grapple in the air as dragons, and finally they fall back exhausted in the shape of pigs. Sinking down into the vat, they drink the mead and fall asleep. Immediately that happens, Lludd is to bundle up the creatures into the silk cover and bury them in a store chest in the strongest place in his kingdom. 'And as long as they remain in that safe place, no foreign oppression shall visit the Isle of Britain.'

Lludd followed the advice, discovering the central point of the Island to be at Oxford (*Rytychen*). All ensued as foretold, and Lludd buried the sleeping beasts at a place called Dinas Emreis (formerly known as Dinas Ffaraon Dandde) in Snowdonia (*Eryri*). Afterwards Lludd ruled in peace and security.

The similarities with the *Historia Brittonum* account will be at once apparent.[2] Clearly a common source must lie behind the kernel of both versions of the Fighting Dragons story, and it seems possible that it rests ultimately on a grain of historical fact.

Vortigern's misguided employment of the Saxons as mercenaries and their subsequent rebellion and invasion is, of course, well known and generally accepted as factual. It is referred to by Gildas, who was writing within two or three generations of an event as starkly important to his contemporaries as was the Norman Conquest in the early Middle Ages. Gildas's words are crucially important, and require careful reading. After describing the foreign invasions to which Britain had been subject after the Roman departure, he continues:

'For counsel is begun as to what best or more advantageous ought to be determined upon to repel such deadly and such frequent irruptions and plunderings of the above mentioned nations. Then all the counsellors, together with the proud tyrant, are blinded – finding protection of such a sort, which was in fact the destruction of the fatherland – so that those most ferocious Saxons of accursed name, hateful to God and to men, were let into the island like wolves into sheepfolds, to beat back the northern nations. Nothing more harmful and bitter ever happened to it. Oh deepest darkness of soul! O hopeless stupidity! They invited in the very people whom when absent they dreaded worse than death, to settle (as one might say) under the same roof! "Foolish princes of Zoan", as is said, "giving to Pharaoh senseless counsel".'

Thus far the invitation. Gildas then continued:

. . . 'a brood of whelps, bursting out of the barbaric lioness's lair, borne in three ships . . . under favourable sails, first set their terrible claws in the eastern part of the island, acting as if about to fight for the fatherland at the hapless tyrant's bidding, but in fact intended to attack it. With unshakeable faith they credited an [or the?] omen and prophecies (*omine auguriisque*), which foretold their domination over the country towards which their prows were directed for a period of three hundred years, the first hundred and fifty of which would be devoted to devastation.'

A moment's reflection reveals the close parallel between this account and that of the *Historia Brittonum*. In the latter, Vortigern on the advice of his *consilium* extends an invitation to the Saxons to act as mercenaries in order to repel the northern invaders (Picts and Scots). He then witnesses the augury of the dragons, whose interpretation is that the Saxons will enjoy an initial prolonged period of triumph, but that ultimately the Britons will prevail and drive them back across the sea. The implication of the prophecy in both cases is identical, and one can only assume that the *Historia Brittonum* version is a garbled or more elaborate version of that to which Gildas refers, and which has gathered a considerable accretion of folklore material over the centuries.

It is perfectly conceivable, then, that a prophecy detailing the struggle of Britons and Saxons was really promulgated at the time of the invitation to Hengist. It was not haphazard rumour, moreover, but a formal vaticination performed according to whatever rites were customary. In the *Historia Brittonum* version the ritual is supervised by *magi*, which the Irish version renders by the word *druid*. There seems no reason to quarrel with this identification: human sacrifice and prophecy were regular druidic practices in classical times, and in a parallel Irish tale the sacrifice of a miraculous youth is supervised by druids.[3]

Perhaps the Council which made the momentous decision to invite the Saxons included druids, whose advice was given in the form of the gloomy prophecy which the Saxons then impudently appropriated to their own use. It looks too as if the druids opposed the invitation. Their attitude is matched in a comparable incident occurring at about the same time in Ireland. The seventh-century Latin *Life of St Patrick* by Muirchu tells of pagan apprehensions in Ireland, when rumours of impending Christian missionary activity from Britain began to spread. Muirchu says that druids and soothsayers prophesied the disruption and overthrow of the old ways. A verse foresaw the coming of a tonsured bishop with his flock:

> 'Adze-head will come
> With his crook-headed staff [crozier],
> And his house [chasuble] holed for his head.
> He will chant impiety from his table
>   in the east of the house.
> His whole household will respond to him,
>   "so be it, so be it",'

This rather charming little verse certainly represents what the druids were considered likely to have said, and in fact there is no strong reason for rejecting its authenticity.[4]

It may be objected that, while we might expect the pagan King

Loegaire mac Niall to consult with his druids on the hill of Tara, a similar situation would not be conceivable in the predominantly Christian society of sub-Roman Britain. But there is no justification for believing mid-fifth-century Britain to have been a monolithically Christian community. Indeed, Gildas refers to this as a time when men turned *en masse* 'to darkness instead of the sun, to receiving Satan as an angel of light', words which seem to imply a revival under stress of public paganism. Nor is there any necessity for believing Vortigern to have been a Christian.[5] And even if he was, the times were such that despairing men were likely to turn to the comforting rites of their ancestors. When Alaric and the Goths were at the gates of Rome, thirty years earlier, it was Pope Innocent himself who yielded to pagan pressures, agreeing that the ancient heathen auguries should be consulted.[6]

Vortigern's dealings with the Saxons took place in Southern Britain, where one would also expect the consultation with the druids to have occurred. That the Saxons adapted the double-edged augury to their own ends suggests that it was uttered, if not in their hearing, at least where it was likely to come to their ears. As mercenaries, Hengist and some of his followers may have formed part of Vortigern's train. In those dangerous times, when the kings of Britain regarded each other in the main with suspicion and hatred, such a bodyguard might have played a useful rôle.[7]

The revelation of the Fighting Dragons in the *Book of the Blessed Germanus* is located among the remote mountains of Snowdonia, which appears from the general setting of events an improbable site. In fact there is much evidence to suggest that the incident was relocated in the storyteller's tradition. As independent Celtic Britain shrank in the West to what is now Wales, it was common for events belonging to the common British heritage to be geographically resited within the borders of Wales. There was also a tendency for events to be duplicated, often where an early redactor failed to identify variant versions of the same episode.[8]

In *The Contention of Lludd and Llevelys*, the dragons are discovered at the exact geographical centre of Britain. The concept of the country's Centre possessed great ritual significance in early cosmogony. The Greeks believed that Delphi was the 'navel' (*Omphalos*) or centre of the Earth. The Celts held to a similar belief. Caesar says that at a certain time of the year all the Gaulish druids assembled at a site in the land of the Carnutes which was 'reckoned to be the centre of all Gaul', and there pronounced judgment on matters of great moment. The site is probably that now dominated by the Cathedral of Chartres, and the time the assembly of the Festival of Lug on 1st August. In Ireland the *Omphalos* or sacred centre was held to be at Uisnech in County Westmeath, and there is abundant evidence that these Centres (which were not of course the real geographical centres) were replete with religious significance. The spiritual cohesion and security of the country depended on the continuance of appropriate rituals on this magical site.[9]

Such a setting would have been entirely appropriate for so momentous an event, at which auguries were consulted whose interpretation might decide the fate of Britain. Britain must certainly, like Gaul and Ireland, have once possessed her own *Omphalos*, and the reference in *Lludd and Llevelys* doubtless retains a lingering memory of its one-time significance, though the site was presumably no longer identified in the storyteller's source. (The identification with Oxford must be an interpolation, since it was a city of late Saxon foundation and can have played no part in so archaic a Celtic conception as the Sacred Centre). We are told, however, that Lludd obeyed an instruction to remove the dragons to Dinas Emrys in Snowdonia, and reinter them there in a stone chest. This move appears both pointless and anachronistic (since Lludd and Llevelys were held to have lived long before Emrys) in the context of the story, and evidently stems from a desire to reconcile the narrative with that in the *Historia Brittonum*.[10]

It seems likely, therefore, that an earlier version of *Lludd and Llevelys* told of the discovery of the dragons at the British *Omphalos*. The story of their migration was added later, coming about as a response to that other tale which asserted that they were discovered at Dinas Emrys. However, there are indications that Dinas Emrys also entered the *Historia Brittonum* as a geographical relocation. There is marked internal evidence to suggest this likelihood.

Firstly, the reason given for Vortigern's seeking refuge in Snowdonia is his desire to escape the Saxons' treacherous intention to extend their dominion beyond the bounds of Kent. A flight to North Wales appears absurd in this context.[11] Secondly, it is necessary to consider the significance of Vortigern's Collapsing Castle. Two mythical or folklore elements are present here. There is the belief, strongly attested both from legend and archaeological discovery, that a human (frequently child) sacrifice and foundation burial was essential to the survival of a newly-erected building.[12]

Secondly, there is the element of aetiological speculation, which seeks to provide an explanation for a curious but inexplicable phenomenon.

The story obviously arose from a desire to explain some unusual ruin, dilapidated for no known reason, and possibly resulting in bizarre effects. It is hard to see how this could apply to Dinas Emrys. Though occupying a strong natural position, the fortress was never very imposing structurally. The rather scanty archaeological evidence suggests that it had been in continuous occupation up to the seventh century and beyond, thus precluding any need for speculation on the state of its construction. In any case, the spoliation of hillforts must have been a matter of such familiarity in the Dark Ages as to make fantastic suggestions concerning their cause superfluous.

The explanation must lie elsewhere, and an Irish legend provides a striking analogy. Irish mediaeval sources tell of a pagan god Cenn Cróich, to whom human sacrifices used to be offered. The place of blood was at Mag Slécht, and there the first-born of each family were given over to the god. Then after many centuries there came St Patrick, who did away with the cruel superstition. He struck the chief idol with his crozier, so that it leaned over to the west and thenceforth bore the crozier's mark on its side.

'And the earth swallowed the other twelve idols up to their heads, and they are in that state as a sign of the miracle.'

The reader will already have guessed the origin of the legend. It had grown up as an *ad hoc* explanation of the state of a megalithic monument in Mag Slécht.[13]

On this analogy we might expect the original traditional site of Vortigern's Collapsing Castle to have been some ruined monument of long-forgotten days, probably with dressed stones lying about as if gathered by masons preparatory to work or dispersed by a mysteriously destructive nocturnal force. It was unlikely to have been any building in regular use in the early Dark Ages (such as a hillfort), as that should have been recognised for what it was. Possibly, too, the ruin carried some intangible aura of magic or dread, as no doubt did the megalithic circle on Mag Slécht.

But why was it Dinas Emrys that the storyteller fastened upon, when he relocated the Vortigern saga in North Wales? The answer probably relates to the discovery of a stone cistern at that fortress, which became associated with the dragons' pool of the legend.[14] The author of the *Historia Brittonum* account has tried to rationalise the association, by stating that Vortigern after his discomfiture bestowed the (unbuilt) castle on the youth Emrys.

The author of *Lludd and Llevelys* also answers the question that must have occurred to many: what was Dinas Emrys called before the Fighting Dragons incident gave it its name? 'Before that it was known as Dinas Ffaraon Dandde', *i.e.* 'the fortress of Fiery Pharaoh'. The allusion is probably to Vortigern, who is being likened to Pharaoh in *Exodus*, vii, 8–13. Pharaoh 'called the wise men and the sorcerers' who created enchanted serpents, which were however swallowed up by the serpent created by Aaron's rod. The parallel is obvious, though whether it was this that Gildas had in mind when he castigated Vortigern with a Biblical reference to another Pharaoh's being guided by unwise counsellors is unclear.[15]

The *Historia Brittonum* makes the Fatherless Boy identify himself as Ambrosius, adding the comment that 'he was seen to be Embreis Guletic', and further that his father had been a Roman consul. This attempt to identify the sacrificial victim with the Romano-British military leader whose victories are extolled by Gildas is a self-evident gloss. It is phrased like one, and absurdly contradicts the earlier statements by the Boy and his mother that he had no father. It was at a later stage in the development of the story that someone identified him with the famous Ambrosius of Gildas, who was also a contemporary of Vortigern. What is most interesting here is the indication that the Fatherless Boy was indeed styled Ambrosius, for otherwise there would have been no cause for the later mistaken identification.

Such discrepancies are in fact very useful to the modern investigator, since they frequently enable us to catch invaluable glimpses of earlier strata of the legends. Even the tantalising *History of the Kings of Britain* by Geoffrey of Monmouth, who abused his sources unscrupulously, can on occasion be tested by this method. Geoffrey tells the story of Vortigern's Collapsing Castle in much the same terms as the *Historia Brittonum*, with the one striking difference that he substitutes the name of Merlin for that of Ambrosius in the rôle of Fatherless Youth.

Geoffrey, however, appears to have known another version of the story, which appears as a transparent duplicate later in his *History*. This time it is connected with Ambrosius, also confused with the political leader named by Gildas. The British nobles who had died in the treacherous massacre staged by Hengist had been interred 'in a cemetery which is near the Monastery of Ambrius, an abbot who had founded it.' After the death of Vortigern, the Britons' fortunes revived under his successor Ambrosius, who resolved to erect a fitting memorial to the dead nobles. He summoned together carpenters and masons, who were however for some mysterious reason unable to attempt the task. Baffled, Ambrosius was advised to send for the prophet Merlin, who possessed powers of enchantment.

Merlin arrived from the Fountain of Galabes, and heard all the King's story. The wizard finally responded:

'If you wish to honour the sepulture of these men with an everlasting monument, send for the Giant's Dance, which is in Killaraus, a mountain of Ireland.'

For there was a wonderful structure of vast stones which, if brought across the sea, could be erected on the site and stand there for all eternity. The stones, moreover, possessed curative properties: illnesses and wounds could be cured in water that had washed the stones. Ambrosius was at first incredulous, but he was persuaded, and despatched an army to Ireland. Merlin, who accompanied it, employed his magical arts to transport the Giant's Dance to Britain and re-erect it by the Monastery of Ambrius. Greatly delighted, Ambrosius placed his crown on his head and staged ceremonials lasting for three days. The stones were now set up in precisely the same manner as they had been on Mount Killaraus.

This of course is Geoffrey's famous romance of the erection of Stonehenge, a story the subject of much comment since it was discovered in the present century that the blue stones were indeed transported a colossal distance from the Prescelly Mountains in Pembrokeshire to their present site by the River Avon in Wiltshire. Several converging elements suggest that the Collapsing Castle motif here is a duplication of the one set at Dinas Emrys in the *Historia Brittonum*.

1. They occur at places bearing identical or very similar meaning. *Dinas Emrys* is 'the fort of Embreis'. Geoffrey's *mons Ambrius* is in fact Amesbury in Wiltshire, the nearest settlement of note to Stonehenge, being a bare two miles from that monument. Geoffrey did not concoct the name (as might in other cases be reasonably suspected) from that of Ambrosius. As has been seen, he invented an Abbot Ambrius, indicating that another name already existed. And in fact the name of Amesbury long

antedates Geoffrey's *History*, being recorded as *Ambresbyrig* as early as the ninth century. It signifies 'the fort of Ambres'.[16] It could well be that Geoffrey's *Mons* Ambrius reflects a pre-Saxon name of Stonehenge, the 'hill' indicating the monument's elevated position (Amesbury lies below, on the River Avon).

2. In both cases a person named Ambrosius is connected with a building project, which for mysterious reasons cannot be effected. The *Historia Brittonum* says that Vortigern's workmen 'assembled timber and stones' (*et ligna et lapides congregavit*), while Geoffrey makes Ambrosius 'summon together several carpenters and masons' (*Conucatis itaque undique artificibus lignorum & lapidum*). There is no way in which *carpenters* would be appropriate to the construction of such an edifice as Stonehenge, and this may suggest a common literary source.

3. That such a duplication is likely is indicated by the thirteenth-century English poem *Of Arthour and of Merlin*, where the story of Vortigern's fruitless attempt to construct his castle takes place 'Vpon ye pleyn of Salesbury.'

There is furthermore good reason to suppose that this was the prior location. Geoffrey identifies the source of the Giants' Dance as 'Killaraus', which suggests that a circle of stones like that of Stonehenge, or like a portion of it, was well known to exist in Ireland. Its site is in fact clearly identifiable with the hill of Uisnech, which plays a great rôle in Irish legend. Now, it is a remarkable fact that the Collapsing Castle motif is as firmly attached to a group of megalithic stones at Uisnech as I have suggested it was to Stonehenge! For the stones of Uisnech, having been cursed by St Patrick, never failed to prove the ruin of any structure into which they chanced to be built.[17]

As is well known, Geoffrey of Monmouth's account of the transportation of the stones of Stonehenge from Ireland is strikingly paralleled by the archaeological evidence. As a result it has been suggested that in Geoffrey's story of Stonehenge we may have the only fragment left to us of a native Bronze Age literature.[18] It looks as if the same fragment coupled (indeed, identified) Stonehenge with Uisnech (*Killaraus*), and to both sites there was attached a legend that a magical inhibition had prevented their stones from being properly erected.

Even more remarkable is the fact that a standing stone at Uisnech was, as Giraldus Cambrensis mentioned in the twelfth century, the *Omphalos* or 'navel' of Ireland! The story of *Lludd and Llevelys*

says the Fighting Dragons were found at the *Omphalos* or Sacred
Centre of Britain – the other traditional accounts appear to place
that at Stonehenge – and Geoffrey of Monmouth identifies Stonehenge with the *Omphalos* of Ireland! For my part I have no
hesitation in suggesting:

1. that Stonehenge was the traditional *Omphalos* of Britain;
2. that it was in the fifth century A.D. still regarded as a uniquely
   sacred spot, with special access to the Otherworld; and
3. that Vortigern may have consulted his druids there over the
   momentous decision to invite the Saxons.

In view of all this it may be conjectured that the Fighting Dragons
formed a motif in some kind of Delphic utterance, probably in
verse and perhaps anticipating prophetic verses ascribed to Merlin
in later times. An odd aspect of the story in the *Historia Brittonum*
is the statement that the dragons were discovered inside a tent.
The meaning of the Latin *tentorium* is explicit, and has caused
some puzzlement to scholars. For what can a tent be doing in this
context? Shamanistic practice seems to provide an explanation.
Several peoples in Siberia preserve a conception of the sky as a
huge cosmic tent, the stars being rents in its surface admitting
celestial light. The dragons would in this case be seen as enacting
their ritual beneath an emblematic heaven.[19] Possibly, too, the
'pool' in which the dragons are found is a microcosmic counterpart
of the 'world-lake', over which God warred with the Devil before
raising up the earth from its depths. The Athenians kept a sacred
serpent in the temple of the Erechtheum, where there was also a
tank of water known as 'the Sea of Erechtheus', said to contain
sea-water and to give off the sound of lapping waves; that is, it was
a reflection of the greater ocean without.[20]

Or could one picture the British 'dragons' pool' as inhabited by
a pair of large snakes? Most native British varieties tend to live by
or near water, and to continue frequenting the same spot for long
periods. Adders, in particular, engage in an exotic 'dance', which
is oddly similar to the snakes' combat described in the *Historia
Brittonum*.

'In May', writes a naturalist, 'I was witness to a peculiar dance,
the participants of which were two male adders, which took place
in a shallow half-carpeted ditch. I was drawn to the spot by the
rustling of dead leaves and saw the silver-grey, black-blotched

bodies of two male adders writhing and coiling about each other in a fantastic "dance". Both would sway sideways in contrary directions, then slowly sweep back, the bodies meeting and then crossing so that each ultimately reached the position occupied by the other.

After a series of these slow movements, the contestants became suddenly excited, darting and ducking until one was in a position to force his opponent to the ground. While these rapid head movements were being executed the snakes' bodies were coiled in a series of undulating patterns. After regaining his breath the fallen viper would erect himself again, sidle up to his conqueror and incite him to further strife. I watched the monotonously repeated posturings until the smaller of the two snakes freed himself and made off with amazing celerity, closely pursued by the other until out of sight.'[21]

Of course the similarity may be coincidental, since in both cases the struggle represents a territorial combat! And it is just as likely that the whole account of the dragons' combat existed only in the form of animal symbolism in some early vaticinatory poem. It is interesting for example to note that, according to *The Contention of Lludd and Llevelys*, the dragons as they subsided into the vat would turn into 'two little pigs' (*deu barchell*). This at once calls to mind the 'little pig' to whom Myrddin is represented as addressing his prophecies (*Oian aparchellan*).

If the hypothesis be correct, Stonehenge was like Delphi the *Omphalos* or Sacred Centre of Britain, and like Delphi it was resorted to by those requiring oracular responses. I have suggested that Vortigern relied upon it in the mid-fifth century in order to seek authority for his proposed invitation to Hengist. This does not necessarily argue continuity of use under the Romans. So significant and literal a centre as the *Omphalos* could remain known in popular consciousness for centuries, and its oracular function revived at an exceptional moment of crisis.

Now, in the account of the Prophetic Dragons given in the *Historia Brittonum*, the prophecy is explained by the Fatherless Boy, named as Embreis. Who was this Embreis (later *Emrys*)? Some confusion undoubtedly was caused by the similarity of his name to that of the Romano-British military leader Ambrosius, who was also a contemporary of Vortigern.[22] The clumsy attempt by a glossator to identify them in the *Historia Brittonum* serves only to show their

essential disparity. I have argued that originally the scene of the
Dragon Conflict was set at Stonehenge, which Geoffrey of Monmouth terms *Mons Ambrii*, 'the hill of Ambrius'. He too implicitly
separates this *Ambrius* (after whom the unbuildable building is
named when complete) from the historical Ambrosius who author-
ised the construction. Thus both accounts unintentionally corrobo-
rate the fact that the structure was *already* known by some such
name as 'the mound (or stronghold) of Ambrius (or Embreis)'.

In the context one would expect the name to be that of some
divine or semi-divine being, with whom the site was associated.
This is suggested by a Welsh legend which claimed that the head
of Emrys was buried at Dinas Emrys – a clear allusion to the Celtic
belief in a divine talismanic head.[23] The Welsh name Emrys
derives from the Latin *Ambrosius*, a well-known personal name.[24] But it
may be more appropriate to look to the adjective *ambrosius*,
meaning 'immortal', 'divine', which in turn would reflect a translation of a Celtic epithet of similar meaning.[25] Could it be that
ritual at Stonehenge was presided over by a succession of priests
(druids?) or priest-kings, who in succession bore this name or
epithet? And was it such a functionary who expounded the mystery
to Vortigern?

This is speculation, though sufficiently suggestive not to be
ignored. The possibility of some survival of extraordinarily archaic
lore centred on Stonehenge and surviving into the still semi-pagan
early Dark Age is by no means incredible.

'If we accept the implications contained in the foregoing argument we must also accept a literary survival which though meagre
and barbaric, would nevertheless be of the same order as that
of the Mycenaean elements preserved in Homer, . . . a literature
which would be as natural an outcome of a heroic culture such
as the Wessex Bronze Age (or that of Mycenae, with which
indeed it traded), as are the gold-hilted daggers of the warriors,
but so infinitely more perishable. We may have a story of the
builder, and of the building of the great monument to the
spiritual and political ascendancy of Bronze Age Wessex, handed
down as part of the sacred lore of its priests long enough to
ensure its incorporation in the legends accumulating round
another Wessex leader, a Roman of the Dark Ages; then preserved in the myths of the Celtic west and finally entering the
body of written record of the Middle Ages among the legendary
miscellanea of a romantic medieval ecclesiastic who may have
fancied it as a fairy-tale.'[26]

Geoffrey of Monmouth's linking of Merlin with the British leader Ambrosius involves a characteristic anachronism. The Ambrosius mentioned by Gildas would have been living in the second half of the fifth century A.D., while Merlin is connected with the battle of Arderydd (A.D. 573). Despite this, the linkage of the two names appears persistent and early. About the year 1153–1154, John of Cornwall in his *Prophecy of Merlin* wrote of 'Ambrosius Merlinus', and the Welsh *Stanzas of the Graves* mention 'the chief magician Merddin Embrais'. These and other combinations of the two names could possibly derive from Geoffrey's passing allusion to 'Merlin, who was called Ambrosius'. But Geoffrey himself appears confused, and his clumsiness may betray his consciousness of the necessity to explain a character who was both Merlin and Ambrosius.[27] There is in any case another reference by Geoffrey to be considered.

In the later *Vita Merlini*, Merlin asks his sister to construct him a curious building in the wilds:

'Before the other buildings build me a remote one to which you will give me seventy doors and as many windows, through which I may see fire-breathing Phoebus with Venus, and watch by night the stars wheeling in the firmament; and they will teach me about the future of the nation.'

A circular or polygonal building is envisaged, surrounded by apertures for observation of the heavens. But why, in addition to the windows, are there seventy *doors*?

The mind is drawn again to Stonehenge, with its lintelled circle of trilithons made of eighty gigantic blocks of sarsen. To an untutored eye the trilithons at once suggest giant doorways; certainly one can conceive of no other building so similar in reality to the description of Merlin's observatory. The first description of Stonehenge, that of Henry of Huntingdon (*c.* 1130), states that 'stones of an amazing size are set up in the manner of doorways, so that one door seems to be set upon another'. And in Thomas Hardy's *Tess of the D'Urbervilles*, when Tess and Angel Clare stumble upon Stonehenge in a mist they cannot at first make out what strange building they have entered. 'The place was all doors and pillars, some connected above by continuous architraves.'

It looks as if, without realising its identity, Geoffrey had picked up another floating traditional account of Stonehenge and incorporated it into his story. Without realising it, because he had done so he would surely have made its purpose consistent with his earlier account in which the monument had been erected by Merlin and Ambrosius as a memorial to the nobles treacherously slain by Hengist. If so it would have been a remarkably tenacious tradition which preserved a memory of Stonehenge as an observatory, and it could be that we have stumbled upon evidence of its purpose, a purpose now accepted by many modern scholars.[28]

Finally, could Merlin's lament for his nineteen apple trees recall the Silver Apples of the Moon, with its nineteen-year cycle?

The historical Merlin cannot have been a contemporary of Vortigern or Ambrosius the British war-leader, unless he really attained the longevity early tradition ascribed to him. Nor on the face of it is it likely he could have been directly concerned with Stonehenge, which had probably passed into the hands of the West-Saxons by the middle of the sixth century. But if Embreis, Emrys or the like were an epithet or title of the custodians of Stonehenge over the centuries, and Merlin regarded as their heir, then he might indeed have been known as 'Myrddin Embreis'.[29]

There was certainly a time when Merlin was regarded as possessing some sort of unique spiritual authority or significance in Britain. A triad in *The White Book of Rhydderch* explains that, 'The first name that this Island [Britain] bore, before it was taken or settled: *Clas Merdin*', i.e. 'Myrddin's Precinct'. Another tradition knew of him as 'Annuab y Llaian', 'the nun's son'[30], the implication being probably that his mother was a virgin and his father unknown: that is, he was the son of a god.

A similar legend is told of the birth of St David. His mother was a nun who was raped (a common hagiographical theme, rationalising an earlier conception of virgin birth), and conceived a son. It was prophesied by the visiting St Gildas that 'the son of the nun' would 'have privilege and rule over all the saints of Britain forever'; and a local tyrant, taking this to mean that his 'power would fill the whole country', according to his druids' prophecies (*ex magorum vaticinio audiebat*), resolved to slay the child when born. The myth of Merlin's birth has here been appropriated by the hagiographer in order to stress that his hero possesses powers as great as any heathen.[31]

This myth is virtually identical to that related of the birth of Christ, when Herod, angered by the prophecy of the Magi, resolved to slay the new-born Babe. It was told of the Celtic god Lug and probably also of the Celtic Apollo, Mabon. This British Sun God was called Maponos son of Matrona, i.e. 'Son, son of Mother.' In a Welsh story he was said to have been taken from his mother when only three days old, and like Merlin to have suffered a magical imprisonment.

The evidence indicates, therefore, that, as priest, prophet and magician, Merlin was the incarnation of a god[32] or was held to have been such. He stood as heir to an extraordinarily rich and varied mythological tradition, partially understood memories of which miraculously survived long enough to be committed to writing in the early Middle Ages.

Another tradition tells how Merlin acquired the Thirteen Treasures of the Isle of Britain, 'and went with them to the Glass House, and they remain there for ever'. The Thirteen Treasures (which the earliest version declares 'were in the North') are listed elsewhere in variant forms, and consist of various objects possessing miraculous powers.[33] The Glass House (*Tŷ Gwydr*) represents a conception of the Otherworld, generally located under the sea. An allusion to this has been detected in the Welsh name of Merlin (*Myrddin* ‹ *Moridunon* = 'fortress of the sea'), suggesting that we have a further echo of the idea of the *Clas Merdin* as the island fortress of Britain herself, hemmed in by the transparent walls of the ocean.[34] Islands enjoyed a reputation for sanctity among the Celts, and Britain herself was identified at times with the Otherworld. As early as the sixth century there existed a belief in Brittany that the souls of the dead were wafted across the Channel in unmanned boats. On the British shore they saw no one, but heard a voice name them all, one by one.[35] It seems that the Britons of old may, like Shakespeare's John of Gaunt, have regarded their Island as,

> 'this little world;
> This precious stone set in the silver sea,
> Which serves it in the office of a wall;'

in which case the name of Myrddin was simply a homonym for Britain, explaining the significance of *Clas Merdin*: 'Precinct of the Sea Fortress'.

It is likely that in early times the coastal perimeter of Britain was regarded in much the same mythical light as were city walls and other defensive lines; long before they were military erections, they formed a magic defence, marking out the middle of a 'chaotic' space, peopled with demons and phantoms; an enclosure, a place that was organised; in other words, provided with a 'centre'.[36] In the case of Britain, 'the fairest island in the world' (as it is termed in the tale of *The Dream of Macsen*), it may be that it was looked upon as a particularly sacred place, a microcosm of the larger world. Contemporary evidence suggests that in Merlin's day the Island of Britain was regarded as lying in the direct path of the *axis mundi* which linked the Nail of the Heavens (the Pole Star) to earth and the Underworld beneath. Gildas, writing in the middle of the sixth century, opens his history with the curious statement that Britain 'is poised in the divine (so it is said) balance which sustains the whole earth'.

Many people have felt instinctively that there is something 'special' about the Island of Britain; that there may be something in William Blake's claim in his *Jerusalem* that 'All things Begin and End in Albions Ancient Druid Rocky Shore'. Describing the assembly of the Gaulish Druids at their Sacred Centre in the territory of the Carnutes, Julius Caesar noted that:

> 'It is believed that their philosophy (*disciplina*) was discovered in Britain and transferred thence to Gaul; and today those who wish to study the subject more deeply travel, as a rule, to Britain to learn it.'

A similar belief that the mantic arts originated in Britain is expressed also in the ancient Irish epic tale, *Táin Bó Cuailnge*. There Queen Medb of Connacht encounters a prophetess, Fedelm, who informs her that she has been in Britain to acquire her prophetic skills. This and other evidence has given rise to speculation that Druidism was adopted by the Celts from the pre-Celtic inhabitants of Britain. Pliny noted in the first century A.D. that Britain was given over to magical ceremonies as was no other province in the Empire, and more than five centuries later Gildas recorded a tradition that idols proliferated in pre-Christian Britain, 'almost surpassing those of Egypt in number.'[37]

In mediaeval times much of this aura of sanctity or other-worldliness stemmed from the magical Arthurian cycle of 'The Matter of Britain'. The Grail, according to Robert de Boron, was brought from the Holy Land to the *vaus d'Avaron* (Avalon, in Somerset); and in due course it was Merlin who foretold the grace that would fall upon 'those who are in the company of the vessel they call Grail'. The Grail cup or chalice bears a strong resemblance to the Cup of Sovereignty offered to King Conn at Tara, when Lug prophesied each of his successors in turn. The Spear, which Chrétien de Troyes and others associated with the Grail, also recalls Lug's magical spear.[38] The most satisfactory explanation of these mysterious symbols derives them from Celtic motifs, and they in turn are bound up inextricably with the story of Merlin and related myths of divine sacrifice.

Behind the darkness of history and cloak of legend, we may dimly perceive a sacred place, 'the fairest isle that is in the world', set apart in the ocean, and 'poised in the divine balance which sustains the whole earth'[39]. It was beneath the sun a place of rare beauty; it was also a theophany – *Merlin's precinct* – with its Thirteen Treasures, archetypal symbols of Forms of Otherworld perfection and profusion. And at its Centre was Merlin: to be seen as Trickster and Master of Beasts, Lord of the Wild Hunt, psychopomp and devil; and, emerging from the wilderness chaos, the Incarnation of Divinity, Guardian of the Grail, and sacrificial Saviour and Victim.

9

The Riddle of Stonehenge

Stonehenge, I have argued, was regarded in early times as the *Omphalos*, Navel, or Sacred Centre of Britain and was traditionally connected with Merlin. It was believed to have been the prophet's observatory, with its seventy doors and windows. Moreover Merlin bore an epithet, *Embreis*, identical with that of the Mons *Ambrius*. As the Northern Merlin of history is unlikely on the face of it to have been directly associated with Stonehenge, I suggested that *Embreis-Ambrosius* may in both cases be an honorific epithet.

Whatever its meaning, Embreis seems to have designated both Stonehenge itself and the functionary who was held to have presided over it, presumably a shamanistic figure, chief priest or druid. The nature of Stonehenge as Sacred Centre illumines the rôle of Merlin as its designated Guardian, and the story of the attempted sacrifice of the Fatherless Child is strikingly borne out by archaeological evidence, as are related themes in myth and legend.

The *Omphalos*, as noted in the previous chapter, is a site of unique sanctity and power. All the great civilisations of the past had their World Centre. For the Babylonians it was at Eridu, at the head of the Persian Gulf, where the Sky-god Anu fashioned the first human from clay, and Enki the sea-god breathed into him the breath of life. A temple stood there with a sacred grove, in which stood the sacred *kiskana*-tree. Its roots stretched down into the subterranean waters where Enki had his abode, while its trunk and branches were regarded as stretching up into the sky. At Nippur there was also a Navel of the Earth, and Egypt possessed its 'primordial sandhill' where the Sun-god Atum-Re-Kepri first emerged from the watery abyss.

Moving westwards, we find evidence for Sacred Centres in Syria (at Hierapolis), at Mounts Tabor and Gerizim in Palestine, and at an unidentified point in Phoenicia. In the Mediterranean world there was of course the most celebrated *Omphalos* of all, at Delphi in Greece. Westwards still there was Rome, and beyond that the Celtic lands, each with its own Centre. Indeed, as far afield as Shang Dynasty China, India of the Upanishads, the Khmer city of Ankor Thom, and the Maya civilization of Central America, each empire and kingdom maintained its own Navel.[1]

The *Omphalos* was the original point at which the world was created and from which it spread. It was in some degree literally a navel:

'The Holy One created the world like an embryo. As the embryo proceeds from the navel outwards, so God began to create the world from its navel onward, and from there it was spread out in different directions.'

From that moment it formed a sort of spiritual pole or axis linking the principal elements of the cosmos. Below, as at Eridu, connection was made with the Underworld, the world of the Dead and the waters of the Chaos which preceded Creation. Above, it was connected with the sky, and in Babylonia sanctuaries were known as *Dur-an-ki*, 'bond between heaven and earth'. It was the point where earch reached nearest to heaven. In early times, when a pilgrim ascends the omphalic mountain, 'he is coming close to the centre of the world, and on its highest terrace he breaks through into another sphere, transcending profane, heterogeneous space, and entering a "pure earth".'

When civilisations required their *Omphalos* to be near at hand, artificial mountains – Babylonian ziggurats and Aztec pyramids – were built as ritual substitutes. But what was essential was for man to ascend to where the Centre touched the Sky. The kingdoms of this world were simply reflections of the greater heavenly world above, whose glorious spread was revealed once the Sun-god had left the heavens. Cities in Babylonia and China were consciously constructed according to designs established by the constellations. When Sennacherib founded Nineveh, he described it as that 'ancient foundation, whose duration is forever, whose form was delineated from distant ages by the writing of the heaven-of-stars.' And when the Chinese city of Glak-diang was established, it was announced that 'the King . . . having constructed this great city and ruling from there, he shall be a counterpart to August Heaven . . . and from there govern as the central pivot.'

The central pivot of the heavens, the counterpart to the earthly *Omphalos*, was the Pole Star. With its roots in the Otherworld, the cosmic tree symbolically linked the earthly and celestial *Omphaloi*.

From this tree, the Tree of Life, flowed all the gifts gods confer upon men. Very frequently the Tree of Life was represented at the *Omphalos* temple by a real tree or pillar. From its base had spread the created earth, and round its top rotated the glittering procession of the constellations.[2]

In the last chapter it was shown how scattered clues point to Stonehenge as the British Sacred Centre. Those clues relate to an event which took place in the fifth century A.D., when Stonehenge was already immeasurably ancient. Had it always been the Centre? Every year thousands of people from all over the world are drawn to gaze at its great heaved-up columns, and wonder what mystery lies hidden there. The old monoliths do not give up their secrets easily, but there is good reason to suppose that the identification is very ancient and that it may from the beginning have been fixed upon as the Centre of what was once known as 'Merlin's Precinct'.

The earliest traceable structure at Stonehenge is the bank raised from the exterior ditch, which surrounds the later stone structures with a circle about a hundred yards in diameter. This is dated to the end of the third millennium B.C.[3] Numerous post-holes testify to the existence of wooden structures whose appearance and purpose is impossible to conjecture. But the bank and ditch may well represent the boundary of the sacred spot, outside which forces of chaos threatening the centre of stability could be checked and controlled. On certain festival occasions a king would perhaps mount or walk round the perimeter, and on these or other occasions (an image of) the god was likewise paraded. To the Hindus this protective circle was known as *Mangalavithi*, the Auspicious Way or Path of Blessings. At Tara the mythical Irish high-king Conn used to mount the rampart every day in a ritual designed to deflect the ever-present menace of the hosts of the Otherworld. In this way the balance of forces in an essentially unstable world was restored to equilibrium, and the four quarters into which the world was divided retained within the harmony established by the divine king.[4]

The concept of the World Centre, with its World Pillar or World-Tree rising to Heaven, is central to the shamanism of the North. The Central Pillar is a characteristic element of life among the primitive populations of the Arctic and North America. It is found among the Samoyed and the Ainu, among the tribes of Northern and Central California (the Maidu, the eastern Pomo, the Patwin) and among the Algonquin. The World-Mountain from which the Pillar or Tree rose was named Sumbur by the Mongols,

Buriats and Kalmucks, and located somewhere in Central Asia. But Mountain and Tree were essentially representational, and wherever the shaman conducted his mantic ecstasy, there also was the World Centre. The Tree passed through a central hole in the cosmic vault above, marked by the Pole Star which was known as the Peg or Nail of the Sky.[5]

Shamanism appears to have been a stage of religious expression virtually universal among mankind, and survived in an exceptional state of purity among the hunter-gatherer peoples of northern forests and taiga, and the tundra of the circumpolar North. This is presumably due to ecological reasons. The old way of life continued virtually unchanged until recent times, whereas in more hospitable regions the agricultural revolution of neolithic times and subsequent civilising processes overlaid 'pure' shamanism with other conceptions.[6]

Possibly it was an awareness of a loss of 'purity' and 'innocence' that led the religious mind northwards to the virgin forest and sea-scape, where in his distant leather tent the shaman's bird-soul detached itself from humanity and fluttered up the World Pillar to where God waited beyond the shining Nail of Heaven. It was there, too, above drifting ice-floes in the polar night that the Nail itself was closest to the earth.

It was to this remote 'Hyperborean' region that Aristeas of Proconnesus directed his steps in the seventh century B.C., when he sought to track down the oracular source of Apollonian manticism. The Greek sophist Lucian, five centuries later, claimed that it was a Hyperborean magician who overcame doubts concerning the possibility of ascent to heaven. The oracle of Apollo himself at Delphi, with its access to Otherworld knowledge, was believed to have originated among the Hyperboreans. And Irish tradition taught that the mythical race of deities, the Túatha Dé Danann,

> 'were in the northern islands of the world, studying occult lore and sorcery, druidic arts and witchcraft and magical skill, until they surpassed the sages of the pagan arts. They studied occult lore and diabolic arts in four cities: Falias, Gorias, Murias, and Findias.'[7]

All in all, there is substantial reason for believing it likely that the concept of the World Centre (*axis mundi*) or Navel in Britain was ancient, and perhaps derived from shamanistic beliefs prevalent among the peoples of the palaeo-Arctic three and more thousand years ago. Positive evidence is provided by the remarkable

statement in the *Historia Brittonum* that the oracular display of the
Fighting Dragons consulted by King Vortigern took place in a tent.
This may well refer, as has been shown earlier, to a late survival
of the shamanistic conception of the heavens as a great tent (*yurt*),
the stars being interpreted as light gleaming through rents in its
leather sides.

There is nothing extraordinary in the survival of this archaic
feature into an age and among peoples so far removed from
the hunter-fisher culture of the northern tundra. At the opposite
extreme of the Eurasian land-mass, Korea was colonised in the
prehistoric era by Altaic tribes from Central Asia. Centuries after
their nomadic origins had been forgotten the shaman faith was
(and still is) preserved. And as late as the sixth century A.D. Korean
kings in Old Silla wore crowns bearing stylistic reindeer antlers and
had horse-trappings of birch-bark – lingering vestiges of a remote
past on the steppes of Central Asia.[8]

Stonehenge is the focus for exceptionally numerous clusters of
Bronze Age burials, as well as some fifty-five cremations within
the temple itself. Clearly the general sanctity of the temple was a
strong lure, but it may also be the fact that it was the British
Omphalos which proved an important attraction in the choice of
burial site. Just as the World Navel was the point from which the
earth had spread over the chaos of primeval waters at the moment
of creation, so it was also regarded as the place that would remain
above the flood when the world ended.[9]

Such a Centre must also surely have been the holy island of Iona,
scene of St Columba's mission in the Western Isles. A traditional
verse foretold that:

> 'Seven years before the Judgment
> The sea shall sweep over Erin at one tide,
> And over blue-green Islay,
> But the Island of Columba
> Shall swim above the flood.'

It looks as if Iona was a Hebridean *Omphalos*, but whether
chosen for that reason by Columba, or deriving its sanctity from
his mission, cannot now be known. Numerous Scottish kings, Lords
of the Isles, and other great men were buried on the island, 'becaus
it was the maist honorable and ancient place that was in Scotland
in their dayes, as we reid'. It has been reasonably conjectured that
the prophecy of Iona's survival above the waters on the Day of
Judgment encouraged princes and chiefs to wish to lay their bones

there[10], and it is possible that a like consideration affected the aristocracy of Bronze Age Wessex.

The concept of Stonehenge as an *axis mundi* or World Centre may also afford an explanation of the most remarkable episode in its construction. It is now familiar knowledge that about the year 1700 B.C., Stonehenge was enhanced by the prodigious feat of transporting thither some eighty bluestones, weighing up to four tons apiece, from the Prescelly Mountains in Pembrokeshire. The motive was clearly one of overriding importance. The stones (according to the most likely theory) were dragged on sledges or rollers from the Prescelly heights, down to the sea at Milford Haven. Thence they were transported on rafts westwards along the coast of South Wales, across the Severn estuary to the mouth of the Bristol Avon, up the Avon, overland again on sledges to the Wylye and so to the confluence of the Wiltshire Avon up to the site of Amesbury, finally ascending the hill to where the stones rest today. It was an operation involving huge numbers of men over a long period of time, and must have strained the resources of the most powerful Bronze Age monarch. Clearly the Prescelly stones possessed some unique aura of sanctity, and there was some very particular reason why they had to be at Stonehenge.[11]

The identification of Stonehenge as the Navel of Britain may well provide the answer to this riddle, which has perplexed investigators since the discovery of the source of the bluestones in 1923. They are found as igneous outcrops in a restricted area at the eastern end of the Prescelly range, in an area about a mile square between the summits of Carn Meini and Foel Trigarn. There one may see still tumbled masses of the remaining rocks (known as spotted dolerite), their number being gradually increased by the action of winter frosts on the solid rock of the mountain, any one of which can match the stones now at Stonehenge.

The range dominates the south-western peninsula of Wales, Prescelly Top itself rising to a height of 1,760 feet above sea-level. What gave Prescelly its sacred character was perhaps the view which a pilgrim gained from the height itself. As the wearied traveller gazes about him from that vantage point, he sees spread below the whole of the promontory of south-western Wales (once the kingdom of Dyfed), and as he lifts his eyes to the distant horizon he sees laid out the great arc of Cardigan Bay, culminating in the gaunt fastnesses of Snowdonia; and beyond towards the setting sun the broad, open sea with the shadowy coastlines of Ireland and the Dumnonian peninsula closing it in to West and

South. Clearly visible too are numerous islands, including the Otherworld havens of Grasholm and Lundy.

What the predecessor of the modern hill-climber gazed upon in the eighteenth century B.C. was in fact the major part of the region developed by Atlantic Coast megalith-builders in the Neolithic and early Bronze Ages.[12] All along the facing coasts of Britain and Ireland are found the passage graves, court cairns, portal dolmens and other mighty relics of a forgotten religion that once dominated much of Europe.

There is no other place affording such a panoramic spectacle of this 'culture province', and one may reasonably conjecture that it formed the *Omphalos* for the Irish Sea zone. Just as Iona may have provided the *axis mundi* for the sea-based kingdom of Dalriada (and possibly its Pictish predecessor), so Prescelly was the focus of the sea-borne 'empire' of the Irish Sea megalith-builders. The significance of the world-embracing mountain-top view has been noted previously, and the Prescelly height seems a likely spot for such a sacred Centre.

This likelihood is greatly increased when the circumstances of the removal of the bluestones to Stonehenge are considered. For if the Bronze Age ruler of Wessex, who already possessed his *Omphalos* at Stonehenge, gained the sort of control over south-western Wales that must in any case surely have been necessary for the acquisition of the bluestones, then it would have been a major priority to absorb the Prescelly *Omphalos* into the greater one at Stonehenge. There could not be rival World Centres within the same sphere of power, and so the Prescelly Omphalos was symbolically re-erected within the Sacred Centre at Stonehenge. Thus when a Chinese emperor in early times conquered a new province, objects emblematic of the subjected 'Centre' were transported to the imperial capital, which signified that the entire state had passed into his hands. Similarly, the Cambodian temple-mountain *axis mundi* included forty-nine towers representing provinces of the empire of King Jayavarman VII.[13]

Possibly it was the Prescelly mountain itself that formed the *Omphalos*, from which boulders symbolising the whole were abstracted. It seems more likely, however, that Irish Sea megalith-builders had erected a Navel at some point on the mountain which for obvious reasons is no longer identifiable. It has been clearly established that the Stonehenge bluestones were re-erected after being displaced from some preceding structure, which may have been one standing somewhere on the Prescelly range. But equally their arrangement could have been altered *in situ* after their arrival at Stonehenge, a possibility for which there is some archaeological evidence. But if the transference of the *Omphalos* were merely a symbolic transfer of the mountain, then it could have been achieved in a manner infinitely less extravagant and taxing to the resources of the Wessex ruler.

For intriguing confirmation that it was a pre-existing monument that was moved, we may turn again to the pages of Geoffrey of Monmouth's *History of the Kings of Britain*. In the tenth chapter of his eighth book we read how Ambrosius resolved to build a suitable memorial near Salisbury to the nobles treacherously killed by Hengist. When his labourers failed in their task, he summoned Merlin from his remote refuge at the Fountain of Galabes.

"'If you wish", explained the magician, "to commemorate the sepulture of these men with an eternal memorial, send for the Giant's Dance (*chorea gigantum*), which is in Killaraus, a mountain in Ireland. For there is an edifice of stones there, which none of this age could raise without a profound knowledge of the mechanical arts (*nisi ingenium arte subnecteret*). They are stones of a vast magnitude and unique quality. If they can be placed here in the same manner as there, round this piece of ground, they will stand forever." At these words of Merlin, Ambrosius cried out, laughing, "how is it possible to remove such vast stones from so distant a country, as if Britain in any case were not well supplied with stones suitable for the purpose?" To which Merlin replied, "let not the King be vainly moved to laughter; what I say is far from frivolous. The stones possess mystical power (*Mistici sunt lapides*) and are useful for many healing purposes. The giants at one time brought them from the furthest frontiers of Africa and placed them in Ireland when they lived there. For they designed to take baths among them whenever they were stricken with illness. For they washed the stones and placed their sick in the water, which invariably cured them. Similarly they cured wounds by also applying herbs. There is not a stone there without its healing power.'"

These words convinced the Britons, who set out in a fleet with fifteen thousand troops, accompanied by Merlin himself. In Ireland they were resisted by the youthful King Gillomanius, who was however defeated after a fierce battle. They then marched to Mount Killaraus, where they gazed in wonder at the Giant's Dance. Merlin, in his usual ironical manner, invited his companions to set about removing the structure. Despite every effort with cables and ladders, their struggles were of no avail.

'Merlin laughed at their vain endeavours, and then set about preparing his own engines (*machinationes*). When he had disposed these in the proper way, he took down the stones more easily than one could credit and directed their embarkment on board the ships; and so they set sail joyfully back to Britain.'

There is much in this account, despite its author's deserved reputation for mendacity, which invites respect. Geoffrey knows the stones came by sea from 'Ireland', which is a reasonable enough extension of Pembrokeshire, always subject to Irish influences. The reference to Mount Killaraus is due to a linking of Stonehenge with Uisnech, its counterpart as the Irish *Omphalos*. (The real site of origin was perhaps forgotten because there was nothing left to mark it.) The reference to Africa may reflect a faint memory of the fact that the megalith-builders did indeed come from Spain and North Africa.

Now can also be seen the force behind Merlin's suggestion, and the reason why it was only as a result of war that the Britons of Wessex were enabled to seize the Giant's Dance. For under no other circumstance than military conquest could the transference of a 'national' *Omphalos* have been contemplated. Geoffrey's story, whatever the source, seems to have preserved an accurate tradition of events nearly three thousand years old. The tradition told of an immensely powerful King of Wessex (the resources required to move the bluestones are evidence enough of that), whose armies conquered South Wales as far as St George's Channel. The once-proud 'empire' of the Peoples of the Inner Sea was crushed, a subjection enforced to eternity by the near-miraculous transfer of the Sacred Centre of their territory within the circumference of the *Omphalos* of Britain.

Fitting and probable too is the way in which the operation is supervised by a priest-magician, who may have been a predecessor of the Merlin Ambrosius of latter days. It is worth noting, though, that contrary to an impression frequently given, there is no suggestion that Merlin employed supernatural powers to accomplish the transportation. It is explicitly stated that it was his superior engineering skills which made the feat possible. In view of Geoffrey's apparent access to reliable tradition, we should perhaps also treat with respect some of his other details, such as the curative power ascribed to the stones.

There may be those who find it hard to credit the trustworthiness of an oral record, supposedly preserved for twenty-eight centuries. This is understandable, but even the most hardened sceptic may find it hard to dispose summarily of a further, parallel instance. Chapter Eight recounted the story of the Fatherless Child (identified with Ambrosius, and later Merlin) in the *Historia Brittonum*. Only by the sacrifice of such a one, the druids explained to the king, could his building be enabled to stand secure. The building, as I argued, is to be identified with Stonehenge.

Now, less than two miles from Stonehenge is the site of the equally mysterious structure known as Woodhenge. Discovered by aerial photography in 1925, all that remained were traces of a ditch and bank enclosing a circular grouping of post-holes, indicating that at one time a large timber edifice stood there. Dated by pottery findings to the Secondary Neolithic period (contemporary with the first building of Stonehenge), its proximity and similarity to that temple clearly suggest a connection, one possibly being the prototype of the other. And almost exactly in the centre of Woodhenge, excavators discovered the burial of a young child, about three years of age, whose skull had been cleft before burial, suggesting that the burial was a dedicatory or sacrificial one. Furthermore, this is one of the very few pieces of evidence for human sacrifice in prehistoric Britain.[14] Does it not seem likely that another such tiny skeleton lay (or lies) buried at Stonehenge, ensuring that no malign forces overturn the mighty building which marks the theophany where God and Man may meet?

Thus we have a remarkable example of archaeology explaining legend, and legend clarifying the archaeological record. From the tale of Ambrosius and Vortigern in the *Historia Brittonum* (ninth century A.D.) it may be deduced that the Woodhenge skeleton was that of a boy whose father was unknown, and who was therefore presumed to have had a divine or at any rate supernatural parent. And from the Woodhenge burial it is possible to see more clearly what precisely would have been the fate of the boy Ambrosius had he not been so perspicacious.

The purpose of the sacrifice was doubtless that indicated in the story in the *Historia Brittonum*: to sustain the edifice. Instances of such a belief and practice were given in Chapter Eight. There may also have been another related reason for placing the corpse of the Fatherless Child in the centre of the *axis mundi*. As has already been remarked, an almost invariable concomitant of the World-Navel was the World-Tree or World-Pillar. The Tree was rooted in the *Omphalos*, and was a ladder or bridge to Heaven and Hell, the central or umbilical cord of the cosmos. As a Finnish folk poem puts it, it is:

> 'a bridge to the timeless place
> for a traveller to go
> a man to dark Pohjola
> to the man-eating village
> the village that drowns heroes.
> He has an eternal bridge
> who was eaten without cause
> who was killed without disease
> without the Creator done
> to death, in dark Pohjola
> in the man-eating village:
> there is meat without bones there
> there is calf without gristle
> for the hungry man to eat
> a bite for the one in want.'

In Norse mythology the tree was represented by the famous ash, Yggdrasil, whose branches spread over the whole world and reached up to heaven. Under one of its roots lay Mimir's Well, the source of wisdom acquired by Odin in exchange for the sacrifice of his eye. Among the Yakuts of Siberia was a belief that an eight-branched Tree arose from the World-Navel. It was there that the First Man was born, being suckled by the milk of a Woman emerging from its trunk. Can this conception be related to Myrddin's 'sweet-apple tree', whose 'peculiar power hides it from the men of Rhydderch', and at whose foot was once 'a fair wanton maiden, one slender and comely'?[15]

To return to Stonehenge, the British *Omphalos*: could it too have once been, like its counterparts, the focus of the World-Tree? It has in fact been conjectured that a tree was the original cult-object within the central trilithons[16], and there are indications that this may be so. It certainly looks as if *something* lay at the focus, for the precise and symmetrical design of the building appears to be directed towards that end.[17] Fortunately an Irish legend contains an account of precisely what was expected to be found within a megalithic circle. The story tells how the hero Diarmait came to what is clearly intended as an Otherworld. There, he

'saw a beautiful country spread out before him: a lovely flowery plain straight in front, bordered with pleasant hills, and shaded with groves of many kinds of trees. It was enough to banish all care and sadness from one's heart to view this country, and to listen to the warbling of the birds, the humming of the bees among the flowers, the rustling of the wind through the trees, and the pleasant voices of the streams and waterfalls. Making no delay, Diarmait set out to walk across the plain. He had not been long walking when he saw, right before him, a great tree laden with fruit, overtopping all the other trees of the plain. It was surrounded at a little distance by a circle of pillar-stones; and one stone, taller than the others, stood in the centre near the tree. Beside this pillar-stone was a spring well, with a large, round pool as clear as crystal; and the water bubbled up in the centre, and flowed away towards the middle of the plain in a slender stream.'

Here we have quite clearly the World-Tree rising from the centre of its stone circle. Whether a real tree was planted within a megalithic monument cannot be known. The World-Tree itself is a cosmic myth, and it may be that it was symbolised by the 'one stone, taller than the others', which stood in the centre. A strong candidate for this rôle at Stonehenge would be the so-called Altar Stone, now lying near the centre and measuring sixteen feet in length.[18] This in turn leads to a consideration of the possibility that the Fatherless Child was sacrificed to ensure the stability of the World-Tree and the pillar representing it. Through his divine father he would have ready access to the Otherworld above and below.

To revert to the tale of Diarmait. Feeling thirsty, he drank from the well by the central pillar:

'but before his lips touched the water, he heard the heavy tread of a body of warriors, and the loud clank of arms, as if a whole host were coming straight down him. He sprang to his feet and looked round; but the noise ceased in an instant, and he could see nothing.'

He drank again, heard the same sound, but again saw nothing. Standing still in puzzlement, he glanced up and saw a magnificent golden drinking-horn lying on top of the pillar-stone by the well. Seized by a sudden idea, he took it down, dipped it in the well, and drank from it.

Immediately he saw a giant, clad in armour and wearing a golden crown, striding towards him from the East. This apparition angrily reproved Diarmait for trespassing in his land and drinking from his well. They fought fiercely all day, until at evening the stranger suddenly disappeared down the well. The same encounter repeated itself daily, until on the fourth occasion Diarmait gripped hold of his adversary and descended with him below the earth. There he found himself in the Land below the Billows – possibly the ocean on which the earth rests.[19]

The armed stranger is clearly the Otherworld guardian of the well, perhaps a malign being believed to haunt a place of such associations rather than the deity or power who presided over it. The well corresponds to that of Mimir by Yggdrasil's roots in Norse mythology, and is the source of Otherworld wisdom and knowledge, providing access to the Otherworld itself. In Celtic Ireland the most famous example was the Well of Segais, around which were set hazel-trees whose nuts dropped into the well and travelled up the Boyne every seventh year in the middle of June: they contained the *imbas* which provided the seer with his prophetic gift. The Well of Segais is not identifiable with any real spring, but as the reputed enchanted source of both the Boyne and the Shannon it corresponds to Merlin's spring on Hart Fell, from whose base rise the rivers Clyde, Tweed and Annan. With the horn one may compare the celebrated *Gjallarhorn*, with which Mismir drank from his well of wisdom beside the Norse World-Tree, Yggdrasil.[20]

The whole episode in this adventure of Diarmait presents a close parallel to that in the romance of *Fergus* at the *Noquetran*, when the knight visits the mountain 'where Merlin dwelt for many a year'. One may recognise as common elements the enchanted horn which summons first the sound of the ghostly company (the Wild Hunt), and secondly the grim *genius loci* who calls the rash visitor to account. The great World-fruit-tree also recalls Merlin's apple-tree, 'with its peculiar power'.

Enough evidence has been assembled to show that it is probable that Stonehenge was from earliest times regarded as the British *Omphalos*; that it was sustained by the sacrifice of a Fatherless Child, that it absorbed a rival megalithic *Omphalos* on the Prescelly Mountains, that it centred on a World-tree, possibly represented by the 'Altar Stone' (then upright), and that it continued as a focus of numinous power into the early Dark Ages, when Vortigern consulted the oracle there. Of course this is far from being the extent of Stonehenge's significance. Its rôle as *Omphalos*, the holiest spot in Southern Britain, made it a fitting site for the most sacred ritual observances and an ever-fertile source of knowledge and power. It may be conjectured, for example, that a 'play' of the god Lug took place within the ring of stones, and that early British kings may have been crowned there.

Stonehenge is clearly orientated toward the rising sun, and as the timing of festivals was all-important, it is likely that a study of the cyclic movements of the heavenly bodies formed a major purpose in its construction. What should be stressed is that the Pole Star must surely have been an object of particular interest to the guardians of the temple, since it was directly linked to it by the World-Tree, up which the seer ascended as the only access to heaven.

It is true that Stonehenge is not situated at the geographical centre of Britain, any more than Chartres lies at the centre of Gaul or Mount Tabor at the centre of Palestine. The imagery was symbolic, not literal. It may be that the site's significance as *Omphalos* reflects its positioning at the point of intersection of three of the greatest trackways of prehistoric Britain: the South Downs ridgeway, the Harroway, and the Icknield Way. In particular, the crossing of the east-west Harroway by the north-south Icknield Way could readily have suggested that here was the very nodal point of Britain: quite literally, the point where everyone met. The name of the Harroway possibly derives from the Old English *hearg-weg*, 'temple-road'; but which came first, the construction of the sanctuary at Stonehenge or the development of the road-crossings, would be hard to establish.[21]

In ancient Ireland it was believed that five great roadways, radiating from the sacred centre at Tara, made a magical appearance at the birth of King Conn Céadcathach. The axis from which they derived necessarily bore a numinous quality.[22] In the Isle of Man, for example, Sir John Rhŷs heard from a local inhabitant of a witch whom he had encountered 'carrying on her evil practices at the junction of cross-roads, or the meeting of three boundaries'. On a second occasion the man found her 'at work at four cross-roads, somewhere near Lezayre. She had a circle,' he said, 'as large as that made by horses in threshing, swept clean around her'.[23]

The rôle of Stonehenge as *Omphalos* is not directly mentioned in any source, and has consequently been reconstructed from a multiplicity of concurring evidence whose value the reader must judge for himself. The Sacred Centre may have been a place of great secrecy as well as sanctity. The ancient Persian *Omphalos* was the magnificent city of Persepolis, begun by Darius in 518 B.C. and sacked by Alexander the Great more than two centuries later. Despite the unparalleled splendour of its construction and its significance in the life of the Persian people, 'it was little known outside Persia. There is no reference to it in the Old Testament, or in Babylonian, Assyrian, or Phoenician documents.'[24] There are things which it is not good for prying outsiders to know.

The significance of Stonehenge must have passed from popular consciousness with the Anglo-Saxon conquest and conversion to Christianity. The Christian world knew of but one *Omphalos*, Jerusalem, which was from an early date regarded as the Navel of Palestine. With the Crucifixion this hierophany took on greatly added significance. Golgotha was henceforward the World-centre, and the Cross its Tree of Life. In the third century A.D. the Tree was described as rooted in Calvary, with a bubbling spring at its foot and its branches spreading so as to encompass the whole world. The faithful who drank from the spring would ascend to Heaven by way of the Tree. A legend grew up that God created Adam on the very spot where the Cross was set up, and the Saviour's blood dropping on his skull redeemed the First Man instantly.[25] But the implications of this development must be reserved for another chapter.

10

The Shaman of Hart Fell and the Ritual of Renewal

The previous two chapters represent something of a digression from the central theme, which is here renewed. Evidence suggests that Stonehenge was an archaic *axis mundi*, the Centre or Navel of Britain. A garbled tradition of this rôle, and of the human sacrifice ensuring its efficacy, survived into the Dark Ages. The central rôle of the boy Embreis (Ambrosius) leads to speculation that the Priest or Guardian of the sanctuary bore some such a name or title. The connection of Merlin with this shadowy figure is by no means fully established. Indications of the possibility exist in the early linking of the names of Merlin and Ambrosius in the tale of the Collapsing Castle, and what appears to be an allusion to Merlin's connection with Stonehenge as observatory in the *Vita Merlini*. Certainly, the mysterious allusion to Britain's having been formerly known as *Clas Merddin*, 'Merlin's Precinct', points to his enjoying some rôle central to British heathendom.

There exists in the body of early Welsh poetry a series of 'transformation' or 'shape-shifting' verses, in which the poet is made to boast of his numerous existences in other guises or other times:

> 'I have been a blue salmon,
> I have been a dog, a stag, a
>   roebuck on the mountain,
> A stock, a spade, an axe in the hand,
> A stallion, a bull, a buck. . . .'

> 'I was with my lord in the heavens
> When Lucifer fell into the depths of hell;
> I carried a banner before Alexander;
> I know the stars' names from the

> north to the south,
> I was in the fort of Gwydion,
> In the Tetragramaton. . . .'

This poetry is generally attributed to the sixth-century poet
Taliesin, and much of it appears developed into a tale about the
infant Taliesin at the court of Maelgwn Gwynedd in North Wales.
The legend is redolent throughout of Celtic magic and paganism,
and stands in marked contrast to the figure of the historical *Christian* bard Taliesin. Of course almost anything can happen in the
development of a legend, but it may be asked whether the story
was not originally attached to the figure of Myrddin, and only later
attributed to Taliesin?

The child Taliesin's wise responses to King Maelgwn's questioning recall the behaviour of the infant Merlin before King Vortigern,
and the climax of his poetry at the end of the story is identical with
Merlin's prophecy, with its foretelling of the coming defeat of the
Britons by a serpent out of Germany (the Saxons) and of their
ultimate triumph. And, indeed, when Maelgwn asks the youth his
name at the beginning of their interview, 'Taliesin' is made to
reply:

> 'The Prophet Johannes called me Merlin (*Merddin*),
> But now all kings know me as Taliesin.'

Thus there must once have existed a version in which Merlin was
the protagonist of the story.[1] The priority may receive confirmation
from the fact that the baby Taliesin is discovered by Maelgwn's
son Elphin in a leather bag stranded on a weir at the estuary of
the Conwy. Elphin slit open the bag and saw the boy's forehead,
upon which he exclaimed 'behold the radiant forehead!' (*i.e. tal
iesin*), and thus named the child. But since the first element of
Myrddin's name undoubtedly signified 'sea' it can be seen how
much more aptly he would have fitted into this episode than
Taliesin. It may also be recalled that Merlin's *alter ego* Lailoken
was impaled on a stake in a fishing-weir.[2]

These transformation passages are also of particular interest for
the light they throw on pagan Celtic concepts of transmigration of
the soul. They appear not only in the late Taliesin saga (*Hanes
Taliesin*) just referred to, but also in other poems in *The Book of
Taliesin*. The most interesting of these is that entitled *Cad Goddeu*,
'the Battle of the Trees'. It begins with a characteristic transformation passage:

'I was in many shapes before I was released:
I was a slender, enchanted sword . . .
I was rain-drops in the air, I was stars' beam;
I was a word in letters, I was a book in origin;
I was lanterns of light for a year and a half;
I was a bridge that stretched over sixty estuaries;
I was a path, I was an eagle, I was a coracle in seas;'

and so forth. Suddenly there is a dramatic shift. The poet was in a fortress (*kaer nefenhir*) when suddenly he witnessed the appalling sight that greeted Macbeth at Dunsinane: a forest was advancing menacingly towards him. At once the wizard Gwydion waved his magic wand and, somewhat incongruously invoking the name of Christ, raised up a rival army of trees and shrubs. There followed a fearful conflict, with cherries, birch, ash and elm giving no quarter; 'blood up to our thighs'. Each of the trees is ascribed its own peculiar quality, and the assemblage of the rival hosts is described with vigour and some humour.

Once again the theme changes without warning, and the poet reverts to an account of his previous existence. This time he explains his original creation:

'Not from father or mother was I made;
As for creation, I was created from nine
         forms of elements:
From the fruit of fruits, from the fruit of
         God at the beginning;
From primroses and flowers of the hill,
         from the bloom of woods and trees;
From the essence of soils was I made,
From the bloom of nettles, from water of
         the ninth wave.'

The act of creation from these natural elements was performed by the wizards Math, Gwydion and others;

'Gwydion created me, great magic from
         the staff of enchantment . . .
From five fifties of magicians and teachers
         like Math was I produced . . .
The magician of magicians created
         me before the world. . . .'

The poem continues with a reassertion of the guises and existences the poet has known since that first enchanted moment when the wizard's wand caused soil and vegetation to coalesce and rise up in human form.

> 'I passed time at dawn, I slept in purple;
> I was in the rampart with Dylan Eil Mor,
> In a cloak in the middle between kings. . . .
> I was a snake enchanted on a hill, I
>   was a viper in a lake. . . .
> I shall cause a field of blood, on it a
>   hundred warriors. . . .
> Long and white are my fingers, long
>   have I not been a shepherd;
> I lived as a warrior before I was a man
>   of letters;
> I wandered, I encircled, I slept in a
>   hundred islands, I dwelt in
>   a hundred forts.'[3]

Cad Goddeu is not directly attributed to Taliesin, though elsewhere Taliesin is made to boast that he 'was in the battle of Goddeu with Lleu and Gwydion.' There are, however, indications that it belongs to that earlier phase when, as Taliesin explained to King Maelgwn, the poet was known as Myrddin. Firstly, it should be noted that *Goddeu*, meaning 'the forest', is probably intended as a proper noun. The genuine poems of the sixth-century Taliesin mention a district in the North, next to Urien's kingdom of Rheged, known by this name. From the context, it is conjectured to have been the wild, unreclaimed territory between Hadrian's Wall and the Forth. Other scholars have followed with a more precise identification of Goddeu with the heavily-forested region in Selkirkshire, which in the Middle Ages was simply known as The Forest. Finally it seems that Goddeu is to be identified with that other famous forest which Welsh tradition located on the same spot, the *Coed Celyddon*.[4]

If Goddeu and Coed Celyddon be one, then it is hard indeed not to conceive of Myrddin as the intended narrator of the poem *Cad Goddeu*.[5] Is he gazing out from the summit of Hart Fell, as Cai and Bedwyr once surveyed a vast landscape from the cairn on Plinlimmon, 'in the greatest wind in the world'? All around, almost as far as the eye can see, spreads the mighty forest. Branches sway and toss in the gale, moving in undulating sweeps first in one direction, then another. As their heads turn in unison, they resemble nothing so much as huge columns of marching men advancing and retreating. Now and then there is a splintering crack as a great branch, or even an entire trunk crashes to the ground. Twigs and foliage are hurled about as the savage element rages through the thickets. When at evening the storm subsides and all returns to its former calm, the bard wandering in the forest below sees traces of devastation comparable to that he knew when driven to madness at the battle of Arderydd. His spirit, still troubled by the turmoil, uneasily contemplates what has been and what is yet to be, as he trudges back to his hut by the sacred well. Just as he sees the world in space spread before his gaze from its Centre at the top of Hart Fell, so his vision encompasses all eternity from the Creation to the Final Day.

This is, of course, reconstruction, but there are sections of the poem which may in part substantiate it:

> 'I shall cause a field of blood, on it a hundred warriors;
> Scaly and red my shield, gold is my shield-ring'

could reflect Myrddin's guilt over the slaughter of Arderydd, and his proud recollection of abandoned military prowess. Then again,

> 'Long and white are my fingers; long have I not been a
> *shepherd*;
> I lived as a warrior before I was a man of letters;'

bears no obvious application to Taliesin, but fits Myrddin to a nicety. Myrddin had been both soldier and courtier before taking to the wilds as a prophet. The word rendered in the translation as 'shepherd' is the Welsh *heussawr*, which is more properly expressed as 'herdsman'. In an episode of the story of *Culhwch and Olwen*, Cai and others encounter a giant herdsman named Custennin. He is seated on a mound, dressed in skins, and watches over a countless herd of sheep wandering over the surrounding plain. He is termed *heussawr* which, as he is clearly intended as a divine Lord of the Animals, should be translated 'woodward' or 'Herdsman'.[6] The lines may be read as implying that the poet was formerly a soldier and man of refinement, but is now at once bard and custodian of (wild) animals.

Whether or not *Cad Goddeu* is to be connected with Myrddin must remain uncertain, but it does appear to encapsulate surviving pagan belief. It is not of course in its present form a production of the sixth century, as its incongruous Christian invocations (to say nothing of metre and language) betray. The clash is manifest throughout, indicating that the Christian redactor was not reworking a malleable mass of half-forgotten heathen allusions, but a work whose structure and concept were established in some set form. It includes a clear exposition of the doctrine of metempsychosis (reincarnation), in a manner which it is scarcely conceivable a tenth-century Christian poet would have set about inventing.[7]

Cad Goddeu recounts that, as a result of his supernatural power, the bard is able to change his shape at will into beast, or human, or natural feature. His soul detaches itself from his body, and moves freely; no more bound by time than space, it can range the centuries, 'becoming' in succession great figures of the past, so acquiring at first-hand all knowledge. The purpose of this out-of-body exploration was to answer questions brought to the bard by earnest enquirers. Some of these queries are also preserved in verse:

'Why is a night moonlit, and another (so dark) that thou seest not thy shield out of doors? . . . Why is a stone so heavy? Why is a thorn so sharp? . . . Who is better off (in) his death, the young or the grey-haired? Dost thou know what thou art when thou art sleeping, whether body or soul, or a bright angel? Skilled minstrel, why dost thou not tell me? Dost thou know where night awaits day? . . . What supports the structure of the earth in perpetuity? The soul . . . who has seen it, who knows it?'[8]

The bard can answer these esoteric enquiries because he has actually been an eagle, a serpent, a drop of water; and was himself Dylan Eil Mor in the rampart.

The poetry in which these answers are given is generally, as the extracts quoted show, rambling, allusive and only partially coherent. Such poems were certainly not orally preserved and committed to manuscript for their lyrical quality, even if at times they achieve a momentary mysterious grandeur. One suspects that they may have been little more intelligible when first expounded. In the twelfth century Giraldus Cambrensis wrote this description of certain soothsayers well known in the Wales of his day:

'There are certain persons in Cambria, whom you will find nowhere else, called *Awenyddion*, or people inspired; when consulted upon any doubtful event, they roar out violently, are rendered beside themselves, and become, as it were, possessed by a spirit. They do not deliver the answer to what is required in a connected manner; but the person who skilfully observes them, will find after many preambles, and many nugatory and incoherent, though ornamented speeches, the desired explanation conveyed in some turn or word; they are then roused from their ecstasy, as from a deep sleep, and, as it were, by violence compelled to return to their proper senses. After having answered the question they do not recover till violently shaken by other people; nor can they remember the replies they have given. If consulted a second or third time upon the same point, they will make use of expressions totally different; perhaps they spoke by means of fanatic and ignorant spirits. These gifts are usually conferred upon them in dreams: some seem to have sweet milk or honey poured on their lips; to others (it seems) that a written document is applied to their mouths, and immediately on rising up from sleep after completing their chant, they publicly declare that they have received this gift . . . they invoke, during their prophecies the true and living God, and the Holy Trinity and pray that they may not by their sins be prevented from finding the truth.'

Giraldus's account provides evidence that the prophetic utterances of the *awenyddion* in his day were taken down in writing. The passage 'to others (it seems) a written document is applied to their mouths, and immediately on rising up from sleep after completing their chant, they publicly declare that they have received this gift . . .' seems to indicate that texts of the 'chants' were issued at the scene of consultation.

Here is first-hand evidence for the practice of writing down prophecies at the time, also referred to in the account of Merlin's *alter ego*, Lailoken, who

'predicted much of the future there like a prophet. But because he never repeated what he foretold (though it was extremely obscure and virtually unintelligible), nobody cared to believe him. *But they remembered some apparently idle remarks and committed them to writing.*'[9]

Giraldus actually compares the prophecies of the *awenyddion* of his time with those of Merlin who also, he affirms, 'became frantic' when prophesying. This is the Myrddin of Welsh poetry (Geoffrey of Monmouth gives no indication of his Merlin being in a state of ecstasy when prophesying), a manuscript collection of whose prophecies Giraldus had himself seen in the remote Lleyn peninsula.

Giraldus was thus in an enviably unique position to compare the verses attributed to Myrddin and those composed by the *awenyddion* of his own day. He clearly saw a marked resemblance which led him to presume that Myrddin's prophecies had been uttered and recorded in a similar way.

Now, there is a close relationship between the Celtic bard who achieves prophetic insight through an ecstatic trance or frenzy, and the comparable practices of shamanism as it has survived in Siberia and elsewhere. The comparison throws a flood of light on the mantic tradition of Celtic druids and bards, and on the story of Merlin in particular.

'Shamanism' (the name derives from the Tungus people of Siberia) is a name of convenience used to describe certain religious practices first clearly identified in Siberia. It is not a religion, but 'an archaic technique of ecstasy'. Shamanism can exist alongside another religion or other religious beliefs and practices, and it can form a component part of a complex of religious practices. In fact virtually all the 'advanced' religions have at one time included shamanistic concepts, often as an inheritance of an earlier phase of religious development. The shaman is a specialist, whose function is to establish contact with the Otherworld. Through this unique capacity he acts as intermediary and suppliant for his people with God.[10]

Shamanism is undoubtedly a practice of extraordinary antiquity. Exactly how old it is there is no means of knowing, but it is virtually certain that it was practised by Palaeolithic man, whose way of life can have been little different from that of the Siberian peoples among whom the practice was first identified. The earliest likely evidence for the existence of a 'professional' shaman is probably to be found in the celebrated painting of the so-called 'Sorcerer' in the cave of Les Trois Frères in Southern France. Withdrawn in its innermost recess, he has the appearance of a man bending forward, his eyes big and round like those of a night bird (or a lion, or a 'ghost'), cervic antlers on his head, and the ears and shoulders of a reindeer or stag. The lower part of the back is provided with a horse's tail, below which the sexual parts are seen, rather human in shape, but located where a female's would be. The figure appears in the act of bounding or dancing, and though possibly intended as a god (Lord of the Animals) the evidence suggests that the shaman in his ecstasy in any case identified in part with the god. As with Merlin himself, it is hard at times to distinguish between god and votary. At Star Carr in Yorkshire, a Mesolithic (*c.* 7000 B.C.) site, a number of stag frontlets were excavated whose inner cores had been hollowed out 'for wearing as a kind of mask', very likely during some ritual enactment.[11]

Though it is probable that human societies have almost universally passed through a period of shamanism lasting for thousands of years, we must beware of thinking either that the shamanism of modern Siberia necessarily represents a 'fossilised' survival of similar practices in, say, Palaeolithic Europe, or indeed that there has ever been such a thing as a 'pure' shamanism. But there are undoubtedly identifiable techniques transcending time and distance, particularly in relation to initiation and ecstasy. It is these which parallel aspects of the Merlin legend far too closely to be coincidental.

Briefly, the shaman's selection and function is much as follows. Whether chosen hereditarily or at random, the neophyte becomes suddenly subject to aberrant behaviour, usually taken as akin to some neurotic ailment – 'madness'.

Eventually he retreats to the wilderness where he lives alone like a wild animal, surviving on roots, berries and what wild creatures he may catch, until after some time he returns to his people. His behaviour marks him as a shaman, and he begins to shamanise. This is often preceded by a ritual dismemberment, burial and resurrection, symbolising the seer's rebirth.

He acquires special clothing, usually with animal or bird associations. Dancing and usually beating on a drum, he works himself up into an ecstasy. As the mantic fit comes upon him he ascends the World-Tree which links this and the Otherworld, symbolised by a real tree, a specially prepared wooden pillar, or the central post of a tent (*yurt*). Through an increasingly frantic babble of semi-coherent chanting, he provides a commentary explanatory of the long and arduous journey his soul (usually conceived in the form of a bird) undergoes. There are many dangers and difficulties, which it is not always possible to overcome. The shaman, who often simulates in action his bird-flight, crossing of the Otherworld-bridge, etc., is assisted in his task by attendant spirits in the form of dogs, wolves, horses, etc. Eventually, his journey safely completed, the shaman awakes from his trance exhausted and generally with no recollection of what has passed or been revealed.

The story of Merlin, as it appears in its variant guises (Myrddin-Lailoken-Suibhne), precisely parallels these aspects of the shaman's 'call' and ecstatic vision. Indeed, the parallel is so precise that it is impossible to doubt that the original Merlin saga comprised the story of a late British shaman-figure.

1. *The shaman's 'call'*

This can occur in a number of ways, the most frequent being an abrupt disorientation of character and temporary removal to the wilderness. Among the Yakuts of Siberia, for example, the person destined to become a shaman starts by becoming frenzied. Suddenly becoming possessed, he retires to the forests, living on tree-bark, throwing himself into water and fire and wounding himself with knives. The family then resorts to an old shaman, who undertakes to instruct the distraught youth in the differing species of spirits, and the means of summoning and mastering them. Similarly, among the Manchurian Tungus, the behaviour of the young neophyte sometimes decides and brings about his initiation. He flees to the mountains and stays there for a week or more, living on animals 'captured by him with his own teeth', and returning to his village dirty and bleeding, with torn clothes and tousled hair, 'like a wild man'. It is only after ten days or so that the neophyte breaks into an incoherent babble. His full initiation as shaman follows thereafter.[12]

That this practice survived in Celtic Britain is attested by folk-lore tradition in Wales. There was a belief that if a man spent a night on Cader Idris, he would descend in the morning a bard or a madman. On Snowdon the place to pass the night with a view to the same result was the hollow underneath the huge block called the Black Stone of the Arddu, near the Black Tarn of the Arddu. Yet another tradition recorded a belief that the Wild Hunt careered above Cader Idris every Halloween.

The word *arddu* signifies 'black', 'dark', in the sense of 'looming, threatening, terrifying', and appears in *The Book of Taliesin* as a name for the Otherworld deity. The Black Man encountered by Owain in the tale of the Lady of the Fountain is clearly to be identified with the Celtic horned god in his rôle of 'lord of the wild beasts', and 'The Black Man' was doubtless a reverential euphemism employed to denote a god whose name it was unlucky to utter openly.[13]

The significance of Geoffrey of Monmouth's account of Merlin's 'madness' is clear:

'He threw dust upon his hair, tore his clothes and lay prostrate on the ground, rolling to and fro. . . . Then, when the air was full with these repeated loud complainings, a strange madness came upon him. He crept away and fled to the woods, unwilling that any should see his going. Into the forest he went, glad to lie hidden beneath the ash trees. . . . He made use of the roots of plants and of grasses, of fruit from trees and of the blackberries in the thicket. He became a man of the woods, as if dedicated to the woods. So for a whole summer he stayed hidden in the woods, discovered by none, forgetful of himself and of his own, lurking like a wild thing.'

Merlin's *alter ego*, Lailoken, explained similarly that 'I was torn out of my own self and an evil spirit seized me and assigned me to the wild things of the woods.'

The frenzy of their Irish counterpart, Suibhne, is described in similar terms, with the additional touch that, after fleeing over plains, bogs and thickets, 'he reached Ros Bearaigh, in Glenn Earcain, when he went into the yew-tree that was in the glen'. The incredibly swift flight of the newly-possessed initiate, as well as the ascent of what is clearly a symbolic World-Tree, are paralleled in shamanistic practice. In Ghana, for example, a novice shaman 'is liable to dash off into the bush so swiftly that he may outrun his pursuers'; and among the Sumatran Nias, 'he who is destined to become a priest-prophet abruptly disappears, carried off by the spirits (very likely the young man is taken up into the sky); he returns to the village after three or four days; otherwise they set out in search of him and generally find him at the top of a tree, talking to the spirits. He appears out of his mind, and sacrifices are necessary to restore him to his senses.'[14]

It could scarcely be plainer that descriptions of Merlin's madness and flight to the wilds represent a misunderstood description of his mantic 'call'.[15] His refuge I identified in an earlier chapter with the mountain of Hart Fell in Dumfriesshire. The mediaeval romance of *Fergus* refers to it as the place 'where Merlin dwelt for many a year', and declares it to have been under the guardianship of 'a knight as black as a mulberry' – a dim memory of the Black Man of Welsh tradition. As Cader Idris was associated both with the Black Man and the Wild Hunt, so Fergus in the romance of that name encountered identical phenomena on the Noquetran frequented by Merlin. Clearly the author of *Fergus* drew on local tradition or folklore attached to Hart Fell.[16]

2. *The Shaman's Feathered Dress*

His lonely confrontation with God and the spirits completed, the
shaman returns home to practise his calling. Before this becomes
possible, he is equipped with a special costume in which to shamanise. This is generally highly elaborate, many objects sewn on or
hanging from it being symbols of the various creatures needed to
help him on his spiritual journey. Very frequently he wears a
bird-cloak made of feathers, representing his transformation into
the bird-soul which detaches itself from his body during the ecstatic
trance, and flies aloft to the heavens.[17]

The likening of the human soul to a bird was a belief widespread
in early Europe, and particularly strong among the Celts. Indeed,
early descriptions of druidic practice in Ireland portray a situation
indistinguishable from the shamanism of Siberia. The ninth-century
Glossary of Cormac describes a bard's clothing (*tugen*) as 'made
of the skins of white and many-coloured birds; up to his girdle of
the necks of mallards, and from his girdle up to his neck of their
tufts.' The use made of it is indicated in a unique but highly
significant episode, where the ascension of a powerful druid is
described:

> 'Mog Ruith's skin of the hornless, dun-coloured bull was brought
> to him then and his speckled bird-dress (*enchennach*) with its
> winged flying, and his druidic gear besides. And he rose up, in
> company with the fire, into the air and the heavens.'

Coming closer to the legend of Merlin proper, it is notable that
his Irish counterpart Suibhne is represented not only as flying high
above the trees and clouds, but actually as growing feathers. It is
quite clear that Suibhne is here envisaged as adopting the guise of
'the bird-soul in travail'.[18]

Equally significant are references in early Arthurian literature
to a curious and hitherto unexplained appendage of Merlin himself.
Two mediaeval writers refer to the wizard's connection with an
'*esplumoir*', a word of mysterious origin, whose meaning can only
be guessed from the context. In the *Didot-Perceval* Merlin is said
to have entered a building (*abitacle*) named '*esplumoir Merlin*',
after which he was never more seen by mortal man. The other
reference suggests that the *esplumoir* was to be found at the top
of a crag, '*la plus haute dou mont*': 'the highest in the world'. The
German philologist Nitze derived it from a postulated Latin verb
ex-plumare, 'to pluck out feathers'; and various explanations, all
more or less fantastic, have been advanced to explain the allusion.

It was 'a place where birds are shut up when moulting', a faery dwelling, an enchanted prison – even the place where Merlin wrote his chronicles with a *plume*![19]

Had the critics glanced at the story of Suibhne Geilt, they must have seen immediately that we have here a parallel to Suibhne's feathers. Whatever the original source of the *esplumoir* reference, it surely represented Merlin as donning his 'feathers', *i.e.* a feathered cloak. The Welsh *plufawr*, 'feathers', derives from Latin *pluma* and one can easily see how during translation from either language incomprehension could creep in. The wizard clad himself in his feathered costume, perhaps on top of a high mountain, and flew off beyond the gaze of man. Having no knowledge of such an unusual garb or procedure, the poet imagined Merlin had disappeared into some sort of mysterious 'feathered' building.

This apparently direct reference to Merlin as druid and shaman suggests an archaic stratum to the story, strongly indicative of an authentic Celtic background only partially attested in the surviving Welsh poetry.

3. *Fasting as Shamanist Initiation*

One of the most important factors in a shaman's initiation was a severe fast, generally lasting for several days. Thus, among the Yakuts, 'the future shaman "dies" and lies three days in his *yurt* (tent) without eating or drinking.' Similarly, among the Samoyeds 'a shaman . . . remains unconscious for three days at death's door' before recovering and becoming a full initiate. In North America among the Winnebago a three-days' fast was similarly usual before initiation, and a detailed account of the ordeal of a Blackfeet Indian shows what it entailed:

'Those who underwent this suffering were obliged to abstain from food or drink for four days and four nights. . . . It was deemed essential that the place to which a man resorted for this purpose should be unfrequented, where few or no persons had walked. . . . Such situations were mountain peaks; or narrow ledges on cut cliffs. . . . Wherever he went, the man built himself a little lodge of brush, moss, and leaves to keep off the rain; and, after making his prayers to the sun singing his sacred songs, he crept into the hut and began his fast. . . . Often by the end of the fourth day, a secret helper – usually, but by no means always, in the form of some animal – appeared to the man in a dream, and talked with him, advising him, marking out his course through life, and giving him its power'.

This initiatory process was widespread also among other Indian peoples.[20]

Fasting as a means of inducing ecstatic trance and visions was known also to the Celts and a period of three days and nights was attributed particular sacral efficacy in both Britain and Ireland. In the latter country the three days' fast, absorbed into Church practice, was known as *triduan*.[21]

Now it can hardly be without significance that Merlin too is said to have undergone a three days' fast before taking to the wilderness and becoming a prophetic 'madman':

> 'So for three long days he wept, refusing food, so great was the grief which consumed him. Then, when the air was full with these repeated loud complainings, a strange madness came upon him. He crept away and fled to the woods, unwilling that anyone should see his going.'

And of Lailoken, too, it is said that 'he remained fasting for three days' before prophesying to King Meldred. The episode has been rationalised by redactors who only partially understood the material they were transmitting, but the implication is clear.[22]

4. *Animal Transformation*

Frequently the shaman shamanises in a bird-cloak. Often, too, he is dressed in animal skins; generally the hide and horns of a stag or reindeer. One of the rôles of the personified stag may be that of totemic ancestor, for the mythical animal-ancestor is conceived of as the indestructible original of the life of the species, an original represented by the shaman's costume. But the main purpose is the *becoming* of the animal personified, in order to achieve the shamans' passage to the Otherworld. They speak like animals, feed like them, and dress in their pelts, a process which, for primitive man, was equivalent to being transformed into that animal.[23]

By imitating an animal's gait when donning its skin, one acquires a means of becoming more than human. It is not a question of reverting to a simple 'animal existence': the animal with which one identifies oneself is already vested with a mythology; it was in fact a mythical Animal, an Ancestor or Demiurge. By becoming this mythical animal, man becomes something much greater and more powerful than himself. It is possible to think that this projection into a mythical Being, at the same moment focus of life and universal renewal, arouses the euphoric experience which, before leading on to ecstasy, indicates the presentiment of its strength and brings about a union with cosmic existence. We have only to remember the rôle of exemplary model afforded by certain animals in Taoist mystical techniques to understand the spiritual richness of the shamanist experience which lies behind the memory of the ancient Chinese. By forgetting the limits of humanity, one recovers (given the ability to recapture the habits of animals – their walk, their breathing, their cries, etc.) a fresh perspective on life: one recovers spontaneity, freedom, one is in tune with the rhythm of the cosmos and consequently bliss and immortality.[24]

These beliefs, like so many other shamanist conceptions, survived in full vigour among the insular Celts. It was shown earlier how Geoffrey of Monmouth, recasting a source he only partially understood, represents Merlin as living to the full the life of a stag; eating grass and berries in summer and moss in winter, and careering freely through the forest glades with other stags. The incident of the scoffing bridegroom probably indicates that Merlin himself once bore stag's antlers, and similar qualities are ascribed to Suibhne Geilt.

In the Irish tale of Tuan mac Cairill, the transformation is sketched so vividly (if briefly) that it is almost possible to sense the mantic experience. Tuan is made to describe his flight to the wilderness:

'Then I was from hill to hill, and from cliff to cliff, guarding myself from wolves, for twenty-two years . . . and I hairy, clawed, withered, grey, naked, wretched, miserable. Then, as I was asleep one night, I saw myself passing into the shape of a stag. In that shape I was, and I young and glad of heart.'

It is especially fascinating to learn, in view of the evidence discussed earlier, that before his transformation Tuan had followed precisely the shamanist procedure ascribed to Merlin and Lailoken: 'I fasted my three days as I had always done. I had no strength left.'[25]

5. *Animal Familiars*

When, in his ecstatic trance, the shaman makes his perilous journey to the Otherworld, he is almost invariably accompanied by familiar spirits who assist and guide him on his way. Generally they are represented in the form of animals, birds and fish. Among Siberian and Altaic shamans, for instance, they 'can appear in the form of bears, wolves, deer, hares and all types of birds'. They are invoked in turn in the shaman's rhythmic chant:

'Turn round! Turn round! Turn round!' cries a Tungus
   shaman:
'Upwards! Upwards! Upwards you go!
My dogs, my fast ones
Don't fall behind!
In the direction of light
You run without dispersing . . .
Small creature – my protection
Burbots [a small fish] – my protection . . .
Snake – my ancestress –
At the light of burning birch bark
Showed me.
The place which I reach
Lighted with the gleam of the birch bark.
The snake – my ancestress. . . .
Fox cub – young game
Now the souls are there!'

A traveller's description portrays how vividly these animal familiars manifested themselves:

'Suddenly the shaman commenced to beat the drum softly and to sing in a plaintive voice; then the beating of the drum grew stronger and stronger, and his song – in which could be heard sounds imitating the howling of the wolf, the groaning of the cargoose, and the voices of the other animals, his guardian spirits – appeared to come, sometimes from the corner nearest my seat, then from the opposite end, then again from the middle of the house, and then it seemed to proceed from the ceiling. . . . The wild fits of ecstasy which would possess him during his performance frightened me.'

This was among the Koryak people of Kamchatka. Another account describes a similarly awe-inspiring performance by a Yakut shaman:

'Only the gentle sound of the voice of the drum, like the humming of a gnat, announces that the shaman has begun to play . . . The audience scarcely breathes, and only the unintelligible mutterings and hiccoughs of the shaman can be heard; gradually even this sinks into a profound silence. Then the music grows louder

and louder and, like peals of thunder, wild shouts rend the air;
the crow calls, the grebe laughs, the seamews complain, snipes
whistle, eagles and hawks scream. The music swells and rises to
the highest pitch. The numberless small bells [on the shaman's
garment] rise and clang . . . It is a whole cascade of sounds,
enough to overwhelm all the listeners . . . Then sombrely
the voice of the shaman chants the following obscure fragments:

'Mighty bull of the earth . . . Horse of the Steppes!
I, the mighty bull, bellow!
I, the horse of the steppes, bellow!
I, the man set above all other things!'

In the ensuing prayers the shaman addresses his *amagyat* and
other protective spirits; he talks with the *kaliany*, asks them
questions, and gives answer in their names. Sometimes the
shaman must pray and beat the drum a long time before the spirits
come; often their appearance is so sudden and so impetuous that
the shaman is overcome and falls down.

'When the *amagyat* comes down to a shaman, he rises and
begins to leap and dance . . . and beats the drum uninterruptedly.
Those who hold him by the leather thongs (he is bound) sometimes have great difficulty in controlling his movements. The
head of the shaman is bowed, his eyes are half-closed; his hair
is tumbled and in wild disorder lies on his sweating face, his
mouth is twisted strangely, saliva streams down his chin, often
he foams at the mouth.'[26]

The purpose of these transformations is to enable the shaman
to 'die', to emerge from the prison of the body, and so to pass over
into the Otherworld. In reality, the animals play a rôle not so much
of helpers, but of recipients of the shaman's spirit, which enters
their shadowy forms in order to pursue the dreadful journey
inaccessible to mortal men.[27]

Pigs in particular played an important rôle in shamanistic ritual.
Among the Goldi, the shaman drank the blood of a pig; 'only the
shaman had the right to drink it, the laity could not touch it.' At
the initiatory rites, he, his family and guests, 'sing and dance (it is
necessary to have at least nine dancers) and nine pigs are sacrificed;
the shamans drink their blood, fall down in an ecstatic trance and
shamanize for a long time.'[28]

The Black Book of Carmarthen Hoianau poetry appears perfectly
to reflect this setting. In it Myrddin is represented as addressing

long, confused prophetic stanzas to his 'little pig'; clearly the pig is envisaged both as familiar and source of mantic inspiration. And in the *Vita Merlini*, Merlin apostrophises a wolf, his 'dear companion', whose presence is otherwise unexplained. Merlin fasts, is bound with thongs, 'becomes' a stag, and prophesies with the aid of a pig and a wolf. This is the purest shamanism.

6. *Interment and Dismemberment*

Other shamanist initiatory rituals included burial and dismemberment whose purpose was to demonstrate that the shaman's body had died, been utterly destroyed, and resurrected in a spiritual form. Only by 'dying' could the shaman travel to the Land of the Dead. The ritual was frequently astonishingly realistic, indeed seems actually to have taken place, as reliable eye-witness accounts testify.[29]

In the poem *The Conversation between Myrddin and Gwenddydd his Sister*, mention is apparently made of Myrddin's interment underground, of his subsequent release, and of his consequent knowledge of the books of inspiration (*awen*). The poem is a difficult one, but if correctly interpreted suggests that it may provide yet another echo of shamanism in the Merlin legend.[30]

Dismemberment, the breaking up of the body preparatory to its reassembly and resurrection, was an extended method of liquidating the former *persona*, so ensuring that it was an utterly new being that arose again. At times symbolically enacted, at others it included real acts of fearful self-mutilation, from which European travellers were astonished to see shamans emerge seemingly unscathed.[31] It is possible that a scene in *Buile Suibhne* represents a memory of this rite, when Suibhne is surrounded by a ghastly collection of severed limbs, trunks and heads, from the midst of which he ascends into the sky.

7. *The Sexual Element*

Several peoples in northern Scandinavia and Siberia cherish a belief in a 'young girl of the forest', who is a protectress of birds and in some degree a Guardian of the Animals. At times she is said to appear at night to sleep with a fortunate shaman. Variant versions imbue the relationship with a melancholy tinge:

'In the next part of the song the shaman's meeting with the Spirit (a sort of romantic honeymoon) is over. The Spirit has proved fickle and the shaman wanders about love-lorn, waiting in vain for the lover's return.'

In the *Afallennau* Myrddin laments:

> 'Sweet-apple tree which grows on a river bank . . .
> While I was in my right mind I used to have at its foot
> A fair wanton maiden, one slender and queenly.'

Abundant evidence was assembled earlier to show that Myrddin's retreat was an *axis mundi*, and his apple tree a Tree of Life. The Yakuts believed that the First Man was suckled at the foot of the Tree of Life by a Woman emerging from its trunk.[32]

8. *The Ascent of the World Tree*

Much has already been related of the concept of the World Tree in shamanist thought. The Tree, growing from the World Centre, connected earth with heaven and provided the shaman with the means of ascent to the Otherworld. During his mantic ecstasy the shaman ritually climbed a substitute tree or tent pole.[33]

It is likely that the trees invoked by Myrddin, the apple tree and birch,[34] represent just such a World Tree. The apple tree has overtly divine properties; though mortals approach Myrddin at its trunk, they cannot see him. The parallel story of Suibhne Geilt is still more explicit. For when Suibhne was similarly encompassed about by enemies in a tree, he 'ascended from the tree towards the rain-clouds of the firmament, over the summits of every place and over the ridge-pole of every land.' Like the shaman he was feathered in semblance of the bird-soul which departs the body.

There are too many shamanistic elements present in the Myrddin legend to be fortuitous. In particular, we may single out the sudden accession of mantic frenzy which drives him to the wilderness; his feathered mantle; the three days' fast and the binding with thongs prior to prophesying; his transformation into a stag, together with his enactment of the animal's feeding and other habits; his familiars or psychopomps, the pig and the wolf to whom he addresses himself in his ecstasy; the bird-flight and ascent of the World-Tree. Other possible parallels lie in the connection with the 'young girl of the forest' and the rituals of interment and dismemberment, though these are not so explicit. One may hardly doubt, therefore, that the 'madness' of Myrddin was simply the shaman's ecstasy, and that of their Welsh counterparts, the *awenyddion*.

*

Everything points to the fact that Merlin (Myrddin) was a pre-eminent practitioner of the mantic art. As early as the late sixth century A.D. (assuming the passage in the *Gododdin* not to be an interpolation) his muse was invoked as an epitome of the spirit of the land. In the ninth century it was accepted that he had foreseen and foretold all the future of the British race, and his genuine prophecies, or those attributed to him, were altered and extended to adapt themselves to current events. Precious manuscript collections of his verse were reverently preserved and consulted. Much has clearly perished over the centuries, and the fragmentary pieces surviving must represent only a small residue of what once existed. Equally, the early Middle Ages probably knew a swollen and corrupt body of pseudo-Myrddin poetry, adapted and expanded from verses very likely composed by the bard himself in the sixth century, and circulated by his disciples or those who came to consult him.

The poem *Cad Goddeu* in *The Book of Taliesin* contains many allusions to the legend of Merlin and may even ultimately derive from genuine verses composed by the prophet. It is also unmistakably a cosmogonic hymn, spanning as it does the whole of creation, the pantheistic doctrine of the transcendence of the inspired prophet in nature, and culminating in an eschatological vision of the three great cataclysms (suitably Christianised) bounding historical time: 'the story of the Flood, and Christ's crucifying, and then Doomsday'. The speaker claims that he 'wounded a great scaly animal', which recalls the cosmic serpent of the ocean wounded by Yahweh in the Old Testament, Thor's attack on the Midgard Serpent which encompassed the earth, and other variants of a world-wide myth.[35] The slaying of a serpent or dragon-demon features significantly as a ritual attendant upon the Irish celebration of the feast of the god Lug, *Lughnasa*.

Generally the recitation of a poem with such a cosmogonic theme formed an important episode in elaborate rituals performed annually in order to ensure the '*start of a new life in the midst of a new creation*'. In Babylonia the New Year's festival centred on the temple of the god Marduk, Esagila, which lay on the site of the world *Omphalos*. One of the principal rituals was the recitation on the fourth day of the Babylonian epic of Creation, *Enuma Elish*, which told how Marduk slew the monstrous Tiamat (representing primeval chaos), separated heaven and earth, and created man. In Egypt rather similar rites took place at Heliopolis, where stood the primeval hill which at the creation emerged from Nun, the primordial waters. In ancient Israel, the New Year Festival included a recitation of the cosmogonic myth, with its account of Yahweh's wounding the serpent-demon Rahab, His creation of the earth and mankind, the catastrophes of the Fall and the Flood, and culminating (Psalm cxxxvi) in His continuing interventions in history as He works out His purpose in mankind.[36]

In ancient Ireland similar ceremonies of cosmic renewal were held at the *Omphalos* (Uisnech) and provincial Navels. The best documented of these is the Assembly of Carmun, which took place at the festival of the god Lug, *Lughnasa*. Through the holding of this assembly the Leinstermen were assured of an abundance of corn and milk, freedom from conquest, the enjoyment of righteous laws, comfort in every house, fruit in great abundance, and plenty of fish in their lakes, rivers, and estuaries. It was the occasion of cosmic renewal, failure to observe which would occasion the disintegration of society and the withering of the fruitfulness of the earth. A mediaeval poem describing the assembly invokes the component parts of the universe:

> 'Heaven, earth, sun, moon and sea,
> fruits of earth and sea-stuff,
> mouths, ears, eyes, possessions,
> feet, hands, warriors' tongues.'

The whole history, too, was surveyed:

> 'the chronicle of women, tales of armies, conflicts,
> Hostels, Prohibitions, Invasions . . .'[37]

It is uncertain where the Assembly of Carmun was held, but generally two important factors deciding the site of a *Lughnasa* Festival were that it should be a Sacred Centre, and that it should command extensive views of the surrounding countryside. Both considerations related to a common conception: the regeneration of the earth must take place at the point where it was originally created; and the wide-ranging prospect allowed the celebrants to see as much as possible of creation spread out around them.

Most dramatic of all sites associated with the celebration of *Lughnasa* in Ireland is Mount Brandon, on the Dingle Peninsula in County Kerry. 3,127 feet high, it is the second highest mountain in Ireland, and from its summit the panorama of ocean, cliffs and mountains is indescribably awe-inspiring. On the very summit is a pillar stone (a symbolic Tree of Life?) and the ruins of a little oratory ascribed to St Brendan. Pilgrims at the season of *Lughnasa* ascended at dawn an old road leading to the peak. There they prayed, passed nine times around the oratory and pillar stone, and drank from the sacred well hard by. An old tradition records that a demon-serpent is confined in a small lake at the base of the mountain. The mediaeval *Lives* of St Brendan preserve a pagan motif in all its purity. The Saint ascended the mountain, where he prayed and fasted for three days. He was then vouchsafed a mantic dream in which an angel promised to guide him to a wonderful island. As a result, the Saint set off on his celebrated voyage into the Western Ocean, traditional home of the Celtic Otherworld.[38] He was likewise recommended to this course by an 'Abbot' Barinthus, who in Geoffrey of Monmouth's *Vita Merlini* appears alongside Merlin as a Celtic Charon, ferrying King Arthur to the Otherworld Island of Apples (where Irish legend placed the birth of Lug).

It is not difficult to imagine analogous ceremonies taking place on the Dumfriesshire mountain of Hart Fell in the sixth century A.D. Merlin's connection with the site and the dovetailing of his legend with the myth of Lug suggest that at the time of *Lughnasa* in *Y Gogledd* rites may well have taken place similar to those witnessed by St Samson about the same time on a hilltop in Cornwall. The British literary record is meagre in comparison with the Irish, but traditions survive indicating that relevant rites were envisaged as occurring on mountain-tops. In the *Mabinogi* of *Culhwch* and *Olwen*, Arthur's companions Cai and Bedwyr are found seated on a cairn on Plinlimmon, a traditional Sacred Centre; while a Welsh Saint's *Life* depicts them again seated on a hilltop in Glamorgan, this time with Arthur himself 'playing at dice' (*cum alea ludentes*). In the context it is probable that the folktale source of this episode referred to the game *gwyddbwyll*, an ancient Celtic boardgame, in some sources described as requiring dice. In the story of *The Dream of Rhonabwy* Arthur plays *gwyddbwyll* with Owain ab Urien. Games of this sort were played for amusement, but could also take on an important ritual aspect.

Merlin's patron Gwenddolau possessed a magical *gwyddbwyll* board on which 'if the pieces were set, they would play by themselves. The board was of gold, and the men of silver'. The game must at one time have been closely associated with the god Lug since he was held in Irish tradition to have invented it. When Lug appeared before the divine race, the *Túatha Dé Danann*, he gained his place by defeating them all at a game of *fidchell* (the Irish name for *gwyddbwyll*). He then made 'the *cró* of Lug', 'Lug's enclosure',[39] by which it seems to be implied that hostile forces were ritually repelled and the central piece on the *fidchell* board preserved from danger – a representation of the protection under which the god laid all Ireland.

The thirteenth-century romance *Fergus* describes how its hero ascends the Black Mountain (*Nouquetran*) where 'Merlin dwelt many a year' ('U Merlins sejorna maint an'), and which I identified with Hart Fell. His task, successfully accomplished, was to retrieve a horn and wimple hanging from a lion's neck, and defeat the Black Knight ('chevalier noir') who guards the place. Fergus ascended the great mountain, gazed on its unequalled view, and entered a marble chapel on the summit. The lion proved to be of ivory, and Fergus took the horn and wimple, survived the peril of the Wild Hunt, overcame the Black Knight, and returned to the Moat of Liddel. As I pointed out earlier, this adventure clearly draws on a traditional account of a visit to a Celtic pagan sanctuary.

Evidence to be examined in the next chapter demonstrates so close a parallel between the legend of Merlin and the myth of Lug as to suggest either that they are identical or, as I argue, that Merlin was the incarnation of the god. In view of this and of the considerations already discussed, it is possible to suppose that the summit of Hart Fell was once the focus of a British *Lughnasa* Assembly. Now the Welsh name for the Irish *Lug* is *Lleu*, which was frequently confused with the word *llew*, 'a lion'.[40] Could it be that the lion encountered by Fergus on the very apex of the Black Mountain represented a confusion of an earlier tradition which placed it under the especial tutelage of the god Lleu? In that case the horn and wimple borne off as trophies might be attributes of the maiden Sovereignty of Ireland encountered by Conn in the Irish *Baile in Scáil*.

William the Clerk, the author of *Fergus*, knew (either at first-hand or through informants) the south-west Lowland region intimately. In compiling his romance he seems to have come across a local story, in which the loft Black Mountain (Hart Fell) featured as a place of sinister repute and magical enchantment, frequented by the wizard Merlin. It was guarded by a dark *genius loci* (*arddu*), and was the haunt of the Wild Troop of Departed Souls. Its summit soared above the clouds, where was reputed to be the sanctuary of 'the lion' – in fact the god Lleu, whom tradition had come to confound with the common noun *llew*. As tapers burned low in the halls of Border peel-towers and wolfhounds growled in their sleep before the hearth, many listeners must have repressed a shudder as they pictured Fergus's ascent of the peak, regularly glimpsed above the forest from the Glasgow road rising northwards into the upland wilderness beyond Annandale.

Passing back another six centuries, one may picture in imagination a scene lying behind the folk-legend. At the time of harvest King Gwenddolau and his hierophants (druids?) ascended Hart Fell in solemn procession to celebrate the Festival of *Lughnasa*. At the summit they found themselves at the very apex of the *Omphalos* of the North, the Centre of all created things. All around, to the distant shimmering sea on the horizon, lay the whole world they knew: *Lleuddiniawn*, 'the country of the stronghold of Lleu'. Then began the mysteries, rites designed to ensure that fruitful creation would renew its waning powers at the moment of rebirth. The *gwyddbwyll* board was taken from its satchel, and the King moved the pegs in their holes until the hostile, disruptive forces of the cosmos were checkmated and the mountain-top became once again Lug's Enclosure; a microcosm of the greater world whose Centre it was, a focus of balance for the Island of the Mighty, Merlin's Precinct.

Then the Prophet stands in the Centre and, arms aloft, chants the liturgical cosmogony. As the world prepares to dissolve into primeval chaos, he places himself at the centre of events, expounding the cyclical procession of time. His story is the history of the world, its creation, chronology and ultimate destruction. But the eschatological process is a *constructive* theme, for though it tells of the world's coming end in fire, flood and cosmic devastation, it concludes with a foretelling of the worn-out earth's renewal in all the greenness, freshness and vigour of an early spring day. Just as the New Year Festival observes the destruction of the old year and the birth of the new out of chaos, so eventually the ageing world itself will be destroyed amid fearful scenes of turmoil – only to emerge once more, green and fresh as at the beginnings. In this way eschatological prophecies of doom may in reality also bear the hope of renewal.[41]

In the twentieth century it should not be difficult to appreciate the value of the annual ritual and accompanying eschatological myth. With every year that passes we wonder whether the next may not bring the ultimate destruction of humanity in an apocalyptic turmoil of blinding light and heat and dust and blast. With a silent shudder we hope that the ageing planet may struggle on a little longer, occasionally nurturing a compensatory hope that *we* may survive into a purged and safer world. For the rest, we simply struggle on blindly, void of any great hope but unable to escape the moving treadmill. For us there is no existence outside the present, no annual purgation, no cathartic ritual of death and rebirth. The explanatory myth finds expression only in millennarist political movements whose followers enter on an otherwise inexplicable frenzy of destruction in the expectation that they will be among the Chosen to survive the havoc.

In the Northern world of antiquity, this expression of cyclical destruction and regeneration found its noblest and clearest expression in the celebrated Icelandic poem *Völuspá*. Composed about the turn of the first millennium A.D., the prophecy is placed in the mouth of a sybil, like Merlin apparently summoned from her grave. In the beginning there was the Void, in which a trinity of gods, Odin and his two brothers, created the earth and mankind. There followed a paradisal dream-time, in which the youthful gods were industrious, joyful and innocent, playing at chess on golden boards. But this archetypal springtime existence was disrupted by malevolent forces, and warfare, greed and corruption flourished increasingly in spite of all the beneficent gods could accomplish. Men grew cruel, abandoned the most sacred family ties to wallow in fornication and adulterous dishonour, and slaughtered their own kindred indiscriminately. These portents heralded the coming end, *Ragnarök*. Wolfish monsters were born, eager for the destruction of gods and men. Terrible scenes arise, horror piled upon horror. The wolf Garmr frees himself from his chains and swallows Odin himself. The sun turns black, the stars vanish, and the repulsive dragon Nidhoggr flaps slowly over fields of corpses. The fighting and chaos grow ever more terrible until the earth disappears beneath the seas, leaving only swirling smoke-clouds and a gigantic flame which licks out towards the sun itself.

But now a profound calm ensues, and a new earth emerges from the ocean, a place of green meadows amid cascades teeming with fish. The gods reappear in all their youthful purity, discover in the grass the magical chess-boards, and live on in everlasting felicity.

It is unlikely that the *Völuspá* was itself recited during rituals of cosmic renewal, but it may reflect mythic materials previously performing such a service. Here it is interesting to compare it with the Welsh poem *Cad Goddeu* and the prophecies of Merlin. So far as the latter are concerned, the similarity was so clear that when the twelfth-century Icelander Gunnlaugr came to translate Geoffrey of Monmouth's *Prophetia Merlini* into Icelandic verse (*Merlinússpá*), he frequently employed the *Völuspá* as a secondary model.[42]

The poem *Cad Goddeu* reads in some ways like the detritus of a Welsh *Völuspá*. As was remarked earlier, it contains all the hallmarks of a cosmogonic composition. It includes references to the creation of man by the wizard Gwydion, the Otherworld enchanter after whom the Milky Way was named, and the wounding of the primeval dragon; hints at a coming struggle against the forces of the Celtic Hades, *Annwfn*; and twice enumerates the cataclysmic cycle of 'the Flood, and Christ's Crucifixion, and then Doomsday'. The poem concludes, however, on an obscurely-phrased note of optimism:

'Golden, gold skinned, I shall deck myself in riches,
And I shall be in luxury because of the prophecy of Virgil.'

According to the Greek ethnographer Posidonius, the Celts, like most other races, believed in the cyclical destruction and rebirth of the earth:

'These men [the Druids], as well as other authorities, have pronounced that men's souls and the universe are indestructible, although at times fire or water may [temporarily] prevail.'

This concept, partially Christianised as in *Cad Goddeu*, certainly survived in the Celtic West into the early Middle Ages. Geoffrey of Monmouth did not invent the prophecy he attributes to Merlin, which reflects a considerable body of Welsh and Cornish vaticinatory verse, attributed to Merlin and circulating in the West in the early twelfth century.[43]

By this period much of the prophetic material had become related to political considerations of the moment, and the eschatological element restricted to a promised restoration of the British monarchy in all its pristine glory. Geoffrey, however, makes Merlin conclude with a passage in which chaos descends upon the earth, the stars and planets are contorted into awesome courses, and the Zodiac transfigured beyond recognition. The penultimate sentence may however hint at a restitution:

'In ictu radii exurgent equora & puluis ueterum renouabitur'

'The seas shall rise up in the twinkling of an eye, and the dust of the ancients shall be restored'

It seems probable that Geoffrey's conclusion is a pastiche of a genuine Celtic prophetic theme, rather than pure invention.[44]

There was a geographical region of Goddeu, identified with the Forest of Celyddon, in which Merlin found his retreat. This was overshadowed by a mythical terrain of the same name.[45] This dichotomy between the spiritual and terrestrial regions appears also in the sixth-century belief that the mountainous country between the two Roman Walls was the refuge of departed spirits. *Cad Goddeu* signifies 'The Battle of the Trees' and in the poem the trees are animated as soldiers engaged in mortal combat. The idea that men were originally created by divinity from trees is archaic, being found in Norse tradition and in Hesiod's *Theogony*. The *Völuspá* opens with the image of the sacred ash *Yggdrasil*, the Norse Tree of Life, and it has been suggested that the references in *Cad Goddeu* 'derive from traditions about sacred trees and sacred groves'.[46]

In view of the associations of the real Forest of Goddeu (Celyddon) with Merlin, one may perhaps picture him reciting an earlier version of *Cad Goddeu* on the peak of Hart Fell overlooking the undulating tree-tops, and suggest that what is essentially the exposition of a cosmogonic myth may have formed a part of the *Lughnasa* assembly there at the beginning of August. In fact, of course, it must be confessed that we possess only a flotsam of assorted materials, and the more precise the reconstruction, the less likely, alas, is its accuracy.

Analogy and inference suggest many possibilities. But of two things it seems we can be reasonably certain. Firstly, Hart Fell mountain was the scene of Merlin's prophetic exile and vision for many years in the second half of the sixth century A.D. The identification rests on a series of converging pieces of evidence, each weighty in itself and together presenting an argument hard to refute.

a. The romance of *Fergus* places Merlin's retreat on the Black Mountain, and both the account of the journey there from Liddel Moat and the description of the unique view from its summit point to this being envisaged as Hart Fell.

b. Hart Fell is in the centre of the Wood of Celyddon, which the Welsh poetry identifies as Merlin's refuge.

c. Hart Fell is ideally suited to have been an archaic *axis mundi*, both on account of its exceptional view and from its being at the point from which spring three great rivers flowing into the seas around the Scottish Lowlands.

d. Merlin's *fons Galabes* is best explained as a chalybeate well, one of which is situated in a dramatic spot on the skirts of the mountain.

e. The mountain itself is called Arthur's Seat, a name traditionally implying a belief that it contained a hollow Otherworld, source of sacred springs and of the Wild Hunt of departed souls heard by Fergus.
f. Hart Fell is in the heart of the territory of the Selgovae, among whom paganism flourished until a late date.
g. *Lleuddiniawn*, the North British name for the Lothians, suggests (as will be seen) an especial local veneration for the god Lug.

Secondly, Merlin displayed in the earliest accounts many important characteristics of the ecstatic technique of prophecy known as shamanism. His 'madness' (the mantic fit), the sudden retreat to the wilds, the identification with a stag, the animal assistants, the feathered cloak, and the prophetic utterances are far too close to shamanist practice for coincidence.

It might be argued that the Merlin story originated from memories of a general tradition of Celtic shamanism, and that this composite picture became personified at some stage in the form of a fictional figure named Myrddin or Lailoken. But the separately attested tradition of a prophet or bard named Myrddin, traceable certainly back to the tenth and possibly to the sixth century, together with the specific location of the story at Hart Fell, makes such a theory improbable. It seems at least likely that political prophecies of the type attributed to Merlin were current at the time when an historical Myrddin might be supposed to have lived. As a distinguished French Celticist has observed of the later prophecies attributed to Merlin:

'Continual re-editing adjusted to the taste of the day, according to misfortunes and hopes, old texts of which the most ancient could go back to the sixth century. Procopius [the sixth-century Byzantine historian, who encountered travellers from Britain] tells us that he has read the Sibylline prophecies: "And at the same time that she predicts the fate of the Romans, she foretells the sufferings of the Britons".'[47]

On the principle of Occam's Razor – that an explanation should be based on the fewest possible assumptions – it is reasonable to hold that Merlin indeed lived, and that he really was a prophet and a poet.

11

The Otherworld Journey and the Threefold Death

As prophet and avatar of the High God, Merlin was a link between the divine and the human, and ultimately a Guide on the road to the Otherworld. Among the Celts there existed a strong sense of the transitoriness of this life, and the corresponding importance of the Afterlife:

> 'We are in a world of grievous wantonness;
> Like leaves from the treetops it will pass away;'

laments a Welsh poem from *The Black Book of Carmarthen*. An Irishman put it still more ominously:

> '. . . this world is profitless, uncertain, a transient possession of everyone in turn, every day. Everyone that has been, everyone that will be, has died, will die, has departed, will depart.'[1]

The Otherworld was omnipresent. It existed in the starry night sky, where the Milky Way (*Caer Gwydion*) provided a celestial ascent to the abodes of the gods; to Caer Arianrhod, where dwells the goddess Arianrhod (Corona Borealis) and Llys Don, palace of the Ancestor-goddess Don (Cassiopeia). The heavens themselves rotated round the Pole Star like a vast mill-wheel, whose axis passed through the earthly Centre or Navel.[2]

But the Otherworld was underfoot as well as overhead. From the earth below gushed forth streams and rivers whose founts lay in the domain of Arawn, King of Annwfn. Every tumulus and deserted hill-fort housed the faery folk. On occasion an unwary traveller might find himself transported into their world; at other times a truculent king would order his people to take spades and attempt a break-in to the faery stronghold. Ravishing maidens lured fortunate youths to palaces below lakes; at times the ethereal palace appeared boldly above ground in a familiar landscape, protected only by an enchanted mist. Very often the Otherworld was located at the bottom of the sea, or on a distant island.

The most striking feature of the Celtic Otherworld was the way in which it impinged so nearly on the world of mortal men. At once alluring yet threatening, it hung intangibly near, like the reflection of a lakeside scene. The dividing line, which was also the point of juncture, provided in time and space a region with uncanny propensities. At fords, mountain-ridges, the frontiers between kingdoms – even stiles – the powers of good and evil possessed potent capacity to intervene in terrestrial affairs. Dawn and dusk, the waxing and waning of the moon, New Year's Day, the Summer and Winter Calends (*Seltaing* and *Samain*), were all occasions when the unseen powers had to be propitiated or warded off. Each represented a dangerous moment of tilt in the cosmos, when supernatural powers might disturb the ordered succession of events. At every turn the Powers of Darkness, personified in Ireland by the *síd* or the *Fomoire*, threatened to irrupt into this precarious world and restore the primeval chaos from which it had arisen.[3]

The Happy Otherworld was a secure haven beyond this unceasing insecurity and struggle:

> 'There are at the western door,
> In the place where the sun goes down,
> A stud of steeds with grey-speckled manes,
> And another crimson-brown.
>
> There are at the eastern door
> Three ancient trees of crimson crystal,
> From which sing soft-voiced birds incessantly
> To the youth from out the kingly *Rath*.
>
> There is a tree in front of the court;
> It cannot be matched in harmony;
> A tree of silver against which the sun shines,
> Like unto gold is its great sheen.
>
> There is a vat there of merry mead,
> A-distributing unto the household,
> Still it remains, constant the custom,
> So that it is ever full, ever and always.'

There are two genres of Irish tale known as *echtrai* and *immrama*, in which heroes set out to find the Happy Otherworld. In *The Voyage of Bran* (*immram Brain*), Bran and his company sail round the Island of Joy whose inhabitants they can see but not converse with. But afterwards they land and savour the pleasures of the Land of Women:

'Thereupon they went into a large house, in which was a bed for every couple, even thrice nine beds. The food that was put on every dish vanished not from them. It seemed a year to them that they were there, – it chanced to be many years.' Returning to the Irish coast, one of the ship's company rashly leaped ashore, but 'as soon as he touched the earth of Ireland, forthwith he was a heap of ashes, as though he had been in the earth for many hundred years.'[4]

St Brendan likewise sailed out towards the setting sun and encountered various wonders, some fantastic and others (such as a volcanic island) presumably based on travellers' tales. From time to time enthusiasts, believing this to represent a real voyage of discovery, have attempted to reconstruct the Saint's Atlantic journey. In fact it is clearly an Otherworld quest, like that of Bran, and it culminates in the boat's arrival at an island surrounded by an enchanted fog. There the pilgrims were greeted by a young man of glorious appearance who told Brendan and his companions that:

'The great river you see here divides this land into two parts. Just as it appears to you now teeming with ripe fruits, so will it remain for all time without any blight or shadow.'[5]

It has been argued convincingly that these accounts represent a 'geographical' account of the passage of the soul after death. Such was doubtless their chief purpose, but as has been pointed out, the Celts in common with other ancient or primitive peoples felt a longing to undertake the Otherworld journey in this life, as well as the next. Thus, though the *Voyage of Brendan* is undoubtedly a legend, drawing on Celtic mythological beliefs, there were people in historical times who endeavoured to undertake such a pilgrimage in reality. Adomnan in the seventh century describes the adventures of a certain Cormac, a friend of St Columba, who sailed beyond the Orkneys on an *immram*, 'wishing to find a desert place in the sea that cannot be crossed'.[6]

Possibly Cormac, like some contemporary journalists, had taken some old *immram* too literally as the log of an actual voyage. Much more common was a consciously ritual enactment of the coming Otherworld journey, as a type of *rite de passage*. One of the most dramatic of these almost literally re-enacted a shamanistic ascent to heaven. Some eight miles off Bolus Head in County Kerry, the gaunt crag of Skellig Michael rises over 700 feet out of the Atlantic. The summit was believed to be an assembly place of the dead, whose souls could be seen on a moonlit night flitting through the sky to the Land of Youth:

> 'Until recently, people used to resort to one of these precipitous little islands to perform a mountain-climbing ritual the symbolism of which is manifestly pre-Christian. Leaving votive offerings at sacred wells at the foot of the mountain, the pilgrim ascended by a narrow track, squeezed himself up through a chimney-like chasm called the Needle's Eye, crossed the "stone of pain" which projected perilously over the sea, and mounted the dizzy pinnacle known as The Eagle's Nest, where stood a stone cross. The ordeal reached its climax with the pilgrim sitting astride a ledge overhanging the sea . . . [700 feet below], and kissing a cross which some bold adventurer had cut into the rock. By making this pilgrimage in life, the pilgrim was believed to expedite the progress of his soul through Purgatory after death.'

It is worth noting that an almost identical practice continues among Buddhist shamans during their ascent of Mount Omine in Japan.[7]

Other related rituals may have taken place in labyrinths and mazes, symbolic representations of the intricate route taken by the dead man's soul, where 'men tried by every means known to them to overcome death and to renew life.' It has been suggested that the concentric pattern of terraces on the slopes of the Glastonbury Tor (legendary home of Gwynn ab Nudd and the faery folk) may have been constructed as a gigantic three-dimensional maze.[8]

The effect of such an anticipatory dramatisation of the Otherworld journey can be profound. St Patrick's Purgatory, a cave on Lough Dearg, was a celebrated entrance to the nether world. A mediaeval legend told of a knight's successful descent and return to Paradise, after passing through many regions of danger and terror. Until the first decades of this century it was the custom for pilgrims to spend a night of prayer in the cave, and since then in a chapel nearby:

> 'The night shadows had fallen and but for two tapers the Chapel was grimly dark. It was something strange and weird, without counterpart on this earth, to look around at the rows of white haggard faces peering in the fragile candlelight. Generations of Gaels have spent a night there . . . for few of the Irish care to

Thong Castle.

The Red Dragon

Merlin Ambrosius with attendant beasts from Thomas Heywood's *Life of Merlin*, 1641.

Above: 'At Merlin's feet the wily Vivien lay'. From Tennyson's *Merlin and Vivien*, engraving by W. Ridgway after Gustave Doré.

Opposite: Page from Welsh annals inserted on the flyleaves of a copy of Domesday Book in the Public Record Office. In the centre column are references to Arthur's victory at Badon and death at Camlann. The second entry from the bottom in the right-hand column reads: 'Annus. Bellum erderit inter filios elifer et Guendoleu filium keidiau in quo bello Guendoleu cecidit Merlinus insanus effectus est'; 'The year [573]: The Battle of Arderyd between the sons of elifer and Gwenddolau the son of Ceidio, in which battle Gwenddolau was killed; Merlin was driven mad.'

<table>
<tr><td>

Amnus · dcssy natat anno xxxi

Dufesti patau de openeaus

Annus

Annus

Annus

Annus

Annus

Annus

Annus

Annus

Annus

Annus

Annus

Annus Domnus bangam epi

Annus

Annus

Annus

Annus

Annus

Annus

Annus

Annus

Annus

Annus

Annus

Annus

Annus

Annus

Annus

Annus

Annus

Annus

Annus

Annus

Annus

Annus

Annus

Annus

Annus

pe iscor ccc l eccius que obiit in xpo

</td><td>

Annus

Annus

Annus

Annus

Annus

Annus

Annus

Annus

Annus

Annus

Annus

Annus

Annus

An bellum badonis in quo rex arthur portauit crucem dni nri ihu xpi tribus diebz 7 tribz noctibz in humeris suis 7 brettones victores fuerunt. In illo p̄lio ceciderunt colgrinus 7 Radulph anglorum duces.

Annus

Annus

Annus

Annus

Annus Columcilla nascitur Sca brigida in xpo obit

Annus

Annus

Annus

Annus

Annus

Annus

Annus

Annus

Annus

Annus

Annus

Annus bellum camlann in quo melet arthur rex brom 7 modredus proditor eius occubuerunt Filipibz corruerut

Annus

Annus

Annus

Annus

</td><td>

An dormis kapaum

Annus

Annus

An portilitelis magna fuit in britannia oralium gumech ob bn̄ eis in hun wallaun en li Ros ac̄ fur̄ lesswelen

Annus

Annus

Annus

Annus

Annus

Annus

Annus

Annus

Annus Cassyran brandomc filius dns̄ bangh ob.

Annus

Annus

Annus colmchilla ex hib vor vent in britannia .

Annus

Annus

Annus mangas galde l hibn

Annus

Annus

Annus gonued victorie ap b tonec cōgregate.

An gildas bronn sapien

Annus

Annus

Annus bellu gdepir me fil oc elifer Guendolen filiu h laum q bello Guendolen cecid cer tm̄ mean aftetna e.

An brendan bejruy ob

Annus

Annus

Annus

Annus

Annus

Annus gurgi 7 pedur fili elifer gouuruui

Annus

Annus

</td></tr>
</table>

Merlin erecting Stonehenge, in an illustration to a 14th-century French romance in the British Museum.

A Siberian shaman: Tulayev of the Karagas people.

ncient churchyard at Hoddom, Dumesshire, traditionally established by Kentigern.

Dumbarton Rock, the Alclut of the Northern Britons and fortress of Merlin's persecutor Rhydderch of Strathclyde.

Door-frame of the Celto-Ligurian sanctuary of Roquepertuse, with niches for skulls and monstrous bird above.

Stonehenge from the air.

elgafell in Iceland, and Glastonbury Tor in Somerset. Both were regarded in early times dwelling places of departed spirits.

Points of departure for the Otherworld: The Skelligs, Co. Kerry, and Rathcroghan Co. Roscommon.

die without a glimpse of what they are coming to. All nights we kept vigil in our prison-house, reciting the next day's Stations by advance . . . With the fall of night the world slipped away. We seemed to stand in a dim place where two worlds meet.'[9]

The rehearsal of the soul's last journey, particularly when undergone in the form of a real passage across country symbolically representative of the Otherworld route, bears a far deeper significance than mere imitation would suggest. The journey itself leads, after attendant hazards and obstacles (real or conceptual), to its symbolic climax, frequently the ascent of a mountain. The pilgrim climbs to the summit, where if fortunate he experiences ecstasy and a visionary ascent to the heavens.[10] The most important aspect of the pilgrimage is its separation from mundane life. As in the ecstatic trance, the neophyte is enabled to exist temporarily on another plane.

A good example of this *rite de passage* is provided by Wordsworth's solitary walk across Salisbury Plain.[11] It was in July or August 1793 that Wordsworth found himself alone on the edge of the great Plain. A wrecked carriage had obliged him to abandon a projected tour of the West Country with a friend, upon which he resolved on the spot to cross the great wasteland on foot. The poem at once establishes his liminal dissociation from workaday life, a process enhanced by the fact that the landscape is literally *boundless*:

> 'The troubled west was red with stormy fire,
> O'er Sarum's plain the traveller with a sigh
> Measured each painful step, the distant spire
> That fixed at every turn his backward eye
> Was lost, tho' still he turned, in the blank sky,
> By thirst and hunger pressed he gazed around
> And scarce could any trace of man descry,
> Save wastes of corn that stretched without a bound,
> But where the sower dwelt was nowhere to be found.'

In the next verse the sense of separation from reality is stressed further, when he shouts against the solitude:

> 'He stops his feeble voice to strain;
> No sound replies but winds that whistling near
> Sweep the thin grass and passing, wildly plain;'

imagery unconsciously invoking with startling aptness a Siberian shaman's description of his soul flight:

'nothing can be seen, and only the wind is whistling loudly.'[12]

Shortly afterwards the sun set, and the walk became an ordeal of terror. A distant view of Stonehenge aroused a horrific vision of bloody rites performed in long-distant time:

> 'when dreadful fire
> Reveals that powerful circle's reddening stones.'

Rain fell heavily in the darkness, and for three hours the traveller 'wildered through the watery storm' across a landscape as feature-less 'as ocean's shipless flood'. A spectral voice evoked in hollow tones grim scenes of slaughter and the passing of the Wild Hunt on 'fiery steeds amid the infernal glooms'.

'At length, deep hid in clouds, the moon rose', and Wordsworth found refuge in a ruined shelter. There he is startled to find a fellow-fugitive, a young woman whose life has been blighted by violence and oppression. The poet indignantly raises his voice in a crescendo of defiance against 'foul Error's monster race' – terrors personified recurrently by 'that eternal pile which frowns on Sa-rum's plain'.

In *The Prelude*, Wordsworth recalled those three strange summer days of his pilgrimage:

> 'There, as I ranged at will the pastoral downs
> Trackless and smooth, or paced the bare white roads
> Lengthening in solitude their dreary line,
> Time with his retinue of ages fled
> Backwards, nor checked his flight until I saw
> Our dim ancestral Past in vision clear . . .'

It was Stonehenge in particular which impressed itself on his consciousness:

> 'a work, as some divine,
> Shaped by the Druids, so to represent
> Their knowledge of the heavens, and image forth
> The constellations . . .'

After this grim journey, the poet walked westwards until he ascended the Wye Valley and passed into North Wales. The climax of the pilgrimage was a nocturnal ascent of Snowdon, and there on the summit of the mountain he underwent an ecstatic experience:

> 'It was a close, warm, breezeless summer night,

Wan, dull, and glaring, with a dripping fog
Low-hung and thick that covered all the sky;
But, undiscouraged, we began to climb
The mountain-side. The mist soon girt us round,
And, after ordinary travellers' talk, pensively we sank
Each into commerce with his private thoughts;
Thus did we breast the ascent . . .
. . . and lo! as I looked up,
The Moon hung naked in a firmament
Of azure without cloud, and at my feet
Rested a silent sea of hoary mist.
A hundred hills their dusky backs upheaved
All over this still ocean; and beyond,
Far, far beyond, the solid vapours stretched,
In headlands, tongues, and promontory shapes,
Into the main Atlantic, that appeared
To dwindle, and give up his majesty,
Usurped upon far as the sight could reach.
Not so the ethereal vault; encroachment none
Was there, no loss; only the inferior stars
Had disappeared, or shed a fainter light
In the clear presence of the full-orbed Moon,
Who, from her sovereign elevation, gazed
Upon the billowy ocean, as it lay
All meek and silent, save that through a rift –
Not distant from the shore whereon we stood,
A fixed, abysmal, gloomy, breathing-place –
Mounted the roar of waters, torrents, streams
Innumerable, roaring with one voice!
Heard over earth and sea, and, in that hour,
For so it seemed, felt by the starry heavens.'

One is irresistibly reminded of Merlin, as he is pictured by Geoffrey of Monmouth, meditating on his mountain (Hart Fell) as the mantic fit comes upon him,

'It was night, and the horned moon was shining brightly; all the vaults of heaven were glittering. The air had an extra clarity, for a bitterly cold north wind had blown away the clouds, absorbed the mists on its drying breath and left the sky serene again. The prophet was watching the stars in their courses from a high hill.'

The sense of some universal power is peculiarly potent on the mountain-top, as Wordsworth experienced on Snowdon's peak:

> 'When into air had partially dissolved
> That vision, given to spirits of the night
> And three chance human wanderers, in calm thought
> Reflected, it appeared to me the type
> Of a majestic intellect, its acts
> And its possessions, which it has and craves,
> What in itself it is, and would become.
> There I beheld the emblem of a mind
> That feeds upon infinity, that broods
> Over the dark abyss, intent to hear
> Its voices issuing forth to silent light
> In one continuous stream; a mind sustained
> By recognitions of transcendent power.
> In sense conducting to ideal form,
> In soul of more than mortal privilege.'

Poets, as Wordsworth emphasises, are attuned to reflect that transcendent power and transmit the experience to others less sensitively endowed:

> 'in a world of a life they live,
> By sensible impressions not enthralled,
> But by their quickening impulse made more prompt
> To hold fit converse with the spiritual world,
> And with the generations of mankind
> Spread over time, past, present, and to come,
> Age after age, till Time shall be no more.
> Such minds are truly from the Deity,
> For they are powers . . .'

Wordsworth's troubled odyssey across the desolate plain, overshadowed by the lowering presence of Stonehenge, with its comprehensive vision of a troubled world, and his dramatic ascent of Snowdon reflect the shaman's ecstatic Otherworld journey with astonishing precision.[13]

It may be that the ascent of the Nouquetran (Hart Fell), scene of Merlin's enchantments, was undertaken in early times as a simulated journey to the Otherworld, a *rite de passage* like those described above. In the thirteenth-century romance of *Fergus*, it is noteworthy that the hero begins his exploit by spending a night at Liddel, scene of Merlin's madness at Arderydd. He then traverses what might have been presumed to be Merlin's route when he fled to the Black Mountain. Though mountain prospects did not provide a notably mediaeval diversion, Fergus scrambled to the very summit where he:

> 'Gazed over the forest great and grand,
> To the distant Sea of Ireland.'

After which he survived the terrors of the dread spot; retrieved a magical horn from a sanctuary, heard the Wild Hunt, and over-came the Black Guardian of the place. It looks a little as if Fergus's pilgrimage bore, or had once borne, a ritual character: the following in Merlin's footsteps, the ascent of the mountain,

> 'Which high as the clouds upreared its head,
> As heaven's high vault is sustainèd;'

and the contest with its supernatural Guardian.[14]

A generation or so earlier, a poet at the other extreme of the Celtic world made a similar pilgrimage to an enchanted spot which had acquired legendary associations with the prophet Merlin. This was the fountain of Barenton in Brittany, where Master Wace travelled in the vain hope of seeing fairies or the stone which, if sprinkled with water, aroused a thunderstorm. By the twelfth and thirteenth centuries such expeditions had possibly degenerated into touristic curiosity or chivalric exploit, but in earlier times they would have borne deeper significance.[15]

Merlin himself appears as an obvious guide to the Otherworld in Malory's *Morte Darthur*. When the noble brothers Balyn and Balan fought and killed each other on a certain island, Merlin appeared and made it a sanctuary:

> 'Than Merlion lette make a brygge of iron and of steele into that ilonde, and hit was but halff a foote brode, and that shall never man passe that brygge nother have hardynesse to go over hit but yf he were a passynge good man withoute trechery or vylany.'

The idea that the Otherworld was accessible only over a narrow and dangerous bridge was common to the Celts and other peoples. John Aubrey recorded a funeral dirge sung in Yorkshire in James I's time, which provides a geographical itinerary for the parting soul:

> 'When thou from hence doest pass away,
> Every night and awle,
> To Whinny Moor thou comest at last,
> And Christ receive thy sawle . . .

From Whinny-Moor that thou mayst pass,
Every night and awle,
To Brig o' Dread thou comest at last,
And Christ receive thy sawle.

From Brig o' Dread, *na brader than a thread*,
Every night and awle,
To Purgatory fire thou comest at last,
And Christ receive thy sawle.'[16]

A charming little verse, dating from the eighth or ninth century
and ascribed to Merlin's Irish counterpart Suibhne Geilt, provides
a glimpse of the Otherworld itself:

'My little hut in Tuaim Inbhir,
a mansion would not be more ingenious,
with its stars to my wish,
with its sun, with its moon.

It was Gobban that made it
– that the tale may be told you –
my darling, God of heaven,
was the thatcher that roofed it.

A house in which rain does not fall,
a place in which spears are not feared,
as open as if in a garden
and it without a wall round it.'

Gobban is the Irish smith-god and here, as Professor O'Rahilly
noted, 'the house that Gobban built appears to be the firmament
of heaven'. It may be significant that he is connected (under his
Welsh name) with Myrddin and the Battle of Arderydd in an early
poem in *The Black Book of Carmarthen*, which speaks of warriors
bearing 'the seven spears of Gofannon', Gofannon being the Welsh
equivalent of Gobban.[17]

Merlin fits too closely into all we know of the shamanistic strain
in Celtic religion to have been a creation of mediaeval fiction. A
'wounded healer', his inspiration came from the primeval forest
and the bare mountain towering above, from the movement of the
stars around the Pole, and the shifting of the seasons. Suspended
between man and nature, he rails against his lot. It is, however,
the circumstances attending the legendary account of his strange

death which illustrate most powerfully the significance of his prophetic rôle.

Merlin's death, according to the variant accounts, took place under
curiously tragic circumstances. Neither Geoffrey of Monmouth nor
the Welsh Myrddin poetry makes any reference to Merlin's end.
But both Lailoken fragments provide descriptions, as does the
Irish tale of Suibhne Geilt. In one version Lailoken foretells the
circumstances of his own death to St Kentigern, and in the other
makes a similar prophecy to a King Meldred. Kentigern ridiculed
the poor madman, who had with apparent inconsistency prophesied
his own death in three distinct forms. He would, he declared on
one occasion, be stoned and clubbed to death. The next time he
announced that his body would be pierced by a sharp stake; and
on a third occasion he said that his life would end by drowning.
He was naturally derided as a false prophet, but in the end all came
about precisely as he explained. For one day he was viciously
beaten and stoned by King Meldred's shepherds. In the moment
of death he slipped down a bank of the Tweed, was impaled on a
stake stuck in the river bed, and simultaneously drowned as his
head passed beneath the water.

It was foretold to Suibhne that he would die of a spear-thrust.
When he was living his fugitive life in the woods, a swineherd's
wife took pity on him and left a puddle of milk for him each day
in a hollowed piece of cowdung (a grotesque touch which may
have arisen from a pun on the Latin version of Myrddin's name,
Merdinus). Unfortunately the swineherd was aroused to unjustified
jealousy by a mischief-making sister:

> 'The herd hearing that became jealous, and he rose suddenly
> and angrily and seized a spear that was within on a rack and
> made for the madman. The madman's side was towards him as
> he was lying down eating his meal out of the cowdung. The herd
> made a thrust of the spear out of his hand at Suibhne and
> wounded him in the nipple of his left breast, so that the point
> went through him, breaking his back in two. (Some say that it
> is the point of a deer's horn the herd had placed under him in
> the spot where he used to take his drink out of the cowdung,
> that he fell on it and so met his death.)'

It seems clear that this account has overlaid an earlier version
which ascribed to Suibhne, as to his North British counterpart
Lailoken, a version of the Threefold Death. The theme itself occurs

elsewhere in earlier versions of the story, just as it does in the Lailoken stories[18], which betrays a consciousness that it was an essential part of the story. It is not hard to see that behind the extant version of *Buile Suibhne* lies a version in which the madman was simultaneously transfixed by a spear, fell forward to be impaled on the concealed deer's horn, and drowned with his face in the milk. If my suggestion for the origin of the cowdung motif be accepted, this may in part account for the particular locale and circumstances of the tragedy.

In the differing versions of the story, then, a Triple Death was ascribed to Lailoken and Suibhne. It seems safe to conclude that Merlin (who is essentially the same figure) was also originally credited with having died the Threefold Death. The motif is introduced as a subsidiary theme in the Suibhne and Lailoken stories. Similarly, it appears in the form of a prophecy uttered by Merlin himself about another, both in Geoffrey's *Vita Merlini* and in the *Merlin* of Robert de Boron. An attribution of the Triple Death to Merlin himself occurs in the distich, apparently of independent origin, quoted in the second Lailoken piece:

'Pierced by a stake, suffering by stone and by water,
Merlin is said to have met a triple death.'

Finally, certain allusions in mediaeval Welsh poetry suggest that there may have been a story according to which Myrddin was transfixed by a stake, as was his counterpart *Lailoken*.[19]

It has been suggested that the Threefold Death represents a popular folktale which was at some point grafted on to the original Wild Man story. The story was certainly a popular one, appearing in different forms not only in Celtic Britain and Ireland but also in other parts of Europe. Doubtless its ingenuity ensured its widespread popularity.[20] But this explanation ignores an essential point. There is abundant evidence that ancient religious practices can survive long after their religious function has been forgotten, and that a mythological theme, based on a sacrificial ritual, can survive as a literary motif. This is what appears to have happened in the case of the Threefold Death motif.[21]

The Commentary on Lucan explains that among the Gauls, victims were sacrificed to the gods in three distinct ways: by hanging, burning and drowning in a vat. The famous Gundestrup cauldron portrays what appears to be a divine figure plunging a man into a vat, and there is abundant evidence to confirm the existence of the differing forms of ritual sacrifice. Of the three forms, killing by a weapon (usually a spear) is frequently substituted for death by burning. Thus in the Irish story of the death of King Muirchertach mac Erca, the King is described as dying simultaneously from a spear-thrust, from burning and from drowning in a cauldron. The theme of Threefold Death as attested fact and incantatory theme in Irish literature is widespread.[22]

Most apposite to the legend of Merlin is the story of the death of the Celtic god Lug, whose rites were still openly honoured in Cornwall in the sixth century A.D. The fullest version is to be found in the Welsh tale *Math vab Mathonwy*. There Lleu (the Welsh version of Lug), nephew of the magician Gwydion, is described as 'the most beautiful youth that man had ever seen'. By his enchantments Gwydion created a maiden, Blodeuedd by name, out of the wild flowers of wood and meadow, a girl of beauty corresponding to that of Lleu, whom she married. But one day when her husband was away, Blodeuedd was unfaithful to him with a visiting chief Gronwy Pevr, Lord of Penllyn. Gronwy was so enamoured that he persuaded his mistress to discover how Lleu might be put to death.

Accordingly when Lleu returned, his wife set to work to wheedle the secret out of him:

'Unless God kill me, it is not easy to kill me.'

Under further pressure he explained the peculiar circumstances necessary to bring about his death:

'"It is not easy to kill me", he said, "without a blow, and it would be necessary to take a year making the spear with which I would be struck, and without making any of it except when they were at Mass on Sunday."'

Furthermore, he went on:

'"I cannot be killed in a house, nor outside; I cannot be killed on a horse, nor yet when I am on foot."'

How then could it be done? The trusting Lleu explained:

'"I will tell you: by making me a bath on the bank of a river, and making a round roof above the vat, thatching it well and closely, and bringing a billy-goat. Place him by the vat, and I place one foot on the back of the goat and the other on the edge of the vat. Whoever should hit me at that point would kill me."'

The treacherous Delilah at once betrayed the whole story to her lover. For a year Gronwy laboured at constructing the spear in the ritual manner described. This done, Blodeuedd asked her husband if he would not show her what precisely was the manner in which he would have to stand in order to be vulnerable to a death-stroke? Lleu good-naturedly agreed, and Blodeuedd assembled the roofed vat as instructed, and gathered a herd of goats on the river-bank. Lleu 'rose from the bath' (implying, though not stating, that he had first immersed himself in it), put on his trousers, and stood with one foot on the bath's edge and the other on the goat's back. The treacherous lover then rose from his hiding-place and flung his spear. Transfixed through the side, Lleu let out a terrible shriek and flew off in the shape of an eagle.

News of this crime was brought to Gwydion, who determined not to rest until he had discovered his nephew. After some time he was put on the track of a wandering sow, which led him to an extraordinary scene. The sow had halted in a valley by a river, where she began grazing at the foot of a tree. Coming close Gwydion saw that she was devouring rotten flesh and maggots, which were dropping from above. Looking up, he saw 'an eagle in the top of the tree, and when the eagle shook himself, the worms and rotten flesh fell from him.' Realising that this was indeed Lleu, Gwydion sang a verse:

> 'An oaktree grows between two lakes
> Darkly overspreading sky and vale;
> If I do not speak falsely,
> These are the limbs of Lleu.'

The eagle crept halfway down the tree, and halted. Gwydion chanted again:

> 'An oaktree grows in the high glade,
> Rain wets it not, nor may heat pierce it,
> Nine score fiercenesses has it undergone,
> In its top is Lleu Llaw Gyffes.'

That is, 'Lleu of the Sure Hand.' A concluding verse brought Lleu down on to Gwydion's knee. The magician struck the eagle form with his wand, and at once Lleu was a man again. But he was in pitiable guise, 'he was nothing but skin and bone.' Eventually, however, he was restored to health and secured his revenge on the faithless wife and lover.

It will be seen that there exist strong parallels in this story to the accounts of the deaths of Lailoken—Suibhne (Merlin). Lleu is the subject of a 'fated death' (in Welsh *dihenydd*),[23] whereby a person is doomed to die in a certain way, and consequently in no other way. Moreover, Lleu's *dihenydd* is an obvious variant of the Threefold Death. He can only be killed by a specially-prepared (magical) spear; neither inside nor outside a house; neither on horseback nor on foot. In the event two of the regular elements of the Threefold Death are introduced: Lleu is pierced by a spear, and stands on a vat. The preconditions make no provision for the vat, and in view of well-attested Celtic tradition, it is reasonable to suppose that Lleu had been drowned in it in an earlier version. One might expect too that originally he was hanged as he slipped over, but there is no trace of this in the tale as we have it. In Ireland the allusion is explicit: Lug (Lleu) was killed at the Sacred Centre (Uisnech) by a *trinity* of deities.

Apart from the likely common incidence of the Threefold Death, two other elements suggest a link between the deaths of Lleu and Merlin. Both take place by a river. In the case of Merlin (Lailoken) it is of course the river in which he drowns, but in Lleu's case no reason is given for setting the scene on a riverbank. More striking is the appearance of the goat on which Lleu is to stand. The logic of this is evident, as it enables him to fulfil the condition of being neither on horseback nor afoot.[24]

This element can be glimpsed also in the composite Merlin legend. The slayer of Suibhne, for example, 'is variously a cowherd, a swineherd, or a shepherd'.[25] And in the Lailoken versions we read that the prophetic madman was stoned and beaten to death near a riverbank by some shepherds. The first account gives no motivation for this, while the second explains, a little improbably perhaps, that the shepherds were incited to their crime by a wicked queen whom their victim had offended some years previously.

Finally, later Welsh sources refer obscurely to some shepherds of King Rhydderch (Myrddin's persecutor in the Welsh poetry) who brought about that battle of Arderydd which drove Myrddin to madness and flight to the Forest of Celyddon.[26] The implications are far from clear, but it is tempting to connect the murderous shepherds by the Tweed with the herd of goats assembled at Lleu's riverside ordeal. And the goat which Lleu mounted before flying in eagle-shape onto the Tree of Life may in turn recall those goats which various mythologies picture as feeding off the Tree of Life.[27] Whatever the explanation, the link between the deathtales of Lleu and Lailoken seems strong.

The story of Lleu as it is preserved in the story of *Math vab*

Mathonwy is a piece of euhemerisation, and it is clear that the storyteller envisaged his characters as human beings, though possessing magical powers. In fact Lleu is a god, and many of the elements in the episode bear a mythological interpretation.[28]

1. *The enchanted spear.*
   Lleu in his Irish guise, the god Lug, possessed a marvellous spear and was known on occasion, as 'Lugaid of the spear'. Strong similarities of circumstance have led to an identification of Lug's spear with the Bleeding Lance which was encountered by Perceval in the Grail Castle, which in other accounts is supposed to be the spear with which the legendary Roman soldier Longinus pierced Christ's side at the Crucifixion.[29]

2. *The goat.*
   Lleu's precarious stance, balanced on the goat and the vat, suggests a ritual posture. In Norse mythology, Thor's chariot is drawn across the heavens by two goats, and a goat and hart feed from the World-Tree, Yggdrasil.[30]

3. *The eagle.*
   When Lleu is pierced by Gronwy's spear, he flies off in the form of an eagle. This must imply that Lleu's spirit left his body in this guise, the concept of the bird-soul being deep-rooted among the Celts, as among other peoples. A silver cup from Lyons bears representations of a sacred mistletoe-bearing tree, a god ('probably Lugus himself') and an eagle.[31]

4. *The eagle on the tree.*
   Still more interesting is the next stage of the story, when Lleu is found by Gwydion in his eagle-form, perched at the top of an oak-tree. For, as Gwydion's incantatory verses make plain, this is no ordinary oak but the World-Tree itself. It overspreads the heaven above and earth below, and possesses the Otherworld characteristics that 'rain wets it not, nor may heat pierce it'. The eagle roosting above is another familiar mythological factor. An eagle 'who knows many things' perched in the branches of the Norse World-Tree Yggdrasil, while the story of *Er Toshtuk* among the Kara-Kirghiz Tartars similarly describes a World-Tree with two young eagles in its top.[32]

It seems that Lleu was envisaged as being pierced by a spear, when he became an eagle. Hanging from the World-Tree, his mortal frame began to 'die', and fell from his bones in the form of rotting flesh to be devoured by the swine below. (Swine were considered Otherworld creatures *par excellence*[33]). His uncle, the wizard Gwydion, brought the wasting body to the ground and resurrected it by his magic arts.

The god Lug (in Welsh Lleu) is generally recognised as corresponding to Odin (Woden) in Teutonic mythology.[34] There is in particular a famous passage in the Norse poem *Hávamál* which reflects strikingly the episode in *Math vab Mathonwy* when Lleu hangs from the tree in eagle-form. The verses (which Odin himself is said to utter) run as follows:

> 'I know that I hung
> on the windswept tree
> for nine full nights,
> wounded with a spear
> and given to Odin,
> myself to myself;
> on that tree
> of which none know
> from what roots it rises.
>
> They did not comfort me with bread,
> and not with the drinking horn;
> I peered downward,
> I grasped the "runes",
> screeching I grasped them;
> I fell back from there.
>
> I learned nine mighty songs
> from the famous son
> of Bolthor, father of Bestla,
> and I got a drink
> of the precious mead,
> I was sprinkled with Othrerir.
>
> Then I began to be fruitful
> and to be fertile
> to grow and to prosper;
> one word sought
> another word from me;
> one deed sought
> another deed from me.'

Odin, like Lug, is wounded by a spear and hangs on a tree. The 'nine full nights' that he hung there are reflected in Gwydion's declaration that Lug's tree had sustained 'nine score fiercenesses'. In addition we learn from a passage in another section of *Hávamál* that when Odin acquired the precious mead of Othrerir (see the third verse above), that is, the source of (poetic) inspiration, he turned himself into an eagle and flew off.[35]

Norse mythology is vastly more richly documented than Welsh, and in consequence Odin's hanging on the tree can be explained in large part by references to other sources. The first thing to note is that Odin, like Lug, is hanging from the World Tree itself, known to the Norsemen as *Yggdrasil*. The name is a compound of two words: *Yggr*, a nickname of Odin recorded elsewhere, and *drasil*, a poetic term for a horse. But the gallows was also known poetically as a horse, upon which its victim 'rode', just as the horse was a symbol of death, carrying men to another world. *Yggdrasil*, like other World-Trees, had its roots in the Otherworld and sustained all of earth and heaven.[36]

The nature of the sacrifice, too, finds clear echoes in other sources. Odin

> 'hung
> on the windswept tree
> for nine full nights,
> wounded with a spear
> and given to Odin.'

Like Lug, Odin possessed a magical spear; it was called Gungnir, and had been forged by dwarves.[37] In the *Ynglinga Saga* Odin is described as being marked on his death-bed with a spear-point before departing to the realm of the gods. Another saga describes the death of a King Vikar, who was sacrificed to Odin by being hanged on a tree and pierced with a spear by the hero Starkadr, who exclaimed 'now I give you to Odin!' This exactly reflects Odin's own words, where he cries out that he has given himself to himself, *i.e.* to Odin. Elsewhere Odin is frequently represented as Lord of the Gallows, learning occult secrets from the dead. Odin himself declares that:

> 'I can do that for the twelfth, if I see a strangled corpse swaying from the gallows-tree, I carve and colour the runes, so that the man comes to life again and speaks with me.'

As a result he was the master of ghosts, leader of the army of the slain. It was he who was seen well on into the mediaeval period leading a spectral army, the Wild Hunt (*Wutanes her*), careering through storm-tossed skies.[38]

What is uncertain is whether Odin's self-sacrifice in order to acquire the knowledge of the Otherworld may be regarded, as Lug's appears to have been, as a version of the Threefold Death. He is represented as simultaneously hanged and pierced with a spear, but the third element is missing. Nevertheless it may be questioned whether it was not originally there, for it has been established that, in general, among Germanic peoples, there were three ways of offering a human victim to the gods; by hanging, drowning and transfixing.[39] At the sacred grove by the heathen temple of Uppsala in Sweden, sacrificial victims were immolated by being hanged, like Odin himself, for nine nights. A mediaeval source adds the information that:

'Near this temple stands a very large tree with wide-spreading branches, always green winter and summer. What kind it is nobody knows. There is also a spring at which pagans are accustomed to make their sacrifices, and into it to plunge a live man. And if he is not found, the people's wish will be granted.'

The tree is clearly a local World-Tree, and victims were both hanged from its branches, and drowned by its side.[40]

The accounts of Lug and Odin hanging on the World-Tree are, despite close similarities, too deeply rooted in their respective mythologies to have been borrowed one from the other. The Celtic and Teutonic tongues derive from a common Indo-European precursor, the parent language spoken (it is now believed) in the fourth and third millennia B.C., and it seems more than likely that related themes of the Threefold Death and the Divine Sacrificial Victim derived from a common tradition three or more thousand years old. The magical spear, for example, which plays so important a symbolic rôle in the sacrifice, represents a significant theme in Indo-European mythology.[41]

Velinas, god of the pagan Lithuanians, appears to have been a figure cognate to Odin, one-eyed, prophetic, a god of hanging and the hanged. Far to the East, but still within the Indo-European cultural tradition, there existed a tradition in Vedic India of the *axis mundi* (the World Centre) as the supreme sacrificial centre. Death was by strangulation, corresponding to Norse practice, and Odin's Indian counterpart, Varuna, was associated with a sacral noose. The concept of the Triple Death is found also among peoples speaking other than Indo-European languages[42], so there can be no doubt that belief in the divine sacrifice at the World-Tree is both ancient and widespread.

There is no means of knowing how far back in time the theme of the Tree of Life originated. What is certain is that from a very early period it was intimately associated with the death of the Saviour God, whose sacrifice achieves the gift of immortality.[43] Nowhere is this symbol more deeply rooted than in the soil of Palestine, and it is there that we find the most remarkable parallel to the Triple-Death sacrifices of Lug and Odin in the wind-swept forests of the North.

In common with neighbouring Near Eastern countries, the Israelites in Old Testament times were familiar with the concept of the World-Tree. Indeed, the worship of sacred trees and representative pillars pre-dates their arrival in Palestine, being associated with the Canaanite goddess Astarte. Though the worshippers of Jehovah were implacably hostile to the old cults, as generally happens they absorbed significant elements into their own practice. Tree-worship was abandoned when the people of Israel returned from their Babylonian exile, but as a religious symbol the Tree of Life continued to flourish: 'the fruit of the righteous was a tree of life' (Proverbs 3, 16–18; 11, 30).[44]

Not surprisingly, soon after the Crucifixion the Cross came to be identified as the Tree. It was the Tree of Life in the Garden of Eden, and legends arose to explain how it had been transferred to Golgotha:

> 'The Tree of Life which was hidden in paradise
> grew up in Marjam, and sprang forth from her,
> and in its shade creation hath repose,
> and it spreadeth its fruits over those far and near;'

ran a Syriac hymn, and another passage makes the identification explicit:

> 'The Tree of Life is the cross
> which gave a radiant life to our race.
> On the top of Golgotha Christ
> distributed life to men.
> And henceforth He further promised us
> the pledge of eternal life.'

The hill at Golgotha was also identified as the *Omphalos*, or Navel of the Earth, and was regarded as the topmost point of the cosmic mountain. The ancient myths of Tree and Centre had entered on a culminating phase of their purpose, the older concept being replaced and sublimated in the *historical* event of the Crucifixion.[45] What is even more remarkable in the context of the present study is the extraordinary similarity between the agony and death of Jesus and the deaths of the gods Odin and Lug.

We may consider the death of Odin first, since the evidence is more explicit than in the case of Lug.

> Odin dies hanging on the World-Tree, as does Christ.
> Whilst on the Tree, Odin is 'wounded with a spear', as is Christ.
> Odin hangs for 'nine full nights', a multiple of three reflecting the three days between Christ's Crucifixion and Resurrection.
> Odin thirsted in his agony, as did Christ (John 19, 28).
> Odin screamed at the moment of truth, just as Christ 'cried with a loud voice' (Matthew 27, 46).
> Above all, Odin was sacrificed to Odin, 'myself to myself'.

A distinguished Norse scholar has stressed:

> 'The sacrifice of Odin to himself may thus be seen as the highest conceivable form of sacrifice, in fact so high that, like many a religious mystery, it surpasses our comprehension. It is the sacrifice, not of king to god, but of god to god, of such a kind as is related in Scripture of the sacrifice of Christ . . . Like Christ, Odin rose from death, now fortified with the occult wisdom which he communicated to gods and men. This thought is conveyed in the last lines of the *Runatal* (str. 145) where it says: this is what . . . [Odin] wrote (*reist*) before men's fates were laid down, where he rose up when he came back.'[46]

Understandably, it was once argued that these aspects of the Odin myth must have been borrowed from Christianity, most likely by Viking settlers in England. However, competent scholars have long been agreed that *all* aspects of Odin's sacrifice listed above are far too deeply embedded in Teutonic mythology to be anything but native to Northern paganism long antedating the arrival of Christianity. The very name of the World-Tree, *Yggdrasil* ('Odin's horse'), is inextricably bound up with Odin. It was probably represented by the sacred column Irminsul, which the pagan Saxons believed upheld the sky and which was destroyed by Charlemagne in 772. The sacrifice of humans to Odin is well-attested, as is the ritual combination of hanging and spear-thrust. The number nine of the nights Odin hung on the Tree was a figure of the highest significance to the pagan Norsemen, and seems to be associated especially with Odin and with sacrifice.[47]

Clearly it is possible that the myth of Odin's self-sacrifice was influenced in some degree by the story of the Crucifixion. But if that occurred, it could only have been because the Christian and pagan motifs were so similar as to invite confusion. Indeed, so close was the similarity that it has been believed to be a principal cause of the relative ease with which the North was converted to Christianity. Christian Anglo-Saxon poetry describing the death of the Saviour unselfconsciously employs Odinic terminology at every turn: Christ hangs on the Rood-tree 'in the wylde wynde'; Christ's Tree had no roots, like that of Odin, and springs from the Cosmic Mountain (*an berge*). The confusion is perhaps most strikingly exemplified by a nineteenth-century folksong from the Shetland Isles. The subject is in fact Christ, but the details are rather more appropriate to Odin:

> 'Nine days he hang   pa de rütless tree;
> for ill was da folk   in' güd wis he.
> A blüdy mael   wis in his side –
> made wi' a lance –   'at wid na hide.
> Nine lang nichts,   i' da nippin rime,
> hang he dare   wi' his naeked limb.
>   Some dey leuch;
>   but idders gret.'[48]

Though the death-tale of Lug appears only in its full form in *Math vab Mathonwy*, enough has been noted to show that a parallel account to the Crucifixion was equally well established among the Celts. Pierced in his side by a spear, Lug hangs on the Tree of Life. His soul had ascended in bird-form (the eagle). Translated into human shape, his body is found on its descent to be 'nothing but skin and bone'. Despite this he was miraculously resuscitated. Both versions, Celtic and Germanic, must surely stem from common Indo-European myth[49], though this of course still bears no obvious relevance to the Crucifixion of Christ.

It was argued earlier in this chapter that the deaths of Lug and Odin, like that of Merlin, represent versions of the Celtic and Teutonic myths of the Threefold Death. Once again there is a marked parallel with the death of Christ. Christ, of course, hung on a tree, and this was the prime cause of his death. He was also pierced in the side by a spear. According to the Gospel of St John (19, 31–35):

'The Jews therefore, because it was the preparation, that the bodies should not remain upon the cross on the sabbath day, (for that sabbath day was an high day,) besought Pilate that their legs might be broken, and that they might be taken away.

Then came the soldiers, and brake the legs of the first, and of the other that was crucified with him.

But when they came to Jesus, and saw that he was dead already, they brake not his legs:

But one of the soldiers with a spear pierced his side, and forthwith came thereout blood and water.

And he that saw it bare record, and his record is true: and he knoweth that he saith true, that ye might believe.'

Though Jesus was already dead when stabbed by the soldier, the context makes it clear that the purpose was to round off a more lingering death caused by the hanging on the Cross. Here is clearly what may be described as a Twofold Death; was there a third element?

Care must be taken not to force the parallel, but a third element may be detectable. When at the ninth hour Christ cried out in agony:

'. . . straightway one of them ran, and took a sponge, and filled it with vinegar, and put it on a reed, and gave him to drink . . .

Jesus, when he had cried again with a loud voice, yielded up the ghost.'

(Matthew, 27, 47–50).

The significance of this episode is not entirely clear, causing disagreement among New Testament scholars. But there is a good case for believing that the 'vinegar' was poison, and that 'this drink is understood as causing premature death.'[50] If so, could this represent a regular third element in Germanic and Celtic Triple-Death motifs: death by 'drowning'?

One thing is certain, and that is that the Crucifixion is saturated with threefold symbolism. Jesus correctly prophesied that 'after three days I will rise again' (Matthew 27, 63; Mark 8, 31). According to Matthew (27, 45–46) and Luke (24, 44), from the sixth hour there was darkness, and Jesus yielded up the ghost 'about the ninth hour.' Mark (15, 25–34) says that he was crucified at the third hour, darkness fell upon the land at the sixth, and he died at the ninth. Finally, Christ was crucified between two other victims, a fact which, it has been conjectured, was not accidental, but had a ritual significance.[51]

It may be, therefore, that the circumstances of Christ's Crucifixion echoed much that was deeply rooted in Near Eastern
mythological belief and practice. But how is one to account for the
fact that, though the Crucifixion has its crucially important mythical
aspect, it was at the same time a factual occurrence, rooted firmly
in time and space? For it would be hard today to find any serious
historian who does not accept the Crucifixion as an undoubted
historical event.[52]

In the improbable, if not impossible, event that the death-tales
of Lug or Odin represent real events in which a divinity cast in
human form was sacrificed, one may readily conceive of the sacrifice
being conducted according to ritual precedent. But this is scarcely
possible in the case of Christ. Neither the Roman nor Jewish
authorities had any incentive for obliging a condemned rebel or
blasphemer in some special manner calculated to gratify his followers' most excited expectations. Crucifixion was in any case
employed as a regular and degrading Roman punishment for se-
dition.[53] The piercing of Jesus' side with a lance-thrust, though like
everything else provided with an Old Testament prophetic parallel,
implicitly takes place from a matter-of-fact motive: to put an end
to Jesus' sufferings. There is in any case no reason to mistrust
the emphatic statement that the episode was recounted by an
eyewitness.

The Threefold Death perhaps reflects the age-old, widespread
conception of a triune deity. Osiris, Isis and Horus comprised the
Egyptian trinity, and among the Indo-Europeans there was a
general tripartition of deities. Belief in the Trinity may be as
old as religious thought.[54] When the risen Christ proclaimed the
doctrine of the Trinity, it was on a mountain in Galilee (Matthew
28, 16–20), which it is tempting to identify with Mount Tabor. It
was the *axis mundi* from which creation had grown, and to which
it would dwindle when time ceased. 'And, lo, I am with you always,
even unto the end of the world.'[55]

The self-sacrifice of god is accompanied by symbols, Tree, Spear
and Water, whose significance can only be guessed at. But the
whole purpose of symbols is to provide expression for what is
essentially incomprehensible. Welling up from the subconscious,
they portray the mystery of which man is too integral a part to
envisage in its totality. The archetype of the Saviour God, the hero
whose death and rebirth bring about the salvation of mankind, is
deeply embedded in the human psyche. Jung believed that 'we can
safely assume that it "originated" at a period when man did not

yet know that he possessed a hero myth; in an age, that is to say, when he did not yet consciously reflect on what he was saying. The hero figure is an archetype, which has existed since time immemorial.'[56] Among the Celtic and Teutonic branches of the Indo-European peoples the archetype expressed itself in the form of the developed parallel myths of the Threefold Deaths of Lug (Lleu) and Odin. The significance of the Crucifixion lies in its introduction of the cosmic event into linear historical time.

It can be seen, therefore, that the Threefold Death motif ascribed to Merlin reflects the myth of the Saviour God, whose self-sacrifice was believed to have occurred in this deeply ritual fashion. Though the motif is certainly of mythological origin, it became like many other myths widely disseminated in folklore. There is no certain means now of distinguishing for certain whether Merlin's end was envisaged as reflecting or imitating the death of the god, or whether the floating folk-tale became attached at some stage to his legend. On the whole, however, the evidence appears to suggest that Merlin was originally regarded as having undergone a sacrificial death. The Threefold Death motif is present in all versions of the Merlin legend (Merlin, Lailoken, Suibhne), indicating that it already existed at an early stage of the legend's development. Other considerations point similarly to its forming an intrinsic part of the history of Merlin.

It is quite likely that Lug's votaries were not only regarded as Lug personified, but also on occasions underwent a sacrifice imitative of that of the god incarnated in their persons. This is certainly what appears to have happened in the case of Lug's Teutonic *alter ego*, Odin.[57] Attention was drawn in an earlier chapter to marked similarities between Lug and Merlin, in view of which it may be conjectured that the Threefold Death ascribed to the latter represents a sacrificial offering comparable to that of King Vikar to Odin. A passage in *The Life of St Samson* describing a pagan assembly in Cornwall about the time Merlin flourished in the North, is (it was also argued) to be compared with the copiously-documented Feast of Lug in pagan Ireland, *Lughnasa*. And as it specifically included the 'death' and resurrection of a youth, it seems possible that the ceremonial at one time included a sacrifice to the god, imitative of his own death.

There is a further consideration. The setting of the poem *Cad Goddeu* in *The Book of Taliesin* was identified with the forest haunted by Merlin in his exile, and there are several reasons for supposing it to represent an adaptation or reflection of an effusion of the bard himself. We know that much of the spurious history of Taliesin (*Hanes Taliesin*) had at an earlier stage been attributed to Merlin, and many of the allusions in *Cad Goddeu* are as appropriate to Merlin as they are inappropriate to the historical Taliesin. His shape-shifting incarnations; his career as a warrior before becoming a guardian of beasts; and the concluding injunction to the druids to prophesy to Arthur: all these bear a strong ring of the legend of Merlin.

What is also noticeable is a parallel identification with Lleu (Lug). The speaker in *Cad Goddeu* declares he was produced by Math, who in the tale of *Math vab Mathonwy* was the putative father of Lleu. He adds that his creation was brought about by Gwydion's magic wand; in the tale Lleu's mother Arianrhod drops him in the form of an afterbirth as she steps over the wizard Gwydion's wand. In a mysterious allusion the poet declares he was 'in the rampart with Dylan Eil Mor'; in the tale, Dylan Eil Ton was Lleu's brother. Again, the poet alludes to two enchanted spears from heaven, and a magical spear was the particular weapon of the god Lug. Most significantly, he asserts that none has dared attack him save 'Goronwy from Doleu Edrywy'. It was of course Gronwy Pevr who seduced Lleu's wife and afterwards transfixed him with a magical spear.[58]

The poem *Cad Goddeu* is obscure in its allusions and difficult in its language, but much of it makes sense if we assume that it is uttered by Merlin as an incarnation of Lug. His eye glances reflectively across all eternity. He sees Gwydion, the primeval magician, bring trees to life with a touch of his wand. He passes in mind through the endless incarnations he and all mankind have known; sees all things past, present and future, the Flood, the Crucifixion and Doomsday. The vision culminates in ecstasy as the prophet sees himself ultimately exalted in a golden form of glory.

This apotheosis was achieved by the ascent of the dangerous path emerging from the Forest to the holy spring in its rocky crevice on Hart Fell, in the heart of Goddeu, the World Centre lying at the base of the Tree of Life whose summit is that bright Nail in the centre of the radiant dome of heaven. As for Merlin himself, his fate was nothing less than a sacrifice in which he, as the god incarnate, underwent the Threefold Death of God Himself, symbolically or in reality.

Tradition places the site of his death and burial a bare dozen miles from his dwelling place on the mountain. Neither Geoffrey of Monmouth nor the Welsh poems refer to Merlin's death, but in the Lailoken fragments he is said to have fallen to his death 'over a steep bank of the Tweed by the fort of Dunmeller'. The allusion has long been taken to point to the village of Drumelzier on the Tweed, and the site of Merlin's grave is still pointed out by villagers. The spot is well within what must have been the bounds of the *Coed Celyddon* and *Goddeu*.

On the other hand, analogy suggests that the sacrifice would have been envisaged as occurring at the apex of the *axis mundi*, the summit of Hart Fell. It may be significant that the only reference to Merlin's death in the Welsh poetry is an allusion to his mountain grave. A verse in the 'Stanzas of the Graves' reads as follows:

> 'Bedd Ann ap lleian ymnewais fynydd,
> lluagor llew Ymrais,
> Prif ddewin Merddin Embrais.'

This I translate as:

> 'The grave of the nun's son on Newais mountain:
> Lord of battle, Lleu Embreis;
> Chief magician, Myrddin Embrais.'[59]

In this verse we seem to possess references to the virgin birth of Merlin and his identification with Lleu (Lug), where both bear the epithet *Embreis*. But Newais mountain remains unidentified, as must for the present the grave of Merlin.

This reconstruction of Merlin's rôle as Prophet and Otherworld Guide and of his relationship to the god Lug is based on a wide variety of sources, but is nowhere recounted explicitly in a single narrative. However, it is paralleled precisely by the tale of a comparable shaman-figure from early Greece. Orpheus (who is in any case linked to Mercury-Lug[60]) was said by Plutarch to have travelled under the aegis of Apollo to the World-Navel at Delphi. There he entered 'the great *krater* from which dreams draw their mixture of truth and falsehood', through which he was enabled to visit the Underworld and return to the earth.[61] We have here a remarkable counterpart to the legend of Merlin, and given the weight of evidence it is likely that the existing references to Merlin represent surviving fragments of a British legend comparable to that of Orpheus.

12

The Trickster, the Wild Man and the Prophet

Few mythological figures enjoy so widespread a provenance as a quirky character known as The Trickster. A many-faceted, complex personality, his traits add up to a rounded and recognisable individual – possibly the first to appear as a 'literary' concept. His attributes have been effectively summarised by the American anthropologist Paul Radin:

> 'Manifestly we are here in the presence of a figure and a theme or themes which have had a special and permanent appeal and an unusual attraction for mankind from the very beginnings of civilisation. In what must be regarded as its earliest and most archaic form, as found among the North American Indians, Trickster is at one and the same time creator and destroyer, giver and negator, he who dupes others and who is always duped himself. He wills nothing consciously. At times, he is constrained to behave as he does from impulses over which he has no control. He knows neither good nor evil yet he is responsible for both. He possesses no values, moral or social, is at the mercy of his passions and appetites, yet through his actions all values come into being.'

Trickster tales are imbued with a picaresque, anarchical quality, frequently revelling in scatological disorder. But there is an evident purpose behind these thematic vagaries. How is one to reconcile a figure at once benefactor, buffoon, and malignant tease; who is at the same time incarnate spirit of destructive mischief, and yet culture hero who teaches man the use of fire and cultivation of plants, a destroyer of monsters and divider of seasons?

The Trickster represents an elemental, whimsical being, whose integration into human society is only partial. There is a dichotomy in his nature, which prevents his ever breaking entirely free of his chaotic, primordial mould. He violates the most sacred taboos of society in a manner not normally contemplated even in myth. He is destructive, even murderous, on occasion; and yet his ready wit at other times leads him to teach his fellows the use of flint or the construction of dwellings. His voracious appetite, his wandering and his unbridled sexuality are always stressed.

Numerous ludicrous episodes illustrate the latter theme. The Winnebago Trickster, Wakdjunkaga, wakes to find himself without a blanket – only to see it floating above him on the end of his giant erect penis. He despatches his penis across a lake to impregnate a bathing girl, only to have an old woman drive a bradawl into it. The whole image is saturated with sex, yet it is a sexuality totally disorganised and unharnessed as yet to social purpose. It is even necessary for a chipmunk to advise him where his penis and testicles should be placed on his body! Subsequently the chipmunk bites at his gigantic penis until pieces are scattered abroad and his organ reduced to human size. On a purely scatological level he emits gas from his rectum which blasts bystanders to the ends of the earth, and ascends a tree defecating to such an extent that the earth is covered with mountains of his own excrement, through which he is forced to struggle until he finds water in which to wash.

Such incidents, humorous in their own right, bear a deeper significance. In a world that has no beginning and no end, an ageless and priapus-like protagonist is pictured strutting across the scene, wandering restlessly from place to place, attempting, successfully and unsuccessfully, to gratify his voracious hunger and his uninhibited sexuality. Though he seems to us to have no purpose, at the end of his activities a new figure is revealed to us and a new psychical reorientation and environment have come into being. Nothing here has been created *de novo*. What is new has been attained either by the sloughing off and rearrangement of the old or, negatively, by the demonstration that certain types of behaviour inevitably bring about ridicule and humiliation and result in pain and suffering where they do not actually lead to death.

But what, we may well ask, is the meaning of this original plot? About this there should be little doubt. It embodies the vague memories of an archaic and primordial past, where there as yet existed no clear-cut differentiation between the divine and non-divine. For this period Trickster is the symbol. Indeed, it has been suggested that the myth derives from that dim prehistoric past when hominid creatures were imperceptibly transforming themselves into man's earliest ancestors.[1]

It is plain that the figure of Merlin perfectly matches the arche-

typal Trickster. In the Winnebago myth, Hare (the Trickster) is
born to a human virgin, the father being unknown.[2] In the *Merlin*
of Robert de Boron, the prophet is similarly conceived by a virgin.
It will be recalled that the devils in Hell arrange for one of their
number to beget a child by a mortal woman who will be half human
and half devil, and who will bring about the destruction of mankind.
The conspiracy is partially frustrated by the holy anchorite, Blaise,
who signs the mother with the cross. As a result the infant Merlin
is born with dual natures. From the devils he receives the power
to view all the past ('those things which had been, and done, and
said, and gone'), and also the hairy skin of an animal. But from
God he received the power to see into the future. Thus he was a
creature half bestial and half spiritual:

> 'he held to whichever he wished, for he saw that he could render
> the devils their due and to Our Lord that which was his: for the
> devils only created his body, and Our Lord placed the spirit
> throughout his body . . .'

Henceforward, like the Trickster, Merlin combined 'the two-fold
function of benefactor and buffoon'. The divinely inspired Merlin
reveals the future to Vortigern, erects Stonehenge, arranges the
succession of Arthur, and recounts the history of that potent if
mysterious palladium, the Grail. In all this he resembles the Trickster in his beneficent aspect, when roaming the earth seeking to
improve it and make life more tolerable for mankind.[3] The demoniac side of the prophet's nature manifests itself in the sardonic
humour accompanying his whimsical displays of supernatural perception. He laughs at the sight of a man weeping at his child's
funeral – because he alone knows that the priest conducting the
ceremony is its real father. He adopts unexpectedly ridiculous
disguises in order to play mischievous tricks, and acts as pander to
Uther's seduction of Igerna. In all this there is much good humour,
but the hairy pelt which is his diabolical heritage terrifies his mother
and other women.

A motif present in most of these impish encounters is the sarcastic
laugh with which Merlin greets the unwitting discomfiture his
knowledge imposes on those about him. It is also the characteristic
laugh of the Trickster in the Winnebago cycle, who laughs at the
dismay of those on whom he has played a trick.[4]

Symbolic of Trickster's efforts to rid himself unavailingly of the
crudely bestial aspects of his nature are violent struggles maintained
within himself, as when his left hand struggles against his right.

Frequently he is made the dupe of his own cunning, when he allows himself to be trapped in the fork of a large tree he was attempting to outwit, burns his own anus under the impression it is a feckless servant's mouth, and is induced by some flies to insert his head in an elk's skull from which it cannot be extracted.[5]

Merlin's tragic end, trapped in a magical prison of his own devising, reflects closely this pattern. Beguiled by the lady Nyneve, the wizard wandered with her into Cornwall. What followed is best told by Malory (drawing on the earlier *Suite du Merlin*):

> 'And so one a tyme Merlyon ded shew hir in a roche whereas was a grete wondir and wrought by enchauntement that went undir a grete stone. So by hir subtyle worchyng she made Merlyon to go undir that stone to latte hir wete of the mervayles there, but she wrought so there for hym that he come never oute for all the craufte he coude do, and so she departed and leffte Merlyon.'

The demoniac aspect of Merlin's nature thus represents an archetype ascending to the period of man's Creation, and surviving as the animal shadow lurking behind man's god-like image, with all its potential for anarchical disorder and evil. The myth arose to exorcise the constant reminder within the unconscious psyche, that man is but a beast erect on his hind legs and endowed with powers of speech and thought. The exorcism is conducted through the familiar medium of ridicule, and Merlin with all his wisdom is frequently made to appear incongruously foolish.

He is born with a hairy animal-skin, and appears later in the guise of a woodman, dressed in 'a short tattered smock, with his hair very shaggy and long, and a very long beard, so that he really looked like a wild man (*home sauvaige*).' The expression 'wild man' relates to a widespread mediaeval conception, which in turn derives from extremely ancient belief.

Wild Men were envisaged as semi-human creatures eking out a brutish life in remote forests, and living on roots, berries, nuts and the raw flesh of wild animals. They dwelt in caves or primitive shelters, and were constantly obliged to defend themselves against other savage denizens of the woods. They were pictured as immensely powerful, savagely aggressive, and only able to command the barest rudiments of language. They believed in no god, being too backward to entertain such a conception and lacking souls in consequence, were greatly given to sating an unbridled sexual appetite, and were frequently regarded as insane. In appearance they were covered with a thick pelt of hair (except on hands, face and feet), and frequently bore a massive untrimmed club as a weapon.[6]

Wild Men proliferate in mediaeval art and literature, and the concept is traceable to the oldest literature in existence. *Gilgamesh*, the great Akkadian epic composed some time in the third millennium B.C., contains a full account of Enkidu, the primordial Wild Man. The tale recounts the history of Gilgamesh, king of Uruk. Though glorious in fame and power, he has taken to oppressing his subjects, who appeal to the gods for aid. They set about creating a rival to Gilgamesh to bridle his arrogance, the valiant Enkidu. Born on the open steppe:

> 'Shaggy with hair is his whole body,
> He is endowed with head hair like a woman.
> The locks of his hair sprout like Nisaba.
> He knows neither people nor land . . .
> With the gazelles he feeds on grass,
> With the wild beasts he jostles at the watering-place –
> With the teeming creatures his heart delights in water.'

Gilgamesh despatches a temple harlot to seduce Enkidu. After a week of fornication, Enkidu found himself weakened physically but possessed of compensatory wisdom. He abandons the wilderness and seeks out Gilgamesh. After a fierce wrestling-bout, in which Gilgamesh is the victor, they become fast friends and set out to slay the dread Lord of the Forest, Huwawa. But a subsequent quarrel with the gods results in Enkidu's death, and Gilgamesh in distress becomes himself a Wild Man and travels on a vain pilgrimage to discover the secret of immortality. Such, in briefest outline, is the epic, as it survives in fragmentary tablets.[7]

Clearly Enkidu represents mankind before civilisation. On the steppe he lives in communion with the wild animals, a communion which is shattered once he knows woman, acquires wisdom, and becomes human:

> 'Carefree became his mood and cheerful,
> His heart exulted
> And his face glowed.
> He rubbed the shaggy growth,
> The hair of his body,
> Anointed himself with oil,
> Became human.

He put on clothing,
He is like a groom!
He took his weapon
To chase the lions,
That shepherds might rest at night.
He caught wolves,
He captured lions,
The chief cattlemen could lie down;
Enkidu is their watchman . . .'

Enkidu, like other Wild Men, represents man in a primitive, brutish condition, before his crude, shaggy frame knew the softening influences of civilised culture and morality. The Wild Man is desire incarnate, possessing the strength, wit, and cunning to give full expression to all his lusts. His life is correspondingly unstable in character. He is a glutton, eating to satiety one day and starving the next; he is lascivious and promiscuous, without even consciousness of sin.[8]

Unlike other fabulous creatures, conceived of as remote in time or space, the Wild Man is conventionally represented as being always present, inhabiting the immediate confines of the community. He is just out of sight, over the horizon, in the nearby forest, desert, mountain, or hills.[9] The implication is clear enough; the Wild Man not only represents man in his early, savage condition, but also that strain of savagery in his nature which is a lingering heritage of his primitive condition. In mediaeval iconography Adam is sometimes portrayed as a Wild Man (there is a fine example carved on a panel in the fifteenth-century French church at Ambierle), and it was Adam's sin which continued to tarnish man made in God's image.

The Wild Man concept is thus to be seen as a variant of the Trickster motif; with the difference perhaps that, whereas Trickster stories portray man's prolonged struggle to free himself from his animal heritage, the image of the Wild Man is simply a reflection of an earlier, unregenerate state, when man dwelt as yet in conditions of unalloyed primitive barbarity. (It is interesting, incidentally, to see this unconscious awareness of man's hominid and pre-hominid existence surviving in the face of virtually all mythologies, which assert man's separate creation.)

It can readily be seen why numerous scholars see the legend of Merlin, particularly the early form preserved in the Lailoken fragments, as a version of the primitive theme of the Wild Man of the Woods.[10] There is however good reason to reject this view, and to stress that though the Wild Man motif is undoubtedly present in the stories of Lailoken, Merlin and Suibhne, it is in a subordinate and accessory relationship.

Firstly, the traditional Wild Man is always represented as a great hunter after game, killing and devouring the raw flesh of his fellow-creatures of the wilderness. The composite Merlin-figure is, in strong contrast, a vegetarian.

Secondly, Wild Men are given over to the crudest sexual indulgence, fornicating like beasts in the absence of any moral restraint. The Merlin-figure is apparently chaste, lamenting his enforced separation from his wife.

Thirdly, and most obviously, Lailoken, Merlin and Suibhne are all characters possessing exceptional intelligence and emotional sensitivity, the latter two continually expressing the utmost distress at being denied the pleasures of cultured society. The true Wild Man is by definition utterly void of these characteristics.

Nothing could be further from this conception than the philosopher-astronomer portrayed by Geoffrey of Monmouth; the broken exile lamenting his former courtly existence, who soliloquises in the Welsh Myrddin poetry; or even the anguished prophet of the Lailoken episodes. Merlin is in truth far nearer to Prospero than Caliban – a connection which is oddly closer than mere analogy. For Shakespeare's Prospero is thought to have been based on the famous alchemist Dr John Dee, who in turn regarded himself and was widely regarded as a sixteenth-century counterpart of Merlin! It is likely too that Spenser's picture of Merlin in *The Faerie Queene* was drawn at least in part from Dr Dee.[11]

There can be no question, therefore, but that the original Merlin-figure was far removed from being a Wild Man. However, this is not to say that he did not acquire some Wild Man characteristics along the way. Living as he did alone in the forest, it was inevitable that his plight would come to be compared with that of those other denizens of the wild. Fortunately it is possible to detect the process at work in the extant texts.

In the *Vita Merlini*, Merlin encounters a madman who had 'for many years lived and gone about the wild places like a beast, without a sense of shame.' Merlin persuades the wretched man, when cured, to join him in his forest refuge. It looks as if Geoffrey of Monmouth, seeing the similarity of their outward existence, had taken care to introduce a Wild Man into the story.

This process may be detected still more clearly in the older

Lailoken stories. Much play has been made by proponents of the theory that the story is in origin merely a version of the Wild Man fable, of the description of Lailoken as 'a naked madman, hairy and completely destitute' (*quidam demens nudus et hirsutus . . .*). The hairy pelt is undoubtedly the characteristic mark of the Wild Man, but critics who use this as evidence that Lailoken was himself a Wild Man cannot have read what follows with full care. After his first encounter with St Kentigern, Lailoken rushes off to the forest. Kentigern, moved by his evident distress, prays to Christ on his behalf these significant words:

> 'Lord Jesus, this is the unhappiest of unhappy men, with the life he leads in this foul wilderness, like a beast among beasts, a naked (*nudus*) fugitive feeding only on plants. Beasts of the wild have bristles and hair as their natural covering and fields of grass and roots and leaves as their proper food. Our brother here is as one with us in naked form and flesh and blood and frailty, (*formam nuditam carnem sanguinem et fragilitatem sicut vnus habens ex nobis*) but lacks all that human nature needs, save only the common air. How then does he live among the beasts of the wood in the face of hunger, cold and constant fasting?'

Nothing could be more emphatically clear. Lailoken is naked, but *not* hairy as are the beasts of the wild. He is in fact a fellow-human in everything but his misfortune. The introductory reference to him as 'hairy' (*hirsutus*) must be an interpolation, since it would have been impossible to have formulated the prayer with its emphasis on hairless nudity had *hirsutus* been present in the original version. It seems certain therefore that the adjective was inserted by a redactor at some stage after the original composition. He had doubtless seen that Lailoken's circumstances corresponded in large part to those of the traditional Wild Man, and accordingly provided him with the traditional hairy pelt.

The evidence seems incontrovertible. The Lailoken of the original story was *primarily* a prophet living in the wilderness, driven there by a traumatic experience. As has been shown in earlier chapters, such a figure perfectly suits what is known of mantic bards and other inspired figures in Celtic and pre-Celtic shamanist tradition. There is no justification at all for arbitrarily altering him into something else, whatever the transient fashions of folklore interpretation. Had Giraldus Cambrensis not been writing as an eyewitness, the ecstatic *awenyddion* he encountered would also doubtless have been classed as Wild Men or similarly picturesque figures.

However, when all is said and done we cannot entirely exclude the intrusive Wild Man from consideration. The redactors who presumed Lailoken must have been hairy, and that Merlin would have been a natural companion for a genuine Wild Man, clearly found that their protagonists matched the mythic mould in significant respects. Indeed, the Wild Man concept is not exclusive, and many Wild Men possess clear shamanistic traits. There is much interplay between the concepts of shaman, Wild Man, Trickster.[12] If Lailoken were not a Wild Man, there was a strong element of the Wild Man in his composition. This, after all, is to be expected. It has been seen how closely the figure of Merlin relates to that popular mythological character, the Trickster. Just as the Trickster represents an indelibly formative epoch in the development of humanity, so too does the Wild Man. The two concepts are closely related.

The Wild Man is the 'beast' in humanity, banished to the unconscious. The banishment can never be total, however, and from time to time the 'beast' surfaces as the archetypal Wild Man. At once menacing, ridiculous and pathetic, he serves both as warning and therapeutic object-lesson. There is thus a Wild Man in everyone, dormant but never totally suppressed. In the character of Merlin he manifests himself in the demoniac aspects of the prophet: his leadership of the Wild Hunt, his refuge in the dark places of the earth, his propensity for mischief, his mocking laughter, his rejection of the whole ethos of civilisation.

All this is in marked contrast to that other Merlin, who dominates the courts of Vortigern, Ambrosius, Uther and Arthur. It is he who intervenes time and again to preserve the British monarchy in its hour of danger, institutes the Table Round (the fulcrum, or *Omphalos*, of civilised order), and directs the chivalry of Britain towards the ennobling quest of the Holy Grail. The course of future events is settled and known in advance to the prophet, but that can allow no slackening of endeavour:

> 'Then *Merlin* thus; Indeed the fates are firme,
> And may not shrinck, though all the world do shake:
> Yet ought mens good endeuors them confirme,
> And guide the heavenly causes to their constant terme'

Thus Spenser in *The Faerie Queene*. For an eye which spanned centuries past and yet to come had ever before it the memory of an older Britain lying close below the present:

> 'But farre in land a saluage nation dwelt,
> Of hideous Giants, and halfe beastly men,
> That never tasted grace, nor goodnesse felt,
> But like wild beasts lurking in loathsome den,
> And flying fast as Roebucke through the fen,
> All naked without shame, or care of cold,
> By hunting and by spoiling lived then;
> Of stature huge, and eke of courage bold,
> That sonnes of men amazed their sternnesse to behold.'

A recent study of the thirteenth-century Robert de Boron's romance of *Merlin* has detailed remarkably close parallels existing between the characters and careers of Merlin, and those of both Antichrist and Christ. The figure of Antichrist was a potent one in the early Middle Ages, and whilst Robert de Boron may have been influenced in his treatment of Merlin by the legend, it may equally be presumed that enough similarity already existed for the resemblance to be remarked.

The parallels are best set out in tabular form.

Merlin	*Antichrist*
Born of a devil and a virgin.	Born of a devil and a virgin.
Mentor to kings and nobles.	Attracts train of kings and princes.
Creates marvels (Vortigern's tower, Stonehenge, the Round Table, Sword in the Stone.)	Performs startling miracles.
Shape-shifter.	Deceives men under various disguises.

Similarities with the life and mission of Christ are similarly striking.

Merlin	*Christ*
Precocious child of virgin and Otherworld being.	Precocious child of Virgin Mary and God.
Brought up by mother in obscurity.	Humble and obscure upbringing.
Vortigern's *magi* seek him out and wish to put the child to death.	Warned by *magi*, Herod abortively seeks to slay Christ-child.

Imposes his will on the Britons by demonstrations of supernatural power.	Performs miracles as demonstration of divine mission.
Stresses supernatural nature of mission.	Sent by His Father in Heaven.
Frequently disappears into forests of Northumberland.	Seeks refuge in wilderness.
Selects Knights of the Table Round to achieve divine purpose.	Chooses disciples to assist and continue mission.

Professor Micha draws a number of other detailed comparisons confirming the similarity of the two figures.[13] It will not be forgotten, either, how close are the parallels between Christ's prophesied death and that of Merlin in the Lailoken story.

At long last we may see the meaning of contradictory elements in Merlin's makeup, alluded to but not explained in earlier chapters. We have seen Merlin as a Celtic Lord of the Beasts; Cernunnos the Horned One, dwelling in the recesses of the forest, animal and master of animals, guide of troubled souls reeling eternally through the sky in the Wild Hunt, Wild Man and deceitful sprite, child of a devil from Hell. But in his dual rôle as Trickster he is also an incarnation of the eternally bright and youthful god Lug, born of a virgin birth, master of all skills and crafts, prophet who foresees and supervises the sacred kingship, and doomed to expiate man's stricken plight by the ultimate self-sacrifice on the World-Tree. This dual nature (Merlin as Lug-Christ, and a Cernunnos-Satan) reflects the dual nature of deity. During his forty days shaman-like initiation in the wilderness, Christ was under the tutelage of the devil, Lord of the unformed, savage earth. It was this that he eventually spurned to emerge as Saviour of Mankind. In an earlier and simpler stage of development the two warring elements were frequently personified as distinct personalities, as in the story of Esau and Jacob. Esau was a true Wild Man, born 'all over like an hairy garment', 'a cunning hunter, a man of the field'. This legend tells how Esau with all his strength and cunning was no match for his brother Jacob, 'a plain man, dwelling in tents' (Genesis, xxv, 27). Eventually the brothers were reconciled, Jacob retaining the mastery through native subtlety and the fact that (through his father's blessing) he was the ordained of God.

Consideration of this theme may help to illuminate an important aspect of the Merlin legend. In the story of *Kentigern and Lailoken* we read of the curious relationship of the Saint and the frantic prophet who lives like a Wild Man in the woods. It is preserved in a manuscript (Cotton MS. Titus A. XIX) in the British Museum. Also in the same manuscript is to be found the preface and first eight chapters of a *Life of St Kentigern*, and it has been plausibly suggested that the Lailoken episode constitutes another surviving extract from the same work, which according to the preface was written by the anonymous author at the request of Herbert, Bishop of Glasgow (1147–64).[14]

The section of the Saint's *Life* treats of his conception and birth. His mother was the daughter of 'a certain King Leudonus, a man half pagan' (*Rex . . . Leudonus, vir semipaganus*). The girl was seduced against her will by a young prince, identified with the famous Northern hero Owain ab Urien. However the author is at pains to stress that, despite the fact that she became pregnant as a result of this incident, the assault took place in such a chancy manner that it must be held that she remained chaste and spiritually a virgin. When the King her father discovered her condition he became exceedingly angry, ordering her death and that of a swineherd in whose care she had been living. The girl miraculously escaped and gave birth to the infant Kentigern; while the swineherd managed to kill the King by lying in wait for him and transfixing him with a javelin through the back.

This story contains much that is archetypal in Celtic mythology. The explanation of the hero's birth reflects an earlier version in which he sprang from a virgin birth. This is a theme recurring elsewhere in Celtic saints' lives (for example, St David), and was probably (as was argued earlier) intended to supersede Virgin Birth tales popular among the pagan Celts. In this case one might suspect that a pagan myth has been adopted wholesale. The girl's father is not only described as 'half-pagan', but bears a name (*Leudonus*) which is an undoubted derivative of the name *Lleu*, i.e. the god Lug.[15]

Most likely the original story told of a hero born to a virgin by the god Lug. For the 'half-pagan' Leudonus dies precisely the death ascribed to Lleu in *Math vab Mathonwy*; an enemy catches him unawares and hurls a spear into his body. And, just as the death of Lug is similar in important respects to that of Merlin, so we find a common motif in the death of King Leudonus. The King's assassin is a swineherd, and it was the swineherd Mongan who treacherously drove his spear into the side of Suibhne Geilt, Merlin's Irish counterpart. One is reminded also of the shepherds who murder Lailoken.[16]

So much for the birth of Kentigern. We now turn to the other surviving fragment of the early *Life of St Kentigern*, the story of *Kentigern and Lailoken*. It opens with the words, 'during the period that St Kentigern used to go into the wilderness . . .', implying that this was his frequent practice. There he meets Lailoken ('some say he was Merlyn'), and was moved to tears by the plight of the madman, whom he terms his 'brother'. Lailoken trailed Kentigern like his shadow, continually interrupting services and prayers with his own wild prophecies. He was a man accursed, driven to 'keep company with the beasts of the wood', and possessed by 'an evil spirit' and 'the angels of Satan'. He repines bitterly at his condition, and pleads with Kentigern to be permitted to receive the Holy Sacrament. Kentigern consents and, weeping once more with compassion, receives Lailoken into the Church. Lailoken then dies the prophesied Threefold Death.

Implicit throughout the story is a deep bond of brotherhood linking the two disparate figures. Indeed, it is clear that Lailoken played a very important rôle in the Saint's life, for the author of the fragment mentions that there is 'much more than is written in this short book' concerning the relationship between the two men. Thus, as in the *Epic of Gilgamesh*, a brilliant hero, born to a divine parent, is the herald of civilised enlightenment in the region over which he presides.

He encounters a Wild Man from the untamed wilderness. After initial hostility the two cement a friendship, the creature of the wild being deeply drawn to the cultured life of the hero. But they are in reality two aspects of the same personality. Kentigern is the divinely-inspired being, harbinger of truth and culture. Lailoken represents the dark element in his unconscious, the 'beast' representative of man in his unredeemed former ape-like condition. It is, moreover, an apparently odd coincidence that St Kentigern was known by an epithet, 'dearest friend', which has virtually the same meaning as a name applied to Myrddin in *The Red Book of Hergest*. Is this not a further suggestion of the interplay between the two characters?[17]

Behind this lies more than a hint of a single, Manichaean figure, man and beast, Lug and Cernunnos, God and Devil, within whom rages the struggle for reconciliation between culture and barbarism, consciousness and unconsciousness. The 'beast' must be drawn out of the darkness of the unconscious (the wilderness) and made a partaker in the New Man.

Any investigation into the British Dark Ages must inevitably proceed from the scanty documentary sources (few of which are in their present form contemporary), to illustration and reconstruction by way of source criticism, analogy, and interpretation based on the vast array of scholarly discussion now available. Faced with a barrage of material from Akkadian to Norse, and appeal to academic disciplines as varied as comparative religion, Indo-European philology and depth psychology, both general reader and professional scholar may well be left with a strong residue of scepticism. The first may wonder whether the whole varied parade is not a delusive exercise in conjuration; mix up a colourful distillation of mythological and historical elements, stir and sift briskly; and as the mist clears from the seething surface – there, lo and behold, appears the fleshed-out figure of Merlin himself! The professional scholar asks the same question in a rather more precise way. Is it really possible to master such disparate materials with any degree of validity? And does the evidence in any case really bear up the superstructure of theory?

To the first objection I can only reply that, so far as is possible, I have avoided disagreement with any scholar in the context of his particular field, and where I have felt obliged to do so I have attempted always to set out the argument in full. My aim has been, so far as is practicable, to indicate to the reader where differences exist, so that he may distinguish between what is controversial and what is generally acceptable to scholars in their own field.

As to the second point, I will be surprised indeed if there are not many experts who will shake their heads gravely. What is Tolstoy about? Can he really expect us to believe that there existed in historical fact, a sixth-century heathen magician and prophet, in an age predominantly Christian, to whom large sections of the population looked for mantic wisdom and prophecy? Could so towering a figure really have flourished even in the darkness of the sixth century, whose very existence was doubted by the world of scholarship for generations? Is not the Merlin of mediaeval writers simply a picturesque concoction, reflecting the needs of their own age of insecurity rather than the realities of a remote past?

Behind this particular objection lies, I suspect, a little of what Sir John Morris-Jones termed the scepticism, 'which is too knowing to be taken in by the truth'. It stems from an instinctive disinclination to accept anything at its face value, particularly if that acceptance by chance reflect a popular conception. *Because* the story of Merlin is one that appeals strongly to romantics and investigative cranks, *therefore* it is to be rejected as one possessing any historical authenticity! One may detect the same process at work with regard to the legend of Arthur. Such a feeling, the more insidious for being largely unconscious, is as antagonistic in its own way to the search for historical truth as is the attitude which aroused it.

With such objections in mind, I have deliberately reserved what is perhaps the most significant piece of evidence of all to this late stage of the discussion. So far the evidence has been presented in a largely circumstantial manner. It was argued on the one hand that there exists no sound reason for rejecting the early mediaeval belief that an important prophet named Merlin flourished in North Britain in the sixth century A.D.; and on the other that so much of the practices and beliefs attributed to him reflects known shamanistic strains in Celtic paganism, that it is consistent and sensible to believe that the later accounts derive from an authentic historical tradition.

There does, however, exist one piece of *near-contemporary evidence* which goes as far as anything to prove the existence, if not of Merlin himself, then of a figure so similar as to validate the whole concept. Mention was made in an earlier chapter of the Latin *Life of St Samson*, a sixth-century Celtic saint who migrated from Wales to Cornwall, and from Cornwall to Brittany, where he established the Bishopric of Dol. The *Life* is generally accepted by Celtic scholars as being of exceptional historical value on account of its age and generally authentic background. According to the anonymous author's introduction, the information contained in it derived from a cousin of St Samson, who had in turn received material both from another cousin and from Samson's mother. Careful study of geographical and personal names included in the *Life* has led philologists to accept the attribution as authentic, concluding that the original document was presumably put together in the first quarter or first half of the seventh century.[18]

The *Life* begins with an account of Samson's birth, an account as has been seen ultimately deriving from his mother, Anna. Anna and her husband Amon lived in South Wales. Though by no means past the age of child-bearing, Anna was concerned at her failure to bear children (her sister had already borne three sons). What followed is best expressed in the words of the text:

'Now it came to pass that on a feast day they went together to church, and there, among the many people to be discussed, they heard a discussion concerning a certain *librarius* who lived in a remote land in the North, a man sought out from many regions because all who had consulted him were assured of the truth of all he told them. It happened that many in the congregation were themselves resolving to travel to him for a consultation, and so Amon, who heard what they said with great excitement, decided with Anna to travel with them to the same Master.'

There are two important points to be noted. The Latin word *librarius*, said to have been borne by the soothsayer, means 'scribe', or 'keeper of books'. But its Welsh derivative and equivalent, *llyfrawr*, means '*a magician, possessing the gift of prophecy*'.[19] The implication is presumably that it was in books he derived or recorded his knowledge. Secondly, 'a remote land in the North' (he was *quendam librarium uersus aquilonem longinquam terrem habitantem*) can hardly be referring to North Wales. That is unlikely to have been regarded as 'remote' from Dyfed or Gwent, and would in any case probably have been referred to as *Venedotia*, 'Gwynedd'. The reference must surely be to the land of the Northern Britons beyond Hadrian's Wall, known simply as *Y Gogledd*, 'the North'.

Moreover the journey was a long one:

'And it happened that, at the end of the third day when the fatigue of the journey was over, they reached the place where the Master, the *librarius*, had his abode, and there found the said Master sitting with many people and talking volubly about particular cases.'

Perhaps we should not take the 'three days' too precisely, and in any case it can provide no sure guide to distance. Roman posts averaged some fifty miles a day, but on one occasion the Emperor Tiberius travelled two hundred miles in twenty-four hours![20] The intention is clearly to show it was a long and arduous journey, though it is interesting to note that it could apparently be accomplished without difficulty by a troop of peaceful pilgrims at the end of the fifth century.

The prophet stopped his consultation to listen to the travel-stained couple's anguished plea. But before they could begin, he interrupted to say that he knew precisely why they had called. Demanding a silver rod 'of equal length to thy wife' as recompense, he promised that Anna's wish would be granted. Amon delightedly promised three rods, whereupon the prophet 'made them remain with him in the guest-chamber until they had given their poor bodies rest the following night after their exhausting journey'. That night Anna was vouchsafed a dream, in which she was assured by an angel that she would indeed bear a son, who would enjoy an honourable career. Next morning she and Amon were visited by the Master, who was already fully apprised of the nature of the dream, adding his own prophecy to the effect that 'of the British race there has not been or will be anyone like him, that is as a priest, who will do great good to many'. The couple returned home rejoicing, and in due course the prophecy was fulfilled.[21]

This passage is again of great interest. Anna's dream was not, as the plain description might suggest, a chance visitation. It is clear that it formed a vital part of the Master's prophetic ritual. The details follow a pattern familiar from Celtic and Norse literature, in which, significantly, such dreams were in early times frequently induced in special incubation chambers attached to temples.[22]

At the famous Romano-Celtic temple at Lydney in Gloucestershire, Sir Mortimer Wheeler discovered a narrow building, 183 feet long, consisting of about a dozen small rooms opening onto a verandah. A paved stone corridor passed before the doorways, but each room had an ornamented mosaic floor. Wheeler argued strongly that this building was an incubation dormitory, where those who came to consult the oracle slept when receiving prophetic guidance in the form of specially-induced dreams. A similar building has been found at the temple of Asklepios at Epidaurus in Greece. That building appears to be referred to by the Greek writer Pausanias, who says that 'beyond the temple is the place where the suppliants sleep'. Wheeler concluded that 'it may be that the Long Building was used perhaps to supplement the "chapels" in the temple itself for the purpose of that temple-sleep through which the healing-god and his priesthood were wont to work.'[23]

It seems most likely therefore that the Master whom Anna and Amon visited resided in a temple which possessed a similar resting-place. The whole account is entirely fascinating, when we recall that much of the information in St Samson's *Life* is credibly claimed to have derived from his mother Anna. The visit to the Northern Master is of all sections the most likely to have rested directly on her testimony, and her understandable excitement and relief do in fact seem to ring through the rather stilted prose of the hagiographer.

To recapitulate: in the *Life of St Samson* we possess what is most likely to be a first-hand account of a pilgrimage to a professional soothsayer in the early Dark Ages, whose prophecies were held to be exceptionally accurate. He was no figure of local importance, but one whose fame was so widespread that people from many provinces undertook long and arduous journeys in order to consult him. If, as seems likely, his temple was somewhere in *Y Gogledd*, then Samson's parents travelled some two or three hundred miles for their consultation. It is clear from this and the trend of the discussion which first drew their attention to him, that he enjoyed unique prestige – possibly in the whole of Britain.

The relevance of this historical figure to Merlin is obvious. The chronology would not on the face of it permit us to regard the *librarius* as Merlin himself, tempting though that would be. St Samson attended the Council of Paris soon after the middle of the sixth century, so that his birth must be relegated to the beginning of the century.[24] Merlin, on the other hand, is said to have become 'inspired' after the Battle of Arderydd in 573.

In every other respect, however, the similarity is remarkable. Welsh literary and historical tradition knew of Merlin as the great prophet of the British race, dwelling in the North (*Y Gogledd*) in the second half of the sixth century. From *The Life of St Samson* we learn from what appears to be very sound authority that in the same century and the same region lived a prophet fulfilling an identical rôle. On this basis it would be hard to think of any very pressing reason for rejecting the authenticity of the Welsh tradition, known as it is to preserve many exceedingly archaic strands. In particular, it would explain the reference in the triads which tells how Britain was once known as 'Merlin's Precinct' (*clas Merddin*). It also suggests that there is no reason to reject the authenticity of the verse in the sixth-century epic poem *Gododdin*, which tells how a warrior 'defended the muse of Merlin'.

The *librarius* of *The Life of St Samson* is clearly an early Welsh *llyfrawr*, or prophet-magician. It is interesting in this context to note a comparison between these *llyfyrion* (plural) and the divine sorcerers Lleu (Lug) and Gwydion which occurs in a line in *The Book of Taliesin*;

'neu leu agბydyon a uuant geluydyon neu awdant lyfyryon'

'Do Lleu and Gwydion [who were skilful wizards] know, or do *llyfyrion* know, what they will do when night and storm come?'

Reasons were given earlier for connecting Merlin with the god Lleu (Lug) and his uncle, the enchanter Gwydion. I have suggested that Merlin was regarded as the incarnation or avatar of Lleu, and the implication of the line quoted is surely that the *llyfyrion* were indeed looked upon as the earthly counterparts of the divine enchanters with whom they are classed.

I contend that it is far simpler to envisage Merlin as an historical prophet of the sixth century, than to suppose him an illusory figure arising from ingenious forgery or chance speculation. The *librarius* visited by St Samson's parents was doubtless his predecessor, since it seems likely that Merlin was heir to an extraordinarily ancient tradition. Behind him in a misty past one may glimpse the hierarchy of the druids, and behind that lie shamanist cults of the Upper Palaeolithic, extending twenty and thirty millennia into the darkness. Nor is that the beginning, though in truth it seems there is neither beginning nor end, but a Mystery. In the words of the scholar Heinrich Zimmer:

> 'What is the world to the forest? What is conscious to unconscious? That is a question only Merlin can ask, which only he can answer. What is history, in space and time, to the abyss? . . . The answer is that he allows the forest, the abyss, to swallow him back, and he becomes again the magic wood and all its trees . . .'[25]

It can now be seen, I hope, that Merlin's withdrawal to the forest is not only to be explained in mythological terms but, like the Crucifixion, was also an event rooted in historical time. The unravelling of the evidence made the laborious reconstruction comprising the major portion of this book unavoidable. Only in this way can the reader judge the material for himself, understanding the nature of the evidence. This done, I propose now to set out the results of this enquiry in a reconstructed narrative form.

The collapse of Roman authority in Britain at the beginning of the fifth century A.D. probably had little direct effect on the extreme northern region of the province. This was the area between Hadrian's Wall and the River Forth, known as *Y Gogledd*, 'the North'. There the major tribes had made only nominal acknowledgement of Roman suzerainty. Over a century later they were still in large part pagan, the heirs of the powerful tribe of the Selgovae inhabiting the mountainous wilderness of the central Lowlands being particularly resistant to the gathering influence of Christianity.

Somewhere in this area flourished the celebrated *llyfrawr*, the prophet consulted by St Samson's parents from far-off Dyfed about the year 500. He was one of a line of great prophetic figures, possibly a Chief Druid, of whom Myrddin was his most celebrated successor and perhaps descendant, if the office was hereditary. The *llyfrawr*, so we are told, was consulted by multitudes of people from all over Britain at what was clearly a major temple.

This temple is possibly to be identified with the *locus maponi* of the Ravenna Cosmography, which it is now agreed was situated at Lochmaben in Dumfriesshire. Of the *loci* listed in the Ravenna Cosmography, it was the one most accessible to the Roman civil province, being situated on a major Roman road crossing from Lockerbie to Nithsdale. Five dedications on Roman altar-stones bearing dedications to the god Maponos have been discovered in Northern Britain, from which it is clear that his cult bore particular appeal to military officers of high rank.[26] It was just such a Northern shrine whose fame might have reached South Wales in the way described in the *Life of St Samson*, particularly as Maponos, a Celtic Apollo, was strongly associated with the idea of healing.[27] It may well be that the temple of Maponos was regarded as particularly efficacious in cases of barrenness among women, since the god Maponos was himself the product of a virgin birth.

It has been suggested earlier in this book that Merlin was closely associated with the god Lug (Lleu, in Welsh). Like Lug, he was reputed to have been conceived of a virgin; like Lug he was a Trickster; and like Lug he died the Threefold Death. This might seem to preclude any connection with the shrine of Maponos, but there is reason to believe that Maponos is simply an attributive name for Lug.

Maponos was clearly a god of considerable importance. To educated Romans he bore the charisma and many of the attributes of the great god Apollo. Yet, beyond some scanty traces of his cult in Gaul, remarkably little is known about him. In Welsh tradition he is known as Mabon son of Modron; *i.e.* Maponos son of Matrona, which means 'Son, son of Mother'. Another Mabon is called Mabon son of Mellt, the latter name probably signifying 'lightning'. The reference is clearly to a deity conceived by a virgin birth, Matrona being the Mother Goddess. If, as seems likely, the two Mabons of Welsh literature are to be identified, then *Mellt* probably suggests an aspect of the Celtic Sky-god. In the *Mabinogi* tale of *Culhwch and Olwen* a few further curious details are added: Mabon was possibly celebrated as a great huntsman; he was as old as the oldest creatures on earth – *i.e.* immortal; and he was taken from his mother when three days old to be imprisoned in a fortress beyond the waters, from which he was rescued by Arthur and his warriors.[28]

Like Maponos, Lug was born of a virgin and was pre-eminently associated with the arts of poetry and music – as is Maponos in altar dedications. Remarkable parallels have already been drawn between the birth- and death-tales of Lug and Christ, and Mabon is actually equated with Christ in a poem in *The Book of Taliesin*, where the Magi are described as arriving before the infant Mabon at Bethlehem. Finally, in the Welsh 'Stanzas of the Graves', Mabon and Lug appear to be directly identified:

> 'The grave on Nantlle's height,
> no one knows its attributes, –
> Mabon son of Mydron the swift.'

For *Nantlle* preserves the Welsh name of Lug, *Lleu*, and is the place named in the story of *Math vab Mathonwy* where Lleu was discovered hanging from the Tree of Life.[29]

It seems certain that, if the myths of Lleu (Lug) and Mabon were not identical, they were at least so similar as to invite confusion. The former suggestion appears the most likely. The names *Mabon*, 'son', and *Modron*, 'mother' strongly suggest honorific epithets rather than the true names of deities, perhaps a descriptive name for one whose real name might not be uttered.[30] There may have been some local reason for this particular mode of reverence. Certainly this explanation best suits the fact that Lug, born of a virginal conception, was commemorated by name all over the Celtic world, whilst a separate cult in North Britain sustained important yet local worship of the unnamed Son, son of Mother. In precisely the same way Christ came to be revered both by his own name and as Son of the Father, born of a Virgin. From this analogy we might expect the cult of Maponos to be a particularly devout expression of that of Lug, rather than a divergent conception, and this is indeed what the evidence suggests.

Loch*maben* and the Cloch*maben*stane, a huge granite boulder by the Solway at Gretna, testify to the cult of Mabon in southern Dumfriesshire. This is part of the region known in the early Dark Ages as Rheged, ruled by the famous Urien and his son Owain. Allusions in an early poem in *The Book of Taliesin* suggest that Mabon was regarded as the tutelary deity of the region, and there is mention of 'the land of Mabon' (*G ó latvabon*) which seems to be identified with Rheged.

At the same time it is precisely the same locality which the *Life of St Kentigern* informs us was known as 'Leudonia', which in mediaeval Welsh appears as 'lleudinyawn'.[31] The most likely interpretation of the name is 'land of the stronghold of the god Lleu', but it is at least certain (as was noted earlier) that it is a territorial name containing the element *Lleu*. Thus one and the same region appears to have borne the name of Lleu, and to have been regarded as coming under the special protection of Mabon, 'the Son'.

There also exists evidence that the dynasty ruling over the Solway basin in the late sixth century regarded itself as enjoying a special relationship with the god Lleu-Mabon. It has been concluded that 'an early offshoot from the heroic tradition of Urien Rheged and his son Owain could have been the attribution to Urien of a myth which depicted him as mating with the locally-worshipped goddess *Modron*, and which depicted his son Owain as a fruit of their union.' At the same time, a subsidiary genealogical tradition interpolated into Urien's pedigree the name of the god Lleu as his brother, which again suggests that traditions of Mabon and Lleu were so interchangeable as to make it reasonable to assume that they are identical.[32]

Persuasive arguments have been made to suggest that the sacred place of Maponos, the *Locus Maponi* of the Ravenna Cosmography, is to be identified with the promontory of Loch Maben on which stood Lochmaben Castle; and that it was here that the tale of the virgin birth was preserved. A bank and ditch, seemingly older than the mediaeval remains, is believed to be the surviving enclosure of the *temenos* of the god.[33]

Drawing the evidence together we find:

1. The existence in Roman times of an important site sacred to the Virgin-conceived god Maponos, north of Hadrian's Wall. This is to be identified with Lochmaben, as is Maponos with Lug-Lleu.
2. From the *Life of St Samson* we learn that about the year A.D. 500 there was a famous temple in the North of Britain. A miraculous birth results from the visit of the Saint's parents.
3. Later, the king (Owain) of this very region is credited with being the offspring of a union between his mortal father (Urien) and the Mother of Mabon, the goddess Modron, and the myths of Lleu's miraculous birth and sacrificial death become attached to the figure of the local saint Kentigern.

All this seems to point to the survival into the late sixth century A.D. of a temple at Lochmaben, at which were upheld the cult and ritual of the god Lug-Lleu, son of a virgin Mother-Goddess. To it resorted devotees from all over Britain, in search (as the *Life of St Samson* states) of healing and prophecy, practised by temple 'priests' whom it is not unreasonable to suppose were still termed druids.

The relationship of the dynasty represented by Urien and his son Owain to the god Mabon and his mother Modron strongly suggests a cult of divine kingship, such as was universal in Celtic and indeed virtually all other early societies. In early Ireland the inauguration of a king took the form of the symbolic mating of the new king with the local Earth-Goddess, the most celebrated of these royal fertility rites being the Feast of Tara (*Feis Temro*), which was originally a ritual marriage between the new king of Tara and the goddess Medb. The last Feast of Tara was held by King Diarmait mac Cerbaill as late as A.D. 560. King Diarmait's contemporary in North Britain, Urien Rheged, lived in a society no more Christian, and there can be nothing incongruous in the idea of similar ritual taking place in the *temenos* at Lochmaben.[34]

A significant aspect of these 'coronations' (as I showed in an earlier chapter) was a prophecy uttered by the Chief Druid, in which he set out the coming succession of kings. No more suitable exponent for this rôle could be imagined than the *llyfrawr*, whom the *Life of St Samson* describes as presiding over the temple. Equally appropriate, of course, is the prophet *par excellence*, Myrddin son of Morfryn.

In the poem *Cyfoesi Myrddin a Gwenddydd ei Chwaer*, ('The Conversation of Myrddin and Gwenddydd his Sister'), Myrddin is represented as foretelling the coming order of kings in the form of successive replies to queries put by his sister Gwenddydd. In its existing form the poem is perhaps to be dated to the tenth, eleventh or an even later century, and its purpose is clearly to legitimise and exalt the claims of the dynasty of Hywel Dda, a great tenth-century Welsh king named in the poem. Myrddin is represented as expounding in prophetic form the succession of the dynasty from his own time to that of Hywel and beyond. The accuracy of the list is borne out by an early court pedigree tracing Hywel's family back to Maelgwn Gwynedd, a great sixth-century king of North Wales, whom the composer of the poem would have known to be roughly contemporary with Myrddin.[35]

Here one might have expected the prophecy to commence, but

in fact the beginning of the poem is concerned not only with the familiar story of the disastrous death of Gwenddoleu at Arderydd and the subsequent triumph of Myrddin's enemy Rhydderch, but also the succession of a Morgan the Great, son of Sadwrnin, who was to be followed by Urien Rheged. No Morgan ab Sadwrnin appears in the pedigrees, but he is perhaps to be identified with a King Morken who persecuted St Kentigern, and who could there-fore have played a part in the original Myrddin saga. But what are these Northern British princes doing at the head of a pedigree of North Walian kings? The composer of the *Cyfoesi* was familiar with the genealogical material, and must have been quite aware who were the real predecessors of Maelgwn Gwynedd, and that Rhydderch, Gwenddoleu, Morgan and Urien were all more or less his *contemporaries*.

The most likely explanation of this awkwardness is that the genealogical account of Maelgwn and his descendants was tagged on to distinct material dealing with events in the sixth-century North. It is therefore likely that the first section of the *Cyfoesi* represents a reversifying of a genuine sixth-century prophecy, in which the succession of kings in south-western Scotland was fore-told. I have already touched on this question in an earlier chapter, where I noted the marked parallel between the format of the *Cyfoesi* and the early Irish tale of the *Baile in Scáil*, 'the Phantom's Frenzy'. In the latter, King Conn enters an Otherworld building where he encounters a *Scál* of wonderful appearance, together with a maiden. The *Scál* then prophesies the succession of kings to rule in Tara after Conn in the form found in the *Cyfoesi*: as a series of questions and answers between himself and the maiden. More than this, the *Scál* reveals himself to be the god Lug, while the maiden 'was the sovereignty of Erinn for ever', that is, the Mother Goddess of the kingdom whom the king must ritually wed at his inauguration.

We may believe either that there existed mediaeval Welsh forgers of astonishing capacity and resource; or that the Welsh tradition, like the Irish, preserved fragments of pagan lore whose traditional authority was employed to further political interests in later ages. The latter proposition, in view of all the evidence, appears rather more likely.

It may tentatively be suggested that the first part of the dialogue between Myrddin and Gwenddydd preserved in the *Cyfoesi* is based on an incantation recited at the inauguration of a sixth-century North-British prince. Myrddin, personifying the god Lleu (Lug), prophesies the future succession in a ritual exchange with the Mother Goddess Modron (Matrona). Was she personified by a priestess, Gwenddydd, who was in reality or by virtue of her office Myrddin's 'sister'? One may venture an alternative suggestion. Welsh tradition records that Gwenddydd was also the name of the Morning Star, the planet Venus. Among the Norsemen Venus was known as Frigg's Star, just as the Latin *dies Veneris* ('Venus's day') became *Frigedaeg*, Friday. Frigg was the wife of Odin, who himself was regularly compared with the Roman god Mercury, and it was Mercury too with whom Roman authors identified the Celtic god Lug. Now, it is noteworthy that among Asiatic peoples the planet Venus excites unique reverence as the shaman's source of prophetic inspiration, even being credited with originating the power to shamanise. Representations of Venus are regularly depicted on shamans' drums.[36]

In Geoffrey of Monmouth's *Vita Merlini*, Merlin requests his sister to construct for him an observatory with seventy windows and doors:

> 'through which I may see fire-breathing Phoebus (the sun) with Venus, and watch by night the stars wheeling in the firmament; and they will teach me about the future of the nation.'[37]

Scant reliance can be placed upon a literal interpretation of Geoffrey's text; yet there is something curious about the fact that it is his sister who erects the astrological observatory, and who eventually joins him there as a prophetess. There is a temptation to suppose that, at the sacred marriage of king and country, Myrddin invokes the Mother Goddess, identified as Venus, the brightest star in the firmament, and incarnated as a prophetess. By her inspiration he was able to utter the prophecy which assured the king of a fruitful reign, and guaranteed the due succession of his heirs. It is a moving sensation to stand today in the enclosure of the sanctuary, gazing on the still waters of Loch Maben as they reflect the glittering Morning Star, and reflect on the possibility of solemn ceremonies taking place there fourteen centuries ago and more.

It has been suggested that, if Lochmaben was the *temenos* of the god Maponos, then the Clochmabenstane was his *fanum*. If so, informed conjecture might locate there *ludi* or sacred games associated with the Feast of Lug at the beginning of August. It was about the time of Myrddin's prophesying that St Samson witnessed the rites taking place in Cornwall. There was formerly a stone circle around the solitary boulder which gives the Clochmabenstane its name,[38] and one could not imagine a more appropriate setting for the veneration of the eternally youthful god.

Myrddin may have been the *llyfrawr* in residence at the temple of Lleu or Mabon at Lochmaben. He was the heir to a very ancient tradition, and his functions can now be described with some precision. He was prophet and healer, Chief Druid presiding over the inauguration of kings. An indistinct memory of this last rôle is perhaps reflected in the significant part he was later accorded in the accession of King Arthur. He it was who supplied the sword in the stone, a magical test of fitness for sovereignty, and it was he who presided over the king's coronation.

Himself born of a virgin and destined to die the Threefold Death, Merlin was an incarnation or avatar of the divine Lleu. He bore the epithet *Embreis*, one of obscure significance borne also by the greatest of all megalithic temples at Stonehenge. He presided over official auguries, and the holy games of Lleu by the shores of Solway. In an increasingly Christian land the age-old rites maintained their sway, and the temple at Lochmaben was resorted to by devotees from far and wide. He was a man of wealth and power, coming under the special protection of King Gwenddolau ab Ceidio, whose fortress by the Esk gazed over the mouth of Solway and guarded the sacred stones of the Clochmabenstane.

Then came the dynastic crisis culminating in the great slaughter of Arderydd and the death of Gwenddolau. Rhydderch Hael, 'defender of the faith', now dominated the Western Lowlands and the old faith was subjected to rigorous exclusion from open practice. According to the twelfth-century *Life of St Kentigern* by Joceline of Furness, the Saint had been obliged by the arrant paganism of a contemporary King Morken (possibly the Morgan the Great of Myrddin's prophecy) to take himself off into exile abroad. Now the Christian Rhydderch invited him to return and assist in establishing the faith. Kentigern returned, founding a see first at Hoddom and afterwards at Glasgow.[39]. Hoddom is a mere eight miles south-east of Lochmaben, and one may suspect therefore that the purpose of its foundation was to overawe and eclipse the rival pagan temple at Lochmaben.

The transition from paganism to Christianity was probably eased by common traditions underlying both creeds. The myth of Lleu was very close to that of Christ, as has been seen, and Christ and Mabon are actually equated in a poem in *The Book of Taliesin*.[40] The myth of Lleu, preserved by the priesthood at Lochmaben, became absorbed into that of Christ. In the *Lives* of Kentigern we find a full-blown retelling of Lleu's death-tale, and an appropriation of the Virgin Birth. The latter story was to cause great offence to the pious in later generations, who instinctively recognised its pagan character and deemed it 'perverse and opposed to the faith.'[41] In the same way Kentigern was credited with the magical powers of Lleu's chief druid: like Myrddin, he held mastery over stags and other wild beasts, and 'delivered a prophecy concerning the Britons and the Angles so true that it bore witness to the faith before all England.'

How far this confusion represents a conscious attempt by the Church to win over those of the older faith, or the result of a popular or literary admixture of traditions in the sixth or succeeding centuries, is impossible now to detect. At the time we may suspect that there were elements both of compromise and hostility. Joceline describes Kentigern converting the heathen in multitudes at Hoddom, at the same time repelling large numbers of recalcitrants who dashed off at speed in the shape of horrible and gigantic phantoms. This may derive from a lingering tradition of an historical clash between the rival temples at Hoddom and Lochmaben, or may equally be sententious hagiographical convention.

In the case of Myrddin we may conjecture that he departed up the Annan in sorrow and anger, to take up his refuge on the slopes of the sacred mountain of Hart Fell in the heart of the Caledonian Forest. No more the companion and mentor of kings, the mantic 'call' came upon him. He vanished into the forest depths, returning in wild but impressive guise as an inspired prophet, the greatest of *awenyddion*. He has fallen from the state of conscious man, represented by the god of light and culture Lleu, back to the older sphere of the unconscious, the world of nature, of the forest and the wild animals. Now he is close to Cernunnos, Lord of the Animals and Leader of the Wild Hunt. At the same time, as eternal Trickster he straddles both worlds; swooping from a time when man was one in his instinctive responses with the beasts, on to the full glory of consciousness, when God reveals himself to man in the form of his Divine Son, and then back again.

According to the Myrddin legend he lived in dread of the men of Rhydderch. There may have been good reason for this, as there is a suggestion that the seer for a time at least attempted to avenge the death of Gwenddolau at Arderydd. The Welsh poem *Peiryan Vaban* is one of the small corpus attributed to Myrddin. It is preserved only in a unique manuscript of the first half of the fifteenth century, together with copies of the other more celebrated Myrddin poetry. It bears one marked distinction from the other poetry, in that it appears to refer only to persons and issues (in so far as they are identifiable) of Myrddin's own time.

The language and allusions of *Peiryan Vaban* are obscure, but its overall theme is clear: *Peiryan Vaban*, which could mean 'commanding Youth', is a figure invoked by Myrddin in verses breathing real passion and purpose. Aedan mac Gabran, King of Dalriada (the Scots settlement in Argyllshire), is on his way with an army to make war on Rhydderch. Once Myrddin dwelt in a king's hall, clad in fine robes, but now the land is filled with the threat of war. Soon there will be a dreadful battle, and Gwenddolau will be avenged. Gwenddydd has lent inspiration to Myrddin's prophetic voice, and the *Peiryan Vaban* is assured of triumph after sorrow.[42]

There are intimations that the poem represents a reworking of a genuine sixth-century effusion. Outside the context of that time it has neither relevance nor meaning. It is full of a vivid urgency, concerned with events imminent but whose outcome is as yet unknown. The conflict between Aedan and Rhydderch to which it alludes it also attested in independent Welsh tradition. One of the triads tells how Aedan came to Rhydderch's court at Alclut (Dumbarton), laying it waste. If this is an allusion to the conflict anticipated in *Peiryan Vaban*, the latter knows nothing of it; all hangs still in the balance.

With its combination of prophecy and exhortation, *Peiryan Vaban* looks very like a prototype on which subsequent prophecies (such as *Armes Prydein*) were modelled and attributed to Myrddin. We may suppose, then, that an earlier version of the poem was composed in or after the year 573. After the disaster of Arderydd, Myrddin incited the remaining great power of the region to intervene. As Aedan succeeded to the throne of Dalriada the year after Arderydd, and as Rhydderch is known to have appealed in the midst of pressing dangers to the apostle and bishop of Dalriada, St Columba, other likely speculations might be made concerning the political background.

There is one suggestive element in the poem *Peiryan Vaban* worth glancing at here. Who exactly was this titular figure, to whom Myrddin addresses the whole programme of intervention, and whom he assures the period of sorrow is over and a time of sweet repose on its way? *Maban* means 'youth' or 'boy', and is cognate with the name of the youthful god Mabon.[43] It is hard to see why

Myrddin should have addressed his exhortations to an anonymous if sympathetic teenager, but nothing could be more appropriate than an invocation to the god Mabon. His fame and faith might be slighted by the Christian Rhydderch, but vengeance was on its way, borne by the fleet and army of Dalriada!

One must of course avoid any attempt to reconstruct a precise chronological history from materials which, after all, comprise only the tantalising detritus of full-blown saga. In the case of a poem like *Peiryan Vaban*, as also with the *Cyfoesi*, *Hoianau*, *Afallennau* and *Cad Goddeu* (poems which, I have argued, bear direct relevance to the original Myrddin-story), language and metre have been so altered or recast as to remove any satisfactory means of dating the original composition.[44] On the other hand it is hard to see what relevance the contents of *Peiryan Vaban* could have had to the bards who recited it or the copyists who later committed it to writing, except as a piece believed to be a genuine effusion of the great sixth-century proto-prophet. Equally, it is difficult to picture a poet in a later age possessed of both the skill and the incentive to concoct a poem which so breathes an atmosphere of contemporary crisis, and which at the same time leaves the hearer or reader in total suspense as to the outcome. What would be the point of a retrospective concoction of this sort? It might be suggested that it was composed in imitation of earlier pieces; but that would introduce an unnecessary complication, it being simpler to suppose that *Peiryan Vaban* itself reflects one of those earlier pieces. In general, as the rest of the Myrddin poetry testifies, later reciters could not resist the temptation of adding verses or allusions applicable to events of their own day. In short, however far one carries back the composition of pseudo-prophecies, there must once have been an initial reason for wishing to attribute them to a prophet named Myrddin. The most likely reason is the prior existence of a surviving body of genuine vaticinatory material.

The Myrddin legend preserved in the Welsh poetry tells a consistent story of the exiled prophet's fear and hatred for Rhydderch Hael. Since the battle of Arderydd he has been compelled to live in the Caledonian Forest, suffering all the privations of life in the untamed wilderness while Rhydderch feasts in his brightly-lit hall. It may be that this aspect of Myrddin's exile arose in part from a misunderstanding of his plight, and that 'the call of the wild' had more to do with circumstances of mantic inspiration than with simple flight and exile. The verses in the *Afallenau* containing the most explicit references to Myrddin's plight suggest at first sight that the exile is pictured as hunted or thinking himself hunted by Rhydderch and his followers. But the lines:

'Sweet-apple tree which grows in a glade,
Its peculiar power hides it from the men of Rhydderch;
A crowd by its trunk, a host around it,
It would be a treasure for them, brave men in their ranks'

suggest rather that there is a mystery in the Forest, centred on the apple-tree, whose secret Rhydderch will be unable to penetrate. And it is a magical power, rather than the inaccessibility of Myrddin's sylvan retreat, which prevents the King's men from achieving their purpose.

Both Geoffrey of Monmouth's *Vita Merlini* and the Kentigern legend suggest an ambivalent relationship between woodland Prophet on the one hand, and King and Saint on the other. In the *Vita Merlini* Rhydderch makes every effort to entice Merlin into residing at his court, and is anxious to take advantage of his prophetic powers. According to the *Life of St Kentigern* by Joceline, the seer actually took up residence as a member of the royal household, and both in that source in the Lailoken fragments (excerpted from an earlier *Life* of the Saint) stress is laid on the accuracy of his prophecies.

Pure conjecture might suggest that Kentigern's church at Hoddom absorbed much of the reverence and prestige previously accorded to the pagan temple at Lochmaben. This would certainly account for the intrusion of the myth of Lleu into the subsequent birth-tale of Kentigern. One recalls Pope Gregory's advice to St Augustine a few years later, in which he advised the Bishop to convert the heathen English gently and by degrees. In particular he urged that pagan temples be converted to churches, the idols within alone being destroyed. The Pope stressed that pagan practices should be adapted to Christian usage:

'so that, changing their hearts, they should lay aside one part of the sacrifice while retaining another. Whilst offering the same beasts they sacrificed before, they now sacrificed them to God instead of idols, which would make them no longer the same sacrifices.'[45]

How much more efficacious would have been this sensible approach in the case of Kentigern at Hoddom! For he was himself a North Briton, doubtless familiar from childhood with the cherished pagan myth which bore such startling resemblance to that of the White Christ. It was Merlin who seceded, in part at least, from the cult of Mabon to that of Cernunnos. And the horned god of the wilderness approached nearly to the Christian conception of the Devil; not only from his attributes of horns and hairy pelt and from his domicile in the wilderness, but also in his older and deeper guise as Lord of the Forest and the Beasts; guardian of man's spirit in his pre-conscious state, when he was still one with natural creation. But in truth Merlin was Cernunnos *and* Lleu, Devil *and* Christ. The harsh laugh heard in the thickets of the *Coed Celyddon* is that of the Trickster, a being whose nature encompasses both the flesh and the spirit breathed into it . . .

'As for creation, I was created from nine forms of elements:
From the fruit of fruits, from the fruit of God at the beginning,
From primroses and flowers of the hill, from the blooms of
   woods and trees;
From the essence of soils was I made . . .
Druids, wise one, prophesy to Arthur;
There is what is before, they perceive what has been.
And one occurs in the story of the Flood
And Christ's crucifying and then Doomsday . . .'

Epilogue

The Oracle and the Source

'Sing, Heav'nly Muse, that on the Secret top
Of *Oreb*, or of *Sinai*, didst inspire
That Shepherd, who first taught the chosen Seed
In the Beginning, how the Heav'ns and Earth
Rose out of Chaos . . .'

(Milton, *Paradise Lost*)

As befits his rôle as archetypal Trickster, Merlin remains an enigma.

He was, I have argued, a genuine prophet whose oracle lay at a sacred spring on that Mountain-Centre, from whose skirts flowed the great rivers of the North. A glimpse of his unhappy story is detectable among all the accretions of the later poetry attributed to him. It seems likely that his prophecies concerned the tribulations and ultimate triumph of the British nation, and the coming succession of kings on whose divine fitness to rule that destiny depended. Such a figure may be presumed to have lived and died in the second half of the sixth century A.D.

Then, too, there was another Merlin; a figure who transcends the centuries; who in the *Vita Merlini* boasts that he is as old as the most venerable oak in the Caledonian Forest, and that:

'I was taken out of my true self, I was as a spirit and knew the history of people long past and could foretell the future. I knew then the secrets of nature, bird flight, star wanderings and the way fish glide.'

This was the Merlin who incarnated the Lord of the Animals, Shepherd (*heussawr*) of the wild creatures and of untamed matter; dark spirit of the earth, before God transfused it with his presence. But Merlin incarnates that presence, too. He is Lug, the brightness which brings dawning self-awareness, culture and the approximation of man to God. And ultimately he dies the sacrificial death of Lug, the ultimate self-sacrifice of God who suffers vicariously, redeeming the plight of man created in His image.

The figure of Merlin has fascinated successive generations for nine centuries and more. As each layer is peeled away, the Trickster peers out at us in new disguise. The secret is well-guarded, and it is unlikely we will ever know the true Merlin in all his complexity, but it is not possible to conclude a study of the myth without at least an attempt to assess its larger significance. If Christ is God reaching out to man, then we may see in Merlin the reflected image of man raising his consciousness to cosmic awareness. A mystery is not to be properly revealed in terms of factual research, but a general picture can be attempted in the light of all that has gone before.

The character of Merlin in the mediaeval Grail-romances is in many ways surprisingly consistent with what is indicated more allusively in the older Celtic sources. Whether this is because it derives ultimately from authentic tradition, or because archetypal verities repeat themselves in poetry, there is no means of knowing. It is a powerful image.

Merlin is the patron of writing, a gift which bears in itself a power of enchantment. For writing is both preserver and destroyer of traditional lore. Existence is circumscribed by the art in time and space. He legitimises genealogies, is historian and guardian of literature, and sets bounds to history; just as his magical etchings scattered around the Kingdom of Logres establish its geographical boundaries. The Welsh word for a wizard, *llyfrawr*, derives from the Latin *librarius*; and Merlin's omniscience, enshrined in his books of enchantment, accords him a power of control over all that is said and done in Britain. It is useless to attempt to evade his power, as he warns repeatedly, since his omniscience ensures that all lies within his compass. As poet, Merlin records the history in which he plays his part, whilst as prophet he stands boldly outside history, an anomaly epitomised by the fact that, whilst it is he who legitimises kings by revelation of their genealogies, he himself is fatherless, possessing no genealogy. As embodiment of a literature which encompasses the human experience, he is to humanity what the author is to a book. Ultimately he is ensnared by his own art, for it is through the repetition of his own formulaic charm that Viviane is empowered to imprison him in the enchanted chamber.

Merlin's gifts enable man to see himself. When he enters the story, it is by *naming* himself to Vortigern's messengers that the Wise Child germinates that succession of events which was to become the Matter of Britain. By making history coterminous with genealogy, he placed man in the succession of linear time. At the same time, a purpose of genealogy is to engross mankind in a perpetual cyclical 'return to the beginnings'.

Order and purpose are brought to the land through the power of language, the recorded word. Literature provides a continual reaffirmation of society's central values, together with the capacity for engineering and controlling change. Recorded change is the essence of history, and it is the coming of history which is the watershed between the conscious existence of cultured man, and the unconsciousness of his primitive predecessors' elemental existence.

It was Merlin who presided over order and purpose in human society. He assisted Uther Pendragon to re-establish the monarchy; provided the magical test of fitness which proved Arthur his legitimate successor; founded the Order of the Table Round which resolved disharmony among the nobles; and instituted the Quest of the Holy Grail, which brought an ennobling purpose to society.

At the same time it is Merlin who, time and again, warns of the dire consequences of any rupture of the magical forms and processes binding the community in common purpose;

> 'To us will be years and long days
> With false kings and withering fruit-crops',

he foretells ominously in the Welsh poem *Hoianau*. It is the false kings who will *cause* the failure of crops, since the rupture in dynastic legitimacy is a signal of the break-up of society. The alternative to the legitimate order is disorder, barrenness and chaos. Everything reverts to its pre-cultured state, and the moral and physical landscapes become the Waste Land of the Arthurian romances.[1]

Merlin, then, is the guardian of culture and civilised order, of poetry and kingship, of writing and genealogy. It is in this capacity that he frequently utters prophetic warnings of the consequences of any abrogation of the harmony of the social structure. More than this, as Guardian of Beasts, he also presides over the Waste Land itself. In Robert de Boron's *Merlin*, the wizard appears among civilised men without warning to counsel or admonish, and then reverts as suddenly to his wilderness retreat. It is this behaviour which characterises Merlin as the archetypal Trickster. With a foot in each camp, Merlin stands at the focal point of culture and nature, of consciousness and unconsciousness, of God and man. He spans the ages before and after the Creation, and to understand his real significance it is necessary to consider the deeper implications of that pre-historical Beginning.

Jung, in *Answer to Job*, suggested that the purpose of the Creation was 'an objectivisation of God'. This came about because in no other way could God fulfil Himself satisfactorily;

> 'Loudly as his power resounds through the universe, the basis of his existence is correspondingly slender, for it needs conscious reflection in order to exist in reality. Existence is only real when it is conscious to somebody. That is why the Creator needs conscious man . . .'

Furthermore, since love (and related emotions of aesthetic rapture) is the most sublime and least explicable factor in the human psyche, we may suppose that the creation of conscious man arose from God's desire to love and be loved. Or, as Blake put it, eternity is in love with the productions of time because eternity of itself can produce nothing. Time in turn, while creating its wonderful work of highest beauty, longs to return to rest in eternity.[2]

The necessity for divinity to be expressed in humanity and the subsequent need for man in turn to differentiate himself from unconscious creation impressed an indelible imprint on the human psyche. A 'memory' of this process of emergence from unconsciousness is preserved in dreams experienced by every individual in every generation, whose purpose is therapeutic and serves to stabilise the fretful wakenings of the psyche by reminders of the 'beginnings'.[3] As has been seen, primitive mythology undertakes the same healing process through representation of a figure personifying the original transformation. In the words of the anthropologist Paul Radin,

> 'Why should a deity wish to bring culture to mankind? I think the answer must be that if he does so, this is not his primary purpose. It is incidental to his desire to express and develop himself. He cannot attain development in a void, and he consequently first attempts to bring some differentiation into this void. It is at this point that man intervenes. The latter cannot, quite correctly from his viewpoint, permit a deity to attain differentiation unless the possibility for man's differentiation is also

provided. Thus man is more or less forcibly injected into the picture. He becomes merged with the gods and the gods with him, and the differentiation and education of the gods becomes as much the education of men as it does that of the gods. Since man begins as a completely instinctual being, non-social and undomesticated, dominated by sex and hunger, so also the gods must begin or, better, so the gods are forced to begin.'

The differentiation is expressed in myth by the shambling, semi-human, semi-divine figure of the Trickster who looks back to the time when man emerged from a hominid condition and attained consciousness.[4] In the higher mythologies he is personified by figures such as Hermes-Mercury and Loki, and above all by the archetypal figure of Merlin. This crucial rôle was instinctively sensed by Spenser, who in *The Faerie Queene* portrays his heroes as struggling forward from unknown origins towards hidden destiny, guided only by the prophet Merlin who has knowledge both of past and future.

Man has been some four million years in the making. It was about that long ago that our ancestors began to walk upright, a development dramatically illumined by the discovery of footprints of three hominids of that period imprinted in cemented volcanic ash at Laetoli in northern Tanzania.[5] Tool-making developed a million or more years later, coinciding with an 'explosive development' of the human brain which nearly doubled its size. Development of the region of the skull known as Broca's area resulted in the acquisition of the power of speech, enabling early man to extend enormously the range of his social relations, and presumably to pass some acquired information from one generation to the next.[6] However, it seems likely that human linguistic skills remained at a rudimentary level for hundreds of thousands of years, and were indeed not yet generically different from those of ape communication.[7]

It is speech that provides the essential distinction between man and the rest of the animal kingdom. For from speech proceeds almost certainly all the other qualities that distinguish man as a species. Speech is not just the unique attribute of humanity, but the single factor which drew us from a pre-conscious, instinctual level of being to one where we became beings conscious of the world about us, and of our place in it. Only through language can concepts be formulated and detached from emotions and sensations. Only by doing so can man stand back and reflect on himself; that is, he is enabled to act *consciously*, because he is aware of what he does and who he is.[8] Neanderthal man appears to represent a strain which failed to transcend this state of *potentially* full consciousness.[9]

Language bestowed on man the intellectual versatility, the *freedom*, to adapt to different environments and ultimately in large part to dominate them. To achieve this he had to shed most of the rigidly instinctive responses formerly shared with other primates.[10] It is reasonable to suppose that hominid intelligence was analogous to that of the other higher vertebrates with whom he shared a common ancestry. A great deal of study has been devoted to analysing the abilities of apes, dogs, rats and other quick-witted animals, as well as birds with surprising capacity for intelligence or mimicry, such as pigeons and parrots. In general, observers have recorded remarkable achievements and unsuspected capacity for memory and abstract conception. At the same time it appears that there are fairly strict limits to the extent of their development. Baboons, dogs, cats and chimpanzees have been shown to possess memories lasting weeks or even months; the more intelligent apes display a capacity to adapt sticks and other objects lying to hand as rudimentary tools, and can manipulate boxes and branches as a means of reaching inaccessible food. Attempts to teach chimpanzees to speak have however produced disappointing results, achieving vocabularies of no more than three or four words, with virtually no capacity to formulate them into syntactical use. The fact appears to be that most existing species of vertebrates have successfully adapted to the ecological rôles they occupy, and there is little evolutionary pressure for further development.[11]

It seems safe to assert that animals lack consciousness, in the sense that they are incapable of being aware of their own existence as an abstraction, or indeed of being anything but the particular dog, cat or chimpanzee they happen to be. Part of the human mind is continually aware of itself as a feature in a conceptual landscape, and this there is no reason to believe an animal ever does. One may guess that 90% or so of the higher animals' responses are instinctual (that is, programmed from birth as part of the phylogenetic process), but that there exists also a residue of individual responses. It is instinctive for a dog to devote himself to a particular human, but there will undoubtedly be moments when he sees his master as something beyond himself. Thus it seems that an animal's responses are almost entirely subjective. As Konrad Lorenz observed, because the higher apes cannot *objectivise* their environment (that is, separate themselves from it) they cannot innovate.[12]

There must have been a dawning of the elements of consciousness during the millennia over which man developed his first linguistic skills. But the capacity for full self-expression and communication appears to have been achieved quite suddenly and relatively recently. It is in the Upper Palaeolithic era, some 50 or 60,000 years ago, that evidence becomes available for the swift development of human consciousness. Of the population explosion of some 40,000 years ago, which relatively swiftly brought about the colonisation of the globe, J. D. Clark asks: 'Was it . . . culture – *language* and technology – that was the catalyst behind Modern Man's dispersal? I suspect it was.' The classic indications of the development of consciousness are: burial of the dead (awareness of mortality), personal ornamentation (development of individuality), and the practice of art (which 'implies a capacity not merely to visualise the outer world, but to conceptualise and in a sense to recreate it in the imagination'). Alexander Marshack has discovered widespread evidence of calendrical notations carved on bones and other objects, indicating appreciation of the passage of time. Finally, the philologist Morris Swadesh hazarded an estimate that the known languages of the world diverged from a common original some 40 to 100,000 years ago. Historically, as already indicated, the displacement of Neanderthal man about this time by Cro-Magnon man, ancestors of the present population of Europe, may have resulted from the latter's 'explosive' break-through in mental capacity.[13]

We know in what consciousness consists, and can date its appearance in the human psyche with some plausibility. But what it is and where it comes from remains mysterious – at least, in terms of mechanistic science. The 'memory' of the brain (which in this respect may be likened to a computer) is contained in one or two million modules, each including up to ten thousand neurones. These complex structures are then 'read' by the conscious mind, which 'plays through the whole liaison brain in a selective and unifying manner'. The activity of the conscious mind is perceptible, for example, in the moment of waking from sleep. Numerous disparate floating images can be detected being swiftly 'sorted' and brought under control in a coherent pattern.

The brain-modules from which the conscious mind retrieves information and then arranges into mental patterns are physical entities contained within the cortex of the brain. But what and where is the conscious mind itself?

This is the question put by the great neurobiologist Sir John Eccles, to which his reply is that it 'is unanswerable in principle', and that self-consciousness does not belong to the physical and biological properties of the brain. There is no satisfactory evolutionary theory to explain this irruption of the god into the machine, and Eccles is accordingly 'constrained to believe that there is what we might call a supernatural origin of my unique self-conscious mind or my unique selfhood or soul . . . By this idea of a supernatural creation I escape from the incredible improbability that the uniqueness of my own self is genetically determined. There is no problem about the genetic uniqueness of my brain. It is the uniqueness of the experienced self that requires the hypothesis of an independent origin of the self or soul, which is then associated with a brain, that so becomes my brain'.[14]

The existence of an overriding non-physical factor in evolution suggests that the universe possesses a purpose, which it could only have if it were itself created by a conscious agent which transcended it. We would then expect all created things to participate in some degree in the nature of that transcendent conscious being, a being impossible to encompass within our understanding. 'God cannot be an object of knowledge, because in the act of knowing man cannot rise above God', as Berdyaev observed. The most striking manifestation of the non-physical transcendent element in the universe must surely be the otherwise inexplicable injection of consciousness into the human psyche; a consciousness which enabled man's vision to encompass the universe in its turn.[15]

It cannot be said that it was the ability to speak which brought about the change from unconscious to conscious thought. The one reflects the other, and the process arose out of some other motivating factor.[16] There are indications that the consciousness which distinguishes *homo sapiens* from his predecessors was acquired, in evolutionary terms, quite 'suddenly'. It did not replace his former pattern of purely instinctual responses, but 'overlaid' them. Thus there is a Jekyll and Hyde in all of us; and a selection of appropriate DNA over untold millennia has brought about the unconscious unconditioned reflexes which in large part govern our behaviour. These reflexes include obvious basic propensities, such as the requirement to satisfy drives of sex, appetite and aggression. Intelligent thought, on the other hand, is infinitely flexible and adaptable when considered on its own, and accounts for man's extraordinary cultural, moral and ethical advances of the past few thousand years.[17] Within every personality there exists a conscious intelligence, unique in each individual, which directs his activities and dictates his view of the world around. Concealed beneath this, and first identified by Freud, lies the inherited unconscious whose latent powers and effects are best described by Jung:

'Man's unconscious . . . contains all the patterns of life and behaviour inherited from his ancestors, so that every human child is possessed of a ready-made system of adapted psychic functioning prior to all consciousness. In the conscious life of the adult as well, this unconscious, instinctive functioning is continually present and active. In this activity all the functions of the conscious psyche are prefigured. The unconscious perceives, has purposes and intuitions, feels and thinks as does the conscious mind. We find sufficient evidence for this in the field of psychopathology and the investigation of dream-processes. Only in one respect is there an essential difference between the conscious and the unconscious functioning of the psyche. Though consciousness is intensive and concentrated, it is transitory and is trained upon the immediate present and the immediate field of attention; moreover, it has access only to material that represents one individual's experience stretching over a few decades. A wider range of 'memory' is an artificial acquisition consisting mostly of printed paper. But matters stand very differently with the unconscious. It is not concentrated and intensive, but shades off into obscurity; it is highly extensive and can juxtapose the most heterogeneous elements in the most paradoxical way. More than this, it contains, besides an indeterminable number of subliminal perceptions, the accumulated deposits from the lives of our ancestors, who by their very existence have contributed to the differentiation of the species. If it were possible to personify the unconscious, we might think of it as a collective human being combining the characteristics of both sexes, transcending youth and age, birth and death, and, from having at its command a human experience of one or two million years, practically immortal. If such a being existed, it would be exalted above all temporal change; the present would mean neither more nor less to it than any year in the hundredth millennium before Christ; it would be a dreamer of age-old dreams and, owing to its limitless experience, an incomparable prognosticator. It would have lived countless times over again the life of the individual, the family, the tribe, and the nation, and it would possess a living sense of the rhythm of growth, flowering, and decay.'

Jung argued that it is impossible to overestimate the strength of the unconscious. 'Theoretically it should be possible to "peel" the collective unconscious, layer by layer, until we came to the psychology of the worm, and even of the amoeba.' It is not a question of 'inherited ideas', he hastened to emphasise, but 'rather a question of inherited *possibilities* of ideas, "paths" that have gradually been traced out through the accumulative experience of our ancestors'. As a result, 'the mind, as the active principle in the inheritance, consists of the sum of the ancestral minds, the "unseen fathers" whose authority is born anew with the child'.

The process not only flows through history and prehistory, but can be observed in the microcosm of each individual.[18] According to Piaget, the idea of reality evolves between the ages of three to eleven from a completely subjective view of the world to a reasonably objective one. Initially, 'the child puts the whole content of consciousness on the same plane and draws no distinction between the "I" and the external world.' As the first decade of its life passes, it gradually learns to divide 'this protoplasmic consciousness into two complementary universes – the objective universe and the subjective'.[19]

Through observation of one's own children it is possible for everyone to be a witness of a microcosmic demonstration of what the entire human race passed through as it emerged from hominid existence to conscious purpose as *homo sapiens*. It is an experience common to all that very little of our first years of existence is retained in the memory, despite the fact that we were as bright, lively and inquisitive as children invariably are. All that can be recalled, in Jung's words, 'are islands of consciousness which are like single lamps or lighted objects in the far-flung darkness'.

'Psychic birth', Jung explained, 'and with it the conscious differentiation from the parents, normally takes place only at puberty, with the eruption of sexuality . . . Until this period is reached the psychic life of the individual is governed largely by instinct, and few or no problems arise.' He also suggested that 'in extreme old age, we descend again into . . . the unconscious, and gradually vanish within it.' This psychic birth, the evolution of consciousness in a manner comparable to that of developing children, is surely what took place among the ancestors of the human race within the last 100,000 years. Before that man was in a state of 'wholeness', of unity with his surroundings, an integral part of the natural order. Primitive man enjoyed in large measure 'that unconscious wholeness' which 'the wild animal possesses to perfection'.[20] The story in Genesis of the Fall of Man represents in mythological terms a perfect expression of the primitive passage of 'psychic birth'. The Garden of Eden provides an idyllic picture of primordial man living in a state of harmony with the animals, and the conversation with the serpent suggests that they communicated in a state of intellectual equality.[21]

Subsequently man is harshly separated from the rest of creation by eating the Fruit of the Tree of Knowledge of Good and Evil. As the serpent explained, 'your eyes shall be opened, and ye shall be as God, knowing good and evil'. This awakening is presented as a curse, the end of purely natural man, even though it is seemingly inevitable and places man on a level with God. The immediate effect lies in Adam's shame at his nudity, and his discovery of sexuality, paralleling the onset of conscious thought in the child at the time of puberty. In Babylonian myth, too, the primordial Wild Man Enkidu lives as a wild animal until he lies with the temple harlot and learns the ways of civilisation. 'Thou art wise, Enkidu, art become like a god!' she exclaims. Later Enkidu curses her for seducing him from his original simple life.[22] Again, one sees a clear analogy with the individual child's emergence into consciousness at puberty. There is a therapeutic memory of the time before the Fall; in Dostoevsky's words, 'without something holy and precious carried over from childhood, one cannot even live.' And Tolstoy recalls from his childhood that at the age of five, when he emerged from the nursery to the company of his elders, 'my heart was terribly sad, I knew I was irreparably losing my innocence and happiness; and only a feeling of doing my duty upheld me.'[23]

It was axiomatic to early man that the imposition of conscious intelligence on the elemental psyche was brought about by divine intervention. Mythical accounts of the creation represent a remarkably convincing picture of the 'event', preserved and transmitted in the collective unconscious. Its elemental truthfulness is evident when contrasted with the scientific explanations of the Greeks and their rationalist heirs, which were largely based on aetiological speculation.[24] Today progressive churchmen claim that it is essential to discard the 'superstitious', 'divisive' elements of religion in order to bring forth the core of truth lying beneath a rag-bag of cultic accretions no longer necessary to sophisticated twentieth-century man. Like most overly 'rational' beliefs, this view is both false and dangerous.

In fact religion is a product of the unconscious, and reveals itself almost exclusively through revelatory symbols, liturgical language, and rituals re-enacting a Mystery which is essentially inexpressible.[25] In one sense it is plain rationality to identify the implanting of consciousness in the human psyche as the action of divinity. Humanity was transformed, placed outside the rest of creation, and henceforth possessed of powers which, however limited, are comparable to those ascribed to God. There is scarcely a limit to what man's mind can conceive, and if one wishes to conceptualise the spirit of God transcendent in a material cosmos, then it must be, as Aristotle saw, in the form of pure mind and intellect, the highest type of being, and the only one that can be conceived as existing apart from matter.[26] It is unlikely that consciousness was self-generating, and it seems more reasonable than not to believe that rational intelligence was bestowed on man by God, as a reflection of His own omniscience. For the universe is best explained as the creation of God; the fact that it is intelligible to man suggests it was not only created but is also the creation of a Being differing from man only in his freedom from limitations. The *experience* of God is a psychic and biological fact, and his objective reality appears a more likely proposition than not, provided it is not contradicted by other cosmological data. As on balance that data suggests the existence of a first cause and immanent cosmic intelligence, for the purposes of this discussion the existence of God will be presumed; that He created the earth, and that He made man in His own image by bestowing on him a spark of His own omniscience in the form of conscious thought.[27]

Though the attainment of consciousness in man represents the fulfilment of God's purpose, it was an event regarded with doubt, regret and even resentment. It was the Fall. In consequence the conscious mind is continually assailed by a desire to abandon the undesired gift, and fall back in heartfelt contentment onto the unconscious. This manifests itself in the individual in various psychological states, ranging from Freud's 'death-wish'[28], to extreme nostalgia for the vanished world of childhood. During most of adult life the conscious mind is sufficiently active and occupied to operate much of the time clear of the trammels of the unconscious. Hedonistic self-indulgence and obsession with material goods, represent a desire to submerge once more into the material world, of which addiction to achieve personal oblivion through narcotic drugs may be an extreme example. Consciousness must struggle against the shackles of the unconscious, which it can never entirely throw off, and to which it must succumb in the end. For the miraculous fruits of culture are largely products of the conscious mind.

This struggle between the rival claims of unconscious psyche and conscious mind is still more clearly portrayed through the didactic medium of myth. Widespread among many primitive peoples is the concept of the *deus otiosus*, the supreme creator divinity and sky-god, who made the earth and peopled it with human beings. In historical time, however, he is almost entirely withdrawn from human affairs, remaining all-powerful but benevolently remote.[29] Among the Dinka people of the Nilotic Sudan, for example, a myth told how Divinity and earth were originally contiguous. 'They were connected by a rope . . . By means of this rope men could clamber at will to Divinity. At this time there was no death.' Later, however, Divinity became offended with humanity, and the rope was severed. Before that, say the Dinka, 'Divinity stayed with people and was good to them.' The motive for the separation between Divinity and man arose from man's assertion of self-consciousness. 'Complete integration gave security, but that very security involved a closeness to Divinity which Man also found an irksome and restricting dependence . . . Man . . . then asserted a life and will of his own which brought him into opposition to his maker.' As might be expected, Dinka rituals explicitly parallel the original fall from grace with each Dinka youth's passage from boyhood to manhood consciousness. Songs express a deep desire for the restoration of the pristine harmony.[30]

This heartfelt longing, paralleled by an attraction to a presumed golden age in the historical past, is expressed by a worldwide *Myth of the Eternal Return*, as it is aptly named in a celebrated book of that name by Mircea Eliade. Providing a wealth of examples, Eliade shows that 'the periodical renewal of the World has been the most frequent mythico-ritual scenario in the religious history of humanity'. It is a deeply-felt belief 'that the Cosmos may be renewed *ab integro*, and that this renovation involves not only the "salvation" of the World, but also the return of the paradisiacal stage of existence, characterised by an abundance of food obtained without toil. Man once felt himself mystically at one with the Cosmos and knew also that the renewal may be affected by the ritual repetition of the cosmogony, performed either annually on the occasion of cosmic crises, or of historical events.'[31] These rites assume their greatest efficacy when performed at the sacred 'Centre of the World', a meeting-place of the three cosmic regions (heaven, earth and underworld); also the point from which the earth expanded at the creation, and to which it will dwindle at its end. In its earliest form this was the sacred mountain, whose summit is at once central and transcendent. From its peak the Tree of Life, symbol of cosmic renewal, ascended to heaven; whilst from its base, rivers flowed outwards to the periphery of the earth. At the central point, the *Omphalos*, the 'priest' incarnates the Immortals, 'and as such must neither be looked at nor touched. He performs the rites away from men, in absolute solitude. For when the Immortals performed them for the first time, men did not yet exist on earth.'[32]

This figure at the Centre was in earliest times the shaman. Just over forty years ago the Soviet ethnologist N. P. Nikuljshin recorded by the Sym river, in the remotest heart of Siberia, a shaman's song. A month before, the German Army had launched its invasion of Russia; while the shaman's chant carried him back over prehistoric millennia to the moment of Creation:

> 'Come here my children!
> Now there is a soul
> On the sharp peak [of the mountain] of the earth
> There we meet
> On the wretched place of earth
> There where the sharp peak [stands]
> In the very middle of the earth . . .
> It was deemed in olden times
> When [everything came to life]
> After the earth had appeared.
> It was always like this
> When [everything] began to live.
> For the essence of success
> I begin to ask.
> Say something!
> At the camp-fire I want to shamanize . . .
> To the centre of the earth
> To mother morning.
> With the search of animals
> Manifest yourself somehow!'[33]

It is hard to exaggerate the antiquity of shamanism, which may almost go back to the emergence of *homo sapiens*. The earliest representation of a shaman is that of the famous 'Sorcerer' in the

Cave of the Trois Frères in southern France. With a deer's head crowned with antlers, he has an owl's face, wolf's ears, chamois' beard, bear's paws and a horse's tail. Only his legs and dancing gait are human, and clearly the animal characteristics are designed to acquire the strengths of different beasts, the psychopomps helping the dancer to be at one again with natural creation before man discovered consciousness and death. About two feet six inches high, the figure is painted on a wall on a high rock pulpit about twelve feet above the floor. Around the walls of this sanctuary are painted wonderfully realistic representations of bison, mammoth, deer, woolly rhinoceros and other creatures of the Upper Palaeolithic era, all dominated by the imperious gaze of the Sorcerer. To reach the sanctuary it is necessary to walk for nearly half an hour through an intricate succession of passages and chambers, many containing magnificent frescoes of animals, birds and cryptic signs. The paintings are thought to date from around 12,000 B.C.[34]

The most likely explanation of the so-called 'Sorcerer' is that it is a representation of the primordial shaman, he who first re-established the link between god and man after the passing of the pre-conscious Dreaming. For it was the First Shaman who established the ritual technique of ecstasy and the means of returning to the beginning by re-enactment of the cosmogonic myth, a version of which doubtless took place in the torch-lit cavern. The shaman is a specialist. Originally, the myths explain, there was a time when Earth and Sky were linked by a rope, tree or mountain. Man and God were joined. Then came the fatal separation. Henceforward contact was broken, the Sky-god distanced himself from concern with man, and only in death did man return to divinity. Thenceforward certain gifted figures retained the power to ascend to heaven at will. They included kings and holy men, and above all the shaman who by means of his ecstatic trance detached himself from the world of conscious mortality and made the now perilous ascent to heaven. It is a concept preserved in the fable of the Indian rope-trick and, appropriately enough, in the children's fairy tale of Jack and the Beanstalk.[35]

Many people have undergone a sensation of the soul's detaching itself from the body, in certain traumatic circumstances similar in some ways to the objective experience attested by every shaman. Of late, much research has been conducted into 'out-of-body' experiences, which are far too widely attested and similar in their essentials to rest on mere illusion. These can occur under almost any conditions, most frequently when a person is near to death.

An army officer, whose car was struck by a shell from an anti-tank gun, stated:

'I was conscious of being two persons, one lying on the ground . . . the other "me" ("double") was floating up in the air, about twenty feet from the ground . . .' A patient in hospital 'heard the doctors say that I was dead, and that's when I began to feel as though I were tumbling, actually kind of floating, through this blackness, which was some kind of enclosure. There are not really words to describe this. Everything was very black, except that, way off from me, I could see this light. It was a very, very brilliant light, but not too large at first. It grew larger as I came nearer and nearer to it . . . I said to myself, "If this is it, if I am to die, then I know who waits for me at the end, there in that light."'

In the majority of such cases 'feelings of peace, tranquillity, a vanishing of all worries' were experienced, as well as sensations of returning to something familiar, of being 'surrounded by an overwhelming love and compassion'. It is clear to all who have undergone the experience that the spirit is separate from the body to which it is attached, and when the appropriate moment arrives slips out of it without regret.[36] Normally death is the moment of release, and for this reason the shaman's initiation centres on a ritual of death and rebirth.

In the famous palaeolithic cave-sanctuary at Lascaux there is a representation of what some prehistorians believe to be a dead shaman with a bird's head or mask, lying by a slain bison. Nearby a bird perched on a pole represents the shaman's bird-soul ascending the World-Tree.[37] This and similar pictures date from a period when man, though very much *homo sapiens*, was still not fully emerged from the spontaneous existence of the wild beasts. Small hunting communities probably maintained a symbiotic relationship with the reindeer herds they hunted, whose skins comprised their clothing.[38] In the Middle Ages in Wales the Celtic Lord of the Animals was described (in *Culhwch and Olwen*) as dressed in skins, and Geoffrey of Monmouth's representation of Merlin as living the life of a stag must draw on an earlier version where the seer dressed in deerskins and wore an antlered helm.

Early man, moving in small, huddled bands of up to perhaps five hundred men, women and children[39] on the tracks of the reindeer herds, inhabited a world redolent with mysterious power. It was a world still dominated by the animals, among whom he was becom-

ing an outsider. Only his remarkable energy, skill and adaptability
enabled him to sustain his hold on an environment so dangerous
and indifferent to his survival. His was a precarious niche in
cave and encampment, watching in awe as mammoth and woolly
rhinoceros broke their way through thicket and scrub with irresist-
ible momentum, and hurriedly breaking camp in the path of vast
herds of bison or reindeer. With his increasingly sophisticated
weaponry, the hunter could trap and kill the unwary herbivore.
But he in turn was stalked by wolves, tigers and other predators
of equal cunning and superior strength. Above all there was the
awe-inspiring shadow of the cave-bear, a figure almost human in
its capacity to stand upright, its facial expression, and its domestic
life with wife and child; but superhuman in size, strength and
preternatural cunning, and only to be referred to by oblique allusive
expressions.

Beyond the tundra and grasslands lay the unknown: impenetrable forests, towering mountains with glaciers between them,
the boundless sea. To the North the habitable world ended before
a wall of ice. Above was the dome of heaven, with its nightly
glittering display reflected in still lakes and sluggish rivers. Man
felt himself an integral part of the cosmos on a level inaccessible
to introspective dwellers in modern cities. He was acutely aware
of the necessity to preserve the balance of the natural world, which
he sensed was poised in harmony. As the face of the Sky-god
was withdrawn, his earthly creation turned to a more immediate
divinity. This was the Lord of the Forest, a being with human and
animal attributes who presided over the beasts and birds on whose
existence as prey man depended. He was a being who spoke in a
high, distorted voice, laughing eerily, and far bigger than common
mortals. He was not God but the guardian of the hunting culture,
a being who looked after the welfare of animals and apportioned
game among hunters worthy of his beneficence.[40]

Possibly he was a being originating from or related to the Primordial Shaman, who first mediated between God and man after their
separation. Like the shaman, he wore antlers and skins, and was
envisaged as possessing a special relationship with the wild deer.
His guardianship of the animals ensured that, despite man's dependence on them for his survival, none was killed without ritual
preparation and propitiation. The underlying concept was one of
a harmonious natural order, which could only be violated of strict
necessity and with due sacrifice to the god who sustained this
balance. As an Eskimo shaman put it, 'the First People made

sacrifices through love of universal harmony, through love of great things, immeasurable things, unfathomable things.'[41] Despite the fact that the earth was stocked with a superfluity of game, primitive man possessed an inspired sense of what would now be termed ecological balance.

This conception of a unifying moral and natural order survived into barbarian and early civilised societies. To the Ancient Egyptians it was known as *Maat*, to the Indians as *Rta*, to the Greeks as *Themis*, and to the early Irish as *fír flatha*. At the Creation God mounted the primordial hill. Out of Chaos he created Order, binding Himself and His Creation by law which henceforth would sustain that Order. Thereafter it was violated only at great peril. If a king governed without due regard for truth and justice, the land would be scourged by plague, famine and foreign invasion.[42]

Next to man's realisation that all of nature was bound by a cosmic code was the discovery of his own mortality. As the word implies, death was the defining principle of conscious man at his beginning. Once again it was the shaman whose rôle it was to ensure that death was deprived of its finality. He assisted man in his fallen state, facilitating the departure of the soul from the body, and accompanying it in its ascent to the Otherworld. This was accomplished by way of the single link at the symbolic World Centre, represented by the World-Tree, the ladder, staircase, chain of arrows or other symbol of the original link between earth and the heaven of the creator Sky-god. It is in this context that we must see the 'brygge of iron and of steele' which Merlin provided as access to a magical (Otherworld) island:

> 'and hit was but halff a foote brode, "and there shall never man passe that brygge nother have hardynesse to go over hit but yf he were a passynge good man withoute trechery or vylany"'.

And it was as psychopomp that Merlin accompanied the stricken Arthur in the ship that bore him to the Celtic paradisal Island of Apples.[43]

Mortality was the necessary condition of humanity, since without it man too would have been a god. And, in becoming detached from God, man became aware of a third, related, reality: the presence of God. This has been experienced in all ages, occurring spontaneously in what has become known as Sacred Time or Sacred Place. In his celebrated work *The Idea of the Holy*, the German theologian Rudolf Otto adopted the neologism 'numinous' to identify this unique sensation 'felt as objective and outside the self'.

The 'numinous' is 'the deepest and most fundamental element in all strong and sincerely felt religious emotion . . . we shall find we are dealing with something for which there is only one appropriate expression, *mysterium tremendum*. The feeling of it may at times come sweeping like a gentle tide, pervading the mind with a tranquil mood of deepest worship. It may pass over into a more set and lasting attitude of the soul, continuing, as it were, thrillingly vibrant and resonant, until at last it dies away and the soul assumes its "profane", non-religious mood of everyday experience. It may burst in sudden eruption up from the depths of the soul with spasms and convulsions, or lead to the strangest excitements, to intoxicated frenzy, to transport, and to ecstasy. It has its wild and demonic forms and can sink to an almost grisly horror and shuddering. It has its crude, barbaric antecedents and early manifestations, and again it may be developed into something beautiful and pure and glorious. It may become the hushed, trembling, and speechless humility of the creature in the presence of – whom or what? In the presence of that which is a Mystery inexpressible and above all creatures.'[44]

A characteristic aftermath of this experience of the numinous is a desperate feeling of separation, of 'otherness', from a sublimity which man senses is always near, yet elusive. It is 'out there', to be reached again if only one had the means. From this stems the sensation of indescribable awe gripping the inner consciousness as one gazes out into limitless space on a starry night. Though reason and astronomy tell us that the material universe consists only of blazing globules of gas and dead specks of rock floating in the intergalactic vacuum, there must be scarcely anyone who can look upon it without an overpowering sensation of its being imbued with an ineffable, transcendent presence. It is a presence deeply concerned with our being, yet veiled from sight.

Man feels a deep dissatisfaction with this state of things. In Eliade's words, he is 'torn and separate'. 'He often finds it difficult properly to explain to himself the nature of this separation, for sometimes he feels himself to be cut off from "something" *powerful*, "something" utterly *other* than himself, and at other times from an indefinable, timeless "state", of which he has no precise memory, but which he does however remember in the depths of his being: a primordial state which he has enjoyed before Time, before History.'

The primordial state reasserts its force under certain evocative conditions. These are the *emptiness* of vast, lonely landscapes; the *silence* of true solitude; and the *semi-darkness* of a starry or moonlit night, of forest glades or vaulted halls. For these are conditions which detach man from the clay of which he is made, and place him once more in face of the *mysterium tremendum*.[45]

It can hardly be doubted that it was instinctive considerations of this sort which drove Palaeolithic man to celebrate his most potent mysteries in caverns far beneath the ground, remote and difficult of access.[46] Nor was it chance that made him express his feeling of the numinous through art, in the form of the wonderful cave-paintings of France and Spain. Justly admired today as great art, they undoubtedly originated as an expression of religious feeling; though it is impossible to doubt that intense aesthetic pleasure accompanied their execution. It is no coincidence that the world's first cathedrals were also the first art galleries.

Despite the institutionalising and secularisation of both, true art and religion remain as essentially dual reflections of a single perceived truth as they did in the caves of Lascaux and Altamira twenty thousand years ago. Through art man fulfils the divine mould, reaching out to the ultimate perfection from which his unconscious reminds him he is sprung. In doing so he commits a religious act, enabling his fellow-men to glimpse a piece of the divine perfection, concealed from sight since the sundering of the rope that linked heaven and earth. It was, after all, Orpheus alone of men who was enabled to enter the Underworld and return in safety; and this he achieved by the power of music.

Thus the missions of artist and prophet are in this respect indistinguishable. The privilege of divine afflatus enables them to reach out to God, and in return to bring a part of God to conscious man. The nature of his prophetic rôle has always been apparent to the artist. The 'great task' Blake set himself was:

'To open the Eternal Worlds, to open the immortal Eyes of Man inwards into the Worlds of Thought; into Eternity Ever expanding in the Bosom of God, the Human Imagination.'[47]

Wordsworth saw himself, like Merlin, as one who 'looks before and after', and shaman-like used his ecstatic vision to transcend 'the limiting constrictions of the human condition, the limits of time, place, and corporeal reality'. He also knew the dangers. Just as the materialist anthropologist explains the shaman as a man 'suffering from a psychosis which becomes steadily worse', and as Merlin became known in mediaeval tradition as *wyllt* ('the wild') and *insanus*[48]; so Wordsworth was condemned by prosaic contemporaries:

> 'Some call'd it madness: such, indeed, it was,
> If child-like the fruitfulness in passing joy,
> If steady moods of thoughtfulness, matur'd
> To inspiration, sort with such a name;
> If prophecy be madness; if things view'd
> By poets in old time, and higher up
> By the first men, earth's first inhabitants,
> May in these untutor'd days no more be seen
> With undisorder'd sight.'[49]

Finally, if one may take the modern poet who perhaps stands closer than any other to the tradition of Merlin, it was W. B. Yeats who saw the poet's rôle as explicitly shamanistic:

> 'I know now that revelation is from the self, but from that age-long memoried self, that shapes the elaborate shell of the mollusc and the child in the womb, that teaches the birds to make their nest; and that genius is a crisis that joins that buried self for certain moments to our trivial daily mind. There are, indeed, personifying spirits that we had best call but Gates and Gatekeepers, because through their dramatic power they bring our souls to crisis. . . .'[50]

From classical times onwards the rôles of prophet and poet have become increasingly distinct, but in an earlier period the distinction was entirely lacking. The ecstatic utterances of the shaman are chanted in verse, and poetry constituted the expression of prophecy. Thus for untold millennia poetry was primarily the creation of shamanism. Gradually poetry became an autonomous art, but it was long before it shed its mantic associations. The Sumerian myths of Inanna's descent to the Underworld, and the parallel Akkadian tale of Ishtar's similar descent must ultimately derive from shamanist beliefs, as does Gilgamesh's summoning of the shade of Enkidu from the Nether World. The latter makes reference to Gilgamesh's *pukku* and *mikku*, possibly a magical drum and drumstick employed by the shaman when working himself up into his ecstasy.[51] Many of the earliest Greek legends also betray unmistakable traces of shamanist myth. One thinks of the visits of Orpheus and Odysseus to the Underworld, and it has even been suggested that the entire theme of the *Odyssey* derives from the perilous adventures and safe return of a shaman hero.[52]

In ancient Israel and among the early Semites in general, prophet and poet appear to have been synonymous. In their rites of initiation, ecstatic frenzy and poetic mode of utterance, the Hebrew prophets were true shamans. In so far as some of the books of the Old Testament represent authentic works of the prophets, they too may be regarded as inspired by shamanist modes of thought.[53]

Both historical tradition and linguistics combine to show that a similar conjunction of poetic and prophetic powers existed in early Celtic society. The Old Irish word for 'poet' is *fili*, related to Middle Welsh *gwelet*, 'to see', and in its original conception meant 'seer, wise man'. Similarly the second element in the Welsh words for 'druid', *derwydd*, is connected with the Latin *videre*, 'to see'. The poet and druid were men with a special perception. Other words make it clear that it was a magical or supernatural perception. The Old Irish verb *canid*, meaning 'to sing', 'chant', 'recite' is applied not only to poetry, but to charms, magical formulas, and even legal pronouncements. Its equivalents in Latin, *canere*, 'to sing', and *carmen*, 'a song', are closely associated with prophetic and magical incantations. Again, the Irish word for 'poetry', *creth*, is found in Welsh in *prydydd*, 'poet'. Cognate forms in related Indo-European languages make it clear that in the original context these words for poet and poetry were indissolubly connected with magicians and magic.

There is another set of related words which is equally illuminating. In Old Irish, the words *fáth*, *fáith*, stand for 'prophecy', 'prophet'. The Welsh equivalent is *gwawd*, 'poetry', and both forms are related to the Latin *vates*, also meaning 'a prophet' (hence the English word 'vaticination'). There is a set of words in the Germanic languages of the same origin: Anglo-Saxon *wóth*, 'sound, melody'; *wódnes*, 'madness'; Old High German *wuot*, 'mad'; German *wüten*, 'to rage'. All this derives from an Indo-European root meaning 'to blow', and hence metaphorically 'to inspire' (cf. the Latin *spiro*, 'I breathe'). Behind this common vocabulary lies a conception of the poet as an ecstatic prophet, his *inspiration* being *breathed* into him by a deity.[54] As the conception formed part of the common Indo-European heritage, its origins lie in all probability somewhere in the third millennium B.C.

The early Irish tradition, isolated on the fringe of Europe and untouched by Roman civilization, preserved many archaic features of the Indo-European parent society. From it we may deduce what was the conception of the poet in early times. His esoteric knowledge derived from the source of wisdom in its perfection, the Otherworld. Normally inaccessible to man, an imperfect reflection of that wisdom could be attained by specialists under special conditions. Mythical tales expounded the form in which the source of knowledge manifested itself. Certain springs and wells brought occult knowledge bubbling up from within the earth.[55]

In the Otherworld itself there was a wonderful cauldron, the possession of the Supreme Father of the gods, the Dagda, 'the good god'. In an early Welsh poem in *The Book of Taliesin*, describing an expedition made by Arthur to the Otherworld (*Annwn*), we learn that the cauldron was dark blue and kindled by the breath of nine maidens. (Nine maidens awaited Merlin on the Otherworld Island of Apples when he guided Arthur there.) From it the inhabitants of the Otherworld drew unlimited sustenance, and it was also the source of poetic inspiration:

> 'Mine is the proper Cauldron of *Goiriath*,
> warmly God has given it to me out of the mysteries of the
>   elements;
> a noble privilege which ennobles the breast
> is the fine speech which pours forth from it.'[56]

By the time this verse came to be written, the cauldron had become a metaphor for the inspiration to be found within the body of the poet himself. The metaphor was perhaps assisted by the fact that the Otherworld cauldron of poetic inspiration was originally regarded as a head. Odin's powers of prophecy came from the head of Mimir, which he kept in a sacred well. The cauldron in the Otherworld to which Arthur made his expedition in the ship Prydwen was known as *peir pen annбfyn*, 'the cauldron of the Otherworld (*Annwn*) Head'. It looks as if the original idea of mantic inspiration as 'breathed' from the Otherworld into the seer came to be conceptualised as deriving from the seat of knowledge, the Head of the Primordial Poet in the Otherworld. The legend of Orpheus, obviously in origin a god of poetry, relates how his head was buried in the sanctuary of Dionysos on the island of Lesbos, where it gained wide fame as an oracle. *Orpheus* is explained as 'the skilful one', and is identified with the name *Rivros* on an ancient Gaulish calendar, who in turn is to be identified with the Celtic god Lug, master of all arts and skills.[57]

Mention of the god Lug, the Celtic deity who was master of all creative arts and skills, introduces yet another aspect of the early mantic poet as one divinely inspired, 'mad'. The Old English word *wód*, 'mad', is, as we saw, cognate with Old Irish *fáth*, 'prophecy' and other words of Indo-European origin ranging in meaning from 'prophecy' and 'poetry' to 'madness', 'frenzy'. A derivative of *wód* is the name of the Germanic god Woden, Odin. Nothing could be more appropriate, since Odin in Norse mythology is the god of poetry. He is even said to speak entirely in verse, which he brought from the Otherworld and conferred upon men. His rôle as divine source of mantic power is very archaic, as the root of his name suggests. Much of his myth represents the purest shamanism.[58]

It is generally agreed that Odin in Norse mythology corresponds to Lug among the Celts, Hermes (Mercurius to the Romans) among the Greeks, and Varuna in Vedic India.[59] The archetypal figure personified in these parallel myths is the divine inspirer, through poetry and prophecy, of those arts which permit man momentarily to approximate himself once more to divinity. He is the medium by whom man and god are able to communicate. And, thirdly, he is a thief and deceiver; at times employing his cunning to assist men, and at others to delude them.

All these characteristics are manifest in the fullest version of the myth, the Greek story of Hermes. He was 'the immortal Guide' to the Otherworld, a bringer of dreams, and a prophet who acquired powers of divination from three virgin sisters – reminding one of the nine virgins who kindled the Otherworld Cauldron in Celtic myth. He created the lyre from a tortoiseshell, sang entrancingly to its accompaniment, and invented fire-sticks and fire. He also mischievously stole the gods' cattle, driving them backwards across a sandy tract in order to deceive his pursuers, and establishing an alibi by passing edgeways through a keyhole into his bedroom at home. 'Go to then', cried his mother, who detected him; 'your father [Zeus] got you to be a great worry to mortal men and deathless gods'. But he remained incorrigible: 'he consorts with all mortals and immortals: a little he profits, but continually throughout the dark night he cozens the tribes of mortal men.' It is then he is found, 'pondering sheer trickery in his heart – deeds such as knavish folk pursue in the dark night-time.'[60]

As psychopomp, Otherworld-messenger, inspirer of prophecy and poetry, and instigator of the arts among humans, this Hermetic figure known variously as Mercurius, Odin, Lug or Varuna clearly fulfils the role of a shaman. But as a god and inspirer of mortal shamans, he is clearly much more. He is in fact the primordial First Shaman who, in cosmogonic myth, established the pattern from which succeeded the race of mortal shamans.[61]

Yet he is even more than this. For at the most archaic level of symbolism the shaman originates from the oldest archetype of all, the Trickster. If the shaman personifies the bridge between the conscious and unconscious, between man and God, it is the Trickster who stands at the original point of dislocation. The Trickster myth, as was shown earlier, represents a 'return' to an earlier, primitive state of consciousness, when indeed the conscious mind first emerged from the unconscious. His is the two-fold function of benefactor and buffoon, culture-hero and spirit of disorder, saviour roaming earth 'to teach people on earth a better life', and yet as 'ape of God', a 'reverse' figure or Devil. His relationship to the shaman is apparent not merely in his outward panoply of racoon-skin and antlers, but in his relationship with the saviour, as the wounded sufferer is the agent of healing, and the sufferer takes away suffering. The likeness to Mercurius-Hermes is evident, as it is to his counterparts Lug and Odin, and we see in these figures an example of the familiar process of the original religious experience acquiring human traits in a myth; the human has become a deity.[62]

The purpose of the Trickster myth is to remind man of his first attainment of the gift of consciousness. At the same time he cannot shed the unwanted inheritance of the unconscious, and the myth again is intended to warn him of the consequences of allowing the unconscious to suck him back into a morass of instinctual wilfulness. Among primitive peoples the Trickster myth seems to have survived in much of its pristine purity. In societies little evolved from that of the Palaeolithic era, its therapeutic benefits remained fully valid. It holds the earlier low intellectual and moral level before the eyes of the more highly developed individual, so that he shall not forget how things were formerly. Elsewhere, however, society became increasingly ordered and sophisticated, and rational, conscious modes of thought drove the older being deep down towards the position it occupies today, the unconscious psyche.[63] The Trickster evolved into a god, and his generic characteristics became the individual traits and adventures of an identifiable personality.

But this development carried with it a certain awkwardness. The incongruities of the Trickster's nature are acceptable to the Winnebago Indian, because his myth confers direct therapeutic effects of which he is unconsciously aware. With increasing sophistication, however, there was a tendency to separate the Trickster figure's disparate functions. His carnal nature, his anarchical amor-

ality, his identification with the earth and the brute beasts of
whose company he was so recently a member are seen as clashing
intolerably with his god-given social, moral and cultural achievements. Dr Jekyll began to deny his identity with the repulsive Mr
Hyde, and instinctual man was provided with a separate personality.

The story of Hermes is of special interest in that it largely
preserves the older stratum. He was both culture-hero and destructive imp. We note in particular that Zeus appointed him 'lord over
all birds of omen and grim-eyed lions, and bears with gleaming
tusks, and over dogs and all flocks that the wide earth nourishes,
and over all sheep.'[64] Thus he was the Master of Animals or Lord
of the Forest, protector of beasts, birds and fish, and by extension
a deity with power over 'things of this world'. Among primitive
hunting peoples the Master of Animals was a being who controlled
the wild, whom it was essential to propitiate for success in the
chase, and who though portrayed in semi-human guise is frequently
identified with the untamed forest itself.[65]

In other Indo-European mythologies it seems that this aspect of
the Trickster-god has been hived off onto another, darker deity.
In Vedic India the counterpart of Hermes was Varuna who, whilst
retaining some dark attributes, was essentially a benevolent, om-
niscient sky-god. The rôle of Lord of the Beasts devolved onto
Shiva, 'a mysterious, lustful being who wanders through the forest
and mountains giving birth to all forms of life, creating new worlds
and new beings through the rhythm of his dance, the sound of his
drum . . . Shiva's image, arising in the depth of prehistory, appears
to be that of the most ancient of all the gods.'[66]

Among the Celts, Hermes' equivalent is Lug, the bright god,
bringer of culture to mankind and himself master of all civilising
arts and skills. The rôle of Lord of the Beasts is accorded to another
god, named Cernunnos, 'the horned one', in one inscription.
Antlers or horns form the regular insignia of the Lord of the
Beasts from a very early period. An Elamite cylinder seal from
Mesopotamia portrays a massive erect bull, who may well be a
Lord of the Beasts, since two lions are paying enforced obeisance
to him. Possibly this bull is the terrifying Humbaba, slain by
Gilgamesh in the Akkadian epic:

'To safeguard the cedar forest,
As a terror to mortals has Enlil appointed him.
Humbaba – his roaring is the storm-flood,

His mouth is fire, his breath is death! . . .
Weakness lays hold on him who goes down to the forest.'

In Europe representations of the Master of Animals in the form of a horned god date, as we have seen, from the Palaeolithic period.[67]

I mentioned earlier that the figure of Hermes appears to date from a period before the rôles of culture-hero and saviour on the one hand, and Master of Beasts on the other, had divided into separate representative deities. Possibly Hermes had acquired so marked a personality and cult in early times that he survived in his integrity. Nevertheless traces of the process may still be detectable in Greek myth. The bright side of Hermes' nature, his musical prowess, his powers of prophecy, and his gifts of fortune, are largely duplicated in the person of Apollo – a relative late-comer to the Greek mythological scene. Perhaps the ambivalent character of Hermes no longer satisfied as it had done.

One may also postulate an association of some of Hermes' darker, earthier attributes with a secondary figure. The son of Hermes was Pan, whose reed-pipes were so often heard by shepherds shrilling from within a thicket, or faintly echoing down the rocky defile. A child of the wilderness, he was half animal himself, with his goat's hooves and horns, and his spotted lynx-skin cloak. He is a typical Lord of the Forest, and as such virtually indistinguishable in function from the Celtic horned god, Cernunnos.[68] His rôle may accordingly be compared with that of the British Lord of the Forest, such as the Brown Man of the Muirs encountered by two young men near Elsdon in County Durham. The Brown Man was 'a dwarf very strong and stoutly built, his dress brown like withered bracken, his head covered with frizzled red hair, his countenance furious, and his eyes glowing like those of a bull. After some parley, in which the stranger reproved the hunter for trespassing on his demesnes and slaying the creatures who were his subjects, and informed him how he himself lived only on whortle-berries, nuts and apples, he invited him home.'[69]

The Brown Man's identification with and mastership of the wild, together with his vegetarianism and inability to cross water, recall in turn the figure of Merlin. Indeed, one may go further and see in Merlin both a Celtic counterpart of Pan, and in Merlin's relationship to the god Lug an echo of Pan's kinship to Hermes. At Pan's birth, for example, 'when the nurse saw his uncouth face and full beard, she was afraid and sprang up and left the child,' just as the women attending at Merlin's birth were disquieted by the appearance of his hairy pelt, 'such as they had never seen on another child'.[70]

Small wonder that the Christian Church in early times identified the horned Lord of the Forest with the Devil of the Bible. Indeed, it could be argued that the Church had unwitting justification for its identification, in so far as the Devil personifies man's carnal nature which he shares with the beasts of the wild.[71] In Robert de Boron's romance Merlin is made a devil's son by a mortal woman; and as I attempted to demonstrate earlier, this account reflects an earlier version in which the prophet was conceived of as the son of a god by a human virgin.

Like Pan and Merlin, man is part beast and part god, and much mythology reflects a struggle to reconcile his disparate inheritance. The struggle is played out in Pythagorean and Gnostic dualism; in Virgil's belief that it is the earthy nature of man which drags him down; in the primitive's view of the world as having lower, more material qualities, in contrast with the upper, more remote sky which is associated with the Creator and spirituality in general; and in the doctrine of dualism characterising many religious beliefs.[72]

Thus this ineradicable dualism came to be personified in a series of Trickster figures: the Egyptian god Seth, Samson, Prometheus, Loki, Lug, or Merlin. He is both son of God and his opponent, demiurge and rival divinity. Ultimately he suffers a terrifying fate; but, as the story of Prometheus reveals most clearly, he has stolen fire from heaven and bestowed on the corporeal clay an element of eternity.[73] He represents struggle and reconciliation: he must drag himself free of his brute antecedents – in achieving consciousness he approaches and rivals God who bestowed the gift upon him; ultimately, despite the literally titanic effort to scale the heights of heaven, he succumbs to the inevitable and becomes a scapegoat. The Lord of the Forest or Master of Beasts represents not only the unconscious animal creation and the wilderness it occupies, but also that primal state which existed before the Trickster began his undignified scramble out of the abyss.[74]

The universality of shamanism is co-extensive with that of the Trickster myth and, as Jung explained:

'There is something of the trickster in the character of the shaman and medicine-man, for he too, often plays malicious jokes on people, only to fall victim in his turn to the vengeance of those whom he has injured. For this reason his profession sometimes

puts him in peril of his life. Besides that, the shamanistic techniques in themselves often cause the medicine-man a good deal
of discomfort, if not actual pain. At all events the "making of a
medicine-man" involves, in many parts of the world, so much
agony of body and soul that permanent psychic injuries may
result. His "approximation to the saviour" is an obvious consequence of this, in confirmation of the mythological truth that the
wounded wounder is the agent of healing, and that the sufferer
takes away suffering.'

The Trickster, then, 'is a forerunner of the saviour' and,

'If, at the end of the trickster myth, the saviour is hinted at, this
comforting premonition or hope means that some calamity or
other has happened and been consciously understood. Only out
of disaster can the longing for a saviour arise – in other words,
the recognition and unavoidable integration of the shadow create
such a harrowing situation that nobody but a saviour can undo
the tangled web of fate.'[75]

The Saviour is simultaneously God and Man, and intermediary
between both. Among the Mandari people of the Nilotic Sudan he
is called Logobong. Logobong is seen as 'in the heavens with
Creator', and also as 'the first man, the child of Creator'. He is the
mediating third of a Trinity, whose other members are the principles of 'Maleness' (Kulun) and 'Femininity' (Agoya). The Mandari say that when a man and his wife enter their hut, 'Logobong
is present and Kulun or Agoya', reminding one of the symbolic
presence of Christ at the marriage service. Logobong's rôle is to
unite elements of a differing order. Every month the Mandari
perform a ritual designed to purge themselves of sin and bring
about new hope of the future. It was Logobong whose intervention
made this possible. As the people say:

'Logobong carries sin with him to the west, because his journey
was made in the east-west direction, once and for all time:
Logobong did not return back.'[76]

Among the Dinka, the saviour-mediator is called Aiwel Longar.
According to the Dinka myth, Aiwel was born to a mortal mother
who had been impregnated by a river-divinity when wading. As a
baby he exhibited extraordinary precocity, and was possessed of
prophetic powers. A time came when he summoned the elders of
the village and offered to guide them to the wonderful pastures of
Lual Aghony, the promised land of the Dinka. The people spurned

his offer; Aiwel Longar then left the Dinka, and Divinity placed a barrier of mountains and rivers between him and them. The people nevertheless set off and eventually arrived at a river, which by implication was that associated with Aiwel's conception. There they found the only crossing to be a narrow dyke made by Divinity out of reeds. As the people attempted to cross this precarious bridge, Aiwel Longar struck them with the fishing-spear he bore as his emblem. Eventually this obstacle was overcome by a tribal hero who wrestled with Longar. The latter submitted, and invited the people to cross over in safety. With the Dinka sitting around him in the Elysian Fields, Longar expounded the original myths and tribal customs by which the Dinka thenceforward governed themselves. He then disappeared, explaining that he would no longer intervene in their affairs except on special occasions.

The explanation of the myth is as follows. 'When Aiwel Longar prevented people from crossing the river, he was denying them life, which was in his power to give; and the image of them as fish trying to evade the spear, and as men wanting to cross the river, both refer to an effort, and sometimes a risk, to be taken in order to take advantage of the conditions for life which the river provides . . . He offers to lead people to fine pastures, but turns upon them as they cross the river with which, by the circumstances of his birth, he is identified. He kills them or threatens them with death. Then, when he is finally mastered, he makes available the blessing and the "life" which is in him. He thus both kills and gives life, as in a simple physical sense the river does . . .'

A further significant element is that Aiwel Longar is generally considered to have been the 'eldest son' in the framework of this myth, or the 'first created'. All in all, Aiwel provides a bridge between human and superhuman forces and influences, and transcends the polarity of the Dinka world.

According to another Dinka account, Aiwel Longar was sacrificed by his father, Divinity; 'he took the fishing spear of the moon and transfixed Aiwel through the head and through the whole body so that he was pinned to the ground. Earth and sky were joined by this fishing-spear, and Aiwel was unable to get off it by moving up or down . . . And where Aiwel was, the earth was darkened. It became the colour of storm-clouds, and Aiwel disappeared . . . The people found *mac* (Fire/Flesh) in a gourd where Aiwel had been transfixed, and those who found it took it and it became their clan-divinity. All the people were afraid of giving offence to those who had Flesh and Fire as clan-divinity. In the past, Flesh used to glow like Fire and it is the same as Fire.'[77]

This is clearly a version both of the Prometheus-myth, and of a divinity's self-sacrifice on behalf of humanity. Prometheus was punished by being bound or nailed (Lucian says he was crucified) to Mount Caucasus, with a shaft driven through his middle. Every day an eagle devoured his liver, which was restored each night.[78] It is true that Prometheus was being punished for stealing fire from heaven, whereas in the case of Aiwel Longar it looks as if he gained it for men by *means* of the suffering itself. A South American Indian myth tells how the divine hero Kumaphari stole the primeval fire from a vulture. Observing that the bird fed on carrion, he died and rotted. After two vain efforts, in which the vultures preyed on his flesh, Kumaphari lay down on a great slab of stone and died again. He spread out his arms, and they penetrated like roots into the ground and then came forth again in the shape of two bushes, each of them with five branches springing from a single point of the stem. When the vulture came to devour the rotting corpse, he said to himself, "In these forked branches is a nice place for my fire." With this he put the firebrand in Kumaphari's hand. The hero clutched it and jumped up: fire was now in his possession.[79]

These versions are based on the conception that suffering and death are the means of achieving the supreme goal; in this case fire, of crucial importance to primitive humanity both for itself and as a symbol of enlightenment. In view of the frequency with which that archetypal figure of redemptive suffering, the Trickster, is depicted as the bringer of fire and light to mankind, it may be suspected that this is the older belief, and, perhaps in an earlier version of the Greek myth, Prometheus was a divine figure whose sufferings brought fire to mankind.[80]

Thus we find a consistent myth spread over different continents and centuries. The separation *ab initio* of earth and heaven results in the ordinary lot of man becoming continual deprivation and suffering. Eventually god, or the son of god, appears in human guise on earth. By suffering a terrible death, sacrificing 'himself to himself', he brings salvation to men and restores the former link with heaven.[81] The myth perhaps derives from an unconscious awareness that God, in extrapolating himself into the material cosmos through the creation of man in his image, imposed a meed of suffering as an inevitable condition of consciousness. However this may be, what is essentially unknowable can be recognised only through symbols, and the sacrifice of the saviour-god is rich in symbolism.

More often than not, for example, the supreme sacrifice takes place at the World Centre, the point where heaven is umbilically linked to earth. Prometheus was pinned to Mount Caucasus, 'loftiest of ranges' whose peaks 'neighbour the stars', and one can hardly doubt that whichever peak was envisaged was also regarded as the Centre of the World.[82] We have seen in earlier chapters how Odin, Lug and Christ were held to have died on the World-Tree linking heaven and earth, and that Golgotha became the *Omphalos*. The Dinka myth has Aiwel Longar impaled by a divine spear, and we are told that 'earth and sky were joined by this fishing-spear, and Aiwel was unable to get off it by moving up or down'.

Here we may note too the remarkable diffusion of the spear-symbol as a motif in the divine self-sacrifice. Christ, Odin and Lug were pierced by spears, as was Aiwel Longar; and Zeus drove a shaft through Prometheus' belly. The significance of the spear is imbued with numinous qualities, as a symbol of male generation, lightning-flash emanation of deity, and so forth. What is perhaps the oldest pictorial representation of a myth in existence is found in the remotest recess of the subterranean Palaeolithic sanctuary at Lascaux. A disembowelled bison is lying by a bird-headed (or masked) human figure, near whom is a bird perched on a pole. Across the scene has fallen a huge spear, broken short of its haft.[83]

Whatever the significance of these symbolic elements, the theme as a whole is that of death as the gateway to life. It must be remembered that in early times death was not the sinister finality it has become to neurotic modern man. To primitives 'death is an initiation', comparable to the *rites de passage* of birth, adulthood and marriage.[84] The attendant symbols play an indefinable part in explaining the inexplicable: the tainted, earth-bound husk of conscious humanity has been discarded, and the purified spirit has returned to God.

The myth was made most explicit at the crowning moment of its becoming reality. The birth of Christ was an historical event, yet attended by all the familiar circumstances of myth. His birth is prophesied; he is the son of a Virgin; he is a child of astonishing precocity; he must be concealed from the murderous intentions of a treacherous king; and so forth.[85] His mission began with the shamanistic initiation of the forty days' fast in the desert, 'with the wild beasts' (Mark 1, 13). There the devil tempted him with the offer of 'all the kingdoms of the world, and the glory of them' (Matthew 4, 8). It was not for nothing that the Temptation took place in the Wilderness, for here the devil represents an aspect of the Guardian of Animals; that of lord of the earthly creation, before and outside man's receipt of the ambivalent gift of divine consciousness. Christ, however, must reject the offer, since he has come precisely for the purpose of liberating man from his earthly trappings. Perhaps it was to this occasion that he was alluding when he told the seventy that, 'I saw Satan as lightning fall from heaven'. (Luke 10, 17).[86]

The myth of the *Heilbringer*, the Saviour who is himself sacrificed in order to bring salvation, has surfaced again and again with its accompanying symbolism from man's psyche. Christ himself fulfilled in many ways the role of the Trickster[87], and (in Jung's words) 'although his birth was an event that occurred but once in history, it has always existed in eternity . . . Christ is God and man at the same time and . . . he therefore suffers a divine as well as a human fate. The two natures interpenetrate so thoroughly that any attempt to separate them mutilates both. The divine overshadows the human, and the human being is scarcely graspable as an empirical personality.' Jung goes on to explain God's appearance as man in these terms:

'All the world is God's, and God is in all the world from the very beginning. Why, then, the *tour de force* of the Incarnation? one asks oneself, astonished. God is in everything already, and yet there must be something missing if a sort of second entrance into Creation has now to be staged with so much care and circumspection. Since Creation is universal, reaching to the remotest stellar galaxies, and since it has also made organic life infinitely variable and capable of endless differentiation, we can hardly see where the defect lies . . . One should make it clear to oneself what it means when God becomes man. It means nothing less than a world-shaking transformation of God. It means more or less what Creation meant in the beginning, namely an objectivation of God. At the time of the Creation he revealed himself in Nature; now he wants to be more specific and become man.'

The Incarnation of God in Christ took place at a concrete point in chronological historical time, but as God in his omniscience must be able to oversee that and all other eventualities, the event existed from the Beginning. Accordingly there float up from the unconscious psyche – that is, from God himself – myths portraying the event on a cosmic, atemporal scale:

'The intimations and prefigurations of the Incarnation must strike one as either completely incomprehensible or superfluous, since all creation *ex nihilo* is God's and consists of nothing but God, with the result that man, like the rest of creation, is simply God become concrete. Prefigurations, however, are not in themselves creative events, but are only stages in the process of becoming concrete.'[88]

The myth, that is, provides an image of an event which is cosmic and eternal, and yet local and particular; attuned to the inherited circumstances of an historically defined community.

It was in the person of Christ that myth attained fruition, expressing itself in history. It is this central fact which provides the Gospel story with its inescapable impact, and enables it to survive intact all the dissections of exegetical scholarship.[89] I hope I may be excused for indulging in a final quotation from that noblest of myths, Jung's *Answer to Job*, which gives expression to the *mysterium* so clearly and succinctly,

'Myth is not fiction: it consists of facts that are continually repeated and can be observed over and over again. It is something that happens to man, and men have mythical fates just as much as the Greek heroes do. The fact that the life of Christ is largely myth does absolutely nothing to disprove its factual truth – quite the contrary. I would even go so far as to say that the mythical character of a life is just what expresses its universal human validity. It is perfectly possible, psychologically, for the unconscious or an archetype to take complete possession of a man and to determine his fate down to the smallest detail. At the same time objective, non-psychic parallel phenomena can occur which also represent the archetype. It not only seems so, it simply is so, that the archetype fulfils itself not only psychically in the individual, but objectively outside the individual. My own conjecture is that Christ was such a personality. The life of Christ is just what it had to be if it is the life of a god and a man at the same time. It is a *symbolum*, a bringing together of heterogeneous natures . . .'[90]

And so we return to the beginnings. For it is in this light that I believe we must view the figure of Merlin. Like Christ, whose incarnation he so clearly paralleled, the British Prophet lived a demonstrably historical existence, while acting out at the same time the myth which is central to man's existence: the objectivisation of

God; the emergence from unconsciousness to the reflected daylight of divine consciousness, and the return to absorption once again in transcendent divinity.

The historical Merlin played a shadowy yet identifiable rôle in events in sixth-century North Britain, of which a dim memory has been handed down to us. He played a central part in the affairs of this world, presiding over the destinies of the Monarchy of Britain[91], an earthly reflection of the supremacy of the Sky-god. He was a poet, and also a prophet. At the battle of Arderydd in 573 his patron Gwenddolau was killed; Merlin fled to wretched exile in the Forest of Celyddon, where he had reason to fear the persecutions of Rhydderch of Strathclyde. This was the historical Merlin, born of a mortal mother and honoured in later ages as the Prophet *par excellence* of the British race.

This Merlin is overlaid by the palimpsest of an archetypal figure fulfilling a mythical rôle. As with Christ in Jung's terminology, 'the archetype fulfils itself not only psychically in the individual, but objectively outside the individual.' There is thus no incongruity in supposing that the essential outline of Merlin's existence is simultaneously the biography of a remarkable individual *and* the enactment of a myth. If his mother was a mortal, his father was the god Lug, pre-eminent among the deities of the Celtic pantheon, master of those arts which raise man closest to divinity, divine prototype of human kingship and whose epithet *Lamhfhada*, 'of the long arm' reflects the transcendence of the Indian god Savitar 'of the wide hand', whose hand reaches out to control the heavenly bodies and regulate the succession of day and night.[92]

Everything suggests that Merlin was regarded as an incarnation of Lug, and that his inspiration (*awen*) was an expression of divine consciousness. Then came the moment of Gwenddolau's downfall, when Merlin was submerged in ecstatic 'madness', and plunged into the darkest recesses of the forest. The forest here is both a real area of thickets and mountains focusing on Hart Fell in the historical region of Goddeu, and also a symbol of immanent unconsciousness. As Master of Beasts and Lord of the Forest, Merlin appears incarnated a second time as Cernunnos, 'the horned one' who presides over the unconscious creation, the wilderness beyond the daylight regions of waking man. This dual aspect of the wilderness as geographical entity and transliminal limbo of the unconscious dates back at least to the time of the historical Merlin, as Procopius' account of the region north of Hadrian's Wall makes explicit. *Y Gogledd*, the region between the two Roman walls, signifies in Welsh not only 'North' but also 'on the left hand', 'sinister'.[93] Similarly, when Welsh tradition tells of Merlin's descent at his end into the mysterious *tŷ gwydr* or 'house of glass'[94], we perceive a Celtic Otherworld conception and a symbolic representation of the ultimate fate of all men, when 'the conscious mind, advancing into the unknown regions of the psyche, is overpowered by the archaic forces of the unconscious . . .'[95] Thus Canaanite myth envisaged the creation of the world as the result of God's triumphant rolling back of the formless ocean.[96] Man's consciousness emerges briefly from the unindividuated unity of the unconscious, to subside into it once more at the end.

That these are the essential outlines of the Merlin story to me at least seems clear. But there remains much that is tantalisingly concealed. The establishment of any part of the story rests, as the reader will have become painfully aware, on complex questions of source-criticism. All research is in a continually developing state, and some Celtic scholars will wish to challenge my interpretations or conclusions. It is essential to bear in mind that no argument is worth more than the evidence on which it rests. The Matter of Britain survives only in shattered images and broken shards, a ruined city glimpsed beneath the darkened waters of a mountain lake.

Fourteen centuries have passed since Merlin's mocking laugh died in the rocky defile of Hart Fell, but in crags above, the echoes linger. He has returned to the darkness of the Forest whence he came. The anguished strains of his mantic ecstasy live on, and sound through the encrustation of centuries in the poetry of the *Afallennau* and the *Hoianau*. The oaks of the Coed Celyddon have fallen, but among the darkness of their rotted trunks the saplings spring up. That other Merlin, too, survives, whose inward eye traversed the centuries, legitimising the British Monarchy and foretelling the destiny of the Island of the Mighty. Aspects of the myth of Merlin – his virgin birth, his prophecy, his power over the creatures of the wild and his suffering the triple fate of Lug – were variously incorporated into the legends of the founders of Christianity in Wales and Scotland, David and Kentigern. There was no return to darkness (there had never been any darkness); only a foreshadowing of the light.

Appendix

I am grateful to Professor A. O. H. Jarman for providing the following translations of the sections of the Welsh Myrddin poetry which refer to the early legend.

The Dialogue of Myrddin and Taliesin
(Black Book of Carmarthen Text)

Myrddin: How sad I am, how sad,
            For what befell Cedfyw and Cadfan!
            The battle was flashing and tumultuous,
            Shields were bloodstained and shattered.

Taliesin: It was Maelgwn that I saw in combat,
            The retinue is not silent before the host.

Myrddin: Before two men in two groups they gather,
            Before Errith and Gwrrith on pale white steeds,
            Slender bay horses without doubt will they bring,
            Soon the host with Elgan will be seen,
            Alas for his death, they have come a great journey.

Taliesin: One-toothed Rhys, whose shield was a span,
            To thee there came the blessing of battle.
            Cyndur has fallen, beyond measure will they grieve,
            Generous men, while they lived, have been slain,
            Three men of note, greatly esteemed by Elgan.

Myrddin: Over and over, in throng upon throng they came,
            From yonder and yonder there came to me fear for Elgan;
            In his last battle they slew Dywel,
            The son of Erbin, and his men.

Taliesin: Maelgwn's host, swiftly they came,

Battle-warriors in the glitter of slaughter.
It is the battle of Arfderydd whence comes the cause,
Throughout their lives they are preparing.

Myrddin: A host of spearsmen in the bloodshed of battle,
A host of mighty warriors, mortal will they be,
A host when broken, a host when put to flight,
A host retreating, under attack.

Taliesin: The seven sons of Eliffer, seven proven warriors,
Will not avoid seven spears in their seven battle-sections.

Myrddin: Seven blazing fires, seven opposing armies,
In every first onset Cynfelyn will be among the seven.

Taliesin: Seven piercing spears, seven rivers full,
With the blood of chieftains will they swell.

Myrddin: Seven score men of rank lapsed into madness,[1]
In the forest of Celyddon they perished:
Since it is I, Myrddin, after Taliesin,
Whose prophecy will be correct.

[1] *gwillon*

The *Afallennau* ('Apple-trees')
(Black Book of Carmarthen text)

1. Sweet-apple tree with sweet branches
Fruit-bearing, of great value, famous, belonging to me . . .
2. Sweet-apple tree, a tall, green tree,
Fruit-bearing its branches and fair trunk . . .
3. Sweet-apple tree, a yellow tree,
Which grows at the end of a hill without tilled land around it . . .
4. Sweet-apple tree which grows beyond Rhun,
I had contended at its foot for the satisfaction of a maiden,
With my shield on my shoulder and my sword on my thigh,
And in the forest of Celyddon I slept alone;
O! little pig why didst thou think of sleep?
Listen to the birds, their imploring is heard . . .
5. Sweet-apple tree which grows in a glade,
Its peculiar power hides it from the lords of Rhydderch;
A crowd by its trunk, a host around it,
It would be a treasure for them, brave men in their ranks.
Now Gwenddydd loves me not and does not greet me

– I am hated by Gwasawg, the supporter of Rhydderch –
I have killed her son and her daughter.
Death has taken everyone, why does it not call me?
For after Gwenddolau no lord honours me,
Mirth gives me no delight, no woman visits me;
And in the battle of Arfderydd my torque was of gold,
Though today I am not treasured by the one of the aspect of swans.

6. Sweet-apple tree with gentle flowers,
   Which grows hidden in the woodlands;
   I have heard tidings since early in the day
   That Gwasawg the supporter of . . . has been angered,
   Twice, thrice, four times in one day.
   O Jesus! would that my end had come
   Before I was guilty of the death of the son of Gwenddydd.

7. Sweet-apple tree which grows on a river bank,
   The steward, approaching it, will not succeed in obtaining its fine fruit;
   While I was in my right mind I used to have at its foot
   A fair wanton maiden, one slender and queenly.
   For ten and twenty years, in distressful outlawry,
   I have been wandering with madness and madmen.[1]
   After goodly possessions and pleasing minstrels
   Now want afflicts me with madness and madmen.[2]
   Now I sleep not, I tremble for my prince,
   My lord Gwenddolau, and my fellow-countrymen.
   After enduring sickness and grief in the Forest of Celyddon
   May I be a blissful man with the Lord of Hosts.

8. Sweet-apple tree with gentle flowers,
   Which grows in the earth, its branches unequal in length,
   The wild man[3] foretells the tidings which will come . . .

9. Sweet-apple tree, a red-flowered tree,
   Which grows hidden in the Forest of Celyddon,
   Though it be sought it will be in vain owing to its peculiar quality
   Until Cadwaladr comes to his meeting with the battle-hosts . . .

[1] & [2] *gan willeith a gwyllon*
[3]*Disgogan hwinleian*

The *Oianau* ('Greetings')
(Black Book of Carmarthen text)

1. O little pig, a happy pig,
   Do not burrow thy lair on the top of a mountain,
   Burrow in a hidden place in the woodlands
   For fear of the hunting-dogs of Rhydderch Hael, defender of the
   Faith,
   And I prophesy, and it will be true . . .

2. O little pig, it were necessary to go
   Before the huntsmen of the court, if one dared,
   For fear we should be pursued and seen,
   And if we escape we shall not complain of our weariness,
   And I prophesy before the ninth wave . . .
3. O little pig, I do not sleep easily,
   From the agitation of the sorrow which is upon me;
   For ten and forty years I have endured pain,
   A woeful appearance is upon me.
   May I receive from Jesus the support
   Of the Kings of Heaven of the highest lineage!
   He was not born with good fortune, of the children of Adam,
   Who does not believe in God in the last day.
   I have seen Gwenddolau, a glorious prince,
   Gathering booty from every border;
   Beneath the brown earth now he is still,
   Chief of the kings of the North, greatest in generosity.
4. O little pig, a prayer were needed
   For fear of five sovereigns from Normandy . . .
5. O little pig, be not drowsy,
   Sad tidings will come to us . . .
6. O little pig, a wretched pig,
   The wild man[1] tells me strange news,
   And I prophesy . . .
7. O little pig, a bright pig
   The wild man[2] told me news which frightens me . . .
8. O little pig, hail, greetings!
   If needful, God would make reversions.
   The pig which is alive will be mine,
   And the one which is dead, let him seek it.
9. O little pig, it is broad daylight,
   Listen to the call of the water-birds with their loud cries,
   For us there will be years and long days . . .
10. O little pig, with sharp claws,
    A rude bedfellow when thou didst go to lie.
    Little does Rhydderch Hael know tonight in his feast
    What sleeplessness I suffered last night,
    Snow up to my hips among the wolves of the forest,
    Icicles in my hair, spent is my splendour . . .
    And unless I receive from my Lord a portion of mercy
    Alas for me that it has befallen me, wretched my end.
11. O little pig . . .
12. O little pig, a bright pig,
    Do not sleep in the morning, do not burrow in the thicket,
    Lest Rhydderch Hael and his trained dogs come:
    Before thou findest the woods thy sweat will run!

13. O little pig, a bright pig,
    Hadst thou seen as much harsh violence as I have seen
    Thou wouldst not sleep in the morning, thou wouldst not burrow the hill,
    Thou wouldst not seek the wilderness from a desolate pool (?) . . .
14. O little pig, listen now . . .
15. O little pig, the mountain is green,
    My cloak is thin, it is not sufficient for me,
    My hair is grey, Gwenddydd does not visit me . . .
16. O little pig, a lively pig,
    Do not burrow thy lair, do not consume increasingly,
    Do not desire the meadow, be not devoted to play . . .
17. O little pig, the thorns are flowering,
    The mountainside is green, the earth is beautiful,
    And I prophesy . . .
18. O little pig, a great wonder
    Will be in Britain, but it will not concern me . . .
19. O little pig, how strange
    That not for one moment is the world the same! . . .
20. O little pig, listen to the deer,
    And the twitter of birds by Caer Rheon . . .
21. O little pig, there will be a troubled world . . .
22. O little pig, small and speckled,
    Listen to the call of the sea-birds, of great energy . . .
    A wild man[3] from afar has told me
    That kings with strange connections,
    Goidels and Britons and Romans,
    Will make adversity and disorder . . .
23. O little pig, small, strong-legged,
    Listen to the cry of the sea-birds of great clamour . . .
24. O little pig, there is for me no purpose
    To hear the call of the water-birds of clamorous sound,
    The hair of my head is thin, my cloak not warm,
    The meadows are my barn, my corn is not plenteous.
    My summer store does not sustain me . . .
25. O little pig, a lustful (?) pig,
    My cloak is thin, it is not sufficient for me.
    Since the battle of Arfderydd I care not
    Were the sky to fall and the sea to overflow . . .

[1] & [2] *hwimleian*
[3] *gwyllon*

The Translations of '*Gwyllon*' and '*Gwyllt*'

Professor Jarman, at the points indicated, has translated the words *gwyllon* and *hwimleian* by 'madmen', 'madman'. Earlier scholars, such as Thomas Stephens and Edward Anwyl, preferred the meaning 'shades', in the sense of 'spirits', 'ghosts'.[1] Professor Jarman's preference rests on the facts that *gwyllt* appears in Welsh poetry seemingly invariably in the familiar sense of 'wild', 'mad',[2] and concludes that the *gwyllan* are therefore madmen; that is, the Wild Men of mediaeval folklore. *Hwimleian* he translates as 'pale wanderer' and presumes from the context to be synonymous with *gwyllon*.[3]

There are however reasons for preferring Anwyl's interpretation, and for regarding the *gwyllon* as beings possessing supernatural attributes far removed from the conception of the Wild Man of mediaeval tradition.

1. The *gwyllon* of the *Hoianau* and *Afallennau* are an important source of Myrddin's prophetic inspiration.[4] The implication must surely be that they possess access to Otherworld knowledge denied to the prophet himself; *i.e.* that they are beings of an altogether different nature. The alternative, that one 'madman' acquired his craft from another, seems improbable.

2. A recurrent theme of the poetry is Myrddin's extreme loneliness in his forest retreat, arousing the pathetic plaint in the *Afallennau* that,
'Death has taken everyone, why does it not call me?'
Yet two verses later he is made to complain that he has for thirty years been living among the *gwyllon* who are still with him:
'Nv nev nam guy guall gan wylleith a gwyllon'.[5]
It is quite clear that the poet regarded Myrddin as generically different from the *gwyllon*, and that they were not to be counted as (human) companions.

3. One cannot make too much of the exact sense of so obscure a poem as the *Ymddiddan Myrddin a Thaliesin*, but nevertheless its last verse seems to imply that the *gwyllon* were conceived of as the ghosts of the slain at Arderydd. To say that
'Seven score men of rank lapsed into madness,
In the Forest of Celyddon they perished',
appears something of a non-sequitur;[6] whereas the two clauses
   . . . *a aethan y gwyllon*
   . . . *y daruuanan*
make sense rather than otherwise if they are homologous:
   . . . they became *gwyllon*
   . . . they perished.

4. Procopius in the sixth century says that the inhabitants of Britannia described the region between the Roman Walls as a wilderness frequented only by wild beasts, and popularly regarded as the home of departed spirits. This is precisely the region where tradition located the *Coed*

Celyddon, and in the *gwyllon* of the Myrddin poetry is surely preserved a lingering memory of the belief reported to the Byzantine historian by travellers from Britain.

In the Irish Mirabilia in the Norse *Speculum Regale* there is a famous passage describing how certain cowardly men were wont to go mad with fear in battle and betake themselves to the forests. Known as *gelt*, they lived in a savage condition until they gradually acquired a coat of feathers. Unable to fly, they could nevertheless outstrip a greyhound on the level sward, and 'run along the trees almost as swiftly as monkeys or squirrels'.[7]

There is no means of knowing how this complex notion originated, but a likely surmise is that it reflects a belief that the spirits of men slain in battle flew off in bird-form (a familiar Celtic concept)[8] to live in the remotest depths of the forests. For Myrddin's Irish *alter ego*, Suibhne, was one such *geilt*. At the height of the battle of Magh Rath he ascended into the air and after long and arduous wanderings in out-of-the-way places, 'reached ever-delightful Glen Bolcain. It is there that the *gealta* used to go when their year of being *geilt* was complete, that glen being a place of great delight for *gealta*. For it is thus Glen Bolcain is: it has four gaps to the wind, likewise a wood very beautiful, very pleasant, and clean-banked wells and cool springs, and sandy, clear-water streams, and green-topped watercress and brooklime bent and long on their surface . . .'[9]

Here and in further references we have all the hall-marks of a typical Irish Otherworld refuge, and we see that the *gealta* were men doomed to pass a year in the wilderness being *gealta*, until their time was up and they were permitted to enter their particular elysium. Because their death in battle was sudden and frequently unattended by the appropriate rites, it may be that the slain were envisaged as compelled to flit about in bird form for a time as a sort of purgatorial prelude to entering the Otherworld. Alternatively, if the element of cowardice be original, one might regard this as the specific cause of the year's prefatory ordeal.

In the poem *Ymddiddan Myrddin a Thaliesin* we learn that 'seven rivers' were 'full with the blood of chieftains . . .

Seven score nobles became *gwyllon*,
In the Forest of Celyddon they perished.'

These *gwyllon* parallel the *gealta* of the cognate story of Suibhne Geilt, and once again it looks as if the fate of the slain 140 nobles was to haunt (for a term?) the nearby Forest of Celyddon as wandering shades or ghosts. They were presumably the followers of Myrddin's defeated patron Gwenddolau, and it was from them or kindred *gwyllon* that Myrddin acquired prophetic information. Having passed over to the realm of the dead, they had access to its occult knowledge.

The epithet *gwyllt* borne by Myrddin himself connotes the frenzy of the inspired prophet (as Giraldus Cambrensis recognised), possessed by shamanistic ecstasy enabling his spirit to leave his body and travel in search of Otherworld knowledge. It is the induced and temporary frenzy of the

Phantom in *Baile in Scáil*, that Irish prophecy whose format so closely parallels the *Cyfoesi Myrddin a Gwenddydd y Chwaer*.[10]

The context suggests, therefore, that the *gwyllon* of the Forest of Celyddon were Otherworld beings, possibly the spirits of the slain, who were possessed of prophetic knowledge which they imparted to the exiled seer. The *hwimleian*, or 'pale wanderer' was a being of similar or identical powers encountered in the Forest.

Since Myrddin's rôle as shaman has been made plain, the rôle of the *gwyllon* becomes clear too. In the prophetic poems *Cyfoesi Myrddin* and *Gwasgarddgerdd vyrddin* references are made to *wylon mynyd*,[11] which Phillimore translated as 'mountain sprites' and J. J. Parry as 'ghosts of the mountain'.[12]

In view of the deeply shamanistic nature of Myrddin's 'call' it is instructive to recall the prevailing belief among Lapp shamans that their prophetic inspiration derived from *passevare olmai*, 'holy mountain men' . . .
'these spirits who lived in sacred mountains called the Lapp into the shamanic office. When the shaman wanted their council he sent for them through his *saiva leddie* . . . a bird spirit at his service . . . A female *saiva* spirit, called *saiva nieidie* ("supernatural virgin"), strengthened the shaman with water . . .' And elsewhere we learn that these mountain sprites appeared to the shaman in his dreams.[13] Finally,
'these *saivo* spirits as a general rule were believed to be souls of departed Samic shamans. In regard to all ideas of this kind we have moreover found that they do not stand alone in the religion of the Lapps, but are encountered among primitive peoples all over the world. Thus the Jibaro Indians in the virgin forests east of the Andes in Ecuador and Peru have exactly the same ideas about the spirits which according to their belief inhabit the high mountains: they are souls of sorcerers who after death have taken up their abode in the mountains, and they are invoked with conjurations by the sorcerers, when they are exercising their art.'
Thus the Lapps regarded mountains as the abode of the departed, holding at the same time that it was they who imparted shamanic knowledge to the shaman who resorted to the mountain for prophetic inspiration.[14]

This remarkably close parallel accords perfectly with what in any case is a reasonable *prima facie* interpretation of the references to *gwyllon* in the Welsh Myrddin poetry. On this analogy the Pale Wanderer (*hwimleian*) may possibly be envisaged as the British equivalent of the Lapp Mountain Virgin (*saivo nieide*).

List of Primary Sources

In order to save repetition in the notes, the editions of early texts regularly referred to in the narrative are listed here. More precise reference may be readily found through their respective indices.

Adomnan: Alan Orr Anderson and Marjorie Ogilvie Anderson (ed.), *Adomnan's Life of Columba* (Edinburgh, 1961).

Black Book of Carmarthen: J. Gwenogvryn Evans (ed.), *The Black Book of Carmarthen* (Pwllheli, 1906).

Book of Taliesin: J. Gwenogvryn Evans (ed.), *Facsimile & Text of the Book of Taliesin* (Llanbedrog, 1910).

de Boron: Alexandre Micha (ed.), *Robert de Boron; Merlin: roman du XIIIe siècle* (Geneva, 1980).

Fergus: Ernst Martin (ed.), *Fergus: Roman von Guillaume le Clerc* (Halle, 1872).

Geoffrey of Monmouth: Acton Griscom (ed.), *The Historia Regum Britanniæ of Geoffrey of Monmouth* (New York, 1929).

Gildas: Theodor Mommsen (ed.), 'Gildae Sapientis De Excidio et Conqvestv Britanniae . . .', *Monvmenta Germaniae Historica*, xiii, *Chronica Minora*, iii (Berlin, 1894).

Giraldus Cambrensis: J. S. Brewer *et al.* (ed.), *Giraldi Cambrensis, Opera* (London, 1861–91).

Gododdin: J. Gwenogvryn Evans (ed.), *Facsimile & Text of the Book of Aneirin* (Pwllhelli, 1908).

St Kentigern: Alexander Penrose Forbes (ed.), *Lives of S. Ninian and S. Kentigern. Compiled in the Twelfth Century* (Edinburgh, 1874).

Lailoken: H. L. D. Ward, 'Lailoken (or Merlin Silvester)', *Romania* (Paris, 1893), xxii, pp. 504–26.

Layamon: G. L. Brook and R. F. Leslie (ed.), *Lazamon: Brut* (Oxford, 1963).

Mabinogion: J. Gwenogvryn Evans (ed.), *The White Book Mabinogion: Welsh Tales & Romances Reproduced from the Peniarth Manuscripts* (Pwllheli, 1907); John Rhŷs and J. Gwenogvryn Evans (ed.), *The Text of the Mabinogion and Other Welsh Tales from the Red Book of Hergest* (Oxford, 1887).

Malory: Eugene Vinaver (ed.), *The Works of Sir Thomas Malory* (Oxford, 1948).

Nennius: Theodor Mommsen (ed.), 'Historia Brittonvm cvm Additamentis Nennii', *Monvmenta Germaniae Historica*, xiii, *Chronica Minora*, iii (Berlin, 1894).

Of Arthour and of Merlin: O. D. Macrae-Gibson (ed.), *Of Arthour and of Merlin* (Oxford, 1973–79).

Red Book of Hergest: J. Gwenogvryn Evans (ed.), *The Poetry in the Red Book of Hergest* (Llanbedrog, 1911).

St Samson: R. Fawtier (ed.), *La vie de Saint Samson: Essai de critique hagiographique* (Paris, 1912).

Suibhne: J. G. O'Keefe (ed.), *Buile Suibhne (The Frenzy of Suibhne) Being The Adventures of Suibhne Geilt: A Middle-Irish Romance* (London, 1913).

Triads: Rachel Bromwich (ed.), *Trioedd Ynys Prydein: The Welsh Triads* (Cardiff, 1961).

Vita Merlini: Basil Clarke (ed.), *Life of Merlin; Geoffrey of Monmouth: Vita Merlini* (Cardiff, 1973).

Wace: I. D. O. Arnold and M. M. Pelan (ed.), *La Partie Arthurienne du Roman de Brut* (Paris, 1966).

Chapter Notes

Notes to Pages 21–41

One *The Matter of Britain*

1 For Dimilioc and Tintagel, cf. W. Howship Dickinson, *King Arthur in Cornwall* (London, 1900), pp. 51–70.

2 R. L. Graeme Ritchie, *Chrétien de Troyes and Scotland* (Oxford, 1952), p. 16.

3 T. D. Kendrick, *British Antiquity* (London, 1950), pp. 1–4; Austin Lane Poole, *From Domesday Book to Magna Carta* (Oxford, 1951), pp. 247–50. Geoffrey certainly provided Britain with 'a glorious past', but he was really concerned with contemporary issues and his 'principal object was to amuse' (Antonia Gransden, *Historical Writing in England c. 550 to c. 1307* (London, 1974), pp. 204–8.)
For the eschatological view of history in the Middle Ages, cf. S. G. F. Brandon, *History, Time and Deity: A Historical and Comparative Study of the Conception of Time in Religious Thought and Practice* (Manchester, 1965), p. 208. The appearance of the *HRB* coincided with a time of intensive but fruitless enquiry into early British history (R. William Leckie, jr., *The Passage of Dominion: Geoffrey of Monmouth and the Periodization of Insular History in the Twelfth Century* (Toronto, 1981), p. 41). Geoffrey's pro-British bias was acceptable to the Norman ascendancy because it shewed the Saxons in a poor light, distinguished the Welsh from their predecessors the Britons, and bestowed much credit on the *Bretons*, many of whom had accompanied William the Conqueror to England in 1066 (ibid., pp. 69–71).

4 E. K. Chambers, *Arthur of Britain* (London, 1927), p. 112.

5 Chambers, op. cit., pp. 258–60; A. B. Scott and F. X. Martin (ed.), *Expugnatio Hibernica: The Conquest of Ireland by Giraldus Cambrensis* (Dublin, 1978), pp. 64, 92, 96, 106, 174, 226–28; John J. Parry and Robert A. Caldwell, 'Geoffrey of Monmouth', in R. S. Loomis (ed.), *Arthurian Literature in the Middle Ages* (Oxford, 1959), p. 79.

6 Thomas Jones, 'The Black Book of Carmarthen "Stanzas of the

Graves,"' *The Proceedings of the British Academy* (London, 1967), liii, p. 127.

7 William A. Nitze (ed.), *Robert de Boron: Le Roman de l'Estoire dou Graal* (Paris, 1927), p. 112.

8 Eugène Vinaver, *The Rise of Romance* (Oxford, 1971), p. 104.

9 Cf. Kendrick, op. cit., pp. 34–38; also Edmund Reiss, 'The Welsh Versions of Geoffrey of Monmouth's Historia', *The Welsh History Review* (Cardiff, 1968), iv, p. 98. For Welsh 'prophecies' of the reigns of 'Henri' and the 'Virgine Queene', see J. G. Evans (ed.), *Report on Manuscripts in the Welsh Language* (London, 1898–1902), i, pp. 580, 581; the *cywyddau brud* however drew on an older and broader tradition than the *HRB* (Glanmor Williams, 'Proffwydoliaeth, prydyddieth a pholitics yn yr oesoedd canol', *Taliesin* (Llandybie), xvi, pp. 31–39). For the revival of Geoffrey's reputation, cf. Sydney Anglo, 'The British History in early Tudor propaganda', *The Bulletin of the John Rylands Library* (Manchester, 1961), xliv, pp. 17–43; and for Merlin as popular prophet in Elizabethan times, Keith Thomas, *Religion and the Decline of Magic: Studies in popular beliefs in sixteenth and seventeenth century England* (London, 1972), pp. 394, 397–403, 405, etc.

10 Cf. my review of Robert B. Stoker's *The Legacy of Arthur's Chester* (London, 1965) in *Irish Historical Studies* (Dublin, 1966), xv, p. 82.

11 E. K. Chambers, *William Shakespeare: A Study of Facts and Problems* (Oxford, 1930), i, p. 466. Merlin was subsequently hero of an inferior play by William Rowley, *The Birth of Merlin* (published in 1662) (E. J. Miller, 'Wales and the Tudor Drama', *The Transactions of the Honourable Society of Cymmrodorion* (1948), p. 174).

12 Bernard Capp, *Astrology and the Popular Press: English Almanacs 1500–1800* (London, 1979), p. 190.

13 *Vivien* understandably aroused some scandalised comment at the time (J. Philip Eggers, *King Arthur's Laureate: A Study of Tennyson's Idylls of the King* (New York, 1971), pp. 83–85). For a comprehensive survey of modern literature employing Merlin as a character, cf. Beverly Taylor and Elisabeth Brewer, *The Return of King Arthur: British and American Arthurian Literature since 1800* (Cambridge, 1983).

14 C. Morine Krissdottir, *John Cowper Powys and the Magical Quest* (London, 1980), pp. 127–70.

Two *Merlin The Prophet*

1 For descriptions and datings of the manuscripts, cf. J. G. Evans (ed.), *Report on Manuscripts in the Welsh Language* (London, 1898–1902), i. pp. 297–99, 300–2; ii, pp. iv, 1–29; Ifor Williams (ed.), *Canu Aneirin gyda Rhagymadrodd a Nodiadau* (Cardiff, 1938), pp. xii–xiv; A. O. H. Jarman (ed.), *Llyfr Du Caerfyrddin gyda Rhagymadrodd Nodiadau*

Testunol a Geirfa (Cardiff, 1982), pp. xiii–xxiv (note by Dr. E. D. Jones). For Welsh translations of the *Prophetia Merlini*, cf. Brynley R. Roberts, 'Copiau Cymraeg o Prophetiae Merlini', *Cylchgrawn Llyfrgell Genedlaethol Cymru* (Aberystwyth, 1977), xx, pp. 14–39.

2 Translation by Professor A. O. H. Jarman, *The Cynfeirdd: Early Welsh Poets and Poetry* (Cardiff, 1981), pp. 109–10.

3 Idem, *The Legend of Merlin* (Cardiff, 1960), p. 16.

4 Rachel Bromwich, 'The Character of the Early Welsh Tradition', in N. K. Chadwick (ed.), *Studies in Early British History* (Cambridge, 1959), pp. 125–26.

5 H. M. Chadwick and N. K. Chadwick, *The Growth of Literature* (Cambridge, 1932–40), i, pp. 105–14, 123–32; P. L. Henry, *The Early English and Celtic Lyric* (London, 1966), pp. 25–26; A. O. H. Jarman, 'Early Stages in the Development of the Myrddin Legend', in Rachel Bromwich and R. Brinley Jones (ed.) *Astudiaethau ar yr Hengerdd* (Cardiff, 1978), pp. 343–45; Kenneth Jackson, 'The Motive of the Threefold Death in the Story of Suibhne Geilt', *Féil-sgribhinn Eóin mhic Néill* (ed. Eóin ua Riain) (Dublin, 1940), p. 546; Patrick Sims-Williams, 'The evidence for vernacular Irish literary influence on early mediaeval Welsh literature', in Dorothy Whitelock *et al.* (ed.), *Ireland in Early Mediaeval Europe* (Cambridge, 1982), p. 237.

6 J. Lloyd-Jones, 'The Court Poets of the Welsh Princes', *The Proceedings of the British Academy* (London, 1948), xxxiv, pp. 3–4; cf. Rachel Bromwich, 'Y Cynfeirdd a'r Traddodiad Cymraeg', *The Bulletin of the Board of Celtic Studies* (Cardiff, 1966), xxii, pp. 30–37; Nikolai Tolstoy, 'Merlinus Redivivus', *Studia Celtica* (Cardiff, 1983–4), xviii–xix, pp. 11–29.

Three *The Kings of the North*

1 '*Gwelais*', 'I have seen', is not to be taken literally but as an expression of the poet's visionary power (Sir Ifor Williams, *Lectures on Early Welsh Poetry* (Dublin, 1944), p. 7).

2 Rachel Bromwich, *Trioedd Ynys Prydein: The Welsh Triads* (Cardiff, 1961), pp. 380, 471.

3 H. Munro Chadwick, *The Heroic Age* (Cambridge, 1912), pp. 365, 425.

4 Sir John Morris-Jones, 'Taliesin', *Y Cymmrodor* (London, 1918), xxviii, p. 196. The expression 'o wawl hyt weryt' is found in *The Book of Taliesin*.

5 P. C. Bartrum (ed.), *Early Welsh Genealogical Tracts* (Cardiff, 1966), pp. 72–73.

6 I. A. Richmond (ed.), *Roman and Native in North Britain* (Edinburgh, 1958), pp. 56, 64, 76, 88–89.

7 David J. Breeze, *The Northern Frontiers of Roman Britain* (London,

1982), pp. 159–60; J. C. Mann, 'Hadrian's Wall: the last phases', in P. J. Casey (ed.), *The End of Roman Britain* (Oxford, 1979), pp. 159–60.

8 Ifor Williams (ed.), *Canu Aneirin* (Cardiff, 1938), pp. liii–lviii; K. H. Jackson, *The Gododdin: The Oldest Scottish Poem* (Edinburgh, 1969), pp. 13–16.

9 Cf. Kenneth Jackson, 'Angles and Britons in Northumbria and Cumbria', *Angles and Britons* (Cardiff, 1963), p. 68.

10 It used to be thought that 'Eitin' referred to Edinburgh (cf. H. M. Chadwick, *Early Scotland: The Picts, the Scots & the Welsh of Southern Scotland* (Cambridge, 1949), pp. 144, 145), but it now seems more probable that Cynon and his father came from within or near the bounds of Rheged (Rachel Bromwich, 'Cynon fab Clydno' in Rachel Bromwich and R. Brinley Jones (ed.), *Astudiaethau ar yr Hengerdd* (Cardiff, 1978), p. 159.)

11 W. F. Skene, *The Four Ancient Books of Wales* (London, 1868), i, pp. 172–73; ii, p. 406; *Y Cymmrodor*, xxviii, pp. 74–75. Of course there can be no certainty; cf. Professor Jackson's caution (*The Welsh Historical Review* (Cardiff, 1963), i, p. 84).

12 V. E. Nash-Williams, *The Early Christian Monuments of Wales* (Cardiff, 1950), p. 14. Professor A. C. Thomas has argued persuasively that sub-Roman episcopal dioceses of the Lowlands reflect the four great tribal areas ('The Evidence from North Britain', in M. W. Barley and R. P. C. Hanson (ed.), *Christianity in Britain, 300–700* (Leicester, 1968), pp. 111–16).

13 This broad picture of life in Dark-Age Britain draws on a variety of sources, some later than the sixth century in their extant form, but I believe sufficiently representative of an exceedingly archaic and conservative society. For the ramparts of a *din* or *llys*, cf. Leslie Alcock, '*By South Cadbury is that Camelot . . .*' *The Excavation of Cadbury Castle 1966–1970* (London, 1972), pp. 175–78; idem, *Arthur's Britain: History and Archaeology AD 367–634* (London, 1971), pp. 222–25. The smithy is enumerated in the Welsh Laws: Melville Richards (ed.), *Cyfreithiau Hywel Dda: O Lawysgrif Coleg yr Iesu Rhydychen LVII* (Cardiff, 1957), pp. 18–19, 51–52. For thatched roofs and fire hazards, cf., ibid., p. 54; Leslie Alcock, *Dinas Powys: An Iron Age, Dark Age and Early Medieval Settlement in Glamorgan* (Cardiff, 1963), pp. 44–47, 216–19; 'gnaðt kael to yg gweunud' (Kenneth Jackson (ed.), *Early Welsh Gnomic Poems* (Cardiff, 1935), p. 26). The diet of the poor is assessed by Michael E. Jones, 'Climate, Nutrition and Disease: An Hypothesis of Romano-British Population', in Casey, op. cit., p. 233. The teeth of a six year old child buried at Dinas Powys (5th century A.D.) contained 'no conclusive evidence of the long term disturbance which might be expected from a diet deficient during a season' (*Dinas Powys*, p. 207); cf. Ludwig Bieler (ed.), *The Irish Penitentials* (Dublin, 1963), p. 60. For their life and labour, glancing allusions are to be found in *Early Welsh Gnomic Poems*, pp. 27, 28, 30; Ifor Williams

(ed.), *Canu Llywarch Hen gyda Rhagymadrodd a Nodiadau* (Cardiff, 1935), p. 23. For the gatehouse lantern, cf. A. O. H. Jarman, 'The Delineation of Arthur in Early Welsh Verse', in Kenneth Varty (ed.), *An Arthurian Tapestry: essays in memory of Lewis Thorpe* (Cambridge, 1983), p. 12. Porters' lodges were found at Castle Dore (C. A. Ralegh Radford, 'Report on the Excavations at Castle Dore', *Journal of the Royal Institution of Cornwall* (Truro, 1951), i (appendix 1951), pp. 66–67, 96. For literary references to this generally surly tribe, cf. Richards, op. cit., p. 5; J. Gwenogvryn Evans (ed.), *The Black Book of Carmarthen* (Pwllheli, 1906), p. 94; John Rhys and J. Gwenogvryn Evans (ed.), *The Text of the Mabinogion and Other Welsh Tales from the Red Book of Hergest* (Oxford, 1887), p. 162; T. Mommsen (ed.), *Monumenta Germaniae Historica*, xiii, *Chronica Minora*, iii (Berlin, 1894), iii, pp. 98–99, 173. The blazing fire and brightly lit hall is found in *The Gododdin: The Oldest Scottish Poem*, p. 138, and for the structure of the hall, cf. *Arthur's Britain*, pp. 225–27; '*By South Cadbury is that Camelot . . .*', pp. 177–80; *Journal of the Royal Institution of Cornwall*, (appendix 1951), pp. 61–64. For Irish Parallels, cf. Kenneth Jackson, *The Oldest Irish Tradition: A Window on the Iron Age* (Cambridge, 1964), pp. 20–21. Seating arrangements were skilfully elucidated by Proinsias Mac Cana, *Branwen Daughter of Llyr: A Study of the Irish Affinities and of the Composition of the Second Branch of the Mabinogi* (Cardiff, 1958), p. 74, and references to various types of food appear in Jackson, *The Gododdin*, pp. 33–37; *Dinas Powys*, pp. 36–40, 50–52; Richards, op. cit., pp. 53, 66–67. For the importance of the winter's hospitality as a social function, cf. Ifor Williams (ed.), *Canu Taliesin* (Cardiff, 1960), p. 51; Richards, op. cit., p. 93; Jackson, *The Gododdin*, pp. 39–40, 120, 132; T. M. Charles-Edwards, 'The Authenticity of the *Gododdin*: An Historian's View', *Astudiaethau ar yr Hengerdd*, pp. 46–47, 57–61; *Y Cymmrodor*, xxviii, p. 172. For chivalry and the position of women, cf. Jackson, *The Gododdin*, pp. 40–41, 100, 116, 128, 143; Richards, op. cit., p. 63; and for sports and games, ibid., pp. 13, 65 (*gware raffan*); J. Gwenogvryn Evans (ed.), *The White Book Mabinogion: Welsh Tales and Romances Reproduced from the Peniarth Manuscripts* (Pwllheli, 1907), p. 12 (*broch yg got*). Some beautiful lines by a 16th-century Irish poet convey an idyllic impression of the pleasures of Celtic court life (James Carney, *The Irish Bardic Poet* (Dublin, 1967), p. 29).

14 C. A. Ralegh Radford, 'Imported Pottery found at Tintagel, Cornwall', in D. B. Harden (ed.), *Dark-Age Britain* (London, 1956), pp. 59–70; Charles Thomas, *Britain and Ireland in Early Christian Times* (London, 1971), pp. 85–88.

15 The late John Morris does seem to have hit the mark for once with a remarkably ingenious point ('Dark Age Dates', in M. G. Jarrett and B. Dobson (ed.), *Britain and Rome: Essays Presented to Eric Birley on his Sixtieth Birthday* (Kendal, 1965), p. 184.)

16 Anne Ross, *Everyday Life of the Pagan Celts* (London, 1970), p. 113.
17 Thomas D. O'Sullivan, *The De Excidio of Gildas: Its Authenticity and Date* (Leiden, 1978), pp. 28, 78.
18 *Y Cymmrodor*, xxviii, pp. 13–14; J. E. Caerwyn Williams, 'Gildas, Maelgwn and the Bards', in R. R. Davies *et al.* (ed.), *Welsh Society and Nationhood: Historical Essays Presented to Glanmor Williams* (Cardiff, 1984), pp. 19–34.
19 F. Kerlouégan, 'Le Latin du De Excidio Britanniae de Gildas', Barley and Hanson, op. cit., pp. 151–76.
20 Nash-Williams, op. cit., pp. 92, 93.
21 S. Burt, *Letters from A Gentleman in the North of Scotland to His Friend in London* (London, 1754), ii, pp. 161–2, 276; Archibald Arbuthnot, *The Life, Adventures, And Many and Great Vicissitudes of Fortune of Simon, Lord Lovat* (London, 1747), pp. 58–59.
22 John Strachan and J. G. O'Keefe (ed.), *The Táin Bó Cúailnge from the Yellow Book of Lecan* (Dublin, 1912), p. 79. This may be no mere hyperbole: 'One of the most frequently demonstrated effects of a mental state on a body condition is that of the formation of blisters at a designated spot as a result of hypnotic suggestion' (J. B. Rhine, *New World of the Mind* (London, 1954), pp. 31, 215–16).
23 Ifor Williams, *Lectures on Early Welsh Poetry* (Dublin, 1944), pp. 9–11.
24 Richards, op. cit., pp. 17–18.
25 *Canu Taliesin*, pp. xvii–xxiii, xxxv; *Y Cymmrodor*, xviii, p. 182.
26 Kenneth Jackson, *Studies in Early Celtic Nature Poetry* (Cambridge, 1935), pp. 52, 74.

Four *The Battle of Arderydd*

1 Kenneth Jackson, *Studies in Early Celtic Nature Poetry* (Cambridge, 1935), pp. 50, 53–55, 73; Melville Richards (ed.), *Cyfreithiau Hywel Dda; O Lawysgrif Coleg yr Iesu Rhydychen LVII* (Cardiff, 1957), pp. 57, 73, 75, 76–83; Leslie Alcock, *Dinas Powys; An Iron Age, Dark Age and Early Medieval Settlement in Glamorgan* (Cardiff, 1963), pp. 37, 40–42. For the seasonal migrations cf. Frederic Seebohm, *The Tribal System in Wales* (London, 1904), pp. 46–47; Melville Richards (ed.), *The Laws of Hywel Dda (The Book of Blegywryd)* (Liverpool, 1954), pp. 139–40. 'Winter's Day, the stags are thin . . . the summer dwelling ("hauot") is deserted' (Kenneth Jackson (ed.), *Early Welsh Gnomic Poems* (Cardiff, 1935), p. 28). For an excavation of *hafotai* of later date but very likely unchanging pattern, cf. C. B. Crampton, 'Hafotai Platforms on the North Front of the Brecon Beacons', *Archaeologia Cambrensis* (Cardiff, 1966), cxv, pp. 99–107. I do not think it has been remarked before that Gildas vouches for the practice in the sixth century: 'campis late pansis collibusque amoeno situ locatis,

praepollenti culturae aptis, montibus alternandis animalium pastibus maxime convenientibus' (T. Mommsen (ed.), 'Gildae Sapientis De Excidio et Conqvestv Britanniae . . .', *Monvmenta Germaniae Historica*, xiii, *Chronica Minora*, iii (Berlin, 1894), p. 28).

2 Richards, op. cit., p. 52; Kenneth Jackson, *The Gododdin: The Oldest Scottish Poem* (Edinburgh, 1969), p. 118; Ifor Williams (ed.), *Canu Taliesin* (Cardiff, 1960), pp. 58–59, 69.

3 Ibid., p. 33; J. Vendryes, 'Saint David et le roi Boia', *Revue Celtique* (Paris, 1928), xlx, pp. 141–72. Professor Jackson has summarised the light thrown on sixth-century warfare by the fullest 'contemporary' account (*The Gododdin*, pp. 28–33, 37–41). Cf. also H. Munro Chadwick and N. Kershaw Chadwick, *The Growth of Literature* (Cambridge, 1932), i, pp. 85–95; and A. O. H. Jarman, 'The Heroic View of Life in Early Welsh Verse', in Robert O'Driscoll (ed.), *The Celtic Consciousness* (New York, 1982), pp. 161–68.

4 M. Miller, 'The Commanders at Arthuret', *Transactions of the Cumberland and Westmoreland Antiquarian and Archaeological Society* (Kendal, 1975), lxxv, pp. 96–98; Rev. John Williams ab Ithel, *Annales Cambriae* (London, 1860), p. 5.

5 Professor Jarman says that 'the form *Merlinus*, used here, derives from Geoffrey's *Historia*, but the information contained in the statement does not in its entirety come from either of Geoffrey's works'. ('Early Stages in the Development of the Myrddin Legend', in Rachel Bromwich and R. Brinley Jones (ed.), *Astudiaethau ar yr Hengerdd* (Cardiff, 1978), pp. 337–8). However there is no justification for the assertion that it was Geoffrey who coined the form *Merlinus*. The Domesday Book *Annales Cambriae* version could be a synchronistic gloss pre- or post-dating Geoffrey, or could even originate from the earlier chronicle Dr Kathleen Hughes showed to have been compiled from the late eighth century at St David's ('The Welsh Latin Chronicles: *Annales Cambriae* and Related Texts', *The Proceedings of the British Academy* (London, 1973), lix, pp. 11–12). The 'Domesday' Annals include independent and seemingly authentic 6th-century entries, and do not draw on Geoffrey (ibid., 13–15), but the details certainly read like a gloss—of unknown provenance and date. The *Annales Cambriae* passage could as readily be a source of inspiration for Geoffrey's *Vita Merlini* as a derivative, and its monkish chronicler even more likely to have jibbed at the transliteration *Merdinus*. The name *Merlinus* is in fact recorded in an Italian document of 1128, eight years before Geoffrey issued the *Historia* (John J. Parry and Robert A. Caldwell, 'Geoffrey of Monmouth', in Roger Sherman Loomis (ed.), *Arthurian Literature in the Middle Ages: A Collaborative History* (Oxford, 1959), p. 91).

6 William F. Skene, *Celtic Scotland: A History of Ancient Alban* (Edinburgh, 1876), i, pp. 157–59; J. Rhys, *Celtic Britain* (London, 1884), p. 145; R. Cunliffe Shaw, *Post Roman Carlisle and the Kingdoms of the*

North-West (Preston, 1964), pp. 29–30); John Morris, *The Age of Arthur: A History of the British Isles from 350 to 600* (London, 1973), pp. 218–19, 232; *Transactions of the Cumberland and Westmoreland Antiquarian and Archaeological Society*, lxxv, pp. 101–17; Kenneth Jackson, 'O Achaws Nyth yr Ychedydd', *Ysgrifau Beirniadol* (Cardiff, 1977), x, pp. 45–50.

7 W. F. Skene, op. cit., i, p. 157.

8 H. M. Chadwick, *Early Scotland: The Picts, the Scots & the Welsh of Southern Scotland* (Cambridge, 1949), p. 145.

9 Cf. J. Loth, 'Une généalogie des rois de Stratclut remontant de la fin du IXe au Ve siècle', *Revue Celtique* (1930), xlvii, p. 180.

10 W. H. Davies, 'The Church in Wales', in M. W. Barley and R. P. C. Hanson (ed.), *Christianity in Britain, 300–700* (Leicester, 1968), Maelgwn 'is accused of sin, but not of paganism' (Thomas D. O'Sullivan, *The De Excidio of Gildas: Its Authenticity and Date* (Leiden, 1978), p. 115).

11 A. W. Wade-Evans, *The Emergence of England and Wales* (Cambridge, 1959), pp. 23–26.

12 Sir John Morris-Jones, 'Taliesin', *Y Cymmrodor* (London, 1918), xxviii, pp. 46–48; Edward Anwyl, *Celtic Religion in Pre-Christian Times* (London, 1906), p. 61; Jakob Haury (ed.), *Procopii Caesariensis Opera Omnia* (Berlin, 1963), ii, pp. 596–97).

13 Barley and Hanson, op. cit., pp. 97–111; J. E. Lloyd, *A History of Wales from the Earliest Times to the Edwardian Conquest* (London, 1911), p. 119.

14 The *englynion* place Urien's death at Aber Llew ('yn aber lleu llad uryen') (J. Gwenogvryn Evans (ed.), *The Poetry in the Red Book of Hergest* (Llanvedrog, 1911), p. 13), which is identified with the little brook of Ross Low, opposite Lindisfarne, where the *Historia Brittonum* places Urien's death (Ifor Williams, 'The Poems of Llywarch Hên', *The Proceedings of the British Academy* (London, 1932), xviii, p. 24; Kenneth Jackson, 'The Poems of Llywarch the Aged', *Antiquity* (Gloucester, 1935), ix, p. 325). Such an ephemeral record must surely rest on a very early source, most likely a *marwnad* for Urien missing from the Taliesin canon, which Sir Ifor Williams reasonably suggested may lie behind the *Historia Brittonum* account (*Lectures on Early Welsh Poetry* (Dublin, 1944), p. 51).

15 For different unsatisfactory explanations for the decapitation of Urien's corpse, cf. *The Growth of Literature*, i, p. 94; *The Proceedings of the British Academy*, xviii, p. 23; Patrick K. Ford, *The Poetry of Llywarch Hen* (Los Angeles, 1974), pp. 43, 103; N. J. A. Williams, 'Canu Llywarch Hen and the Finn Cycle', *Astudiaethau ar yr Hengerdd*, pp. 250–59. Nearly 200 years ago Owen Pughe enquired shrewdly: 'Does it not allude to some custom peculiar to the Britons?' (*The Heroic Elegies and Other Pieces of Llywarç Hen, Prince of the Cumbrian Britons* (London, 1792), p. 25).

16 Rev. Denis Murphy (ed.), *The Annals of Clonmacnoise being Annals of Ireland from the Earliest Period to A.D. 1408* (Dublin, 1896), p. 88; cf. William M. Hennessy (ed.), *Chronicum Scotorum. A Chronicle of Irish Affairs from the Earliest Times to A.D. 1135* (London, 1866), p. 56; Standish H. O'Grady (ed.), *Silva Gadelica* (London, 1892), ii, p. 88. This Diarmait mac Cerbaill was the last king to hold the pagan 'Feast of Tara' (*Feis Temro*), 'from which we may infer that the Tara monarchy was not Christianized – at any rate not fully Christianized' (D. A. Binchy, *Celtic and Anglo-Saxon Kingship* (Oxford, 1970), p. 11). The Ahenny cross bears a carving of a headless corpse being borne on horseback in procession, with an attendant bearing the head (Seán P. Ó. Riordáin, 'The Genesis of the Celtic Cross', in Séamus Pender (ed.), *Féilscríbhinn Torna* (Cork, 1947), p. 111 and Fig. 2). Another Irish example is that of Cormac mac Cuilennán, and we learn that it was 'the usage of victorious Irish kings' to place the head 'under his thigh' (Whitley Stokes (ed.), *Three Irish Glossaries* (London, 1862), p. xi). It is striking that the bard of the Urien *englynion* is made to say that 'I carry a head by my thigh', 'Penn aborthaf tu mordwyt'. In Ireland, 'the head of a buried hero is a security for the land' (A. C. van Hamel, 'Aspects of Celtic Mythology', *The Proceedings of the British Academy* (London, 1934), p. 7). In Britain, one of the best-known mythological tales concerns the death of Bendigeid Vran in Ireland, who ordered his followers to take his head back to Britain and inter it as such a defensive palladium (J. Gwenogvryn Evans (ed.), *The White Book of Rhydderch* (Pwlheli, 1907), pp. 29–30). The custom was not confined to the Celtic world (cf. Sir James Frazer, *The Dying God* (London, 1923), pp. 202–3).

17 *Y Cymmrodor*, xxviii, pp. 198–99; cf. R. S. Loomis, *Arthurian Tradition and Chrétien de Troyes* (New York, 1949), pp. 269–70. For other possibilities of Owain's pagan connections, cf. Ross, op. cit., pp. 253, 331; *The Growth of Literature*, i, pp. 224–25, 439.

18 'keneu menrud a vu neidyr vlô ydyn am y vanôgyl' (J. G. Evans (ed.), 'Pedigrees from Jesus College MS. 20', *Y Cymmrodor* (1887), viii, p. 88, cf. Alfred Anscombe, 'Indexes to Old-Welsh Genealogies', *Archiv für Celtische Lexicographie* (Halle, 1906), iii, p. 101; Gwilym Peredur Jones, 'A List of Epithets from Welsh Pedigrees', *The Bulletin of the Board of Celtic Studies* (Cardiff, 1926), iii, p. 34). The practice of twining a snake round the necks is widely recorded in Southern Africa (cf. Rev. Joseph Shooter, *The Kafirs of Natal and the Zulu Country* (London, 1857), p. 191; S. G. Lee, 'Spirit Possession among the Zulu', in John Beattie and John Middleton (ed.), *Spirit Mediumship and Society in Africa* (London, 1969), p. 139. Readers of Rider Haggard's fine novel, *Finished*, will remember the end of the Dwandwe wizard, Zikali.) In ancient Greece certain snakes used to lick the ears of Melampus, so conveying to him prophet powers (Hugh G. Evelyn-White (ed.),, *Hesiod: The Homeric Hymns and Homerica* (London,

1914), p. 262; Sir James Frazer (ed.), *Apollodorus: The Library* (London, 1921), i, p. 86; ii, p. 49), and from Shang China there are 'many references to the shaman's wearing of snakes on one or both ears' (K. C. Chang, *Art, Myth, and Ritual: The Path to Political Authority in Ancient China* (Harvard, 1983), pp. 73, 114).

19 Cf. Anne Ross, *Pagan Celtic Britain: Studies on Iconography and Tradition* (London, 1967), pp. 167, 306.

20 Ross, op. cit., p. 266. Cf. E. Anwyl, 'The Value of the Mabinogion for the Study of Celtic Religion', *Transactions of the Third International Congress for the History of Religions* (Oxford, 1908), ii, p. 241; Rachel Bromwich (ed.), *Trioedd Ynys Prydein: The Welsh Triads* (Cardiff, 1961), p. 69.

21 J. Vendryes, 'L'oiseau qui arrache les yeux', *Revue Celtique* (Paris, 1928), xlv, pp. 334–37; Brynley F. Roberts, 'Rhai o Gerddi Ymddiddan Llyfr Du Caerfyrddin', *Astudiaethau ar yr Hengerdd*, pp. 309–11.

22 Ross, op. cit., pp. 270–73; E. O. G. Turville-Petre, *Myth and Religion of the North: The Religion of Ancient Scandinavia* (London, 1964), p. 58; Isabel Henderson, *The Picts* (London, 1967), plate 41. For geese as shamanist psychopomps, cf. Joan Halifax, *Shaman: The Wounded Healer* (London, 1982), p. 86. Odin exchanged his eye for a draught of the water of wisdom in Mimir's well (Anthony Faulkes (ed.), *Snorri Sturluson: Edda, Prologue and Gylfaginning* (Oxford, 1982), p. 17). Among the Maya of Central America there was an 'expression *colop u ich*, "pulling out of the eye", which occurs so frequently in the Ritual of the Bacabs, frequently as the title of a god' (J. Eric S. Thompson, *Maya History and Religion* (Norman, Oklahoma, 1972), p. 337).

23 The region around the Solway estuary seems to have remained a semi-pagan enclave until a very late period. As late as the eighteenth century the primitive custom of the *couvade* survived near Langholm (Thomas Pennant, *A Tour in Scotland and Voyage to the Hebrides* (London, 1776), i, pp. 90–91; on which cf. the comments of Marie-Louise Sjoestedt (*Gods and Heroes of the Celts* (London, 1949), pp. 27–28), and Sir John Rhŷs, *Celtic Folklore, Welsh and Manx* (Oxford, 1901), p. 654).

24 William Forbes Skene, 'Notice of the Site of the Battle of Ardderyd or Arderyth', *Proceedings of the Society of Antiquaries of Scotland* (Edinburgh, 1866), vi, pp. 91–98. Liddel Moat had been visited and described nearly a century before Skene by the topographer Thomas Pennant (op. cit., i, p. 85).

25 Lloyd, op. cit., p. 167; A. O. H. Jarman, *The Legend of Merlin* (Cardiff, 1960), p. 20; Bromwich, op. cit., p. 379. As the Chadwicks note, Gwenddolau's name was preserved in the place-name Carwinley almost within living memory of the battle of Arderydd, since the district fell into English hands in the early part of the seventh century (*The Growth of Literature*, i, p. 134). For the history of subsequent mediaeval strongholds, whose ruins can still be seen at Liddel Moat, cf.

T. Thornton Taylor, 'Liddel Strength', *Dumfriesshire and Galloway Natural History & Antiquarian Society . . . Transactions* (1931), xvi, pp. 112–19.

26 For evidence of the hostility of the Selgovae to Rome, cf. H. M. Chadwick, *Early Scotland: The Picts, the Scots and the Welsh of Southern Scotland* (Cambridge, 1949), p. 153; I. A. Richmond (ed.), *Roman and Native In North Britain* (Edinburgh, 1958), pp. 76, 94; S. N. Miller (ed.), *The Roman Occupation of South-Western Scotland* (Glasgow, 1952), p. 226; Eric Birley, *Roman Britain and the Roman Army* (Kendal, 1961), p. 40; Sheppard Frere, *Britannia: a history of Roman Britain* (London, 1967), pp. 58, 107–8, 121–22, 126, 129, 150, 164; Myles Dillon and Nora K. Chadwick, *The Celtic Realms* (London, 1967), p. 21; Barley and Hanson, op. cit., pp. 112, 113. That *Selgovae* = 'hunters' is accepted by the best authorities (Edmund McClure, *British Place-Names in their Historical Setting* (London, 1910), p. 99; William J. Watson, *The History of the Celtic Place-Names of Scotland* (Edinburgh, 1926), pp. 27–28; Kenneth Jackson, *Language and History in Early Britain* (Edinburgh, 1953), p. 476.) For the local cult of the horned head, cf. Ross, op. cit., pp. 81–82, 155–56, 162, 181; cf. the map on p. 370 and plate 21a.

27 *Transactions of the Cumberland and Westmoreland Antiquarian and Archaeological Society*, lxxv, pp. 104–15.

28 Bromwich, op. cit., pp. 29–60; D. A. Binchy, *Celtic and Anglo-Saxon Kingship* (Oxford, 1970), p. 17; 'it is not usual for defence after the fall of the chieftain' (Nessa ní Shéaghdha (ed.), *Tóruigheacht Dhiarmada agus Ghráinne* (Dublin, 1967), p. 44). As Dr Bromwich points out to me, 'a fortnight and a month' is a conventional expression, occurring for example in *Mabinogi Branwen*.

29 Ross, op. cit., p. 331.

30 Whitley Stokes (ed.), *Lives of Saints from the Book of Lismore* (Oxford, 1890), pp. 68–69; W. J. Gruffydd, *Math vab Mathonwy* (Cardiff, 1928), p. 123; Eugene O'Curry, *Lectures on the Manuscript Materials of Irish History* (Dublin, 1861), pp. 447–48; M. A. O'Brien, 'Fled Bricrenn', in Myles Dillon (ed.), *Irish Sagas* (Dublin, 1959), pp. 70–72; Alwyn Rees and Brinley Rees, *Celtic Heritage: Ancient Tradition in Ireland and Wales* (London, 1961), p. 74. Norse wizards and witches also possessed the power to raise enchanted mists (Venetia Newall (ed.), *The Witch Figure* (London, 1973), pp. 23, 169). For the appropriation of the art by early Welsh saints, cf. J. W. James (ed.), *Rhigyfarch's Life of St David* (Cardiff, 1967), pp. 9–11; J. Vendryes, 'Saint David et le roi Boia', *Revue Celtique* (1928), xlv, pp. 155–56; A. W. Wade-Evans (ed.), *Vitae Sanctorum Britanniae at Genealogiae* (Cardiff, 1944), pp. 8, 74.

31 John Strachan and J. G. O'Keefe (ed.), *The Táin Bó Cúailnge from the Yellow Book of Lecan* (Dublin, 1912), p. 106; K. Meyer, 'The Expulsion of the Dessi', *Y Cymmrodor* (1901), xiv, p. 120; *Chronicum*

Scotorum, pp. 52–54; *Lives of Saints from the Book of Lismore*, p. xxviii; *Adomnan's Life of Columba*, pp. 404–6.

Five *The Mountain Seer*

1 As my old friend James Carney has pointed out, the visionary battle in the sky is implicit in *Buile Suibhne* ('Suibhne Geilt' and 'The Children of Lir', *Éigse* (Dublin, 1950), vi, pp. 89–90). After the battle of the Catalaunian Plains in 451, ghostly armies were said to have continued the struggle for three whole days and nights (E. A. Thompson, *A History of Attila and the Huns* (Oxford, 1948), p. 142). For other examples, cf. A. W. Wade-Evans (ed.), *Vitae Sanctorum Britanniae et Genealogiae* (Cardiff, 1944), p. 232; Jennifer Westwood, *Albion: A Guide to Legendary Britain* (London, 1985), pp. 317–8; Alexander D. Murdoch (ed.), *The Grameid: An Heroic Poem Descriptive of the Campaign of Viscount Dundee in 1689* (Edinburgh, 1888), pp. xxxviii–ix, 17–19; Peter Young, *Edgehill 1642: The Campaign and the Battle* (Kineton, 1967), pp. 162–64.

2 D. Justin Schove, 'Visions in North-West Europe (A.D. 400–600) and Dated Auroral Displays', *The Journal of the British Archaeological Association* (London, 1950), xiii, p. 42. Several peoples of the Arctic North believe the Aurora Borealis to be an apparition of dead warriors battling in the sky (Ivar Paulson, Åke Hultkrantz and Karl Jettmar, *Les Religions Arctiques et Finnoises* (Paris, 1965), p. 258).

3 Kenneth Jackson, 'The Motive of the Threefold Death in the Story of Suibhne Geilt', in Eóin ua Riain (ed.), *Féil-sgríbhinn eóin mhic néill* (Dublin, 1940), pp. 547–48; James Carney, *Studies in Irish Literature and History* (Dublin, 1955), pp. 151–52. For a valuable general discussion, cf. Basil Clarke, 'Calidon and the Caledonian Forest', *The Bulletin of the Board of Celtic Studies* (Cardiff, 1969), xxiii, pp. 191–97.

4 Thomas Jones, 'Datblygiadau Cynnar Chwedl Arthur', ibid. (1958), xvii, pp. 239–42. Cf. Kenneth Jackson, 'Once Again Arthur's Battles', *Modern Philology* (Chicago, 1945), xliii, pp. 48–49.

5 *The History and Chronicles of Scotland: written in Latin by Hector Boece, Canon of Aberdeen; and translated by John Bellenden, Archdeacon of Moray, and Canon of Ross* (Edinburgh, 1821), i, pp. xxx, xxxix. It may be that the Caledonian Forest stretched as far as Hadrian's Wall in Roman times, and that its name was retained locally in the exceptionally wild and remote area of upper Annandale and Tweeddale (*Féil-sgríbhinn eóin mhic néill*, p. 547; *Modern Philology*, xliii, p. 48) which was also known simply as The Forest in mediaeval times (G. W. S. Barrow, *Robert Bruce and the Community of the Realm of Scotland* (London, 1965), p. 20). It is interesting to note that Boece's family origins probably lay in Dumfriesshire (A. Cameron Smith, 'The Dumfriesshire Origin of Hector Boece', *Dumfriesshire and Galloway Natu-*

ral History and Antiquarian Society . . . Transactions (Dumfries, 1946), xxiii, pp. 75–81).

6 Cf. the map of sub-Roman North Britain in M. W. Barley and R. P. C. Hanson (ed.), *Christianity in Britain, 300–700* (Leicester, 1968), p. 115.

7 Alexandre Micha, 'Miscellaneous French Romances in Verse', in R. S. Loomis (ed.), *Arthurian Literature in the Middle Ages* (Oxford, 1959), pp. 377–78.

8 M. Dominica Legge, 'Some Notes on the Roman de Fergus', *Dumfries-shire and Galloway Natural History and Antiquarian Society . . . Trans-actions* (1950), xxvii, pp. 168–69.

9 Cf. John Robson (ed.), *Three Early English Metrical Romances* (London, 1842), p. 67.

10 The exploits of Don Quixote's precursors are described by R. S. Loomis, 'Arthurian Influence on Sport and Spectacle', *Arthurian Literature in the Middle Ages*, pp. 553–59. A striking parallel is Wace's (12th-century) expedition to Merlin's springs at Barenton, where he fruitlessly 'sought for the marvels' (N. K. Chadwick, *Early Brittany* (Cardiff, 1969), p. 300).

11 *The New Statistical Account of Scotland* (Edinburgh, 1845), iv, p. 104.

12 Máire MacNeill, *The Festival of Lughnasa: A Study of the Survival of the Celtic Festival of the Beginning of Harvest* (Dublin, 1962), pp. 67, 428. This sense of mountain-top communion with the Infinite is not of course confined to 'primitive' religious experience. Cf. William James, *The Varieties of Religious Experience: A Study in Human Nature* (London, 1903), pp. 66–67.

13 John Rhŷs and J. Gwenogvryn Evans (ed.), *The Text of the Mabinogion and other Welsh Tales from the Red Book of Hergest* (Oxford, 1887), p. 132; A. W. Wade-Evans (ed.), *Vitae Sanctorum Britanniae et Geneal-ogiae* (Cardiff, 1944), p. 26. For the folklore account of Plinlimmon, cf. Sir John Rhys, *Celtic Folklore, Welsh and Manx* (Oxford, 1901), pp. 391–92. In the Highlands of Scotland a sacred copse by a well was an object of awe and dread (M. Martin, *A Description of the Western Highlands of Scotland* (London, 1703), pp. 140–41), and 'the wildest recess of some lonely waterfall' was the customary resort of a diviner (T. F. O'Rahilly, *Early Irish History and Mythology* (Dublin, 1957), p. 324).

14 Ibid. For different versions of the Sacred Centre as source of rivers, cf. Mircea Eliade, *Patterns in Comparative Religion* (London, 1958), pp. 282, 284–85, 293, and for the Sacred Mountain, pp. 99–102, 107–11. The sacred spring is normally 'guarded by monsters. It is to be found in places which are hard to get to, and belong to some sort of demons or divinities' (ibid., p. 193). Buchanan in the 16th century noted the source of the three great Lowland rivers in one mountain (James Aikman, (ed.), *The History of Scotland, Translated from the Latin of George Buchanan* (Glasgow, 1827), i, p. 22).

15 *Early Brittany*, pp. 292–332.
16 Anne Ross, *Pagan Celtic Britain: Studies in Iconography and Tradition* (London, 1967), pp. 20–38; Sir James George Frazer, *The Dying God* (London, 1923), pp. 79, 80; Eliade, op. cit., p. 202; A. B. Cook, *Zeus: A Study in Ancient Religion* (Cambridge, 1914–40), i, pp. 76–77.
17 Roger Sherman Loomis, *Arthurian Tradition and Chrétien de Troyes* (New York, 1949), pp. 269–93. The 12th-century Welsh poet Gwalchmai considered Arderydd to be in or bordering on Lothian (Rachel Bromwich (ed.), *Trioedd Ynys Prydein: The Welsh Triads* (Cardiff, 1961), pp. 208–210).
18 Cf. *The New Statistical Account of Scotland*, iv, pp. 106–7; Frederick A. Pottle, *James Boswell: The Earlier Years 1740–1769* (London, 1966), pp. 21–22.
19 On the face of it *in natione gewisseorum* can only mean 'in the territory of the West Saxons' (Rachel Bromwich, 'The Character of the Early Welsh Tradition', in Nora K. Chadwick (ed.), *Studies in Early British History* (Cambridge, 1959), p. 109; cf. H. E. Walker, 'Bede and the Gewissae: The Evolution of the Heptarchy and its Nomenclature', *The Cambridge Historical Review* (Cambridge, 1956), xii, pp. 174–86). Historically the identification is of course an absurd anachronism. Though Geoffrey was fully capable of perpetrating any error, it seems more likely that he confused the well-known Gewissae of Bede with an obscure place-name associated in the *Historia Brittonum* with Vortigern. After the tyrant's discomfiture at Dinas Emrys he fled with his druids to a place called Guunnessi: 'et ipse cum magis suis ad sinistralem plagam pervenit et usque ad regionem, quae vocatur Guunnessi, adfuit et urbem ibi, quae vocatur suo nomine Cair Guorthigern, aedificavit.'

It must surely be the otherwise unknown Guunnessi for which Geoffrey substituted the familiar but inappropriate *Gewissae*. Guunnessi remains unidentified, but in the ninth century it was believed to lie somewhere in the Scottish Lowlands, *Y Gogledd* (Kenneth Jackson, 'Nennius and the Twenty-Eight Cities of Britain', *Antiquity* (Gloucester, 1938), xii, p. 48). Elsewhere in *HB* we are told that Vortigern's 'authority extended as far as the Wall' (cf. H. M. Chadwick, *Early Scotland: The Picts, the Scots & the Welsh of Southern Scotland* (Cambridge, 1949), p. 149), which would explain the course of his flight.

Early Welsh tradition knew of 'the open land of Gwynassedd' (*lleutir Guynnassed*) which was linked with the North of Britain (*Priden*), and appears in a verse contiguous to one referring to the grave of Vortigern (Thomas Jones, 'The Black Book of Carmarthen "Stanzas of the Graves"', *The Proceedings of the British Academy* (London, 1967), liii, p. 124; for other possible Northern associations, cf. Ifor Williams (ed.), *Canu Aneirin* (Cardiff, 1938), p. 367; P. C. Bartrum (ed.), *Early Welsh Genealogical Tracts* (Cardiff, 1966), p. 57).

Geoffrey himself may have known of a tradition that Guunnessi was in the North, reflected in his references to a 'Gunuasius rex orcadum', who appears in the Bruts as 'Guinwas urenhin Orc' (Henry Lewis (ed.), *Brut Dingestow* (Cardiff, 1942), pp. 153, 158). A gloss in the *Historia Brittonum* places Vortigern's Northern refuge at 'Guasmoric iuxta Lugubalium', *i.e.* near Carlisle (cf. Ferdinand Lot (ed.), *Nennius et l'Historia Brittonum* (Paris, 1934), i, p. 183). Interestingly, this Guasmoric was associated with a 'Pictish' King Rodric (McClure, op. cit., pp. 137–39), by whom may be intended Rhydderch of Strathclyde.

On the other hand there is a Gwynnys in North Wales not far from 'Vortigern's valley' (Nant Gwrtheyrn) (Melville Richards, 'Nennius's "Regio Guunnessi"', *Caernarvonshire Historical Society . . . Transactions* (1963), xxiv, pp. 21–27). The indications that the original Guunnessi was to be found in Northern Britain are however so strong as to suggest that this is either coincidence or another example of the relocalisation of North British tales in Wales. To Robert de Boron, Merlin's refuge lay in the impenetrable forests of Northern Britain, referred to under the generic name of 'Norhombellande'. Finally, it is perhaps worth noting that the Northern Guunnessi was regarded in the ninth century as a place where *magi* were likely to betake themselves in an emergency.

20 There appear to be few, if any, *invented* names (as opposed to eponymous concoctions) in the *HRB*, though of course there are numerous misspellings and misinterpretations. As Stuart Piggott has shown with the king-lists, it seems to have been Geoffrey's policy to use names from extant sources, and where he found them in a series to retain that series. Professor Piggott sees in this 'retention of . . . meaningless lists of names . . . the vestige, perhaps the only vestige, of an historical conscience' ('The Sources of Geoffrey of Monmouth', *Antiquity* (1941), xv, pp. 280–81).

21 Cf. E. K. Chambers, *Arthur of Britain* (London, 1927), pp. 221–32; Rev. J. A. Bennett, 'Camelot', *Proceedings of the Somersetshire Archaeological and Natural History Society* (Taunton, 1890), xxxvi, pp. 2, 4; T. Gwynn Jones, *Welsh Folklore and Folk-Custom* (London, 1930), pp. 87–89; Cook, op. cit., i, p. 116. The Arthur who presides over the hall of the dead in the mountain-heart was clearly once (or has replaced) a god (cf. Edwin Sidney Hartland, *The Science of Fairy Tales: An Enquiry into Fairy Mythology* (London, 1891), p. 229).

22 G. E. Bentley (ed.), *William Blake's Writings* (Oxford, 1978), pp. 1247–48.

Six *The Last of the Druids?*

1 Cf. the description of the Green Knight's chapel, which is in any case clearly related to the Fairy Fountain motif (J. R. R. Tolkien and E. W. Gordon (ed.), *Sir Gawain and The Green Knight* (Oxford, 1930),

pp. 66–68). The 'position by a fountain, at the head of a rough and rugged ravine' was its traditional characteristic (Jessie L. Weston, *The Legend of Sir Gawain: Studies upon its Original Scope and Significance* (London, 1897), p. 105).

2 In Ireland Credé, daughter of Cairbre, possessed a magical apple-tree, as did St Kevin (Eugene O'Curry, *Lectures on the Manuscript Materials of Ancient Irish History* (Dublin, 1861), p. 311; Standish H. O'Grady (ed.), *Silva Gadelica* (London, 1892), ii, p. 121; Kuno Meyer, 'The Irish Mirabilia in the Norse "Speculum Regale"', *Ériu* (Dublin, 1908), iv, p. 9). In *Echtra Connla* the hero eats a magic apple; Maelduin on his voyage found three magic apples; Conchobar possessed three enchanted apples on a rod of silver; and Oisin on his way to the Land of Youth saw a maid bearing a golden apple (Kuno Meyer and Alfred Nutt, *The Voyage of Bran Son of Febal* (London, 1895), i, pp. 145, 150, 169, 204, 205; Whitley Stokes, 'Tidings of Conchobar mac Nessa', *Ériu*, iv, p. 30). Cú Roí's 'external soul' was located in a golden apple in a salmon (Thomas F. O'Rahilly, *Early Irish History and Mythology* (Dublin, 1957), p. 321), and it is interesting to compare with this the local belief that the 'external souls' of boys at Aargau in Switzerland were supposed to be bound up with the life of an apple-tree (J. G. Frazer, *Balder the Beautiful: The Fire-Festivals of Europe and the Doctrine of the External Soul* (London, 1930), ii, p. 165). With regard to the apostrophised *Afallennau* and *Hoianau*, one may note the juxtaposition of the three magic apples and pig's skin sought by the sons of Tuirenn, and the enchanted apple-devouring swine found by Maelduin (H. Munro Chadwick and N. Kershaw Chadwick, *The Growth of Literature* (Cambridge, 1932), i, p. 259; Myles Dillon and Nora K. Chadwick, *The Celtic Realms* (London, 1967), p. 266). Apples grew on a certain ash-tree by the Wye (Theodor Mommsen (ed.), *Monvmenta Germaniae Historica*, xiii, *Chronica Minora*, iii (Berlin, 1894), p. 215); *Aballava* (near Carlisle) may imply an orchard with sacred connotations (A. L. F. Rivet and Colin Smith, *The Place-Names of Roman Britain* (London, 1979), p. 238; cf. Constance Bullock-Davies, 'Lanval and Avalon', *The Bulletin of the Board of Celtic Studies* (Cardiff, 1969), xxiii, pp. 133–42).

3 Cf. Kuno Meyer and Alfred Nutt, op. cit., i, pp. 236–37.

4 Cf. Sir James George Frazer, *Folk-Lore in the Old Testament: Studies in Comparative Religion, Legend and Law* (London, 1918), i, pp. 46–48; idem (ed.), *Apollodorus: The Library* (London, 1921), i, pp. 218–20; and the words of Euripides, quoted by Jane Ellen Harrison, *Themis: A Study of the Social Origins of Greek Religion* (Cambridge, 1912), p. 432. In Valhalla the Norse gods retained their youth by eating the magic apples of Iduun (Anthony Faulkes (ed.), *Snorri Sturluson: Edda, Prologue and Gylfaginning* (Oxford, 1982), p. 25). This conception may be of Celtic origin (cf. E. O. G. Turville-Petre, *Myth and Religion of the North: The Religion of Ancient Scandinavia* (London,

1964), p. 175, 186–87). A bronze bucket in the famous Oseberg ship-burial was found to have contained apples (H. R. Ellis Davidson, *Scandinavian Mythology* (London, 1982), pp. 90–91).

5 Jessie L. Weston, 'The Apple Mystery in Arthurian Romance', *The Bulletin of the John Rylands Library* (Manchester, 1925), ix, pp. 1–14; Alwyn Rees and Brinley Rees, *Celtic Heritage: Ancient Tradition in Ireland and Wales* (London, 1961), pp. 90–91; Mary Williams, 'Notes on Perlesvaus', *Speculum* (Cambridge, Mass., 1939), xiv, p. 200; Anne Ross, *Pagan Celtic Britain: Studies in Iconography and Tradition* (London, 1967), pp. 34, 38, 130, 214.

6 Thomas Stephens took the *Afallennau* to be 'probably an address to the tree of liberty'! (*The Literature of the Kymry* (London, 1876), p. 236). Professor Jarman suggests that the apple-trees in the *Myrddin* poetry derive from the trees which his counterpart Suibhne ascended when flying, but to do so has to explain away the fact that Myrddin-Merlin is nowhere accorded the power of levitation, and that the trees Suibhne ascends are not apple-trees (A. O. H. Jarman, 'The Welsh Myrddin Poems' in R. S. Loomis (ed.), *Arthurian Literature in the Middle Ages* (Oxford, 1959), pp. 27–28).

7 Ross, op. cit., pp. 308–21, 352; T. Rice Holmes, *Ancient Britain and the Invasions of Julius Caesar* (Oxford, 1907), p. 284; E. Anwyl, 'The Value of the Mabinogion for the Study of Celtic Religion', *Transactions of the Third International Congress for the History of Religions* (Oxford, 1908), ii, p. 239; idem, *Celtic Religion in Pre-Christian Times* (London, 1906), pp. 24–25, 30–31. The pigs of the Celts were 'noted for their height, and pugnacity and swiftness' (J. J. Tierney, 'The Celtic Ethnography of Posidonius', *Proceedings of the Royal Irish Academy* (Dublin, 1960), lx, p. 268). For a stimulating discussion, cf. Próinséas ní Chatháin, 'Swineherds, Seers and Druids', *Studia Celtica* (Cardiff, 1979/80), xiv/xv, pp. 200–11. V. Gordon Childe, *Prehistoric Communities of the British Isles* (London, 1940), p. 217; Kenneth Jackson, *The Oldest Irish Tradition: A Window on the Iron Age* (Cambridge, 1964), p. 35. O'Rahilly showed that pork was the principal food of the Celtic Otherworld (op. cit., pp. 122–23), as of the Norse Valhalla (Faulkes, op. cit., p. 32). The carving of the roast pig was an elaborate ritual affair: cf. A. O'Sullivan, 'Verses on Honorific Portions', in James Carney and David Greene (ed.), *Celtic Studies: Essays in memory of Angus Matheson* (London, 1968), pp. 118–23. It is curious, though, to note that Sir Walter Scott (*Waverley*, cap. xix) noted the Highlanders' *aversion* to pork. This may have been due to economic motives (S. Burt, *Letters from a Gentleman in the North of Scotland to His Friend in London* (London, 1754), i, pp. 141–43; but cf. ii, p. 343). In the Teutonic North (where boars were sacred to Freyr, goddess of fertility (Turville-Petre, op. cit., pp. 166, 168, 175–76), boars' flesh was eaten in the belief that the consumer acquired some of the god's power (ibid., p. 255). Cf. H. Munro Chadwick, *The Origin of the English Nation*

(Cambridge, 1907), p. 246. For St Patrick's pork (*immolaticum enim erat*), see Whitley Stokes (ed.), *The Tripartite Life of St Patrick, with Other Documents Relating to that Saint* (London, 1887), p. 495; Kathleen Mulchrone (ed.), *Bethu Phátraic: The Tripartite Life of Patrick* (Dublin, 1939), i, p. 15. Cf. the passage in O'Davoren's Glossary *s.v. Lupait* (W. Stokes (ed.), *Three Irish Glossaries* (London, 1862), p. 103). For sites chosen by pigs, cf. W. B. Jones, *Vestiges of the Gael in Gwynedd* (London, 1851), p. 41; J. Gwenogvryn Evans and John Rhŷs (ed.), *The Text of the Book of Llan Dâv* (Oxford, 1893), p. 80; A. W. Wade-Evans (ed.), *Vitae Sanctorum Britanniae et Genealogiae* (Cardiff, 1944), pp. 8, 44. A magical boar led Manawyddan and Pryderi to an enchanted castle (J. Gwenogvryn Evans (ed.), *The White Book of Mabinogion* (Pwllheli, 1907), pp. 34–35). The Bechuana practice is quoted by Sir James George Frazer, *Adonis, Attis, Osiris: Studies in the History of Oriental Religion* (London, 1927), ii, p. 249; cf. A. B. Cook, *Zeus: A Study in Ancient Religion* (Cambridge, 1914–40), i, pp. 539–41. The *clad na muice* appears in the Irish Nennius (A. G. van Hamel (ed.), *Lebor Bretnach: The Irish Version of the Historia Britonum ascribed to Nennius* (Dublin, 1932), p. 32). For other divine pigs, cf. John Rhŷs and J. Gwenogvryn Evans (ed.) *The Text of the Mabinogion and other Welsh Tales from the Red Book of Hergest* (Oxford, 1887), pp. 134–41; cf. Arthur's pursuit of another divine pig, Henwen (Rachel Bromwich (ed.), *Trioedd Ynys Prydein: The Welsh Triads* (Cardiff, 1961), pp. 48, 49–50). Cf. also Myles Dillon (ed.), *Irish Sagas* (Dublin, 1959), pp. 90–91, 144; Gerard Murphy, *The Ossianic Lore and Romantic Tales of Medieval Ireland* (Dublin, 1955), p. 49. The Tsuwo of Formosa had a legend of a pig who diverted a river to prevent a flood (*Folk-Lore in the Old Testament*, i, p. 231), and the belief may have been widespread that boundaries in primitive societies had been marked out by mythical (totemic) monsters (cf. Richard B. Lee and Irven DeVore, *Man the Hunter* (Chicago, 1968), p. 157). For pigs as a guide to the Celtic Otherworld, cf. W. J. Gruffydd, *Math vab Mathonwy* (Cardiff, 1928), pp. 44, 78, 330–31; Proinsias MacCana, *Celtic Mythology* (Feltham, 1970), pp. 50–55, 136. It was the magician Gwydion ab Don who brought swine from the Otherworld (*The White Book of Mabinogion*, p. 42; J. Gwenogvryn Evans (ed.), *Facsimile and Text of the Book of Taliesin* (Llanbedrog, 1910), p. 36). Finally, the boar was frequently adopted as an emblem or totem by the Celts. Tristan bore the image of one upon his shield (J. Loth, *Contributions à l'étude des Romans de la Table Ronde* (Paris, 1912), pp. 14–16).

8 George E. Mylonas, *Eleusis and the Eleusinian Mysteries* (Princeton, 1961), pp. 249–50; cf. ibid., pp. 201, 223; Sir James George Frazer, *Spirits of the Corn and of the Wild* (London, 1925), ii, p. 19; Matti

Kuusi, Keith Bosley and Michael Branch (ed.), *Finnish Folk Poetry Epic* (Helsinki, 1977), pp. 269–70.

9 *Three Irish Glossaries*, p. 25; O'Rahilly, op. cit., p. 325.

10 Merlin's address to the wolf appears without any preamble, apparently as a poetic excerpt. Suibhne Geilt also passed his winters among the wolves. For Merlin's wolf in Breton legend, cf. the discussion by Alexandre Micha, *Étude sur le "Merlin" de Robert de Boron* (Paris, 1980), p. 191.

11 Ross, op. cit., pp. 341–42. For Celtic Saints with pet wolves, cf. H. Idris Bell (ed.), *Vita Sancti Tathei and Buched Seint y Katrin* (Bangor, 1909), pp. 12–14; P. Grosjean, 'Vie de S. Rumon. Vie, Invention et Miracles de S. Nectan', *Analecta Bollandiana* (Brussels, 1953), lxxi, pp. 393–94; Canon G. H. Doble, *The Saints of Cornwall* (Oxford, 1960–70), iv, pp. 77–78. The Koriaks of Siberia regard the wolf as a powerful lord of the tundra (I. Paulson, Å. Hultkrantz and K. Jettmar, *Les Religions Arctiques et Finnoises* (Paris, 1965), p. 178); and there is evidence that wolves were invested with peculiar sanctity among the Indo-European peoples (Folke Ström, *On the Sacral Origin of the Germanic Death Penalties* (Stockholm, 1942), pp. 130–31). Lapp shamans would 'run in the shape of wolves and bears', and it appears that 'the shaman's *saiva*, or assistant spirit, appeared as a wolf'. (Louise Bäckman and Åke Hultkrantz, *Studies in Lapp Shamanism* (Stockholm, 1978), p. 57.)

12 Ross, op. cit., pp. 127–67, 297–98, 310, 333, 334, 338, 341, 353; MacCana, op. cit., pp. 44–48. For the functions of the (Scandinavian) Lord of the Forest, cf. Anna Birgitta Rooth, 'The Conception of "Rulers" in the South of Sweden', in Åke Hultkrantz (ed.), *The Supernatural Owners of Nature* (Uppsala, 1961), pp. 117–22.

13 William Henderson, *Notes on the Folk Lore of the Northern Counties of England and the Borders* (London, 1866), pp. 176, 214; T. D. Kendrick, *The Druids: A Study in Keltic Prehistory* (London, 1927), p. 217; Eilert Ekwall, *The Concise Oxford Dictionary of English Place-Names* (Oxford, 1936), p. 189.

14 John Strachan and J. G. O'Keefe (ed.), *The Táin Bó Cúailnge from the Yellow Book of Lecan* (Dublin, 1912), pp. 26–27; Whitley Stokes (ed.), *The Martyrology of Oengus the Culdee* (London, 1905), p. 72; idem (ed.), *Lives of Saints from the Book of Lismore* (Oxford, 1890), pp. 76, 123, 129; *The Text of the Book of Llan Dâv*, pp. 101–2; Idris Bell, op. cit., pp. 3–5; Wade-Evans, op. cit., p. 204; Doble, op. cit., iii, pp. 90–91, 97. Cf. John MacQueen, 'Roman and Celt in Southern Scotland', in Robert O'Driscoll (ed.), *The Celtic Consciousness* (New York, 1982), pp. 187–88.

15 Lailoken, too, is a vegetarian: 'Hic miserorum miserrimus hominum quomodo in hac squalenti degit solitudine inter bestias vt bestia, nudus et profugus et herbarum tantum pabulo pastus. Sete et pili sunt feris

ac bestijs termina naturalia herbarumque virecta, radices et folia, propria cibaria.'

16 Cf. the summary of Kenneth Jackson, *Studies in Early Celtic Nature Poetry* (Cambridge, 1935), pp. 125–26.

17 It is noteworthy that the three sons of Gilvaethwy were turned by Math's enchantments into a wolf, a stag and a pig (Gruffydd, op. cit., pp. 319–20). In the *Lestoire de Merlin*, Merlin appears disguised as a stag (Richard Bernheimer, *Wild Men in the Middle Ages* (Cambridge, Mass., 1952), p. 142); Timothy Husband, *The Wild Man: Medieval Myth and Symbolism* (New York, 1980), pp. 59–60, and elsewhere he is found in a forest in Northern Britain as an unmistakable Lord of the Animals: 'une grande plante de bestes et un homme molt lait et molt hidos qui ces bestes gardoit' (Alexandra Micha (ed.), *Robert de Boron: Merlin, Roman du XIIIe Siècle* (Paris, 1980), p. 128). For stags as Otherworld animals, cf. Hans Peter Duerr, *Dreamtime: Concerning the Boundary Between Wilderness and Civilization* (Oxford, 1985), pp. 164–5.

18 Alfred Nutt, *The Celtic Doctrine of Re-birth* (London, 1897), pp. 285–301. A three days' fast was traditional before the prophet's vision came upon him (cf. James Carney, *Studies in Early Irish Literature and History* (Dublin, 1955), pp. 166–67). Nutt considered the Tuan Story 'probably a production of the late ninth or early tenth century', and explained Tuan's exposition of Irish history as 'the first attempt to give a rational answer to questions raised by the annalistic scheme' (op. cit., p. 81).

19 John Rhys, *Lectures on the Origin and Growth of Religion as Illustrated by Celtic Heathendom* (London, 1888), pp. 97–98.

20 Charles Plummer and John Earle (ed.), *Two of the Saxon Chronicles Parallel* (Oxford, 1892), i, p. 258. The best study of the Wild Hunt is that of Michael John Petry, *Herne the Hunter: A Berkshire Legend* (Reading, 1972). Cf. also Henderson, op. cit., pp. 97–106; R. L. Tongue, *Somerset Folk-Lore* (London, 1965), p. 228; E. K. Chambers, *The Mediaeval Stage* (Oxford, 1903), i, p. 264; Stith Thompson, *The Folktale* (New York, 1967), p. 257; William Howitt, *The Year-Book of the Country* (London, 1850), pp. 301–3; H. M. Chadwick, *The Cult of Othin: An Essay in the Ancient Religion of the North* (London, 1899), p. 66; Donald J. Ward, 'The Threefold Death: An Indo-European Trifunctional Sacrifice?' in Jaan Puhvel (ed.), *Myth and Law Among the Indo-Europeans* (Berkeley, 1970), p. 124; Ström, op. cit., p. 161; Chambers, *Arthur of Britain*, pp. 227–28; Edwin Sidney Hartland, *The Science of Fairy Tales: An Enquiry into Fairy Mythology* (London, 1891), pp. 233–35; Duerr, op. cit., pp. 36–39, 234–40.

21 Rhys, *Celtic Heathendom*, pp. 84, 537, 559–60; cf. Brynley F. Roberts, 'Rhai o Gerddi Ymddiddan Llyfr Du Caerfyrddin', in Rachel Bromwich and R. Brinley Jones (ed.), *Astudiaethau ar yr Hengerdd* (Cardiff, 1978), p. 312; *The Cambro-Briton* (London, 1820), i, p. 350; Anatole

le Braz, *La Légende de la Mort chez les Armoricains* (Paris, 1928), ii, pp. 293–94; T. Gwynn Jones, *Welsh Folklore and Folk-Custom* (London, 1930), pp. 202–3. Cf. Theo Brown, 'The Black Dog', *Folklore* (London, 1958), lxix, pp. 175–92; Mary Williams, 'A Welsh Version of the William Tell Legend', ibid. (1961), lxxii, p. 318.

22 Cf. Jessie L. Weston, *From Ritual to Romance* (Cambridge, 1920), p. 80.

23 Geoffrey says that Merlin lined up a herd of deer and goats and set off 'driving his columns before him'. This odd arrangement may stem from Geoffrey's misunderstanding of his source, in which Merlin was *pursuing* the deer. A troop of slain soldiers was believed to emerge daily from the Donnersberg (Thor's Mountain) near Worms (Hartland, op. cit., p. 216).

24 The Siberian shaman's animal-dress signifies his identification with the animal, real or fabulous. (Paulson, Hultkrantz and Jettmar, op. cit., p. 132).

25 *Celtic Heathendom*, p. 248.

26 J. S. Brewer, J. F. Dimock and G. F. Warner (ed.), *Giraldi Cambrensis Opera* (London, 1861–91), vi, pp. 62, 124, 196, 216; cf. *The Growth of Literature*, i, pp. 111–13.

27 Margaret Enid Griffiths, *Early Vaticination in Welsh with English Parallels* (Cardiff, 1937), pp. 85–107.

28 Sir John Morris-Jones, 'Taliesin', *Y Cymmrodor* (London, 1918), xviii, p. 7; Ifor Williams, 'The Poems of Llywarch Hên', *The Proceedings of the British Academy* (London, 1932), xviii, p. 6; *The Growth of Literature*, i, pp. 528, 529; Griffiths, op. cit., pp. 73–74.

29 *Giraldi Cambrensis Opera*, v, p. 401; Griffiths, op. cit., p. 104; *The Growth of Literature*, i, pp. 106, 455. The Chadwicks compare the prophecies of Musaios, an early Thracian poet, which appear to 'have been adapted, like the Myrddin poems, to the political exigencies of the hour' (ibid., p. 117); one may also note the updating of the Sibylline Oracles in the Christian era (E. O. James, *The Ancient Gods* (London, 1960), p. 250; Evelyn Jamison, *Admiral Eugenius of Sicily: His Life and Work* (London, 1957), pp. 22–24). In 1307 an Englishman reported that the Scots were making propaganda use of a prophecy by Merlin foretelling Bruce's victory (G. W. S. Barrow, *Robert Bruce and the Community of the Realm of Scotland* (London, 1965), p. 245). The use of prophecy as an incitement to war or rebellion is of course worldwide (cf. Bryan R. Wilson, *Magic and the Millennium: A Sociological Study of Religious Movements of Protest among Tribal and Third-World Peoples* (London, 1973), pp. 226–36).

30 Ifor Williams (ed.), *Armes Prydein o Lyfr Taliesin* (Cardiff, 1955), pp. 1, 6.

31 The *Cyfoesi Myrddin a Gwenddydd y Chwaer* contains references to the battle of Arderydd, Rhydderch Hael, Gwenddolau, Urien Rheged, and Maelgwn Gwynedd (J. Gwenogvryn Evans (ed.), *The Poetry in*

the Red Book of Hergest (Llanbedrog, 1911), p. 1). And in *Peiryan Vaban* Myrddin is interestingly made to refer to a conflict between Rhydderch and Aedan (A. O. H. Jarman, 'Peiryan Vaban', *The Bulletin of The Board of Celtic Studies* (Cardiff, 1952), xiv, pp. 105, 106–7), absent from the Myrddin saga but alluded to in a triad (R. Bromwich, op. cit., p. 147).

32 O'Curry, op. cit., pp. 385–91, 620–22; Francis John Byrne, *Irish Kings and High-Kings* (London, 1973), pp. 54–55; *The Growth of Literature*, i, pp. 462–63; Gerard Murphy, 'On the Dates of Two Sources Used in Thurneysen's Heldensage', *Ériu* (Dublin, 1952), xvi, pp. 149–51.

33 T. D. Kendrick, op. cit., pp. 212, 214–15, 281, 219, 220. Mrs Chadwick notes the close connection 'between prophecy and political propaganda' (Nora K. Chadwick, *The Druids* (Cardiff, 1966), pp. 46, 76, 79–80).

34 Cf. the Druid Nemthes (Kuno Meyer, 'Brinna Ferchertne', *Zeitschrift für Celtische Philologie* (Halle, 1901), iii, p. 44) and, for other examples, Myles Dillon and Nora K. Chadwick, op. cit., p. 244; Anne Ross, op. cit., p. 336; O'Curry, op. cit., p. 284; *Lives of Saints from the Book of Lismore*, pp. 35, 119–20; *The Oldest Irish Tradition*, pp. 11, 23–24; *The Growth of Literature*, i, pp. 464, 612; J. B. Bury, *The Life of St Patrick and his Place in History* (London, 1905), pp. 79–80; Kuno Meyer, 'The Expulsion of the Dessi', *Y Cymmrodor* (1901), xiv, p. 108; Cecile O'Rahilly (ed.), *The Stowe Version of Táin Bó Cúailnge* (Dublin, 1961), p. 142; J. W. James (ed.), *Rhigyfarch's Life of St David* (Cardiff, 1967), p. 5; *Chronica Minora*, iii, p. 181.

35 J. Gwenogvryn Evans (ed.), *Facsimile and Text of the Book of Taliesin* (Llanbedrog, 1910), pp. 18, 76; idem (ed.), *The Poetry in the Red Book of Hergest* (Llanbedrog, 1911), p. 167. Two sixth-century poems mention soothsayers (*sywedydyon*) (*The Book of Taliesin*, p. 64; idem (ed.), *Facsimile and Text of the Book of Aneirin* (Pwllheli, 1908), p. 6), whom Sir Ifor Williams identified with 'druids' or 'druidic bards' (*Canu Taliesin gyda Rhagymadrodd a Nodiadau* (Cardiff, 1960), p. 99; cf. idem, *Canu Aneirin gyda Rhagymadrodd a Nodiadau* (Cardiff, 1938), p. 131).

36 E. Bachelier, 'Les Druides en Gaule romaine', *Ogam* (Rennes, 1959), xi, pp. 295–304. Overt paganism continued in Gaul and Spain into the seventh century (A. H. M. Jones, 'The Western Church in the Fifth and Sixth Centuries', in M. W. Barley and R. P. C. Hanson (ed.), *Christianity in Britain, 300–700* (Leicester, 1968), p. 15; E. A. Thompson, *The Goths in Spain* (Oxford, 1969), pp. 308–10). A fourth-century priest of the temple of Belenus at Bordeaux claimed Druidic descent (Kendrick, op. cit., pp. 219–20), and it has been conjectured that Armorican Druids fomented the *Bagaudae* revolts in fifth-century Armorica (Chadwick, *Druids*, p. 99). In the late fourth century St Martin destroyed a certain 'templum' 'in pago Aeduorum' (Karl Halm (ed.), *Sulpicii Severi Libri qui Supersunt, Corpus Scriptorum Ecclesi-*

asticorum Latinorum (Vienna, 1866), i, pp. 121–25; cf. H. Delehaye, 'Saint Martin et Sulpice Sévère', *Analecta Bollandiana* (Brussels, 1920), xxxviii, pp. 55–56), and Mrs Chadwick has remarked that 'we shall do well, before we lightly dismiss such stories, to remember that this had been a stronghold of Druidism' (N. K. Chadwick, *Poetry and Letters in Early Christian Gaul* (London, 1955, p. 101). For other references to the continuing strength of paganism in late and post-Roman Gaul, cf. eadem, *Early Brittany* (Cardiff, 1969), pp. 296–97; Simone-Antoinette Deyts, 'The Sacred Source of the Seine', *Scientific American* (New York, July 1971), pp. 72–73.

37 D. A. Binchy, 'Patrick and His Biographers: Ancient and Modern', *Studia Hibernica* (Dublin, 1962), ii, pp. 48–49; Kathleen Hughes, *The Church in Early Irish Society* (London, 1966), pp. 45–46; Ludwig Bieler (ed.), *The Irish Penitentials* (Dublin, 1963), pp. 56, 428; James F. Kenney, *The Sources for the Early History of Ireland* (New York, 1929), pp. 170, 273; Bury, op. cit., pp. 167–68. The poem *Fáed Fíada* carries the invocation 'fri brichta ban ocus goband ocus druád' (*The Tripartite Life of Patrick*, p. 50), and a century later St Columba was said to have been opposed by Druids at Tara and to have invoked Christ as 'my Druid' (William Reeves (ed.), *The Life of St. Columba* (Dublin, 1857), p. 74; Hugh Williams, *Christianity in Early Britain* (Oxford, 1912), pp. 50–51). The word *DRVVIDES* appears on a fifth- or sixth-century ogam inscription in Co. Kildare (R. A. S. Macalister (ed.), *Corpus Inscriptionum Insularum Celticarum* (Dublin, 1945), i, pp. 22–24; cf. John Rhŷs, 'Studies in Early Irish History', *The Proceedings of the British Academy* (London, 1903), i, pp. 4–5; Bury, op. cit., p. 305; Kendrick, op. cit., pp. 102–3).

38 Macalister, op. cit., pp. 480–82; cf. Bury, op. cit., p. 11; Kendrick, op. cit., p. 100.

39 Most authorities agree that Broichan the *magus* was a Druid (Reeves, op. cit., pp. 73–74; J. Frazer, 'The Question of the Picts', *Scottish Gaelic Studies* (Oxford, 1928), ii, p. 191; W. Douglas Simpson, *The Celtic Church in Scotland* (Aberdeen, 1935), p. 16; Ross, op. cit., p. 57). Mrs Chadwick dissented (*Celtic Britain* (London, 1963), p. 100), though earlier she had described him as 'the chief Druid' of Bruide's court (H. M. Chadwick, *Early Scotland: The Picts, the Scots & the Welsh of Southern Scotland* (Cambridge, 1949), pp. xii, xvi).

40 Kendrick, op. cit., pp. 87, 88, 105, 138, 147, 148.

41 Bards, *ollamhs* and *fili*, on both sides of the Irish Sea, did much to preserve Druidic traditions and beliefs (*The Growth of Literature*, i, pp. 469–71, 492, 607; James Carney, *The Irish Bardic Poet* (Dublin, 1967), pp. 8–12).

Seven *The Divine Kingship*

1 Rachel Bromwich (ed.), *Trioedd Ynys Prydein: The Welsh Triads* (Cardiff, 1961), p. 241. *Lug* in Welsh is *Lleu*, (cf. W. J. Gruffydd, *Math vab Mathonwy* (Cardiff, 1928), pp. 60–62). For Lug's arrival among the Túatha Dé, see Elizabeth A. Gray (ed.), *Cath Maige Tuired: The Second Battle of Mag Tuired* (Dublin, 1982), pp. 38, 40.

2 For useful summary accounts of the myth and distribution of the cult of Lug, cf. John Rhŷs, *Lectures on the Origin and Growth of Religion as Illustrated by Celtic Heathendom* (London, 1888), pp. 383–430; idem, 'All around the Wrekin', *Y Cymmrodor* (London, 1908), xxi, pp. 4–9; Marie-Louise Sjoestedt, *Gods and Heroes of the Celts* (London, 1949), pp. 42–45; Proinsias Mac Cana, *Celtic Mythology* (Feltham, 1970), pp. 27–29; Antonio Tovar, 'The God Lugus in Spain', *The Bulletin of the Board of Celtic Studies* (Cardiff, 1982), xxix, pp. 591–99.

3 Egerton G. B. Phillimore, 'A Fragment from Hengwrt MS No. 202', *Y Cymmrodor* (1886), vii, pp. 112–21, 151–54.

4 Cf. Rhŷs's perceptive note, *Celtic Heathendom*, pp. 576–77.

5 Arthur West Haddan and William Stubbs (ed.), *Councils and Ecclesiastical Documents Relating to Great Britain and Ireland* (Oxford, 1873), ii, part i, p. 75.

6 Kenneth Jackson, *Language and History in Early Britain* (Edinburgh, 1953), p. 40. 'This Life contains material which must go back to the sixth century, and it was written probably in the seventh century' (Kathleen Hughes, 'Synodus II S. Patricii', in John J. O'Meara and Bernd Naumann (ed.), *Latin Script and Letters A.D. 400–900* (Leiden, 1976), p. 145).

7 J. Loth, 'La vie la plus ancienne de Saint Samson de Dol', *Revue Celtique* (Paris, 1914), xxxv, pp. 285, 295. Cf., for the whole episode, S. Baring-Gould and John Fisher, *The Lives of the British Saints* (London, 1913), iv, pp. 156–58; F. Duine, *Questions d'hagiographie et vie de S. Samson* (Paris, 1914), p. 30; Gilbert H. Doble, *The Saints of Cornwall* (Oxford, 1970), v, pp. 87–96.

8 Máire MacNeill, *The Festival of Lughnasa: A Study of the Survival of the Celtic Festival of the Beginning of Harvest* (Oxford, 1962), p. 421. Water dripping from the roofs of caves was widely regarded as ritually pure (cf. J. Eric S. Thompson, *Maya History and Religion* (Norman, Oklahoma, 1972), p. 184).

9 MacNeill, op. cit., pp. 402–3, 423, 545–48.

10 Ibid., pp. 143, 254, 305, 319, 326, 328–29, 338, 341, 344–45, 619, 624.

11 Ibid., p. 426.

12 Ibid., pp. 502–25.

13 Cf. J. E. Caerwyn Williams, 'Gildas, Maelgwyn and the Bards', in R. R. Davies *et al.* (ed.), *Welsh Society and Nationhood: Historical Essays Presented to Glanmor Williams* (Cardiff, 1984), p. 29. The image *ritu bacchantium* occurs in Gildas, and may represent a scholarly borrowing

(cf. Neil Wright, 'Did Gildas Read Orosius?', *Cambridge Medieval Celtic Studies* (Cambridge, 1985), ix, p. 33).

14 MacNeill, op. cit., pp. 381–85.

15 J. Loth, 'Remarques à l'Historia Brittonum dite de Nennius', *Revue Celtique* (1932), xlix, pp. 160–61.

16 For the complex relationship between *Gereint* and *Erec*, cf. Idris L. Foster, 'Gereint, Owein, and Peredur', in R. S. Loomis (ed.), *Arthurian Literature in the Middle Ages: A Collaborative History* (Oxford, 1959), pp. 193–96.

17 MacNeill, op. cit., pp. 311–38.

18 Eugene O'Curry, *Lectures on the Manuscript Materials of Ancient Irish History* (Dublin, 1861), pp. 385–91, 620–22. Cf. Robert H. Gartman, 'Mael, Bloc, and Bluiccniu', in D. K. Wilgus (ed.), *Folklore International: essays in traditional literature, belief, and custom in honor of Wayland Debs Hand* (Hatboro, Pa., 1967), pp. 67–70.

19 Roger Sherman Loomis, *Arthurian Literature and Chrétien de Troyes* (New York, 1949), pp. 171–75.

20 T. F. O'Rahilly, 'On the Origin of the Names *Érainn* and *Ériu*, *Ériu* (Dublin, 1943), xiv, pp. 14–21. Cf. Maartje Draak, 'Some Aspects of Kingship in Pagan Ireland', *La Regalità Sacra: Contributi al Terna dell' VIII Congresso Internazionale di Storia delle Religioni* (Leiden, 1959), pp. 651–63.

21 K. A. H. Hidding, 'The High God and the King as Symbols of Totality', ibid., pp. 54–62; D. A. Binchy, *Celtic and Anglo-Saxon Kingship* (Oxford, 1970), pp. 9–10; Mircea Eliade, *A History of Religious Ideas* (London, 1979), i, pp. 75, 123–24.

22 Thomas F. O'Rahilly, *Early Irish History and Mythology* (Dublin, 1957), p. 284; Heinrich Wagner, 'The Origin of the Celts in the Light of Linguistic Geography', *Transactions of the Philological Society* (Oxford, 1969), p. 245.

23 William F. Skene, *Celtic Scotland: A History of Ancient Alban* (Edinburgh, 1876), i, pp. 490–91; M. Martin, *A Description of the Western Islands of Scotland* (London, 1703), pp. 240–41. Cf. Davies, op. cit., pp. 31–33. In a letter to me, Dr Rachel Bromwich makes an intriguing point: 'With the list of Conn's royal successors I always think one should compare the vision shown to Banquo in Macbeth of the kings to be descended from him, though I do not think anyone has quoted a source for this.' Another episode perhaps reflecting a Celtic source is the soliloquy of the surly porter.

24 Byrne, op. cit., pp. 54, 91, 104; Gerard Murphy, 'On the Dates of Two Sources Used in Thurneysen's Heldensage', *Ériu* (Dublin, 1952), xvi, pp. 149–50. For the selection of the king's heir, cf. Binchy, op. cit., p. 26; and for the rôle of the chief druid, Proinsias Mac Cana, 'Regnum and Sacerdotium: Notes on Irish Tradition', *The Proceedings of the British Academy* (London, 1979), lxv, pp. 453, 456; Davies, op. cit., pp. 25–27.

25 H. Munro Chadwick and N. Kershaw Chadwick, *The Growth of Literature* (Cambridge, 1932), i, pp. 462–63. For another example of prophetic revelation provided in a dialogue with a priestess, cf. James Carney, 'The Earliest Bran Material', in O'Meara and Naumann, op. cit., pp. 182–83, 190.

26 *The Proceedings of the British Academy*, lxv, pp. 453, 456, 459; J. E. Caerwyn Williams, 'The Court Poet in Medieval Ireland', ibid. (1971), lvii, pp. 40–46.

Eight *The Fighting Dragons and the FatherlessChild*

1 Understanding of the nature of the *Historia Brittonum* has been revolutionised by the brilliant work of Dr David Dumville in a series of important papers – work soon to culminate in his long-awaited new edition of the texts. Dr Dumville's conclusion is that 'Nennius' was 'a Welsh counterpart of the early Irish synchronising historians . . . one who was struggling with the embarrassment of too little, rather than too much, material', and that 'the implications of his method for the historiographical usefulness of his work are totally damaging . . .' ('On the North British Sections of the *Historia Brittonum*', *The Welsh History Review* (Cardiff, 1976/7), viii, pp. 353–54; cf. the analyses in his '"Nennius" and the *Historia Brittonum*', *Studia Celtica* (Cardiff, 1975–6), x–xi, pp. 78–95; 'Some Aspects of the Chronology of the *Historia Brittonum*', *The Bulletin of the Board of Celtic Studies* (Cardiff, 1974), xxv, pp. 439–45). My own inclination is willingly to adopt the first conclusion while being wary of too eager acceptance of the second. That 'Nennius' was an enthusiastic but incompetent synchronist is clear to all, but the precise nature and value of his sources is less easy to determine. To take but one example: Dr Dumville's rejection of the historicity of the account of Cunedda's migration ('Sub-Roman Britain: History and Legend', *History* (London, 1977), lxii, pp. 181–83), appears in some ways to rest on assumptions as arbitrary as those of the scholars he is attempting to refute, and to ignore some telling points; *e.g.* those made by Sir John Lloyd, *A History of Wales from the Earliest Times to the Edwardian Conquest* (London, 1911), pp. 118–19. What can a sceptic make of mediaeval chroniclers' claims that the Kingdom of Lotharingia was actually named after an historical King Lothaire?!

2 Cf. Brynley F. Roberts (ed.), *Cyfranc Lludd a Llefelys* (Dublin, 1975), pp. xviii–xix.

3 A. G. van Hamel (ed.), *Lebor Bretnach: The Irish Version of the Historia Brittonum Ascribed to Nennius* (Dublin, 1932), pp. 53–61; Nora K. Chadwick, 'Intellectual Contacts between Britain and Gaul in the Fifth Century', in Nora K. Chadwick, (ed.), *Studies in Early*

British History (Cambridge, 1959), p. 195; F. Lot, *Nennius et L'Historia Brittonum* (Paris, 1934), pp. 89–90.
4 Whitley Stokes (ed.), *The Tripartite Life of Patrick with other Documents Relating to that Saint* (London, 1887), pp. 278–79. The prophecy appears in Irish in the Notes on Fiacc's Hymn (ibid., p. 422), and in the *Vita Tripartita* (Kathleen Mulchrone (ed.), *Bethu Phátraic: The Tripartite Life of Patrick* (Dublin, 1939), pp. 21–22). These Irish versions translate Muirchu's *magi* by *druide*, which must be correct (cf. William Reeves (ed.), *The Life of St. Columba* (Dublin, 1857), pp. 73–74). Supporters of the verse's authenticity include Eugene O'Curry, *Lectures on the Manuscript Materials of Ancient Irish History* (Dublin, 1861), pp. 397–98; J. B. Bury, *The Life of St Patrick and his Place in History* (London, 1905), pp. 79–80, 299, 352. For more cautious views, cf. James F. Kenney, *The Sources for the Early History of Ireland: An Introduction and Guide* (New York, 1929), p. 344; Ludwig Bieler, *St. Patrick and the Coming of Christianity* (Dublin, 1967), p. 6.
5 H. Munro Chadwick, *The Origin of the English Nation* (Cambridge, 1907), p. 39. Could 'angelo lucis' be a Gildasian pun for *angelo Lugis*?
6 J. B. Bury, *History of the Later Roman Empire* (London, 1923), i, pp. 176–77. There seems no good reason to reject Zosimus' account, *pace* Stewart Irvin Oost, *Galla Placidia Augusta: A Biographical Essay* (Chicago, 1968), pp. 90–91. Cf. the Roman general Litorius' pagan sacrifice at the siege of Toulouse in 439 (E. A. Thompson, *A History of Attila and the Huns* (Oxford, 1948), p. 68).
7 For later reference to foreign mercenaries in Welsh kings' retinues, cf. Sir Ifor Williams, *Lectures on Early Welsh Poetry* (Dublin, 1944), pp. 30–31, 72–73; Rachel Bromwich (ed.), *The Beginnings of Welsh Poetry: Studies by Sir Ifor Williams* (Cardiff, 1980), pp. 94–95. For evidence that Hengist may have been a homeless adventurer rather than a visiting sea-king, cf. H. Munro Chadwick, op. cit., pp. 52–53.
8 Cf. Thomas Jones, 'The Black Book of Carmarthen "Stanzas of the Graves"', *The Proceedings of the British Academy* (London, 1967), liii, p. 108; Rachel Bromwich, 'Some Remarks on the Celtic Sources of "Tristan"', *The Transactions of the Honourable Society of Cymmrodorion* (London, 1955), p. 49; Nora K. Chadwick, (ed.), *Studies in the Early British Church* (Cambridge, 1958), p. 23.
9 H. W. Parke and D. E. W. Wormell, *The Delphic Oracle* (Oxford, 1956), i, p. 6; T. Rice Holmes (ed.), *C. Iuli Caesaris Commentarii: Rerum in Gallia Gestarum* (Oxford, 1914), pp. 241–42; Anne Ross, 'Chartres: the *Locus* of the Carnutes', *Studia Celtica* (Cardiff, 1979/80), xiv/xv, pp. 260–69; Alwyn Rees and Brinley Rees, *Celtic Heritage: Ancient Tradition in Ireland and Wales* (London, 1961), pp. 146–72; J. Loth, 'L'Origine de la Légende d'Arthur fils d'Uther Pendragon', *Revue Celtique* (Paris, 1932), xlix, p. 136; Françoise Le Roux, *Les Druides* (Paris, 1961), pp. 109–11.

10 Roberts, op. cit., pp. xxxv–xxxvi, xxxviii–xxxix.
11 H. N. Savory, 'Excavations at Dinas Emrys, Beddgelert (Caern.), 1954–56', *Archaelogia Cambrensis* (Cardiff, 1961), cix, pp. 54–55. As Dr D. P. Kirby says, 'the long story of the dealings of Vortigern and his magicians with the boy Ambrosius would appear to be a garbled folk-tale of pagan origin . . . not necessarily a Gwyneddian tale in origin.' ('Vortigern', *The Bulletin of the Board of Celtic Studies* (Cardiff, 1968), xxiii, p. 55). Legends of Gwrtheyrn (Vortigern) were known in Gwynedd and Powys from an early date (cf. Rachel Bromwich (ed.), *Trioedd Ynys Prydein: The Welsh Triads* (2nd ed., 1978), p. 554). It is not certain whether these were 'imported' from Southern Britain during the early Dark Ages, or whether they relate to a different Gwrtheyrn (cf. *History*, lxii, p. 187).
12 For British and Irish traditions of sacrificial foundation burials, cf. Paul Grosjean (ed.), 'The Life of St Columba from the Edinburgh MS.', *Scottish Gaelic Studies* (Oxford, 1928), ii, p. 146; Whitley Stokes (ed.), *Three Irish Glossaries* (London, 1862), pp. xli–xlii; J. Vendryes, 'Saint David et le roi Boia', *Revue Celtique* (Paris, 1928), xlv, p. 166. For the archaeological evidence, cf. Donald Atkinson, *The Romano-British Site on Lowbury Hill in Berkshire* (Reading, 1916), pp. vii–viii, 7–10; Leslie Alcock, 'Excavations at South Cadbury Castle, 1969: A Summary Report', *The Antiquaries Journal* (London, 1970), l, pp. 16–17, 23–24, plate V; Anne Ross, 'The Divine Hag of the Pagan Celts', in Venetia Newall (ed.), *The Witch Figure* (London, 1973), p. 158; Sir Ian Richmond, *Hod Hill* (London, 1968), ii, p. 16, plates 6, 7A. For the practice elsewhere and its implications, cf. S. Baring-Gould, *Strange Survivals: Some Chapters in the History of Man* (London, 1892), pp. 1–35; T. Rice Holmes, *Ancient Britain and the Invasions of Julius Caesar* (Oxford, 1907), p. 293; S. R. Driver, *Modern Research as illustrating the Bible* (London, 1909), pp. 69–72; Sir James George Frazer, *Folk-Lore in the Old Testament: Studies in Comparative Religion, Legend and Law* (London, 1918), i, pp. 421–22; iii, pp. 13–15, 18; idem, *Taboo and the Perils of the Soul* (London, 1927), pp. 89–92; idem, *Balder the Beautiful: The Fire-Festivals of Europe and the Doctrine of the External Soul* (London, 1930), i, pp. 326–27; E. O. James, *Sacrifice and Sacrament* (London, 1962), p. 95. An Indian scholar reproached a British engineer in the Himalayas for not securing his road with a touch of human sacrifice (Rudyard Kipling, *Letters of Travel (1892–1913)* (London, 1920), p. 186).
13 Mícheal Ó Duígeannaín, 'On the Medieval Sources for the Legend of Cenn (Crom) Cróich of Mag Slécht', in Rev. John Ryan (ed.), *Féilsgríbhinn Eóin Mhic Néill* (Dublin, 1940), pp. 296–306; cf. T. Gwynn Jones, *Welsh Folklore and Folk-Custom* (London, 1930), pp. 93–94. Sir John Rhŷs appears to have been the first to explain the story (*Lectures on the Origin and Growth of Religion as Illustrated by Celtic Heathendom* (London, 1888), pp. 200–202).

14 Cf. *Archaeologia Cambrensis*, cix, pp. 44–48, 54–56.

15 Bromwich, op. cit., p. 24; Ifor Williams (ed.), *Cyfranc Lludd a Llevelys* (Bangor, 1910), p. 30; Brynley F. Roberts, op. cit., pp. xxxv–xxxvii. The adjective 'fiery' possibly refers to the tradition that Vortigern was destroyed 'per ignem missum de caelo' (Mommsen, op. cit., p. 191).

16 J. E. B. Gover, Allen Mawer and F. M. Stenton, *The Place-Names of Wiltshire* (Cambridge, 1939), pp. 358–59.

17 *Celtic Heathendom*, pp. 192–94. A building which is magically destroyed after three days' building occurs in the *Uita Sancti Bernachii* (A. W. Wade-Evans (ed.), *Vitae Sanctorum Britanniae et Genealogiae* (Cardiff, 1944, p. 6). Jacob Hammer argued that Geoffrey's description of the building of Stonehenge was influenced by biblical phraseology ('Geoffrey of Monmouth's Use of the Bible in the "Historia Regum Britanniae"', *Bulletin of the John Rylands Library* (Manchester, 1947), xxx, p. 16).

18 Stuart Piggott, 'The Sources of Geoffrey of Monmouth: II. The Stonehenge Story', *Antiquity* (Gloucester, 1941), xv, p. 319.

19 To an 11th-century Icelandic poet the sky was 'the sun's awnings' (Diana Edwards, 'Christian and Pagan References in Eleventh-Century Norse Poetry: The Case of Arnórr Jarlaskáld', *Saga-Book of the Viking Society* (London, 1982–3), xxi, p. 38). Cf. Ivar Lissner, *Man, God and Magic* (London, 1961), p. 168; Ivar Paulson, Åke Hultkrantz and Karl Jettmar, *Les Religions Arctiques et Finnoises* (Paris, 1965), p. 39; Mircea Eliade, *Le Chamanisme et les Techniques Archaiques de l'Extase* (Paris, 1951), p. 236. Sir Ifor Williams tentatively emended *tentorium* to *tentura*, 'a curtain' ('Hen Chwedlau', *The Transactions of the Honourable Society of Cymmrodorion* (London, 1948), pp. 57–8), in which case one may recall the curtain behind which an Eskimo shaman withdraws when conducting his Otherworld journey (Nevill Drury, *The Shaman and the Magician* (London, 1982), p. 19).

20 I. Paulson, Åke Hultkrantz and K. Jettmar, op. cit., pp. 43–44. For the Erechtheum, cf. Sir James George Frazer (ed.), *Apollodorus: The Library* (London, 1921), ii, pp. 78–79; idem, *The Dying God* (London, 1923), p. 87; A. B. Cook, *Zeus: A Study in Ancient Religion* (Cambridge, 1914–40), iii, pp. 764–76.

21 Malcolm Smith, *The British Amphibians and Reptiles* (London, 1969), pp. 248–49.

22 Cf. *Celtic Heathendom*, pp. 154–55.

23 Bromwich, op. cit., p. 346; for the cult of the head, cf. Anne Ross, *Pagan Celtic Britain, Studies in Iconography and Tradition* (London, 1967), pp. 126, 252.

24 Henry Lewis, *Yr Elfen Ladin yn yr Iaith Gymraeg* (Cardiff, 1943), pp. 4, 21.

25 *Celtic Heathendom*, pp. 158, 161. A poem in *The Black Book of Carmarthen* contains a reference to 'the lords of Emrys', and Dr Rachel Bromwich conjectures that *Emrys* may be employed here 'symbolically,

with some such meaning as "the lords of Britain"(?)' ('Celtic Elements in Arthurian Romance: A General Survey', in P. B. Grout *et al.* (ed.), *The Legend of Arthur in the Middle Ages* (Cambridge, 1983), pp. 45, 231).

26 *Antiquity*, xv, pp. 318–19. Professor Piggott also notes a striking parallel with the story of the retrieval of Bran's head from Ireland and its interment in Britain as a protective talisman in the tale of *Branwen uerch Llyr* (ibid., pp. 309–12); for the practice cf. Sir James George Frazer, *The Dying God* (London, 1923), pp. 202–3. For Geoffrey's access to a genuine tradition of Stonehenge, cf. also H. J. Fleure, 'Archaeology and Folk Tradition', *The Proceedings of the British Academy* (London, 1931), xvii, pp. 12–13; Glyn E. Daniel, 'Who are the Welsh?', ibid. (1954), xl, p. 154; C. F. Arden-Close, 'Time and Memory' in W. F. Grimes (ed.), *Aspects of Archaeology in Britain and Beyond* (London, 1951), p. 29.

27 Michael J. Curley, 'A New Edition of John of Cornwall's *Prophetia Merlini*', *Speculum* (Cambridge, Mass., 1982), lvii, p. 236; Thomas Jones, 'The Black Book of Carmarthen "Stanzas of the Graves"', *The Proceedings of the British Academy* (London, 1967), liii, p. 136; J. Lloyd-Jones, *Geirfa Barddoniaeth Gynnar Gymraeg* (Cardiff, 1931–63), pp. 474–75; Acton Griscom (ed.), *The Historia Regum Britanniae of Geoffrey of Monmouth* (New York, 1929), p. 382. Hugh Williams claimed that Ambrosius and Merlin were identified 'very early, possibly in the sixth or seventh century' (*Christianity in Early Britain* (Oxford, 1912), p. 338). His argument appears confused, but Geoffrey's awkwardness may suggest something of the sort. The statement that 'Merlin . . . was called Ambrosius' seems at first glance designed to pre-empt criticisms that the Fatherless Boy at Vortigern's castle was named Ambrosius in Nennius's history. But in that case he would surely have placed the sheepish explanation at the appropriate place in his narrative. On the contrary, he betrays no fear that his audience would quote Nennius at him. Coming where it does, the identification adds a needless element of confusion, telling the reader that Merlin and Ambrosius are one at the close of a section in which they have appeared as two separate characters!

28 Cf. John Edwin Wood, *Sun, Moon and Standing Stones* (Oxford, 1978). For possible examples of mythic Celtic observatories, cf. Alwyn Rees and Brinley Rees, *Celtic Heritage: Ancient Tradition in Ireland and Wales* (London, 1961), pp. 149–50. According to Thomas Stephens, Welsh tradition numbered 'the seven score stones at Stonehenge' – citing the poem *Angar Kyvyndawd* (*The Literature of the Kymry* (London, 1876), p. 224). This does not appear in the version in the *Book of Taliesin*.

29 Cf. Rhŷs: 'we must give all the attributes of Emrys and the Merlins to one Merlin Emrys' (*Celtic Heathendom*, p. 152). It might be objected that the terminology *Merlinus Ambrosius* was coined in order to

distinguish the Merlin of *HRB* from the *Merlinus Celidonius* of *VM*; this was how Giraldus Cambrensis accounted for the obvious chronological discrepancy (cf. A. O. H. Jarman, *The Legend of Merlin* (Cardiff, 1960), p. 17). But whilst there is no certainty (interpolation is always a possibility), it does look as if the combination antedates Geoffrey's composition. The verse in the Welsh 'Stanzas of the Graves' which mentions 'Myrddin Embrais' forms part of a compilation assembled 'as early as the ninth or tenth century' (*The Proceedings of the British Academy*, liii, p. 100). John of Cornwall, who refers to 'Ambrosius Merlinus', probably composed his *Prophetia Merlini* in 1153–54 (*Speculum* lvii, pp. 222–23), which certainly derived from independent Celtic (probably Cornish) tradition (ibid., pp. 224–25; Brynley F. Roberts, 'Geoffrey of Monmouth and Welsh Historial Tradition', *Nottingham Mediaeval Studies* (Nottingham, 1976), xx, pp. 39–40). It is highly improbable that John knew of the existence, let alone the contents, of Geoffrey's *Vita Merlini*.

30 *The Proceedings of the British Academy*, lii, p. 136. Cf. the illuminating note by Dr Patrick Sims-Williams, *The Bulletin of the Board of Celtic Studies* (Cardiff, 1978–80), xxviii, pp. 90–93.

31 J. W. James (ed.), *Rhigyfarch's Life of St David* (Cardiff, 1967), pp. 4–5. Cf. D. Simon Evans (ed.), *Buched Dewi: O Lawysgrif Llanstephan 27* (Cardiff, 1959), pp. 3, 30–31. It seems most likely that the British Virgin Birth motif derives from native paganism, and is original to the Merlin story (cf. T. Gwynn Jones, op. cit., pp. 24–25). Robert de Boron's account of Merlin's birth from the union of a mortal mother and supernatural father owes nothing to Geoffrey, and most likely rests on an independent source. The hagiographical virgin birth themes are unlikely to derive from the story of the Nativity – a comparison which proved a subsequent source of embarrassment in view of the potential blasphemy. The original virgin birth tale of St Kentigern was regarded by his later biographer Joceline as 'shockingly blasphemous and heretical, and he tries to gloss it over' (Kenneth Jackson, 'The Sources for the Life of St Kentigern', in N. K. Chadwick (ed.), *Studies in the Early British Church* (Cambridge, 1958), p. 275). It was customary for a druid to foretell the future career of a newly-born infant (cf. Rev. Alexander Cameron (ed.), *Reliquiae Celticae: Texts, Papers, and Studies in Gaelic Literature and Philology* (Inverness, 1894), ii, p. 422).

32 Cuchulain was the son of the god Lug, conceived by a mortal woman (Alfred Nutt, *The Celtic Doctrine of Re-birth* (London, 1879), p. 42). Lug's counterpart, Mercury, bore the celebrated *caduceus* with emblematic entwined serpents. Could the Fighting Dragons/Serpents Merlin revealed to Vortigern reflect a mythic theme attached to the god of whom he was avatar? (cf. Douglas Brooks-Davies, *The Mercurian monarch: Magical politics from Spenser to Pope* (Manchester, 1983), pp. 33–50). In Greece they symbolised the mating of Zeus and Demeter (M. L. West, *The Orphic Poems* (Oxford, 1983), pp. 195, 220). Possibly

they personified the dualistic myth of symbiotic unity/opposition of creation, with its bright (divine) and dark (earthy) aspects. In the British Dark Ages the hated Saxons could readily have fitted into the latter rôle, and a cosmogonic myth have been translated into a contemporary political one.

33 Rachel Bromwich, *Trioedd Ynys Prydein: The Welsh Triads* (Cardiff, 1961), pp. cxxx–cxxxv, 228, 229, 240–49; ibid. (2nd edition, 1978), p. 560; cf. Mary Williams, 'Notes on Perlesvaus', *Speculum* (Cambridge, Mass., 1939) xiv, pp. 201–2.

34 John Rhŷs, *Lectures on the Origin and Growth of Celtic Heathendom* (London, 1888), pp. 160–61, 168. Similarly, the Chief Druid of the people of Nemed in Ireland was Mide, eponym of the province of Meath. He presided over the sacred first fire at Uisnech, the *Omphalos* of Ireland, which 'shed the fierceness . . . for a time over the four quarters of Ireland'. (Alwyn Rees and Brinley Rees, *Celtic Heritage: Ancient Tradition in Ireland and Wales* (London, 1961), p. 156).

35 Myles Dillon and Nora K. Chadwick, *The Celtic Realms* (London, 1967), pp. 135–36.

36 Eliade, *Patterns in Comparative Religion*, p. 371. For the peculiar sanctity of boundaries among the Celts, cf. L. Fleuriot, 'La Grande Inscription Celtibère de Botorrita', *Études Celtiques* (Paris, 1975), xiv, pp. 405–42.

37 Bentley, op. cit., pp. 470, 484; T. Rice Holmes (ed.), *C. Iulii Caesaris Commentarii* (Oxford, 1914), pp. 241–42; John Strachan and J. G. O'Keefe (ed.),*The Táin Bó Cúailnge from the Yellow Book of Lecan* (Dublin, 1912), p. 4; T. D. Kendrick, *The Druids: A Study in Keltic Prehistory* (London, 1927), p. 218. Cf. Julius Pokorny, 'The Origin of Druidism', *The Smithsonian Report for 1910* (Washington, 1911), pp. 583–97; Stuart Piggott, 'The Sources of Geoffrey of Monmouth: II. The Stonehenge Story', *Antiquity* (Gloucester, 1941), xv, pp. 312–19. For the concept of Britain as a 'fairy isle', cf. Peter J. Reynolds, 'The Material Culture of the Pagan Celtic Period', in Robert O'Driscoll (ed.), *The Celtic Consciousness* (New York, 1982), p. 79); Theo Brown, 'Westcountry Entrances to the Underworld', in H. R. Ellis Davidson (ed.), *The Journey to the Other World* (Cambridge, 1975), p. 91.

38 Roger Sherman Loomis, *Arthurian Tradition and Chrétien de Troyes* (New York, 1949), pp. 374–93.

39 Gildas, translated by A. W. Wade-Evans, *Nennius's 'History of the Britons' together with* . . . *'The Story of the Loss of Britain'* (London, 1938), p. 124. The engraving of a masked human figure on a piece of bone found in a Derbyshire cave (now in the British Museum) suggests that shamanistic traditions of inspired prophecy in Britain were thousands of years old when Merlin lived. Cf. Stuart Piggott and Glyn E. Daniel (ed.), *A Picture Book of Ancient British Art* (Cambridge, 1951), pp. 3, 12 and plate 1.

Nine *The Riddle of Stonehenge*

1 Mircea Eliade, *Patterns in Comparative Religion* (London, 1958), pp. 375–76; Alwyn Rees and Brinley Rees, *Celtic Heritage: Ancient Tradition in Ireland and Wales* (London, 1961), p. 160; Joan Halifax, *Shaman: The wounded healer* (London, 1982), pp. 30–31; E. O. James, *The Tree of Life: An Archaeological Study* (Leiden, 1966), pp. 12–13, 140, 142, 148; idem, *Creation and Cosmology: A Historical and Comparative Enquiry* (Leiden, 1969), pp. 15, 24–25; Eric Burrows, 'Some Cosmological Patterns in Babylonian Religion', in S. H. Hooke (ed.), *The Labyrinth: Further Studies in the Relation between Myth and Ritual in the Ancient World* (London, 1935), pp. 45–53; Jane Harrison, *Themis: A Study of the Social Origins of Greek Religion* (Cambridge, 1912), pp. 396–415; Paul Wheatley, *The Pivot of the Four Quarters: A Preliminary Enquiry into the Origins and Character of the Ancient Chinese City* (Edinburgh, 1971), pp. 259–60, 418–27; Henri Frankfort, *Kingship and the Gods: A Study of Ancient Near Eastern Religion as the Integration of Society and Nature* (Chicago, 1948), pp. 151–54; J. Eric. S. Thompson, *Maya History and Religion* (Norman, Oklahoma, 1972), p. 195; Arthur Bernard Cook, *Zeus: A Study in Ancient Religion* (Cambridge, 1914–40), ii, pp. 166–91.

2 Burrows, op. cit., pp. 59–66; Eliade, op. cit., pp. 231–35, 374–79; Wheatley, op. cit., pp. 416–18, 428–36; Cook, op. cit., ii, pp. 45–113; iii, pp. 1116–17.

3 Colin Burgess, *The Age of Stonehenge* (London, 1980), p. 328; Christopher Chippindale, *Stonehenge Complete* (London, 1983), pp. 266–68.

4 Cf. Wheatley, op. cit., pp. 433–34, 440; A. M. Hocart, 'The Life-Giving Myth', in S. H. Hooke, op. cit., pp. 266–67; Alwyn and Brinley Rees, op. cit., p. 156. Mircea Eliade sees in Stonehenge the 'valorization of the sacred space as "center of the world", the privileged place that affords communication with heaven and the underworld' (*A History of Religious Ideas* (London, 1979), i, p. 118).

5 Mircea Eliade, *Le Chamanisme et les Techniques Archaiques de l'Extase* (Paris, 1951), pp. 179, 205, 227, 236–42, 330, idem, *Patterns in Comparative Religion*, pp. 298–300; Ivar Lissner, *Man, God and Magic* (London, 1961), pp. 266–68; H. Munro Chadwick and N. Kershaw Chadwick, *The Growth of Literature* (Cambridge, 1940), iii, p. 144; Halifax, op. cit., pp. 21–22. For a Chukchee 'map' of the heavens, with the Polar Star as their fulcrum, cf. ibid., p. 66. There appears to have been a widespread tradition in the ancient world of a 'journey to a huge mountain in the North to acquire (or receive) wisdom.' (Jan Bremmer, *The Early Greek Concept of the Soul* (Princeton, 1983), p. 38).

6 Cf. Gutorm Gjessing, 'The Circumpolar Stone Age', *Antiquity* (Newbury, 1953), xxvii, pp. 131–36; Stuart Piggott, *Ancient Europe from*

the beginnings of Agriculture to Classical Antiquity (Edinbrgh, 1965), p. 35.

7 J. D. P. Bolton argues persuasively that Aristeas in fact travelled east (*Aristeas of Proconnesus* (Oxford, 1962), p. 116), but the point is that Aristeas himself believed his direction was *northerly*. For Greek traditions of the Hyperborean seers, cf. Morton Smith, *Clement of Alexandria and a Secret Gospel of Mark* (Cambridge, Mass., 1973), p. 242; Eliade, *Le Chamanisme*, p. 349; and for the Irish tradition that magical arts came from the North, Elizabeth A. Gray (ed.), *Cath Maige Tuired: The Second Battle of Mag Tuired* (Dublin, 1982), p. 24. For archaeological evidence of Palaeolithic and Mesolithic survivals in Northern Europe, cf. F. T. Wainwright (ed.), *The Problem of the Picts* (Edinburgh, 1956), p. 55; V. Gordon Childe, *Scotland before the Scots* (London, 1946), p. 42; F. T. Wainwright (ed.), *The Northern Isles* (London, 1964), pp. 24–25, 44–45. Pokorny's theories have received just criticism, but there is certainly something in his overall argument favouring palaeo-Arctic survivals in the Bronze Age and after in the British Isles (cf. 'The Pre-Celtic Inhabitants of Ireland', *Celtica* (Dublin, 1960), v, pp. 228–40).

8 Jon Carter Covell, *Korea's Cultural Roots* (Seoul, 1982), pp. 25–30.

9 Eliade, *Patterns in Comparative Religion*, pp. 233, 376.

10 The prophecy is quoted in Gaelic by Thomas Pennant, *A Tour in Scotland, and Voyage to the Hebrides; MDCCLXXII* (London, 1776), i, pp. 284–85. Cf. *Description of the Western Isles of Scotland, called Hybrides; by Mr. Donald Monro High Dean of the Isles . . . in the year 1549* (Edinburgh, 1774), pp. 20–21; F. Marian McNeill, *Iona: A History of the Island* (Glasgow, 1946), pp. 62–63.

11 W. F. Grimes, op. cit., p. 292; cf. R. J. C. Atkinson, *Stonehenge and Avebury and Neighbouring Monuments* (London, 1959), p. 21; I. Ll. Foster and Glyn Daniel, *Prehistoric and Early Wales* (London, 1965), pp. 84–87; W. F. Grimes, 'The Stone Circles and Related Monuments of Wales', in I. Ll. Foster and L. Alcock (ed.), *Culture and Environment: Essays in Honour of Sir Cyril Fox* (London, 1963), pp. 108–11; R. J. C. Atkinson, *Stonehenge* (London, 1956), pp. 98–110.

12 Sir Cyril Fox, *The Personality of Britain: its Influence on Inhabitant and Invader in Prehistoric and Early Historic Times* (Cardiff, 1959), pp. 44, 88; Michael Herity, 'The Early Prehistoric Period Around the Irish Sea', in Donald Moore (ed.), *The Irish Sea Province in Archaeology and History* (Cardiff, 1970), pp. 30–33.

13 Wheatley, op. cit., pp. 431–32.

14 M. E. Cunnington, *An Introduction to the Archaeology of Wiltshire from the Earliest Times to the Pagan Saxons* (Devizes, 1934), pp. 60–63; R. J. C. Atkinson, *Stonehenge and Avebury*, p. 34.

15 E. O. James, op. cit., pp. 32, 140, 143, 148. For the 'close association of human sacrifice and the *axis mundi*', cf. James L. Sauvé, 'The Divine Victim: Aspects of Human Sacrifice in Viking Scandinavia and Vedic

India', in Jaan Puhvel (ed.), *Myth and Law Among the Indo-Europeans: Studies in Indo-European Comparative Mythology* (Los Angeles, 1970), p. 181. Cf. further Matti Kuusi, Keith Bosley and Michael Branch (ed.), *Finnish Folk Poetry Epic* (London, 1977), p. 267; Anthony Faulkes (ed.), *Snorri Sturluson: Edda, Prologue and Gylfaginning* (Oxford, 1982), p. 17. For representations of the World-Tree, cf. H. R. Ellis Davidson, *Pagan Scandinavia* (London, 1967), plate 46; E. O. G. Turville-Petre, *Myth and Religion of the North: The Religion of Ancient Scandinavia* (London, 1964), plate 39. Could Myrddin's 'fair wanton maiden' be the Forest Guardian known to Estonians and Finns as 'the young girl of the forest' (*metsa-neitsi*)? (cf. I. Paulson, Å. Hultkrantz and K. Jettmar, *Les Religions Arctiques et Finnoises* (Paris, 1965), pp. 178, 186–87; and, for the Yakut tree-woman, Eliade, *Le Chamanisme*, p. 247). Among the heathen Lapps it was a 'mountain-virgin' (*saivo-neide*) who awoke the shaman to ecstasy and strengthened him with '*saivo-tjatse*, the magically powerful water which flows down from the sacred mountain' (Rafael Karsten, *The Religion of the Samek: Ancient Beliefs and Cults of the Scandinavian and Finnish Lapps* (Leiden, 1955), pp. 60, 87). Blood sacrifices sustained the World Tree (ibid., p. 97). For the Tree of Life as World Centre, source of mantic inspiration and sexual fecundity, and its approximation to the Cross of Jesus, cf. Hans Peter Duerr, *Dreamtime: Concerning the Boundary between Wilderness and Civilization* (Oxford, 1985), pp. 213–18. Insular Celtic belief in the Tree of Life is well-attested (cf. Charles Plummer (ed.), *Bethada Náem nÉrenn: Lives of Irish Saints* (Oxford, 1922), i, p. 89; Whitley Stokes (ed.), *Lives of Saints from the Book of Lismore* (Oxford, 1890), p. 128).

16 James, op. cit., p. 62; Cook, op. cit., iii, p. 910.

17 Atkinson, *Stonehenge*, pp. 18, 62.

18 Ibid., pp. 45–46. A North African tale relates how a noted Imam visited an obviously numinous spot: 'they found a place in which there were twelve stones and a tree. In their hearts they strongly sensed that here was the place of the tomb of that pious saint. At that spot they sacrificed a ewe, they said, and its blood rose up to heaven. The tree shook, and their souls were calmed on account of that.' (H. T. Norris, *Saharan Myth and Saga* (Oxford, 1972), p. 157).

19 John Rhŷs, *Lectures on the Origin and Growth of Religion as Illustrated by Celtic Heathendom* (London, 1888), pp. 187–90; for a full translation of the story, see Standish H. O'Grady, *Silva Gadelica* (London, 1892), ii, pp. 301–2. This legendary account receives confirmation from the archaeological record. At Emain Macha (Navan) excavations have shown that about 200 B.C. 'something in the nature of an artificial grove was set up on the hill, the structure consisting of concentric circles of stakes, with one huge and lofty trunk at the centre'. Mr Tómas Ó. Broin suggests that this trunk was an *axis mundi* in the form of a World-Tree, and that the Red-branch Knights (*Curaid na Craebruaide*)

of Ulster legend ultimately represent a group of initiates of the cult at Emain Macha ('"Craebruad": The Spurious Tradition', *Éigse: A Journal of Irish Studies* (Dublin, 1973), xv, pp. 103–13); Bernard Wailes, 'The Irish "Royal Sites" in History and Archaeology', *Cambridge Medieval Celtic Studies* (Cambridge, 1982), iii, pp. 8–10. In ancient Ireland wells were regarded as natural entrances to the Otherworld, and their waters were believed to flow from an underground sea (James Carney, 'The Earliest Bran Material', in John J. O'Meara and Bernd Naumann (ed.), *Latin Script and Letters A.D. 400–900* (Leiden, 1976), pp. 185, 191–92). For a similar belief among the Lapps, cf. Karsten, op. cit., p. 18.

20 Faulkes, op. cit., p. 17. According to the *Prose Edda* the *Gjallahorn* was a drinking-vessel, but in the *Völuspa* it is a musical instrument (*galla* = 'resounding': Sigurdur Nordal (ed.), *Völuspa* (Durham, 1980), p. 91). This ambivalence recurs throughout versions of the sacred spring and attendant horn theme. Cf. also Jacqueline Simpson, 'Mímir: Two Myths or One?', *Saga-Book of the Viking Society* (London, 1962), xvi, pp. 41–53.

21 O. G. S. Crawford, *Archaeology in the Field* (London, 1953), pp. 77–81.

22 Colm O Lochlainn, 'Roadways in Ancient Ireland', in Eoin ua Riain (ed.), *Feil-sgribhinn eoin mhic neill* (Dublin, 1940), p. 470.

23 John Rhŷs, *Celtic Folklore: Welsh and Manx* (Oxford, 1901), p. 295.

24 Wheatley, op. cit., pp. 438–39.

25 K. R. Maxwell-Hyslop, 'The Assyrian "Tree of Life": a Western Branch?', in J. V. S. Megaw (ed.), *To illustrate the monuments: Essays on archaeology presented to Stuart Piggott* (London, 1976), pp. 263–76; A. F. J. Klijn, *Seth in Jewish, Christian and Gnostic Literature* (Leiden, 1977), p. 44; Eliade, *Le Chamanisme*, p. 243; idem, *Patterns in Comparative Religion*, pp. 375, 377–79; S. H. Hooke, op. cit., pp. 53–59; E. O. James, op. cit., pp. 161–62; 'the Temple was destined to become the *omphalos* whither all nations would be gathered under his God's righteous rule' (idem, *The Worship of the Sky-God: A Comparative Study in Semitic and Indo-European Religion* (London, 1963), p. 64).

Ten *The Shaman of Hart Fell*

1 Sir Ifor Williams, *Chwedl Taliesin* (Cardiff, 1957), p. 9. Presumably 'the prophet Johannes' is St John the Divine. For an important recent discussion of the *Hanes Taliesin*, v. Juliette Wood, 'The Elphin Section of *Hanes Taliesin*', *Études Celtiques* (Paris, 1981), xviii, pp. 229–44. An eleventh-century prophecy attributed to Merlin in *The Black Book of Carmarthen* concludes with the peculiar distich 'Since it is I, Myrddin, after Taliesin/Whose prophecy will be correct'. Could this be a further instance of the intrusion of Taliesin into the Myrddin saga? Cf. A. O.

H. Jarman (ed.), *Ymddiddan Myrddin a Thaliesin* (Cardiff, 1951), p. 67; also Roger Sherman Loomis, *Wales and the Arthurian Legend* (Cardiff, 1956), p. 160.

2 Is it possible that the puzzling Ysgolan poem in *The Black Book of Carmarthen* refers to Myrddin? In the poem Ysgolan is denounced as a man whose hostility to the Church earned him a year's penance affixed to a stake in a fishing-weir. The name *Ysgolan* derives from a cognate form of the Irish *scal*, the name given to the god Lug in the Irish tale *Baile in Scáil*, whose prophecy so closely parallels Myrddin's in the *Cyfoesi*. Moreover, Ysgolan is described as *ysgodig*, 'frenzied'; a word synonymous with Myrddin's epithet *gwyllt* (P. L. Henry, *The Early English and Celtic Lyric* (London, 1966), pp. 88–89; cf. A. O. H. Jarman (ed.), *Llyfr Du Caerfyrddin* (Cardiff, 1982), p. lx); Donatien Laurent, 'La gwerz de Skolan et la légende de Merlin', *Ethnologie française*, i, pp. 19–54. There are other suggestions in the early poetry of an unsuccessful attempt (on the part of the Church?) to censor the works of the pagan Myrddin, and in this case it may be that his celebrated death on a stake in a fishing-weir has been translated into a penance undergone by the 'frenzied' 'black one' for his anti-Christian conduct. One of Ysgolan's crimes was 'the drowning of a gift book', and Merlin's Irish counterpart Suibhne Geilt was cursed by a saint for throwing a beautiful psalter into a lake.

3 J. Gwenogvryn Evans (ed.), *Facsimile and Text of the Book of Taliesin* (Llanbedrog, 1910), pp. 23–27; translation by Patrick K. Ford, *The Mabinogi and other Medieval Welsh Tales* (Los Angeles, 1977), pp. 184–87.

4 Sir John Morris Jones, 'Taliesin', *Y Cymmrodor* (London, 1918), xxviii, pp. 281–82; William J. Watson, *The History of the Celtic Place-Names of Scotland* (Edinburgh, 1926), pp. 343–44; Ifor Williams (ed.), *Canu Taliesin* (Cardiff, 1960), p. xxviii; Rachel Bromwich (ed.), *Trioedd Ynys Prydein: The Welsh Triads* (2nd edition, Cardiff, 1978), p. 540.

5 Myrddin's Irish counterpart, Suibhne Geilt, in his sylvan refuge hears the 'hunting-call of a multitude in the verge of the wood', and apostrophises the various trees in a series of verses specifying them by name as in *Cad Goddeu* (J. G. O'Keefe (ed.), *Buile Suibhne . . . The Adventures of Suibhne Geilt* (London, 1913), pp. 62–68). Cf. also note on p. 312. For arboreal battles in Celtic literature, cf. Sir John Rhŷs, 'Notes on the Coligny Calendar together with an Edition of the Reconstructed Calendar', *Proceedings of the British Academy* (London, 1910), iv, p. 139; Françoise Le Roux, *Les Druides* (Paris, 1961), pp. 69–71. See also p. 365.

6 The Black Man in *Owein* is so called: 'Oc wtwart yw ar y koet hwnnw' (John Rhŷs and J. Gwenogvryn Evans (ed.), *The Text of the Mabinogion and Other Welsh Tales from the Red Book of Hergest* (Oxford, 1887), p. 166).

7 *Y Cymmrodor*, xxviii, pp. 240–54; Sir Edward Anwyl, 'Prolegomena to the Study of Old Welsh Poetry', *Transactions of the Honourable Society of Cymmrodorion* (London, 1903–4), p. 75.

8 *Y Cymmrodor*, xxviii, p. 242.

9 For the mantic setting of the *Awenyddion*, cf. J. Gwyn Griffiths, 'Giraldus Cambrensis Descriptio Kambriae, i, 16', *The Bulletin of the Board of Celtic Studies* (Cardiff, 1984), xxxi, pp. 1–16. Sir Ifor Williams (*Lectures on Early Welsh Poetry* (Dublin, 1944), pp. 59–60) suggests that the shape-shifting verses represent 'nonsense verse' extracted from a ninth-century Taliesin saga which formed the nucleus of the much later *Hanes Taliesin*. This is surely putting the cart before the horse: were the *awenyddion* also quoting from the saga? Cf. the sensible caution of Alwyn D. Rees, 'Modern Evaluations of Celtic Narrative Tradition', *Proceedings of the Second International Congress of Celtic Studies* (Cardiff, 1966), pp. 51–52, 56. It may be that the obscurity of *Cad Goddeu* and similar verses was deliberate. Professor Sigurdur Nordal has this to say of the comparable Icelandic *Völuspa*: 'the harder it is to understand, the more powerfully it attracts one. People do not try to plumb the depths of works which let all their treasures float on the surface.' ('Three Essays on *Völuspa*', *Saga-Book of the Viking Society* (London, 1970–71), xviii, pp. 79–80).

10 H. Munro Chadwick and N. Kershaw Chadwick, *The Growth of Literature* (Cambridge, 1932–40), iii, pp. 850–51; Å. Hultkrantz, 'Ecological and Phenomenological Aspects of Shamanism', in V. Diószegi and M. Hoppál (ed.), *Shamanism in Siberia* (Budapest, 1978), pp. 30–31. Cf. Mircea Eliade, *Le Chamanisme et les Techniques Archaiques de l'Extase* (Paris, 1951), pp. 17–22; Andreas Lommel, *The World of the Early Hunters* (London, 1967), pp. 69–74.

11 André Leroi-Gourhan, *The Art of Prehistoric Man* (London, 1968), pp. 132–33, plate 57; J. G. D. Clark, 'Star Carr, a Mesolithic Site in Yorkshire', in R. L. S. Bruce-Mitford (ed.), *Recent Archaeological Excavations in Britain* (London, 1956), pp. 17–19, plate IIa. Antlers have been found in Mesolithic graves (idem, 'In Mesolithic Times', in I. E. S. Edwards, C. J. Gadd and N. G. L. Hammond (ed.), *The Cambridge Ancient History* (Cambridge, 1970), i, pp. 111–12), suggesting a ritual rather than practical purpose. Lommel (op. cit., pp. 148–49) traces the roots of shamanism back to the Alpine Palaeolithic era, 30,000 to 50,000 years ago.

12 Eliade, op. cit., pp. 29–30. Cf. Lommel, op. cit., pp. 36–39; S. I. Vajnstejn, 'The Tuvan (Soyot) Shaman's Drum and the Ceremony of its "Enlivening"', in V. Diószegi (ed.), *Popular Beliefs and Folklore Tradition in Siberia* (Budapest, 1968), pp. 331–32; G. M. Vasilievich, 'The Acquisition of Shamanistic Ability among the Evenki (Tungus)', in ibid., pp. 345–46).

13 John Rhŷs, *Celtic Folklore, Welsh and Manx* (Oxford, 1901), pp. 202–3. This figure, 'too colossal for any house to contain', squatting

on his mountain-top, may be identified with the horned god Cernunnos (p. 552). Cf. idem, *Lectures on the Origin and Growth of Religion as Illustrated by Celtic Heathendom* (London, 1888), pp. 250–51; J. Lloyd-Jones, *Geirfa Barddoniaeth Gynnar Gymraeg* (Cardiff, 1931–63), p. 37; Anne Ross, *Pagan Celtic Britain: Studies in Iconography and Tradition* (London, 1967), pp. 137–38. For the taboo against naming a deity, cf. Sir James George Frazer, *Taboo and the Perils of the Soul* (London, 1927), pp. 387–91.

14 M. J. Field, 'Spirit Possession in Ghana', in John Beattie and John Middleton (ed.), *Spirit Mediumship and Society in Africa* (London, 1969), pp. 4, 9; Eliade, op. cit., p. 136.

15 The Chadwicks appear to have been alone in perceiving this (*The Growth of Literature*, iii, pp. 888–89), though in the case of Suibhne the parallels are discussed by Brigit Beneš, 'Spuren von Schamanismus in der Sage "Buile Suibhne"', *Zeitschrift für Celtische Philologie* (Tübingen, 1960/61), xxviii, pp. 309–34.

16 The 'reference to Merlin in the romance of *Fergus* . . . appears to derive directly from North British tradition in the Arthuret area' (A. O. H. Jarman, 'A Note on the Possible Welsh Derivation of *Viviane*', in *Gallica: Essays presented to J. Heywood Thomas by Colleagues, pupils and friends* (Cardiff, 1969), p. 10). In Iceland it was believed that troops of dead souls entered a sacred mountain, Holyfell (H. R. Ellis Davidson, *Scandinavian Mythology* (London, 1982), p. 42), and among the Lapps 'the land of the departed had become identical with "the land in the interior of the mountains"' (Rafael Karsten, *The Religion of the Samek: Ancient Beliefs and Cults of the Scandinavian and Finnish Lapps* (Leiden, 1955), p. 107); Louise Bäckman and Åke Hultkrantz, *Studies in Lapp Shamanism* (Stockholm, 1978), p. 81.

17 Eliade, op. cit., pp. 125–26, 134, 137, 144, 149–51, 153, 166, 262, 291, 395, 415–19; N. K. Chadwick, *Poetry and Prophecy* (Cambridge, 1942), p. 58; Lommel, op. cit., p. 111; I. Paulson, Å. Hultkrantz and K. Jettmar, *Les Religions Arctiques et Finnoises* (Paris, 1965), p. 132; *Popular Beliefs in Siberia*, pp. 312, 324–25, 336; Ivar Lissner, *Man, God and Magic* (London, 1961), pp. 272, 282–83; M. Ja. Zhornickaya, 'Dances of Yakut Shamans', in V. Diószegi and M. Hoppál (ed.), *Shamanism in Siberia* (Budapest, 1978), p. 304; V. A. Tugolukov, 'Some Aspects of the Beliefs of the Tungus (Evenki and Evens)', ibid., p. 426. The Norse god Loki flew to Jötunheim in Freya's feathered cloak, Freya herself being a practitioner of inspired divination, *seidr* (C. J. Bleeker, *The Sacred Bridge: Researches into the Nature and Structure of Religion* (Leiden, 1963), p. 107).

18 Henry, op. cit., pp. 26–27, 137–49; Peter Gelling and Hilda Ellis Davidson, *The Chariot of the Sun and Other Rites and Symbols of the Northern Bronze Age* (London, 1969), pp. 175–76; Whitley Stokes (ed.), *Three Irish Glossaries* (London, 1862), p. 45; Ross, op. cit., pp.

262–63. The garbled account in the Norse *Speculum Regale* must derive
from this concept, and Suibhne's epithet *geilt* corresponds in some
degree to *uolatiles* (Kuno Meyer, 'The Irish Mirabilia in the Norse
"Speculum Regale"', *Ériu* (Dublin, 1908), iv, p. 12; James Carney,
'"Suibhne Geilt" and "The Children of Lir"', *Éigse: A Journal of Irish
Studies* (Dublin, 1950), vi, pp. 97–100).

19 Arthur C. L. Brown, 'The Esplumoir and Viviane', *Speculum* (Cam-
bridge, Mass., 1945), xx, pp. 426–32; R. S. Loomis, 'The Esplumeor
Merlin Again', *Bulletin Bibliographique de la Société Internationale
Arthurienne* (Paris, 1957), pp. 79–83; Alexandre Micha, *Étude sur le
'Merlin' de Robert de Boron* (Geneva, 1980), p. 22; Pierre le Gentil,
'The Work of Robert de Boron and the *Didot Perceval*', in R. S.
Loomis (ed.), *Arthurian Literature in the Middle Ages: A Collaborative
History* (Oxford, 1959), pp. 259, 261.

20 Eliade, op. cit., pp. 47–50; J. G. Frazer, *Totemism and Exogamy: A
Treatise on Certain Early Forms of Superstition and Society* (London,
1935), iii, pp. 373, 376, 378, 382, 383, 384, 387, 388, 389, 391, 392,
393, 395, 399, 403, 404, 406, 409, 413, 419, 423, 432, 437, 467. For
fasting preparatory to ecstatic or prophetic vision in Classical and early
Christian times, cf. Violet MacDermot, *The Cult of the Seer in the
Ancient Middle East* (London, 1971), pp. 12, 40–42, 96.

21 Kathleen Mulchrone (ed.), *Bethu Phátraic: The Tripartite Life of
Patrick* (Dublin, 1939), pp. 70–71; Whitley Stokes (ed.), *The Tripartite
Life of Patrick with Other Documents Relating to that Saint* (London,
1887), p. 418; Theodor Mommsen (ed.), 'Historia Brittonum cvm
Additamentis Nennii', *Monvmenta Germaniae Historica*, xiii, *Chronica
Minora*, iii (Berlin, 1894), p. 191; S. Baring-Gould and John Fisher,
The Lives of the British Saints (London, 1907), i, pp. 17–21; Whitley
Stokes (ed.), *The Martyrology of Oengus the Culdee* (London, 1905),
p. 68.

22 Lailoken is said in addition to have been 'bound with thongs . . . so
that the king might come to hear something new from him'. Can this
be a reflection of a practice similar to that of the Kharty shamans, who
lay bound upon the floor during their prophetic convulsions? (J. Balázs,
'The Hungarian Shaman's Technique of Trance Induction', *Popular
Beliefs in Siberia*, p. 59; cf. A. A. Popov, 'How Sereptic Djaruoskin
of the Nganasans (Tavgi Samoyeds) Became a Shaman', ibid., p. 139;
Lommel, op. cit., p. 69). A figure carved on a Scandinavian reindeer
horn and dating from about 6000 B.C. represents a shamanistic figure
'seemingly bound and asleep' (Ellis Davidson, *Scandinavian Mythology*, pp. 16, 17).

23 Lissner, op. cit., pp. 272–73; cf. Eliade, op. cit., pp. 30, 97–102, 144,
149, 153, 167; B. Gunda, 'Survivals of Totemism in the Hungarian
táltos Tradition', *Popular Beliefs in Siberia*, pp. 42, 48; ibid., pp.
202–3, 346, 400–401; G. N. Gracheva, 'A Nganasan Shaman Costume',
Shamanism in Siberia, p. 323; Sir James George Frazer, *Folk-lore in*

the Old Testament: Studies in Comparative Religion, Legend and Law (London, 1918), i, pp. 32–35.

24 Eliade, op. cit., pp. 403–4.

25 Nutt, op. cit., pp. 295–99. Cf. Thomas F. O'Rahilly, *Early Irish History and Mythology* (Dublin, 1957), pp. 323–25.

26 G. M. Vasilievich, 'Shamanistic Songs of the Evenki (Tungus)', *Popular Beliefs in Siberia*, pp. 354–55; Lommel, op. cit., pp. 64, 68.

27 Cf. ibid., pp. 49–52, 59–63; Eliade, op. cit., pp. 93–99; *Les Religions Arctiques*, p. 128; Å. Hultkrantz, 'Ecological and Phenomenological Aspects of Shamanism', *Shamanism in Siberia*, pp. 38–40, 337, 343; Nevill Drury, *The Shaman and the Magician: Journeys between the worlds* (London, 1982), pp. 20–21; *The Growth of Literature*, iii, p. 199. Lapp shamans were able 'to run in the shape of wolves and bears', and it seems that 'the shaman's *saiva*, or assistant spirit, appeared as a wolf' (Bäckman and Hultkrantz, op. cit., p. 57).

28 Eliade, op. cit., pp. 81, 115. Pig-sacrifices play an especially important rôle in Korean shamanism (Taegon Kim, *Photographs of Shamanism in Korea* (Seoul, 1981, plates 4, 5, 6, 35, 36; Jung-Young Lee, *Korean Shamanistic Rituals* (The Hague, 1981), pp. 29, 33, 51, 97, 145, plate 203). For the sacrifice of a divine pig in Finnish folklore, see Matti Kuusi, Keith Bosley and Michael Branch (ed.), *Finnish Folk Poetry Epic* (Helsinki, 1977), pp. 269–70. 'The deity . . . is never far removed from his cult animal. He may be encountered in the form of his sacred dog, stag, horse or bird as the case may be . . .' Of one sinister Otherworld figure, it is recorded that 'a pig, black-bristled, singed, was on his back, squealing continually . . .' (Anne Ross, 'The Divine Hag of the Pagan Celts', in Venetia Newall (ed.), *The Witch Figure* (London, 1973), pp. 140, 147).

29 Eliade, op. cit., pp. 64, 73; *Shamanism in Siberia*, p. 385. For the widespread occurrence of initiatory rituals of death and resurrection, cf. J. G. Frazer, *Balder the Beautiful: The Fire-Festivals of Europe and the Doctrine of the External Soul* (London, 1930), ii, pp. 225–78. Christ, of course, was buried in a tomb before His resurrection.

30   'gan unben deßr diarchar
        dy ylodi y dan dayar . . .
        Olochwyt kyuot a thauot llyfreu
        awen heb arsßyt
        achwdyl bun a hun breudwyt.'
(J. Gwenovbryn Evans (ed.), *The Poetry in the Red Book of Hergest* (Llanbedrog, 1911), p. 4). The poem *Gwasgarddgerdd vyrddin yn y bedd* (ibid., p. 5; Egerton G. B. Phillimore, 'A Fragment from Hengwrt MS. No. 202', *Y Cymmrodor* (1886), vii, pp. 151–54) carries the same suggestion of ritual resurrection.

31 Cf. Lommel, op. cit., pp. 54–59; A. J. Joki, 'Notes on Selkup Shamanism', *Shamanism in Siberia*, p. 379; Eliade, op. cit., pp. 47–49, 53–55, 62–67; idem, *The Two and the One* (London, 1965), pp. 140–45.

32 *Religions Arctiques*, pp. 178, 186–87; *Popular Beliefs in Siberia*, p. 343; Lommel, op. cit., p. 61; Eliade, op. cit., p. 247.

33 Lissner, op. cit., p. 267; *Religions Arctiques*, pp. 39–43, 131; *Shamanism in Siberia*, pp. 32–33; Eliade, *Le Chamanisme*, pp. 244–48; B. Gunda, 'Survivals of Totemism in the Hungarian *táltos* Tradition', *Popular Beliefs in Siberia*, p. 42.

34 Each stanza of the *Bedwenni* begins '*Gwin y bid y vedwen*', 'blessed is the birch tree' (Margaret Enid Griffiths, *Early Vaticination in Welsh with English Parallels* (Cardiff, 1937), p. 85). For the 'rich birch-tree' as 'a rung of the ladder connecting earth with heaven' among Shor and other shamans, cf. V. Diószegi, 'Pre-Islamic Shamanism of the Baraba Turks and some Ethnogenetic Conclusions', *Shamanism in Siberia*, pp. 117–18.

35 E. O. James, *Creation and Cosmology: A Historical and Comparative Inquiry* (Leiden, 1969), p. 28; Anthony Faulkes (ed.), *Snorri Sturluson: Edda: Prologue and Gylfaginning* (Oxford, 1982), pp. 43–45; H. T. Norris, *Saharan Myth and Saga* (Oxford, 1972), pp. 10–11; Mircea Eliade, *A History of Religious Ideas* (London, 1979), i, pp. 142–45.

36 Idem, *Patterns in Comparative Religion* (London, 1958), pp. 398–407; James, op. cit., pp. 23–24; Henri Frankfort, *Kingship and the Gods: A Study of Ancient Near Eastern Religion as the Integration of Society & Nature* (Chicago, 1948), pp. 148–59, 313–33; C. J. Bleeker, *Egyptian Festivals: Enactments of Religious Renewal* (Leiden, 1967), pp. 39–40; S. G. F. Brandon, *Creation Legends of the Ancient Near East* (London, 1963), pp. 19–29; E. O. James, *The Tree of Life: An Archaeological Study* (Leiden, 1966), pp. 145–47. As Geo Widengren noted, the seven days allotted to the Creation in *Genesis* may reflect the successive days of the ritual rather than the chronology of the myth. The Babylonian *Enuma Elish* is preserved on *seven* tablets ('Early Hebrew Myths and their Interpretation', in S. H. Hooke (ed.), *Myth, Ritual and Kingship* (Oxford, 1958), p. 175).

37 Alwyn Rees and Brinley Rees, *Celtic Heritage: Ancient Tradition in Ireland and Wales* (London, 1961), pp. 168–72; Nutt, op. cit., pp. 183–86; Eoin MacNeill, *Early Irish Laws and Institutions* (Dublin, 1936), pp. 104–8; Máire MacNeill, *The Festival of Lughnasa: A Study of the Survival of the Celtic Festival of the Beginning of Harvest* (Oxford, 1962), pp. 339–44.

38 Ibid., pp. 101–5. For the absorption of pagan motifs in hagiographical literature, cf. Felim Ó Briain, 'Saga Themes in Irish Hagiography', in Séamus Pender (ed.), *Féilscríbhinn Torna* (Cork, 1947), pp. 33–42; D. A. Binchy, 'A pre-Christian survival in mediaeval Irish hagiography', in Dorothy Whitelock *et al.* (ed.), *Ireland in Early Mediaeval Europe: Studies in Memory of Kathleen Hughes* (Cambridge, 1982), pp. 165–78.

39 For Plinlimmon as a Sacred Centre, cf. Rees and Rees, op. cit., pp. 175, 177. Cf. also A. W. Wade-Evans (ed.), *Vitae Sanctorum Britanniae et Genealogiae* (Cardiff, 1944), p. 26; Bromwich, op. cit., pp. 246–47;

John O'Donovan (ed.), *leabhar na g-ceart, or The Book of Rights* (Dublin, 1847), pp. lxi–iv; H. O'Neill Hencken, 'A Gaming Board of the Viking Age', *Acta Archaeologica* (Copenhagen, 1933), iv, pp. 85–104; Rees and Rees, op. cit., pp. 154–56; Elizabeth A. Gray (ed.), *Cath Maige Tuired: The Second Battle of Mag Tuired* (Naas, 1982), pp. 40, 93–94.

40 *Celtic Heathendom*, pp. 398–403; Gruffydd, op. cit., pp. 60–61.

41 Mircea Eliade, *Myth and Reality* (London, 1964), pp. 50–60; idem, *The Quest: History and Meaning in Religion* (Chicago, 1969), pp. 140–41. For the king as head shaman in ancient China, cf. K. C. Chang, *Art, Myth, and Ritual: The Path to Political Authority in Ancient China* (Harvard, 1983), pp. 44–45. Similarly, 'the king's role as diviner, seer and prophet' was crucial in Babylonia. 'This side of kingship was very important in older times; the king was, as priest-king, mediator between the people and the gods, and by discovering the gods' will and obeying it he ensured peace and prosperity . . . That Ziusudra made a statue of the god of giddiness suggests that he also was able to communicate with the world beyond through ecstasy, and so valued and sought the giddiness that precedes and induces ecstatic trance' (Thorkild Jacobsen, 'The Eridu Genesis', *Journal of Biblical Literature* (Chico, California, 1981), c, p. 523).

42 Cf. E. O. G. Turville-Petre, *Myth and Religion of the North: The Religion of Ancient Scandinavia* (London, 1964), p. 45; idem, *Origins of Icelandic Literature* (Oxford, 1953), pp. 55–64, 200–202; Sigurdur Nordal, 'Three Essays on Völuspá', *Saga-Book of the Viking Society* (London, 1970–71), xviii, p. 81.

43 Virgil was regarded as a prophet in the Middle Ages (Lloyd-Jones, op. cit., p. 505). J. J. Tierney, 'The Celtic Ethnography of Posidonius', *Proceedings of the Royal Irish Academy* (Dublin, 1960), lx, p. 269; Brynley F. Roberts, 'Geoffrey of Monmouth and Welsh Historical Tradition', *Nottingham Mediaeval Studies* (Nottingham, 1976), xx, pp. 39–40; Michael J. Curley, 'A New Edition of John of Cornwall's Prophetia Merlini', *Speculum* (Cambridge, Mass., 1982), lvii, pp. 224–29.

44 Dr Brynley F. Roberts has shown that Geoffrey's overall historical theme is a 'myth of unity, loss and renewal' (op. cit., p. 36), and that he derived this from Celtic originals. It may be conjectured that, under the influence of Christianity and the stress of national humiliation, this cycle had come to overlay an earlier conception of cosmic renovation. Susan M. Schwarz points out: 'In both the Bible and the *Historia Regum Britanniae* we have history accompanied by eschatology' ("The Founding and Self-betrayal of Britain: *An Augustinian Approach to Geoffrey of Monmouth*'s Historia Regum Britanniae', *Medievalia et Humanistica* (Cambridge, 1981), x, p. 49), and the same might be said of Gildas. Though both authors were deeply reliant upon the Bible as model, the adaptation may have been facilitated through inheritance

of the native tradition of *Armes*. See further note 47, *infra*. Parallel historicisations of the Canaanite myth of God's conflict with the dragon and the sea developed among the Israelites (John Day, *God's conflict with the dragon and the sea: echoes of a Canaanite myth in the Old Testament* (Cambridge, 1985), pp. 88–140). Similarly in modern times we have seen former religious millennarist beliefs absored into secular Marxist chiliasm.

45 J. Loth (ed.), *Les Mabinogion* (Paris, 1889), ii, pp. 259–60.

46 Faulkes, op. cit., p. 13; Hugh G. Evelyn-White (ed.), *Hesiod: The Homeric Hymns and Homerica* (London, 1914), p. 13; cf. Edgar C. Polomé, 'Some Comments on *Völuspá*, Stanzas 17–18', in idem (ed.), *Old Norse Literature and Mythology: A Symposium* (Austin, 1969), pp. 265–67; B. Sijmons (ed.), *Die Lieder der Edda* (Halle, 1888), i, p. 3; Ford, op. cit., p. 183.

47 L. Fleuriot, 'Les Fragments du Texte Brittonique de la "Prophetia Merlini"', *Études Celtiques* (Paris, 1974), xiv, p. 56. It is possible that Gildas's *De Excidio Britanniae*, whose title so closely parallels the *ormes brydein* mentioned in the *Cyfoesi Myrddin a Gwenddydd ei chwaer* (cf. Ifor Williams (ed.), *Armes Prydein o Lyfr Taliesin gyda Rhagymadrodd a Nodiadau* (Cardiff, 1955), pp. xxxviii–xli) may have been modelled on native prophetic tradition, such as Gildas's contemporary Procopius implies existed in his time. 'Hactenus cum regibus patriae non minus prophetarum oraculis quam nostris sermonibus disceptavimus', as he writes – his authority being Christian prophets, rather than those of the native heathen. The apostrophising of the five British kings by the names of wild animals may also echo the usages of Celtic vaticination. Robert W. Hanning, in his penetrating study of early British historiography, suggests that it was 'by a strange accident of history' that for five hundred years historians accepted the conceptual framework imposed by Gildas's *liber querulus* (*The Vision of History in Early Britain: From Gildas to Geoffrey of Monmouth* (New York, 1966), pp. 61–62). But though the influence of Eusebius and Orosius is clear – indeed explicit – may it not have been as a Christianised *ormes* that the *De Excidio* became psychically acceptable for absorption into the native tradition?

Eleven *The Otherworld Journey and The Threefold Death*

1 P. L. Henry, *The Early English and Celtic Lyric* (London, 1966), pp. 84–85, 107; T. H. Parry-Williams, 'Welsh Poetic Diction', *The Proceedings of the British Academy* (London, 1946), xxxii, p. 21; J. Lloyd-Jones, 'The Court Poets of the Welsh Princes', ibid., xxxiv, p. 15.

2 Sir John Morris-Jones, 'Taliesin', *Y Cymmrodor* (London, 1918),

xxviii, p. 239; John Rhŷs, *Celtic Folklore, Welsh and Manx* (Oxford, 1901), p. 645; T. Gwynn Jones, *Welsh Folklore and Folk-Custom* (London, 1930), pp. 15–16. Roger Sherman Loomis, *Wales and the Arthurian Legend* (Cardiff, 1956), p. 137; cf. S. V. Spilsbury, '*Traditional Material* in Artus de Bretagne', in P. B. Grout *et al.* (ed.), *The Legend of Arthur in the Middle Ages* (Cambridge, 1983), pp. 187–89. For the Milky Way as *Seelenpfad* and passage for the Wild Hunt, cf. Arthur Bernard Cook, *Zeus: A Study in Ancient Religion* (Cambridge, 1914–40), ii, pp. 36–54, 62–63, 483–84.

3 Alwyn Rees and Brinley Rees, *Celtic Heritage: Ancient Tradition in Ireland and Wales* (London, 1961), pp. 83–94, 156. For the sacred nature of boundaries among the Celts, cf. L. Fleuriot, 'La Grande Inscription Celtibère de Botorrita', *Études Celtiques* (Paris, 1975), xiv, pp. 405–42.

4 Kuno Meyer and Alfred Nutt, *The Voyage of Bran Son of Febal* (London, 1895), pp. 29–33, 155.

5 Carl Selmer (ed.), *Navigatio Sancti Brendani Abbatis from Early Latin Manuscripts* (Notre Dame, Indiana, 1959), pp. 78–81.

6 A. Rees and B. Rees, op. cit., pp. 297, 325. For the *immrama* in general, cf. James F. Kenney, *The Sources for the Early History of Ireland: An Introduction and Guide* (New York, 1929), pp. 409–12; David Dumville, '*Echtrae* and *Immram*: Some Problems of Definition', *Ériu* (Dublin, 1976), xxvii, pp. 73–94; Proinsias MacCana, 'The Sinless Otherworld of *Immram Brain*', ibid., pp. 95–115.

7 A. Rees and B. Rees, op. cit., pp. 97–98; for the site cf. Liam de Paor, 'A Survey of Sceilg Mhichíl', *The Journal of Royal Society of Antiquaries of Ireland* (Dublin, 1955), lxxxv, pp. 174–87. And, for a similar practice among Buddhist shamans in Japan, cf. Joan Halifax, *Shaman: The wounded healer* (London, 1982), p. 73. The shaman's spirit-journey frequently followed recognisable local terrain; cf. H. Munro Chadwick and N. Kershaw Chadwick, *The Growth of Literature* (Cambridge, 1940), iii, pp. 207, 217; Halifax, op. cit., pp. 17–18, and the shaman 'map' reproduced on p. 68.

8 Cf. *Buchedd Collen*, printed by S. Baring-Gould and John Fisher, *The Lives of the British Saints* (London, 1913), iv, p. 377; A. Rees and B. Rees, op. cit., p. 346; C. N. Deedes, 'The Labyrinth', in S. H. Hooke (ed.), *The Labyrinth: Further Studies in the Relation between Myth and Ritual in the Ancient World* (London, 1935), pp. 3–42; Philip Rahtz, 'Excavations on Glastonbury Tor, Somerset, 1964–6', *The Archaeological Journal* (London, 1971), cxxvii, pp. 6–7; C. Kerényi, *Dionysos: Archetypal Image of Indestructible Life* (London, 1976), pp. 90–107; Cook, op. cit., i, pp. 486–90.

9 Quoted by A. Rees and B. Rees, op. cit., p. 304. Initiation into the mystery-cult of Mithras occurred similarly in a cave, representative of the 'world-cave'. (Leroy A. Campbell, *Mithraic Iconography and Ideology* (Leiden, 1968), p. 7).

10 Cf. Morton Smith, *Clement of Alexandria and a Secret Gospel of Mark* (Harvard, 1973), p. 238; Mircea Eliade, *Patterns in Comparative Religion* (London, 1958), pp. 102–8.

11 Cf. J. R. Watson, *Wordsworth's Vital Soul: The Sacred and Profane in Wordsworth's Poetry* (London, 1982), pp. 56–60.

12 G. N. Gracheva, 'A Nganasan Shaman Costume', in V. Diószegi and M. Hoppál (ed.), *Shamanism in Siberia* (Budapest, 1978), p. 318.

13 For Wordsworth's rôle as prophet, cf. Watson, op. cit., pp. 93–96. In the quoted passage from the *Vita Merlini* the imagery is Geoffrey's own, though perfectly consonant with the bardic and druidic tradition. Julius Caesar reported that the druids of Gaul 'have many discussions touching the stars and their movement' (T. Rice Holmes (ed.), *C. Iuli Caesaris Commentarii* (Oxford, 1914), p. 243). Cosmology remained a close concern of Welsh bards in post-Roman Britain (cf. the passages quoted in *Y Cymmrodor*, xxviii, pp. 241–42), and that they studied the stars from mountain tops is suggested by the tradition of Idris Gawr, who 'sat on a mountain-peak to watch the stars' (Rev. William Basil Jones, *Vestiges of the Gael in Gwynedd* (London, 1851), pp. 55–56). It was held of anyone lying on the same peak (Cader Idris) that 'one of two things will happen to him, either he will be a poet of the best kind, or go entirely demented' (Hugh Owen, 'Peniarth MS. 118, fos. 829–837.', *Y Cymmrodor* (1917), xxvii, p. 125). The implication may be that inspired prophets (*awenyddion*) lay on occasion on the summit cairn to study the night sky. St Berach interrupted the druidess Cainech whom he saw 'on top of a mountain [at Glendalough], worshipping the devil and practising druidism' (Charles Plummer (ed.), *Bethada Náem nÉrenn: Lives of Irish Saints* (Oxford, 1922), i, p. 30).

14 A fight with a mountain guardian was one of the ordeals a Tungus shaman had to overcome on his mantic journey (G. M. Vasilevich, 'Shamanistic Songs of the Evenki (Tungus)', in V. Diószegi (ed.), *Popular Beliefs and Folklore Tradition in Siberia* (The Hague, 1968), p. 356).

15 Cf. Paul Piehler, *The Visionary Landscape: A Study in Medieval Allegory* (London, 1971). That the re-enactment of an archetypal journey possessed thaumaturgic significance is an old and widespread idea; cf. the Egyptian Jew who, c. A.D. 55, prepared his followers for an attack on Jerusalem by a trek into the wilderness, a move which was 'probably a way of re-enacting the ancient preconquest experiences of Israel' (David E. Aune, *Prophecy in Early Christianity and the Ancient Mediterranean World* (Grand Rapids, Michigan, 1983), pp. 128–29).

16 Edwin Sidney Hartland, *The Science of Fairy Tales. An Inquiry into Fairy Mythology* (London, 1891), pp. 190–92; Arthur C. L. Brown, *The Origin of the Grail Legend* (Harvard, 1943), pp. 49–50; A. Rees and B. Rees, op. cit., pp. 345–46; William J. Thoms (ed.), *Anecdotes*

and Traditions, Illustrative of Early English History and Literature (London, 1839), pp. 88–91.

17 Kenneth Jackson, *Studies in Early Celtic Nature Poetry* (Cambridge, 1935), p. 3; cf. Thomas F. O'Rahilly, *Early Irish History and Mythology* (Dublin, 1957), pp. 525–26. In view of the 'hut's' clearly otherworld attributes, it is hard to see how Professors Jackson and Carney could have thought it an ordinary dwelling, whether on the ground or in a tree, (Jackson, op. cit., pp. 35, 97, 122–23; idem, 'A Further Note on Suibhne Geilt and Merlin', *Éigse: A Journal of Irish Studies* (Dublin, 1951), vii, p. 115; James Carney, '"Suibhne Geilt" and "The Children of Lir"', ibid. (1950), vi, pp. 87–88). For the 'Seith guaew gowanon' cf. A. O. H. Jarman (ed.), *Ymddiddan Myrddin a Thaliesin* (Cardiff, 1951), p. 16. In an Irish tale Goibniu (Gobban) undertakes to provide spear-points which will slay all whom they touch even though the battle continue for *seven* years (Elizabeth A. Cray (ed.), *Cath Maige Tuired: The Second Battle of Mag Tuired* (Dublin, 1982), p. 50).

18 Kenneth Jackson, 'The Motive of the Three-fold Death in the Story of Suibhne Geilt', in Rev. John Ryan (ed.), *Féil-Sgríbhinn Eóin mhic Néill* (Dublin, 1940), pp. 536–44.

19 Rachel Bromwich (ed.), *Trioedd Ynys Prydein: The Welsh Triads* (Cardiff, 1961), p. 473. The only known Welsh story linking Merlin directly with the story of the Threefold Death appears to be a borrowing from a French literary source (Thomas Jones, 'Chwedl Myrddin a'r farwolaeth driphlyg yng nghronicl Elis Gruffudd', *The Bulletin of the Board of Celtic Studies* (Cardiff, 1956), xv, pp. 184–88). It may also be significant that in *Buile Suibhne* the North British madman Ealladhan tells what appears to be a prophecy of his own Triple Death, since it is this episode which provides implicit acknowledgement of the priority of the North British (Lailoken-Merlin) version of the story. With Lailoken's impalement on a stake in the river, one may perhaps compare the fate of a Lapp shaman whose belly was ripped open by a rival who had transformed himself 'into a pointed stake and hidden himself in a lake' (Rafael Karsten, *The Religion of the Samek: Ancient Beliefs and Cults of the Scandinavian and Finnish Lapps* (Leiden, 1955), p. 74).

20 Kenneth Jackson, 'The Sources for the Life of St Kentigern', in Nora K. Chadwick (ed.), *Studies in the Early British Church* (Cambridge, 1958), pp. 328–30; James Carney, *Studies in Irish Literature and History* (Dublin, 1955), p. 393.

21 Donald J. Ward, 'The Threefold Death: An Indo-European Tri-functional Sacrifice?' in Jaan Puhvel (ed.), *Myth and Law Among the Indo-Europeans* (Berkeley, 1970), pp. 126, 137–38.

22 Cf. Proinsias MacCana, *Celtic Mythology* (London, 1970), p. 26; Puhvel, op. cit., pp. 134–35; Tomás Ó Concheanainn, 'The Act of Wounding in the Death of Muirchertach mac Erca', *Éigse* (1973), xv, pp. 141–44; Brian Ó Cuív, 'The Motif of the Threefold Death', ibid.,

pp. 145–50; Francis John Byrne, *Irish Kings and High-Kings* (London, 1973), pp. 97–102; A. Rees and B. Rees, op. cit., pp. 333–41; Tomás Ó Cathasaigh (ed.), *The Heroic Biography of Cormac mac Airt* (Dublin, 1977), pp. 48–49.

23 W. J. Gruffydd, *Math vab Mathonwy* (Cardiff, 1928), pp. 301–3.

24 Ibid., p. 311.

25 James Carney, *Éigse*, vi, p. 94.

26 Bromwich, op. cit., pp. 207–9.

27 Eliade, op. cit., pp. 272, 276, 279.

28 Kenneth Jackson claims that the various elements present in the story of the plot to kill Lleu derive from international popular tales, and cannot represent a myth (*The International Popular Tale and Early Welsh Tradition* (Cardiff, 1961), pp. 106–13, 128). But this restricted view (cf. Eric P. Hamp, 'Mabinogi', *The Transactions of the Honourable Society of Cymmrodorion* (London, 1975), p. 249) ignores the extent to which folk tales often reflect myths, and indeed in some cases represent the detritus of a decayed mythology. For instance, on pp. 117–18 he cites the story told of Thor, in which the god is fed with goat's flesh, but warned at the same time to break no bones but lay them out on the goats' skins. A bone is broken, however, and when the goats are resuscitated next morning one of them is in consequence seen to limp. The same story is recorded in the *Historia Brittonum* and elsewhere, and obviously existed as an international popular tale.

But this folktale undoubtedly has its origin in myth and ritual. For instance the Tungus of Siberia worship and kill bears. After a feast strict precautions are adopted in order to ensure that the bear's soul survives unharmed.

'It is exceedingly important to keep the bones to one side so that the bear's skeleton can be deposited in a tree or laid out on a platform high above the ground. *No bones must be missing, or the bear's soul will never rest.*'

(italics inserted) (Ivar Lissner, *Man, God and Magic* (London, 1961), pp. 157–58; cf. Å. Hultkrantz, 'Ecological and Phenomenological Aspects of Shamanism', in V. Diószegi and M. Hoppál (ed.), *Shamanism in Siberia* (Budapest, 1978), p. 39; I. Paulson, 'The Preservation of Animal Bones in the Hunting Rites of Some North-Eurasian Peoples', in V. Diószegi (ed.), *Popular Beliefs and Folklore Tradition in Siberia* (The Hague, 1968), pp. 451–57).

29 Thomas F. O'Rahilly, *Early Irish History and Mythology* (Dublin, 1957), pp. 60–61; Roger Sherman Loomis, *Arthurian Tradition and Chrétien de Troyes* (New York, 1949), pp. 379–82; idem, 'The Origin of the Grail Legends', *Arthurian Literature in the Middle Ages: A Collaborative History* (Oxford, 1959), p. 289.

30 Peter Gelling and Hilda Ellis Davidson, *The Chariot of the Sun* (London, 1969), p. 166.

31 Anne Ross, *Pagan Celtic Britain: Studies in Iconography and Tradition* (London, 1967), p. 278.

32 Anthony Faulkes (ed.), *Snorri Sturluson; Edda: Prologue and Gylfa-ginning* (Oxford, 1982), p. 18; cf. Einar ÓL. Sveinsson, 'Svipdag's long Journey', *Béaloideas: The Journal of the Folklore of Ireland Society* (Dublin, 1975), xxxix–xli, p. 316. Heinrich Wagner compares Lleu hanging in the Tree with a verse similarly describing the Mordvine lightning-god Niske in his oak ('Studies in the Origins of Early Celtic Civilisation', *Zeitschrift für Celtische Philologie* (Tübingen, 1970), xxxi, pp. 35–36.) For the Tartar World-Tree, cf. H. M. Chadwick and N. K. Chadwick, op. cit., pp. 87–88. In Siberia it is believed that shamans are born to eagles (B. Gunda, 'Survivals of Totemism in the Hungarian *táltos* Tradition', *Popular Beliefs and Folklore Tradition in Siberia*, pp. 47–48; Joan Halifax, *Shaman: The wounded healer* (London, 1982), pp. 19, 23).

33 Gruffydd, op. cit., p. 144. Lug's father Cian is said to have been slain by a trinity of gods. According to the tale *Oidheadh Chloinne Tuireann* he was in the form of a pig when he was speared through the chest, and on resuming his human shape he was promptly stoned to death. This looks like another version of the Threefold Death of Lug, with the elements of spearing and stoning found in the Lailoken episodes. Could there have been a time when the death of Lug was comme-morated by the ritual sacrifice of a pig, and is this the significance of the pig at the foot of Lleu's tree? It is he who devours all that is mortal of Lleu. But it is uncertain that Cian became a *pig* in the original version (cf. O'Rahilly, op. cit., pp. 310–11).

34 Ross, op. cit., p. 252; *Zeitschrift für Celtische Philologie*, xxxi, pp. 24–25, 29–30; MacCana, op. cit., p. 29.

35 E. O. G. Turville-Petre, *Myth and Religion of the North: The Religion of Ancient Scandinavia* (London, 1964), pp. 36, 42.

36 Ibid., p. 279; H. M. Chadwick, *The Cult of Othin: An Essay on the Ancient Religion of the North* (London, 1899), pp. 73–80; Sigurdur Nordal (ed.), *Völuspa* (Durham, 1978), p. 37. For Snorri's description of *Yggdrasil*, see Faulkes, op. cit., p. 17. Allusions in an Irish legend of Lug's death are very significant: according to a Dindshenchas verse he was killed by a trinity of gods (probably three aspects of the same deity) at Uisnech, the Sacred Centre (*Omphalos*) of Ireland (Máire MacNeill, *The Festival of Lughnasa: A Study of the Survival of the Celtic Festival of the Beginning of Harvest* (Oxford, 1962), pp. 7, 322). A triple death is clearly implied, and the Sacred Centre is the point at which the Tree of Life strikes its roots into the earth.

37 Faulkes, op. cit., p. 50. Cf. the magnificent inlaid spearhead illustrated in H. R. Ellis Davidson, *Scandinavian Mythology* (London, 1982), p. 35. King Athelstane was presented by Hugh Capet with a spear described as that of Charlemagne, but which from its attributes clearly derives ultimately from Odin's spear. It was also (like the spear of Lug

in the Grail Castle) identified with the lance with which Longinus pierced the side of Christ (William A. Chaney, *The Cult of Kingship in Anglo-Saxon England: The Transition from Paganism to Christianity* (Manchester, 1970), pp. 145–46; Thomas D. Hill, 'Longinus, Charlemagne and Ódinn: William of Malmesbury, *De Gestis Regum Anglorum* II, 135', *Saga-Book of the Viking Society* (London, 1982–3), xxi, pp. 80–84).

38 Folke Ström, *On the Sacral Origin of the Germanic Death Penalties* (Stockholm, 1942), pp. 146–50; Chadwick, op. cit., pp. 66–67. A human sacrificial victim of the 1st century B.C. discovered at Tollund (Denmark) in 1951 had been both hanged and drowned (F. M. Bergounioux and Joseph Goetz, *Prehistoric and Primitive Religions* (London, 1965), pp. 54–55). A tenth-century Arab traveller in Russia witnessed the multiple sacrifice of a slavegirl at the funeral of a chief of the Swedish Rus. She was simultaneously strangled and stabbed with a dagger. It is possible, however, that a third form was included, as she was given a drink which made her so 'distracted' she was unable to see which way she was going, and which may therefore have been a very powerful somnific or even poisonous draught (H. M. Smyser, 'Ibn Fadlan's Account of the Rus with Some Commentary and Some Allusions to *Beowulf*', in Jess B. Bessinger Jr. and Robert P. Creed (ed.), *Medieval and Linguistic Studies in Honor of Francis Peabody Magoun, Jr.* (London, 1965), pp. 99–100). Cf. R. I. Page, 'Anglo-Saxon Runes and Magic', *The Journal of the British Archaeological Association* (London, 1964), xxvii, p. 16; Chadwick op. cit., pp. 68–82; Ström, op. cit., pp. 135–50; Turville-Petre, op. cit., pp. 42–50. It has been suggested that it is the liminal moment between life and death which possesses exceptional magical potency (Ström, op. cit., p. 245). Åke V. Ström argues that kings were sacrificed 'as the creator of a new year and as the link between time and eternity' ('The King God and his Connection with Sacrifice in Old Norse Religion', *La Regalità Sacra: Contributi al Tema dell' VIII Congresso Internazionale di Storia delle Religioni (Roma, Aprile 1955)* (Leiden, 1959), pp. 702–15).

39 Puhvel, op. cit., pp. 131, 141.

40 James L. Sauvé, 'The Divine Victim: Aspects of Human Sacrifice in Viking Scandinavia and Vedic India', ibid., p. 177.

41 Winfred P. Lehmann, 'From Phonetic Facts to Syntactic Paradigms: The Noun in Early PIE', in Edgar C. Polomé (ed.), *The Indo-Europeans in the Fourth and Third Millennia* (Ann Arbor, 1982), pp. 140–41; Marija Gimbutas, 'Old Europe in the Fifth Millennium B.C.: The European Situation on the Arrival of the Indo-Europeans', ibid., p. 19.

42 Jaan Puhvel, 'Indo-European Structure of the Baltic Pantheon', in Gerald James Larson (ed.), *Myth in Indo-European Antiquity* (Berkeley, 1974), pp. 84–85; Sauvé, in Puhvel, op. cit., pp. 182–91; Jeannine E. Talley, 'The Threefold Death in Finnish Lore', ibid., pp. 143–46.

43 E. O. James, 'The Tree of Life', in E. C. B. MacLaurin (ed.), *Essays in Honour of Griffithes Wheeler Thatcher 1863–1950* (Sydney, 1967), p. 118.

44 Ibid., pp. 108–11; S. H. Hooke, 'The Myth and Ritual Pattern in Jewish and Christian Apocalyptic', in S. H. Hooke, op. cit., pp. 228–29.

45 E. O. James, *The Tree of Life: An Archaeological Study* (Leiden, 1966), pp. 161–62; MacLaurin, op. cit., pp. 108–14; Mircea Eliade, *Patterns in Comparative Religion* (London, 1958), pp. 292–94, 375, 378–79; idem, *The Two and the One* (London, 1962), pp. 54–55; Geo. Widengren, *Mesopotamian Elements in Manichaeism* (Uppsala, 1946), pp. 124–29. The concept of the Tree of Life is rooted within man himself; cf. Nicolas Berdyaev: 'His roots are in heaven, in God, and also in nethermost depths' (*The Destiny of Man* (London, 1937), p. 46). It is significant too that the chronological and familial procession of man is regularly envisaged in the form of a tree (cf. C. R. Hallpike, *The Foundations of Primitive Thought* (Oxford, 1979), pp. 219–20; R. Howard Bloch, *Etymologies and Genealogies: A Literary Anthropology of the French Middle Ages* (Chicago, 1983), pp. 87–91.

46 Turville-Petre, op. cit., pp. 48–49.

47 Ibid., p. 49; cf. pp. 43–50; *The Cult of Othin*, pp. 72–82.

48 Turville-Petre, op. cit., pp. 42–43, 50; Ellis Davidson, *Scandinavian Mythology*, pp. 111, 124; Mary R. Gerstein, 'Germanic Warg: The Outlaw as Werwolf', in Larson, op. cit., pp. 140–45; Chaney, op. cit., pp. 51–52.

49 Cf. Puhvel, op. cit., p. 183; Jeannine L. Talley, 'Runes, Mandrakes and Gallows', in Larson, op. cit., pp. 163–65, 167. Posidonius in the 2nd century B.C. relates that the Gauls of his day practised 'a unique impiety' in their sacrifices: criminals were kept in custody for five years, and then crucified. (J. J. Tierney, 'The Celtic Ethnography of Posidonius', *Proceedings of the Royal Irish Academy* (Dublin, 1960), lx, p. 229). In an Irish folk-tale Cuchulain (Lug's son) appears as the 'Hung-up Naked Man' on a tree, who is elsewhere identified with Christ (Roger Sherman Loomis, *Celtic Myth and Arthurian Romance* (New York, 1927), pp. 18–21, 51, 135).

50 Matthew Black and H. H. Rowley (ed.), *Peake's Commentary on the Bible* (London, 1962), p. 797.

51 Sir James George Frazer, *The Scapegoat* (London, 1925), p. 413. The evidence that Jesus was regarded as having ascended into Heaven on the third day seems clear (cf. Bruce M. Metzger, *Historical and Literary Studies: Pagan, Jewish and Christian* (Leiden, 1968), p. 22).

52 A. E. Harvey, *Jesus and the Constraints of History* (London, 1982), pp. 3–4, 11; S. G. F. Brandon, *Jesus and the Zealots: A Study of the Political Factor in Primitive Christianity* (Manchester, 1967), p. 1.

53 'The extraordinary paucity of the theme of crucifixion in the mythical tradition, even in the Hellenistic and Roman period, shows the deep aversion from this cruellest of all penalties in the literary world' (Martin

Hengel, *Crucifixion in the ancient world and the folly of the message of the cross* (Philadelphia, 1977), pp. 14–15). This revulsion was most marked in Judaea (ibid., p. 85).

54 J. Gwyn Griffiths (ed.), *Plutarch's De Iside et Osiride* (Cardiff, 1970), pp. 55–56 (cf. Sir James George Frazer, *The Dying God* (London, 1923), pp. 5–6); C. Scott Littleton, *The New Comparative Mythology: An Anthropological Assessment of the Theories of Georges Dumézil* (Los Angeles, 1966), pp. 9–14. For an excellent discussion of the Scandinavian trinity which presided over the Creation, see Edgar C. Polomé, 'Some Comments on *Völuspá*, Stanzas 17–18', in idem (ed.), *Old Norse Literature and Mythology: A Symposium* (Austin, 1969), pp. 264–90. In Ireland Lug was killed by a triple deity (MacNeill, *The Festival of Lughnasa*, pp. 7, 322); did the Triple Sacrifice reflect the death and resurrection of a god in his three aspects? For discussions of the significance of the Trinity, cf. R. C. Zaehner, *Concordant Discord: The Interdependence of Faiths* (Oxford, 1970), p. 413; C. G. Jung, 'A Psychological Approach to the Trinity', in *Psychology and Religion: West and East* (New York, 1958), pp. 107–200; David L. Miller, 'Between God and the Gods – Trinity', *Eranos Jahrbuch 1980* (Frankfurt, 1981), xlix, pp. 81–148. 'Three principles are active in the world: Providence, i.e. the super-cosmic God; freedom, i.e. the human spirit; and fate or destiny, i.e. nature, the solidified, hardened outcome of the dark meonic freedom'. (Berdyaev, op. cit., p. 31). Early Christian tradition represented the Trinity as directly involved in the creation of man (S. G. F. Brandon, *Creation Legends of the Ancient Near East* (London, 1963), plate VIII). Philo of Alexandria held that a right-angled triangle was 'the source from which the universe springs' (Violet MacDermot, *The Cult of the Seer in the Ancient Middle East* (London, 1971), i, p. 29).

55 Michel Aubineau, 'Une homélie grecque inédite sur la Transfiguration', *Analecta Bollandiana* (Brussels, 1967), lxxxv, p. 423.

56 Carl G. Jung, *Man and his Symbols* (London, 1964), p. 73; Eliade, *The Two and the One*, p. 210. For an interesting discussion as to why God might be conceived of as wishing to provide atonement for man's continuing fall from grace in the form of an Incarnation, cf. Richard Swinburne, *The Existence of God* (Oxford, 1979), pp. 239–42.

57 Kings and heroes were regarded as incarnations of Lug (Heinrich Wagner, 'The Origin of the Celts in the Light of Linguistic Geography', *Transactions of the Philological Society* (Oxford, 1969), p. 245), and in Scandinavia the death of King Vikar was intended as a human sacrifice offered 'as an Odin surrogate' (James L. Sauvé, 'The Divine Victim: Aspects of Human Sacrifice in Viking Scandinavia and Vedic India', in Jaan Puhvel (ed.), *Myth and Law among the Indo-Europeans* (Los Angeles, 1970), pp. 180–81.)

58 Elsewhere in *The Book of Taliesin*, Taliesin is made to claim that he 'was in *Cad Goddeu* with Lleu and Gwydion': 'Bum ygkat godeu gan

lleu a gŏydyon' (J. Gwenogvryn Evans (ed.), *Facsimile and Text of the Book of Taliesin* (Llanbedrog, 1910), p. 33). In fact Lleu is not mentioned in the text of *Cad Goddeu*; unless, that is, it is he who is envisaged as the speaker.

59 *The Proceedings of the British Academy*, liii, p. 137. *annuab y lleian*, 'the nun's son', is a regular euphemism for Myrddin (Melville Richards, 'Llwyn Lleiaf', *The Bulletin of the Board of Celtic Studies* (Cardiff, 1972–74), xxv, pp. 272–73; Patrick Sims-Williams, 'anfab² 'illegitimate child': a ghost-word', ibid. (1978–80), xxviii, pp. 90–93). For *lluagor*, *v*. Bromwich, op. cit., p. 98. *Llew*, 'a lion', is regularly substituted in error for *Lleu* (Rhŷs, *Celtic Heathendom*, pp. 398–404; Gruffyd, op. cit., pp. 60–61). In the *Afallennau* and *Hoianau*, Myrddin is said to have received prophetic inspiration from a mysterious *hwimleian*: 'the *hwimleian* prophesies a tale'. Professor A. O. H. Jarman translates this as 'pale wanderer', suggests that the reference is to a forest madman, and shows convincingly that in transference to the Continent the *hwimleian* became the seductress *Viviane*, who entrapped Merlin in his magical tomb ('Hwimleian, Chwibleian', *The Bulletin of the Board of Celtic Studies* (1955), xvi, pp. 71–76; 'A Note on the Possible Welsh Derivation of *Viviane*', *Gallica: Essays presented to J. Heywood Thomas by colleagues, pupils and friends* (Cardiff, 1969), pp. 1–12). It is surely more likely that the 'pale wanderer' is a prophetess, such as Gwenddydd in the *Cyfoesi*; and in view of the native Welsh tradition that Merlin ended his days in an enchanted 'prison', one may suppose too that the Continental story of *Viviane* rested on more than a mere garbling of a name, and probably included an account of Merlin's descent into a magical Otherworld tomb, prison or haven. Alternatively, *hwimleian* may refer to a mountain sprite, the inspiration of Northern shamans. See further the note on pp. 288–90.

60 *Zeitschrift für Celtische Philologie*, xxxi, p. 57.

61 M. L. West, *The Orphic Poems* (Oxford, 1983), pp. 11–13. For Delphi as the World Navel and the Greek concept of the *axis mundi*, cf. pp. 146–47, 239. It remains an open question whether Orpheus actually lived (p. 263).

Twelve *The Trickster, the Wild Man and the Prophet*

1 Paul Radin, *The Trickster: A Study in American Indian Mythology* (London, 1956), pp. ix–x, 142, 166–68; cf. Stith Thompson, *The Folktale* (New York, 1946), p. 319; Mary Douglas, *Purity and Danger: An analysis of concepts of pollution and taboo* (London, 1966), pp. 79–80. 'In the trickster's movement between these two worlds [those of the animals and the wilderness, and that of the transparent order of the High God] the human world takes shape as the fruit of the dialectic of

hierophanies, sacred both as given and as process, both as social enterprise and as divine creation . . . In short, the trickster is the image of man individually and communally seizing the fragments of his experience and *discovering* in them an order sacred by its very whole-ness' (Robert D. Pelton, *The Trickster in West Africa: A Study of Mythic Irony and Sacred Delight* (Los Angeles, 1980), p. 255).

2 Radin, op. cit., p. 63.

3 Radin, op. cit., pp. 52–53, 124.

4 Alexandre Micha, *Étude sur le 'Merlin' de Robert de Boron* (Geneva, 1980), pp. 184–85; Radin,, op. cit., pp. x, 139.

5 Ibid., pp. 17–18, 32–34.

6 Richard Bernheimer, *Wild Men in the Middle Ages* (Cambridge, Mass., 1952), pp. 1–13; Christopher McIntosh, 'The Eternal Wild Man', *Country Life Annual* (London, 1972), pp. 72–73.

7 James B. Pritchard (ed.), *Ancient Near Eastern Texts Relating to the Old Testament* (Princeton, 1969), pp. 72–98, 503–7. For a perceptive discussion of the theme of the nature-culture contrast, cf. G. S. Kirk, *Myth: Its Meaning and Functions in Ancient and other Cultures* (Cambridge, 1971), pp. 132–52.

8 S. G. F. Brandon, *Creation Legends of the Ancient Near East* (London, 1963), pp. 127–28; Jeffrey H. Tigay, *The Evolution of the Gilgamesh Epic* (Philadelphia, 1982), pp. 202–13; G. Komoróczy, 'Berosos and the Mesopotamian Literature', *Acta Antiqua Academiae Scientiarum Hungaricae* (Budapest, 1973), pp. 140–42.

9 Hayden White, 'The Forms of Wildness: Archaeology of an Idea', in Edward Dudley and Maximilian E. Novak (ed.), *The Wild Man Within* (Pittsburgh, 1972), pp. 18–23.

10 A. O. H. Jarman, *The Legend of Merlin* (Cardiff, 1960), p. 12; Kenneth Jackson, 'The Motive of the Threefold Death in the Story of Suibhne Geilt', in Rev. John Ryan (ed.), *Féil-sgríbhinn eóin mhic néill* (Dublin, 1940), p. 544; James Carney, '"Suibhne Geilt" and "The Children of Lir"', *Éigse: A Journal of Irish Studies* (Dublin, 1951), vii, p. 113; Bernheimer, op. cit., pp. 13–14. In order to represent Merlin as a Wild Man, his distinctive traits have to be explained as 'Geoffrey of Monmouth's invention' which 'provide a new venue for wild man symbolism' (Timothy Husband, *The Wild Man: Medieval Myth and Symbolism* (New York, 1980), p. 61).

11 Frances A. Yates, *The Occult Philosophy in the Elizabethan Age* (London, 1979), pp. 77–78, 107.

12 For Wild Men pure and simple, cf. Nynniaw and Peibiaw, Kynedyr Wyllt, and Owain (J. Gwenogvryn Evans (ed.), *The White Book Mabinogion: Welsh Tales and Romances Reproduced from the Peniarth Manuscripts* (Pwllheli, 1907), pp. 125–26, 240–41, 242). Llywarch Hên lived wretchedly off acorns in a forest (Ifor Williams, 'The Poems of Llywarch Hên', *The Proceedings of the British Academy* (London, 1932), xviii, p. 26). But Pádraig ÓRiain's scholarly 'A Study of the

Irish Legend of the Wild Man' (*Éigse* (1972), xiv, pp. 179–206) makes it abundantly clear that shamanistic initiation is the predominating factor among Irish Wild Men, rather than the crude primitivism of the true Wild Man (cf. p. 205). In Wales a hairy pelt was the mark of an 'ugly' (*hagr*) 'devil' (*cythraul*) (Rachel Bromwich (ed.), *Trioedd Ynys Prydein: The Welsh Triads* (Cardiff, 1961), p. 463), and 'ugliness' was also the attribute of Merlin in Welsh literature (ibid., p. 473) and French ('un home molt lait et molt hidos'). The hairy pelt in this context is the mark of the demonic rather than the primitive.

13 Micha, op. cit., pp. 180–83; cf. R. K. Emmerson, *Antichrist in the Middle Ages: A Study of Medieval Apocalypticism, Art, and Literature* (Seattle, 1981), pp. 19–20, 81–82, 293–94.

14 Cf. Kenneth Jackson, 'The Sources for the Life of St Kentigern', in Nora K. Chadwick (ed.), *Studies in the Early British Church* (Cambridge, 1958), pp. 328–29.

15 *Leudonus* is the eponym of *Leudonia*, *i.e.* the Scottish province of Lothian (W. J. Watson, *The History of the Celtic Place-Names of Scotland* (Edinburgh, 1926), pp. 101–3). Leudonus appears in some of the Welsh genealogies, but his 'own genealogy is never given' (H. M. Chadwick, *Early Scotland: The Picts, the Scots & the Welsh of Southern Scotland* (Cambridge, 1949), p. 146); presumably because it was unknown. Geoffrey calls him 'loth' (Acton Griscom (ed.), *The Historia Regum Britanniae of Geoffrey of Monmouth* (New York, 1929), p. 444), which the *Bruts* render 'Lleu' (Henry Lewis (ed.), *Brut Dingestow* (Cardiff, 1942), p. 152). *Lleu* can of course appear as an element in a compound name, but as the likely meaning of *Lleuddin* is 'town of Lug' (cf. *Lugudunum* (W. J. Gruffyd, *Math vab Mathonwy* (Cardiff, 1928), p. 62) the *Brut* version is probably correct. From *Lleuddin* comes *Lleuddiniawn*, the Welsh name for the Lothians, stretching south to the Tweed; *i.e.* 'territory of Lug's fort'. As the Ravenna Cosmography lists a *Lugudunum* in North Britain, this seems likely enough (A. L. F. Rivet and Colin Smith, *The Place-Names of Roman Britain* (London, 1979), pp. 401–2).

16 Bishop A. P. Forbes (ed.), *Lives of S. Ninian and S. Kentigern* (Edinburgh, 1874), pp. 243–52. Some of the features of this tale are found in another told of Ragallach, King of Connacht (Alwyn Rees and Brynley Rees, *Celtic Heritage: Ancient Tradition in Ireland and Wales* (London, 1961), p. 222). Could the 'swineherd' element be linked in some way to the 'Little Pig' apostrophised by Myrddin in the *Hoianau*? For a rather similar example of the hagiographer's treatment of his legendary sources, cf. John MacQueen, 'Roman and Celt in Southern Scotland', in Robert O'Driscoll (ed.), *The Celtic Consciousness* (New York, 1982), pp. 191–92.

17 Forbes, op. cit., p. 169. Kenneth Jackson showed that in fact *Munghu* is not, as Joceline believed, derived from *mwyn*, 'gentle', and *cu*, 'dear', but is in fact a diminutive of Kentigern's British name, *Cunotegernos*

(Chadwick, op. cit., pp. 300–303). But here the point is not its real meaning, but the fact that the name 'was popularly etymologized as meaning "My Dear"' in Cumbric and Gaelic (ibid., p. 302). Juliette Wood suggests plausibly that Taliesin in the *Vita Merlini* has replaced the original figure of Kentigern ('Maelgwn Gwynedd: A Forgotten Welsh Hero', *Trivium* (Lampeter, 1984), xix, p. 113). This may be borne out by Geoffrey's passing reference to the 'saint' protected by Rhydderch, who remains otherwise unidentified in the *Vita Merlini* (John J. Parry, 'Celtic Tradition and the Vita Merlini', *The Philological Quarterly* (Iowa, 1925), iv, p. 206).

18 Kenneth Jackson, *Language and History in Early Britain* (Edinburgh, 1953), p. 40; cf. Susan Pearce, *The Kingdom of Dumnonia: Studies in History and Tradition in South-Western Britain A.D. 350–1150* (Padstow, 1978), pp. 188–89.

19 Ifor Williams (ed.), *Armes Prydein o Lyfr Taliesin* (Cardiff, 1955), pp. xxii, 67.

20 Peter Salway, *Roman Britain* (Oxford, 1981), p. 566.

21 Joseph Loth conclusively refuted Fawtier's claim that the birth-tale of Samson was borrowed from the story of Anna, the mother of the Virgin Mary ('La vie la plus ancienne de Saint Samson de Dol', *Revue Celtique* (Paris, 1914), xxxv, pp. 281–83).

22 Nora Chadwick, 'Dreams in early European Literature', in James Carney and David Greene (ed.), *Celtic Studies: Essays in memory of Angus Matheson* (London, 1968), pp. 38, 39, 47; Gabriel Turville-Petre, *Nine Norse Studies* (London, 1972), pp. 30–51. At the sanctuary of Asculepios at Epidauros, Queen Andromache of Epirus underwent an identical experience to that of Anna at the North British temple; she dreamed that the god revealed a beautiful boy to her, and conceived a son shortly afterwards (C. Kerényi, *Asklepios: Archetypal Image of the Physician's Existence* (New York, 1959), p. 41). A silver rod the height of a man is a reward in the tale of *Branwen verch Llyr*: 'Llathen aryant a uo kyuref a chyhyt ac ef e hun'.

23 R. E. M. and T. V. Wheeler, *Report on the Excavation of the Prehistoric, Roman, and Post-Roman Site in Lydney Park, Gloucestershire* (Oxford, 1932), pp. 49–52; M. J. T. Lewis, *Temples in Roman Britain* (Cambridge, 1966), p. 89.

24 Arthur West Haddan and William Stubbs (ed.), *Councils and Ecclesiastical Documents Relating to Great Britain and Ireland* (Oxford, 1873), ii (pt. i), p. 75. A. W. Wade-Evans suggested a date *c.* 480 for Samson's birth, which is perhaps a decade or so too early (*Welsh Christian Origins* (Oxford, 1934), p. 232).

25 Heinrich Zimmer, *The King and the Corpse* (New York, 1960), pp. 197–98.

26 I. A. Richmond and O. G. S. Crawford, 'The British Section of the Ravenna Cosmography', *Archaeologia* (London, 1949), xciii, p. 19; Rivet and Smith, op. cit., pp. 395–96; Ivan D. Margary, *Roman Roads*

in Britain (London, 1957), ii, p. 194; Eric Birley, 'Maponus, the Epigraphic Evidence', *Dumfriesshire and Galloway Natural History and Antiquarian Society . . . Transactions* (Dumfries, 1954), xxxi, pp. 39–42. It is significant also that 'the shaman was . . . first and foremost concerned with curing (although his ecstatic abilities included other tasks)' (Louise Bäckman and Åke Hultkrantz, *Studies in Lapp Shamanism* (Stockholm, 1978), p. 44).

27 Edward Anwyl, *Celtic Religion in Pre-Christian Times* (London, 1906), pp. 40–41.

28 F. Haverfield and George Macdonald, *The Roman Occupation of Britain* (Oxford, 1924), p. 248; Thomas F. O'Rahilly, *Early Irish History and Mythology* (Dublin, 1957), pp. 52–53. (cf. however the discussion by Professor A. O. H. Jarman, 'The Arthurian Allusions in the Black Book of Carmarthen', in P. B. Grout *et al.* (ed.), *The Legend of Arthur in the Middle Ages* (Cambridge, 1983), p. 103); Bromwich, op. cit., pp. 433–34, 458; Anne Ross, *Pagan Celtic Britain: Studies in Iconography and Tradition* (London, 1967), pp. 208–9, 230, 359–60, 369.

29 Thomas Jones, 'The Black Book of Carmarthen "Stanzas of the Graves"', *The Proceedings of the British Academy* (London, 1967), liii, p. 137; cf. John Rhŷs, *Lectures on the Origin and Growth of Religion as Illustrated by Celtic Heathendom* (London, 1888), p. 404.

30 R. G. Collingwood and J. N. L. Myres, *Roman Britain and the English Settlements* (Oxford, 1937), p. 265. For the taboo against naming a god, cf. Sir James George Frazer, *Taboo and the Perils of the Soul* (London, 1911), pp. 387–91.

31 J. Gwenogvryn Evans (ed.), *Poetry by Medieval Welsh Bards* (Llanbedrog, 1926), p. 196.

32 Bromwich, op. cit., pp. 422–23, 459–60. To this evidence may be added Sir John Rhŷs' likely suggestion that the lion (*llew*) with which Owain is linked in *Chwedyl Iarlles y Ffynnaun* represents an earlier connection with Lleu (*Celtic Heathendom*, pp. 401–4).

33 John MacQueen, 'Maponus in Mediaeval Tradition', *Dumfriesshire and Galloway Natural History and Antiquarian Society . . . Transactions*, xxxi, pp. 54–55; cf. pp. 37–38; Rivet and Smith, op. cit., pp. 395–96. No other remains have yet been detected, but in 1967 a small slab of red sandstone was excavated at the nearby Roman fort at Birrens. It bears the inscription CISVMVCI LO (CO) MAbOMI, interpreted as '(the gift of) Cistumucus from the Place of Mabonus'; together with an incised figure, possibly a sacred serpent (*The Journal of Roman Studies* (London, 1968), lviii, p. 209, plate XIX; cf. Anthony Birley, *The People of Roman Britain* (London, 1979), p. 112). Serpents were traditionally associated with healing (Kerényi, op. cit., pp. 10–15, 18–20; Sir James George Frazer, *Adonis, Attis, Osiris: Studies in the History of Oriental Religion* (London, 1914), i, pp. 80–82); the Birrens slab was presumably bought at the Lochmaben temple.

34 Cf. D. A. Binchy, *Celtic and Anglo-Saxon Kingship* (Oxford, 1970), pp. 9, 11–14; idem, 'A pre-Christian survival in mediaeval Irish hagiography', in Dorothy Whitelock *et al.* (ed.), *Ireland in Early Mediaeval Europe: Studies in Memory of Kathleen Hughes* (Cambridge, 1982), p. 174. For *brenhin* and Brigantia cf. also D. Ellis Evans, 'Continental Celtic and Linguistic Reconstruction', in Gearóid Mac Eoin (ed.), *Proceedings of the Sixth International Congress of Celtic Studies* (Dublin, 1983), pp. 46–47.

35 Egerton Phillimore, 'The *Annales Cambriae* and Old-Welsh Genealogies from *Harleian MS.* 3859', *Y Cymmrodor* (1888), ix, pp. 169–70. The poem *Ymddiddan Myrddin a Thaliesin* implies that Myrddin and Maelgwn were thought to be contemporaries (A. O. H. Jarman (ed.), *Ymddiddan Myrddin a Thaliesin* (Cardiff, 1951), pp. 40–44).

36 J. Lloyd-Jones, *Geirfa Barddoniaeth Gynnar Gymraeg* (Cardiff, 1931–63), p. 745; *Celtic Heathendom*, p. 543; E. O. G. Turville-Petre, *Myth and Religion of the North: The Religion of Ancient Scandinavia* (London, 1964), pp. 72–73, 188; Rees and Rees, op. cit., pp. 143–44; L. Mándoki, 'Two Asiatic Sidereal Names', in V. Diószegi (ed.), *Popular Beliefs and Folklore Tradition in Siberia* (The Hague, 1968), pp. 487–96. In ancient Babylonia omens and prophecies were deduced from the movements of Venus (Erica Reiner and David Pingree (ed.), *Enūma Anu Enlil; Tablet 63: The Venus Tablet of Ammisaduqa* (Malibu, 1975), p. 29). The late Professor Thomas Jones edited a late adaptation of the Myrddin-Gwenddydd prophecy: 'The Story of Myrddin and the Five Dreams of Gwenddydd in the Chronicle of Elis Gruffydd', *Études Celtiques*, viii, pp. 315–45.

37 Merlin's Irish counterpart, Suibhne, also had an observatory (James Carney, *Studies in Irish Literature and History* (Dublin, 1955), p. 392). The Myrddin-Gwenddydd responses recall those of the Delphic Pythia, bride of Apollo (A. B. Cook, *Zeus: A Study in Ancient Religion* (Cambridge, 1914–40), ii, pp. 207–10).

38 Ross, op. cit., pp. 363–64; Watson, op. cit., pp. 180–81.

39 Forbes, op. cit., pp. 212–18. Kenneth Jackson has shown that much of Joceline's work is speculative fiction of a familiar hagiographical type (*Studies in the Early British Church*, pp. 273–357), and rejects both Kentigern's period of exile and his foundation at Hoddom as unhistorical. But the *Life* includes genuinely archaic elements (cf. A. C. Thomas, 'The Evidence from North Britain', in M. W. Barley and R. P. C. Hanson, *Christianity in Britain, 300–700* (Leicester, 1968), pp. 109–10; idem, *Christianity in Roman Britain to A.D. 500* (London, 1981), p. 210), and John Morris has provided remarkable contemporary evidence of Kentigern's activities as a bishop in Gaul in the sixth decade of the sixth century ('Dark Age Dates', in M. G. Jarrett and B. Dobson (ed.), *Britain and Rome: Essays Presented to Eric Birley on his Sixtieth Birthday* (Kendal, 1965), pp. 171, 184). As Professor E. G. Bowen points out, 'there is much to suggest . . . that there was a

very early association of St. Kentigern with Hoddom in Dumfriesshire,
– a tradition possibly revived at this time by a new dedication' (*Saints, Seaways and Settlements in the Celtic Lands* (Cardiff, 1969), pp. 88–89).
40 J. Rhŷs, *Celtic Britain* (London, 1884), p. 302.
41 *Studies in the Early British Church*, p. 275.
42 A. O. H. Jarman, 'Peiryan Vaban', *The Bulletin of the Board of Celtic Studies* (1952), xiv, pp. 104–8. There seems to be an implication that Aedan's forces were based on Man, and that a battle took place in Galloway – both likely possibilities in the circumstances.
43 Cf. John MacQueen, 'The Name Maponus', *Dumfriesshire and Galloway Natural History and Antiquarian Society . . . Transactions*, xxxi, pp. 55–57.
44 Dr David Dumville has argued that there is no palaeographical evidence proving the existence of early Welsh poetry before the year 1100. ('Palaeographical Considerations in the Dating of Early Welsh Verse', *The Bulletin of the Board of Celtic Studies* (1977), xxvii, pp. 246–51). It is surely no derogation of the marvellous philological work accomplished by Morris-Jones, Ifor Williams, Kenneth Jackson, A. O. H. Jarman and others, when it is stressed that the *primary* argument for accepting the genuineness of the works of *Cynfeirdd* is one based on historical consistency and integrity. It was an argument first effectively set out by Sharon Turner in 1803 (cf. the summary by Sir John Morris-Jones, 'Taliesin', *Y Cymmrodor* (1918), xxviii, pp. 13–15), whose relevance remains as apt nearly two centuries later. After all Sir Ifor Williams' penetrating work on the Taliesin poetry, he concludes with the essential point that the Urien of these verses is no figment of poetic imagination, but a figure of flesh and blood, entirely consistent with what can be gleaned from the scanty historical record (*Canu Taliesin* (Cardiff, 1960), pp. xliv–xlv). Cf. Dr T. M. Charles-Edwards: 'Most of the arguments for and against the authenticity of the Gododdin are historical in nature' ('The Authenticity of the *Gododdin*: an Historian's View', in Rachel Bromwich and R. Brinley Jones (ed.), *Astudiaethau ar yr Hengerdd* (Cardiff, 1978), p. 44). It is the absence of any annalistic or other reliable historical yardstick which makes opinions on the historicity of the early Irish literature so fluid and conflicting; cf. James Carney's remarks, 'Early Irish Literature: the State of Research', *Proceedings of the Sixth International Congress of Celtic Studies*, pp. 114–16.
45 Charles Plummer (ed.), *Venerabilis Baedae Historiam Ecclesiasticam Gentis Anglorum . . .* (Oxford, 1896), i, pp. 65–66. Both Mabon and his mother Modron were 'canonized' in popular esteem, becoming dedicatees of churches in Wales (W. J. Gruffydd, *Rhiannon: An Inquiry into the Origins of the First and Third Branches of the Mabinogi* (Cardiff, 1953), p. 98).

Epilogue

1 This analysis owes much to the valuable discussion by Professor R. Howard Bloch, *Etymologies and Genealogies: A Literary Anthropology of the French Middle Ages* (Chicago, 1983), pp. 1–7, 14–18, 34–39, 62, 200–207, 212–15, 234.

2 C. G. Jung, *Psychology and Religion: West and East* (New York, 1958), pp. 373, 401. However, there is no requirement to assume that God was *alone* in the universe before he created man. As the gnostic Marcion argued, surrounded by his creation he cannot be isolated (cf. Ugo Bianchi, 'Marcion: theologien biblique ou docteur gnostique?', *Studia Evangelica* (1968), v, p. 236). For Blake's view, cf. James Olney, *The Rhizome and the Flower: The Perennial Philosophy – Yeats and Jung* (Los Angeles, 1980), p. 52.

3 Carl G. Jung, *Man and his Symbols* (London, 1964), pp. 98–99.

4 Paul Radin, *The Trickster: A Study in American Indian Mythology* (London, 1956), pp. 125–26.

5 Mary D. Leakey, 'Tracks and Tools', in J. Z. Young *et al.* (ed.), *The Emergence of Man* (London, 1981), pp. 95–100.

6 P. V. Tobias, 'The Emergence of man in Africa and beyond', ibid., pp. 43–44; ibid., pp. 3, 50–52, 101; C. G. Phillips, 'The Human Brain', ibid., p. 151; J. Z. Young, 'Some tentative conclusions', ibid., pp. 213, 214–15; R. E. Passingham, 'Broca's area and the origins of human vocal skill', ibid., pp. 167–75.

7 Cf. Philip Lieberman, *The Biology and Evolution of Language* (Harvard, 1984), pp. 226–55. Contrary to what is frequently asserted, there is no *prima facie* reason to associate conscious intelligence (and, by implication, speech development), with pack hunting (Stephen Walker, *Animal Thought* (London, 1983), pp. 204–8).

8 Walker, op. cit., pp. 387–8. Cf. A. J. Ayer (*The Central Questions of Philosophy* (London, 1973), p. 49: 'the very notion of there being a world of such and such a character only makes sense within the framework of some such system of concepts which language embodies . . . our experience is articulated in language, and the world which we envisage as existing at times when we do not is still a world which is structured by our method of describing it.' For a clear definition of consciousness as 'the quality inherent in the contrast between Actuality and Ideality', cf. Alfred North Whitehead, *Adventures of Ideas* (Cambridge, 1935), pp. 347–48). Sir Alister Hardy suggests that religious concepts rest on the development of speech (*The Biology of God* (London, 1975), pp. 171–72).

9 Lieberman, op. cit., pp. 322–24.

10 Konrad Lorenz, *Studies in Animal and Human Behaviour* (London, 1970–71), ii, p. 236.

11 Walker, op. cit., pp. 194–236, 287–340, 343–64.

12 Lorenz, op. cit., pp. 229–31, 238, 239.

13 J. D. Clark, '"New Men, Strange Faces, Other Minds": An Archaeologist's Perspective on Recent Discoveries Relating to the Origin and Spread of Modern Man', *The Proceedings of the British Academy* (Oxford, 1981), lxvii, p. 186; Grahame Clark, *Aspects of Prehistory* (Los Angeles, 1970), pp. 113–21; Alexander Marshack, *The Roots of Civilization: The Cognitive Beginnings of Man's First Art, Symbol and Notation* (London, 1972); Morris Swadesh, *The Origin and Diversification of Language* (London, 1972), p. 226; John C. Eccles, *The Human Mystery* (Berlin, 1979), p. 103; Lieberman, op. cit., pp. 328–29.

14 Karl R. Popper and John C. Eccles, *The Self and its Brain* (Berlin, 1981), pp. 367–80, 478, 507–8, 559–61; *The Human Mystery*, pp. 227–34.

15 J. B. Rhine, *New World of the Mind* (London, 1954), pp. 92–95, 100–102; Rupert Sheldrake, *A New Science of Life: The Hypothesis of Formative Causation* (London, 1981), pp. 202–7; Nicolas Berdyaev, *The Destiny of Man* (London, 1937), p. 14; Hugo Meynell, *God and the World: The Coherence of Christian Theism* (London, 1971), p. 129; Sir Alister Hardy, *The Divine Flame: An Essay towards a Natural History of Religion* (London, 1966), pp. 228–30. C. R. Hallpike argues strongly that primitive theories of causality may arise from genuine (and well-attested) paranormal phenomena. At least, he concludes, we should check whether 'our theories of primitive causality and spiritual beliefs are entirely objective and not distorted by the contemporary orthodoxies of our own culture' (C. R. Hallpike, *The Foundations of Primitive Thought* (Oxford, 1979), pp. 474–79).

16 As Sir John Eccles points out, the invention of writing arose as a belated response to the ever-increasing complexity of Sumerian administration and economy (*The Human Mystery*, p. 110). May not language itself have arisen as a similar response to the 'dire need' for linguistic skills capable of formulating abstract religious conceptions? As Sir Alister Hardy suggests, it may be that consciousness permits man to realise the spirituality latent in unconsciousness (*Darwin and the Spirit of Man* (London, 1984), pp. 233, 242). Cf. also the cogent discussion by Claude Lévi-Strauss, *Totemism* (London, 1964), pp. 95–104.

17 Bernard C. Campbell, *Human Evolution: An Introduction to Man's Adaptations* (London, 1967), pp. 303–4, 320–21; J. Z. Young, *An Introduction to the Study of Man* (Oxford, 1971), p. 129.

18 C. G. Jung, *The Structure and Dynamics of the Psyche* (London, 1960), pp. 349–50; cf. pp. 53–54, 152, 360–63, 390. '. . . one must always remember that every man, in a sense, represents the whole of humanity and its history. What was possible in the history of mankind at large is also possible on a small scale in every individual.' (ibid., p. 250). Jung's image of the mind being 'peeled' down to its unconscious has its physiological parallel: 'The brain is like an onion in that it is

organized in layers. The most primitive parts – the parts that are found in animals that appear to be similar to animals that first evolved a hundred million years or so ago – are in the centre of the brain. The most recent part of the brain, the cortex, is the outer layer of the onion' (Lieberman, op. cit., p. 29). The presence of the unconscious was intuitively sensed long before its discovery. In 1800 Blake explained that: 'In my Brain are studies and Chambers filled with books and pictures of old which I wrote and painted in ages of Eternity, before my mortal life . . .' (G. E. Bentley, Jr. (ed.), *William Blake's Writings* (Oxford, 1978), p. 1541).

19 Jean Piaget, *The Child's Conception of Causality* (London, 1930), pp. 241–44.

20 Jung, *The Structure and Dynamics of the Psyche*, pp. 220, 347, 390–403.

21 S. G. F. Brandon, *Creation Legends of the Ancient Near East* (London, 1963), pp. 126, 129.

22 Ibid., p. 132.

23 A. Boyce Gibson, *The Religion of Dostoevsky* (London, 1973), p. 8; Aylmer Maude, *The Life of Tolstoy: First Fifty Years* (London, 1911), pp. 12–13.

24 Cf. Thomas Cole, *Democritus and the Sources of Greek Anthropology* (Western Reserve, 1967), pp. 1–10.

25 Cf. Martin Johnson, *Time and Universe for the Scientific Conscience* (Cambridge, 1952), p. 27; Jung, *Man and his Symbols*, p. 102–3; idem, *The Structure and Dynamics of the Psyche*, pp. 408–9; Rudolf Otto, *The Idea of the Holy: An Inquiry into the Non-Rational Factor in the Idea of the Divine and its Relation to the Rational* (Oxford, 1926), pp. 62, 67–68; William James, *The Varieties of Religious Experience: A Study in Human Nature* (London, 1903), p. 242; Stewart R. Sutherland, *God, Jesus and Belief: The Legacy of Theism* (Oxford, 1984), pp. 6–11.

26 W. K. C. Guthrie, *A History of Greek Philosophy* (Cambridge, 1962), i, p. 13. Conversely, Sir Karl Popper argues that it is the creation of mind which (in Einstein's words) prevents the universe from being 'merely . . . a rubbish heap' (Popper and Eccles, op. cit., p. 61).

27 Cf. Richard Swinburne, *The Existence of God* (Oxford, 1979), pp. 136–41; Hugo A. Meynell, *The Intelligible Universe: A Cosmological Argument* (London, 1982), pp. 68, 75–76, 118–19.

28 Jung, *The Structure and Dynamics of the Psyche*, pp. 112–13, 210–12; Sigmund Freud, *New Introductory Lectures on Psycho-Analysis* (London, 1946), pp. 138–39.

29 Mircea Eliade, *Patterns in Comparative Religion* (London, 1958), pp. 24–25, 46–50; E. O. James, *The Worship of the Sky-God: A Comparative Study in Semitic and Indo-European Religion* (London, 1963), pp. 8–13. Saliba objects that Eliade's assertion of the near-universality of the *deus otiosus* in primitive societies remains unproved. (John A. Saliba, *'Homo Religiosus' in Mircea Eliade* (Leiden, 1976) pp. 106–8). But one could hardly expect rigid conformity (the record is in any case

fragmentary) of concept or development, and recorded instances are so explicit and widespread as to indicate strong predisposition towards the belief.

30 Godfrey Lienhardt, *Divinity and Experience: The Religion of the Dinka* (Oxford, 1961), pp. 33–41. Further south, the Mandari preserve a similar myth of the former linking of earth and sky by a rope, subsequently severed when man's independent existence began. (Jean Buxton, *Religion and Healing in Mandari* (Oxford, 1973), pp. 22–23; cf. Lucien Levy-Bruhl, *Primitives and the Supernatural* (London, 1936), p. 36); G. Komoróczy, 'The Separation of Sky and Earth', *Acta Antiqua Academiae Scientiarum Hungaricae* (Budapest, 1973), pp. 21–45; Hans Peter Duerr, *Dreamtime: Concerning the Boundary between Wilderness and Civilization* (Oxford, 1985), p. 31. In Vedic cosmogony, it was Varuna who separated earth and heaven, setting himself on high as the universal king. (E. O. James, *Creation and Cosmology: A Historical and Comparative Inquiry* (Leiden, 1969), p. 34), and the Greeks believed that heaven and earth once met on Olympus until Zeus, offended by man's growing wickedness, removed himself (Arthur Bernard Cook, *Zeus: A Study in Ancient Religion* (Cambridge, 1914–40), ii, p. 905). As Jung pointed out, *rites de passage* in adolescence are designed to separate the consciously developing primitive from the claims of the unconscious (*The Structure and Dynamics of the Psyche*, pp. 374–75).

31 Mircea Eliade, *The Two and the One* (London, 1965), pp. 158–59. In China, 'Taoism looks back . . . to a time when what it calls the Great Unity was still unbroken, and man lived in perfect harmony with birds and beasts . . . his life was still perfect and whole because his life was merged in the uninterrupted flow of all natural things' (R. C. Zaehner, *Concordant Discord: The Interdependence of Faiths* (Oxford, 1970), pp. 215–36; D. Howard Smith, *Chinese Religions* (London, 1968), pp. 69–77). For the psychological significance of the need to return *in illo tempore*, cf. Jung, *The Structure and Dynamics of the Psyche*, p. 380.

32 Eliade, *Patterns in Comparative Religion*, pp. 374–79; idem, *The Two and the One*, p. 146. Eliade has been accused of overstating his case for the universality of the desire to 'escape from profane time' (S. G. F. Brandon, *History, Time and Deity: A Historical and Comparative Study of the Conception of Time in Religious Thought and Practice* (Manchester, 1965), pp. 65–70; G. S. Kirk, *Myth: Its Meaning and Functions in Ancient and Other Cultures* (Cambridge, 1971), pp. 255, 257; Saliba, op. cit., pp. 129–31). But Brandon's claim that 'there is no hint of a repetitive cycle of events [in Ancient Egypt], an 'eternal retour' to some primeval situation, such as Professor Eliade conceives' is not borne out by the evidence: 'Apparently, the Ancient Egyptian was above all desirous of the renewal and rejuvenation of the life of the cosmos, of the community and the individual. . . . Thus the ancient

Egyptian festivals came to have the function of *enactments of religious renewal*.' (C. J. Bleeker, *Egyptian Festivals: Enactments of Religious Renewal* (Leiden, 1967), p. 22).

33 G. M. Vasilevich, 'Shamanistic Songs of the Evenki (Tungus)', in V. Diószegi (ed.), *Popular Beliefs and Folklore Tradition in Siberia* (The Hague, 1968), pp. 353, 360.

34 André Leroi-Gourhan, *The Art of Prehistoric Man in Western Europe* (London, 1968), pp. 210–11, 366–67, plate 57; Johannes Maringer, *The Gods of Prehistoric Man* (London, 1960), pp. 74, 105–6. The animal attributes serve to restore the spontaneity and cosmic rhythm which they have not lost (Mircea Eliade, *Le Chamanisme et les techniques archaïques de l'extase* (Paris, 1951), pp. 403–4).

35 Cf. idem, *Myth and Reality* (London, 1964), p. 26; idem, *Le Chamanisme*, pp. 76–79, 227, 438; idem, *The Two and the One*, pp. 160–69; K. C. Chang, *Art, Myth, and Ritual: The Path to Political Authority in Ancient China* (Harvard, 1983), pp. 44–45. Australian aborigines hold that the first Medicine Man (Bundjil, Baiame, Nurundere, Dara mulun, Goin, Birugan) laid down the ritual procedure for 'visiting the sky-world after they had been through a severe experience of death and rising again' (A. P. Elkin, 'Religion and Philosophy of the Australian Aborigines', in E. C. B. MacLaurin (ed.), *Essays in Honour of Griffithes Wheeler Thatcher 1863–1950* (Sydney, 1967), pp. 32–33). In their rock-shelter galleries they paint ritual representations of 'a quasi-human figure', the Wandjina, the Dreaming heroes. The Wandjina have actually 'become' the paintings, which must be continually renewed to maintain their potency. 'In addition, so as to give detail to man's need, those with ritual authority in each local clan paint on the gallery wall designs representing the totems of the clan – natural species and objects whose abundance is desired. These galleries are secret, being visited only by the initiated with the knowledge of the ritual leaders.' (p. 27). Cf. William Henderson, *Notes on the Folk Lore of the Northern Counties of England and the Borders* (London, 1866), p. 307.

36 Raymond A. Moody, Jr., *Life after Life: The investigation of a phenomenon – survival of bodily death* (New York, 1976), pp. 62, 63, 75; Robert Crookall, 'Out-of-the-body Experiences and Survival', in Canon J. D. Pearce-Higgins and Rev. G. Stanley Whitby (ed.), *Life, Death and Psychical Research* (London, 1973), p. 75; Eliade, *The Two and the One*, pp. 73, 183; Jung, *The Structure and Dynamics of the Psyche*, pp. 507–11.

37 Leroi-Gourhan, plate 74; Ivar Lissner, *Man, God and Magic* (London, 1961), pp. 280–82; Maringer, op. cit., pp. 61–62.

38 Grahame Clark, *The Stone Age Hunters* (London, 1967), pp. 64–66, 90; there was 'a deeply felt community between man and the animals he hunted for his food' (p. 86).

39 Cf. Joseph C. Birdsell, 'Some Predictions for the Pleistocene Based

on Equilibrium Systems among Recent Hunter-Gatherers', in Richard B. Lee and Irven DeVore (ed.), *Man the Hunter* (Chicago, 1968), pp. 233, 239.

40 Lissner, op. cit., pp. 160, 232, 249; Åke Hultkrantx, 'The Owner of the Animals in the Religion of the North American Indians', in Åke Hultkrantz (ed.), *The Supernatural Owners of Nature* (Stockholm, 1961), pp. 54–55.

41 Ivar Paulson, Åke Hultkrantz and Karl Jettmar, *Les Religions Arctiques et Finnoises* (Paris, 1965), pp. 86–88, 274, 379.

42 Emile Benveniste, *Le vocabulaire des institutions indo-européennes* (Paris, 1969), ii, pp. 99–105; Heinrich Wagner, 'Studies in the Origins of Early Celtic Civilisation', *Zeitschrift für Celtische Philologie* (Tübingen, 1970), xxxi, pp. 1–45; Fergus Kelly (ed.), *Audacht Morainn* (Dublin, 1976), p. xvii; Tomás Ó Cathasaigh (ed.), *The Heroic Biography of Cormac mac Airt* (Dublin, 1977), pp. 64–65. 'Thus we see that down the centuries this faith is rooted in man's ethical consciousness; he obeys rules because nature herself does so, and this obedience is at the bottom of the essential cohesion in nature and human society, and morality becomes a matter of inner compulsion in response to the operation of Rta in external nature. And, because all this is so, there is peace and harmony in nature. Man, too, in order to have peace and prosperity should observe some fixed principles and behave according to some accepted code of conduct.' (Sukumari Bhattacharji, *The Indian Theogony: A Comparative Study of Indian Mythology from the Vedas to the Puranas* (Cambridge, 1970), p. 30). Cf. also Chang, op. cit., pp. 33–35; David Carrasco, *Quetzalcoatl and the Irony of Empire: Myths and Prophecies in the Aztec Tradition* (Chicago, 1982), pp. 164–65. 'The essential religious insight is that the order of the world, the beauty of the world, and the mastery of evil, are all connected. This is because God is the source of order, as revealed in scientific discovery but also by artistic vision; moral order is one aspect of the general order on the basis of which and towards which God directs the world' (Meynell, *God and the World*, p. 131).

43 Eliade, *Le chamanisme*, pp. 426–29; Eugene Vinaver (ed.), *The Works of Sir Thomas Malory* (Oxford, 1948), p. 91. Cf. Kenneth Varty, 'On Birds and Beasts, "Death" and "Resurrection", Renewal and Reunion in Chrétien's Romances', in P. B. Grout *et al.* (ed.), *The Legend of Arthur in the Middle Ages* (Cambridge, 1983), pp. 206–8; C. J. Bleeker, *The Sacred Bridge: Researches into the Nature and Structure of Religion* (Leiden, 1963), pp. 180–89.

44 Otto, op. cit., pp. 7, 12–13; cf. the quotation by William James (op. cit., pp. 60–61).

45 Eliade, *The Two and the One*, p. 122; Otto, op. cit., pp. 70–71.

46 Grahame Clark and Stuart Piggott, *Prehistoric Societies* (London, 1965), p. 89.

47 J. D. P. Bolton, *Glory, Jest and Riddle* (London, 1973), p. 70; Bentley

(ed.), *William Blake's Writings*, p. 423. Cf. Berdyaev, op. cit., pp. 126–32.

48 Andreas Lommel, *Prehistoric and Primitive Man* (London, 1966), p. 19; Rachel Bromwich (ed.), *Trioedd Ynys Prydein: The Welsh Triads* (Cardiff, 1961), p. 473.

49 Ernest de Selincourt (ed.), *The Prelude, or Growth of a Poet's Mind by William Wordsworth* (Oxford, 1926), pp. 76–79; cf. Watson, op. cit., pp. 96, 102. In the *Phaedrus*, Plato envisaged four categories of madness, all gifts from God. The first three are prophetic inspiration, religious inspiration and poetic genius; while the fourth is the Love by which the immortal soul is winged for its passage to heaven (J. A. Stewart (ed.), *The Myths of Plato* (London, 1905), p. 306). Cf. Blake's view that, 'If it were not for the Poetic or Prophetic character the Philosophic and Experimental would soon be at the ratio of all things, and stand still, unable to do other than repeat the same dull round over again.' (Bentley, op. cit., p. 13).

50 Quoted in George Mills Harper (ed.), *Yeats and the Occult* (Canada, 1975), p. 102. Cf. Olney, op. cit., p. 156: 'Yeats and Jung were both excellent examples of a certain type . . . labelled the "shaman".'

51 For the texts, cf. James B. Pritchard (ed.), *Ancient Near Eastern Texts Relating to the Old Testament* (Princeton, 1969), pp. 52–57, 97–99, 107–9; also *A Vision of the Nether World* (pp. 109–10). Professor Tigay, however, interprets *puqqu* as referring to a game (Jeffrey H. Tigay, *The Evolution of the Gilgamesh Epic* (Philadelphia, 1982), p. 190). Rhythmical music and other typically shamanistic aids to ecstasy recur as the techniques of Old Testament prophets (David E. Aune, *Prophecy in Early Christianity and the Ancient Mediterranean World* (Grand Rapids, 1983), pp. 86–87); H. W. F. Saggs, *The Encounter with the Divine in Mesopotamia and Israel* (London, 1978), p. 166.

52 Lommel, *The World of the Early Hunters*, pp. 105, 145. For Orpheus as a shaman-figure, cf. M. L. West, *The Orphic Poems* (Oxford, 1983), pp. 4–7, 143–50, 259.

53 Alfred Guillaume, *Prophecy and Divination among the Hebrews and other Semites* (London, 1938), pp. 243–59; H. H. Rowley, *Prophecy and Religion in Ancient China and Israel* (London, 1956), pp. 4–5, 14–15.

54 Cf. Sir Ifor Williams, *Lectures on Early Welsh Poetry* (Dublin, 1944), p. 7; Calvert Watkins, 'Indo-European Metrics and Archaic Irish Verse', *Celtica* (Dublin, 1963), vi, pp. 213–16; *Zeitschrift für Celtische Philologie*, xxxi, pp. 46–57. Professor Wagner's discussion is of enormous value, but his attempt to dissociate the 'wildness' element from *Wotan* rests on too many adjustments of accepted meanings to carry conviction. Cf. the parallel Greek *mantis*, 'a seer', and *mainomai*, 'I rage' (ibid., p. 47), and Professor J. E. Caerwyn Williams' remarks ('The Court Poet in Medieval Ireland', *The Proceedings of the British Academy* (London, 1971), lvii, pp. 22–23). There appears to be in

reality a physiological relationship between breathing patterns and poetry (Lieberman, op. cit., pp. 109–10).

55 Thomas F. O'Rahilly, *Early Irish History and Mythology* (Dublin, 1957), pp. 318–25. An Irish verse contains an account of a druid who detaches his spirit (*fiss*) from his body, despatching it up into the high clouds, where it reaches 'a pure well in which there is the equipment of a band of hundreds of [Otherworld] women' (James Carney, 'The Earliest Bran Material', in John J. O'Meara and Bernd Naumann (ed.), *Latin Script and Letters A.D. 400–900* (Leiden, 1976), pp. 182, 184).

56 Marie-Louise Sjoestedt, *Gods and Heroes of the Celts* (London, 1949), pp. 38–40; Roger Sherman Loomis, *Wales and the Arthurian Legend* (Cardiff, 1956), pp. 135, 156–58; P. L. Henry, 'The Caldron of Poesy', *Studia Celtica* (Cardiff, 1979/80), xiv–xv, pp. 114–28; Liam Breatnach, 'The Caldron of Poesy', *Ériu* (Dublin, 1981), xxxii, pp. 45–93. The Kogi of the Sierra Nevada believe that the Universal Mother possesses nine daughters, 'each one representing a certain quality of arable soil', reflecting in turn the nine stages of the cosmic egg (Mircea Eliade, *The Quest: History and Meaning in Religion* (Chicago, 1969), p. 140).

57 *Zeitschrift für Celtische Philologie*, xxxi, pp. 56–57; cf. Eliade, *Le Chamanisme*, pp. 350–52. For the Celtic cult of the head, cf. Anne Ross, *Pagan Celtic Britain: Studies in Iconography and Tradition* (London, 1967), pp. 61–126. In Indo-European mythology the Godhead 'authorizes' the poet's words, which thereby achieve cosmic reality (Benveniste, op. cit., ii, pp. 35–42).

58 E. O. G. Turville-Petre, *Myth and Religion of the North* (London, 1964), pp. 35–41; Eliade, *Le Chamanisme*, pp. 342–48.

59 Proinsias MacCana, *Celtic Mythology* (Feltham, 1970), p. 29.

60 Hugh G. Evelyn-White (ed.), *Hesiod: The Homeric Hymns and Homerica* (London, 1914), pp. 364, 366, 368–76, 396–98, 404; cf. also Sir James George Frazer (ed.), *Apollodorus: The Library* (London, 1921), ii, pp. 5–11. For the significance of the cattle-stealing motif in Indo-European mythology, cf. Leroy A. Campbell, *Mithraic Iconography and Ideology* (Leiden, 1968), pp. 250–52.

61 Cf. Eliade, *Myth and Reality*, pp. 26–28; Joan Halifax, *Shaman: The wounded healer* (London, 1982), pp. 29, 38. The rôle of the shamanistic function is to carry initiates back to the beginnings (Nevill Drury, *The Shaman and the Magician: Journeys between the worlds* (London, 1982), pp. 9–10).

62 Joseph L. Henderson, 'Ancient myths and modern man', in *Man and his Symbols*, p. 151; Paul Radin, *The Trickster: A Study in American Indian Mythology* (London, 1956), pp. 195, 196; cf. Otto, op. cit., pp. 202–3. For Odin and Loki as Tricksters, cf. H. R. Ellis Davidson, 'Loki and Saxo's Hamlet', in Paul V. A. Williams (ed.), *The Fool and the Trickster: Studies in Honour of Enid Welsford* (Cambridge, 1979), pp. 3–11.

63 Radin, op. cit., pp. 203–4, 207.

64 Evelyn-White, op. cit., p. 404.

65 Cf. Paulson, Hultkrantz and Jettmar, op. cit., pp. 75–76, 170–71.

66 Bhattacharji, op. cit., pp. 33–34; E. O. James, *The Ancient Gods: The History and Diffusion of Religion in the Ancient Near East and the Eastern Mediterranean* (London, 1960), p. 52; Alain Daniélou, *Hindu Polytheism* (London, 1964), p. 192. Shiva's manifestation as Lord of Beasts is the Herdsman, Pasupati (ibid., pp. 208–210; MacCana, op. cit., p. 38).

67 Beatrice Laura Goff, *Symbols of Prehistoric Mesopotamia* (Yale, 1963), figure 276. For a similar Master of Animals in Minoan Crete, cf. Martin P. Nilsson, *The Minoan-Mycenean Religion and its Survival in Greek Religion* (Lund, 1968), pp. 357–68, 513 (identified by C. Kerényi with Dionysos (*Dionysos: Archetypal Image of Indestructible Life* (London, 1976), p. 81)) Pritchard, op. cit., p. 79.

68 Evelyn-White, op. cit., pp. 443–47. Cf. the Rheims stele, where the identification is disputed (John Ferguson, *The Religions of the Roman Empire* (London, 1970), plate 33.)

69 Henderson, op. cit., pp. 213–14.

70 Evelyn-White, op. cit., p. 444; Alexandre Micha (ed.), *Robert de Boron: Merlin; roman du XIIIe siècle* (Geneva, 1980), p. 51. 'The Great Pan, who had been revealed to the natural man of antiquity, was driven to take refuge in the uttermost depths of nature. A gulf now separated the natural man from the man who had entered upon the path of Redemption.' (Nicolas Berdyaev, *The Meaning of History* (London, 1936), p. 115.)

71 F. M. Bergounioux and Joseph Goetz, *Prehistoric and Primitive Religions* (London, 1965), p. 100; John Rhŷs, *Lectures on the Origin and Growth of Religion as Illustrated by Celtic Heathendom* (London, 1888), pp. 97–98. Margaret Murray (*The God of the Witches* (London, 1933), pp. 13–38) lists some useful evidence, which her conclusions have wildly outstripped. Seth was not only the archetypal Trickster of Egyptian mythology (H. te Velde, *Seth, God of Confusion: A Study of his Role in Egyptian Mythology and Religion* (Leiden, 1977), pp. 7, 56–57, 84), but became the personification of evil (ibid., pp. 11, 66–67) and demon of death (pp. 93–94); *i.e.* the Devil (pp. 142–43). For the Devil as lord of this world, cf. Jeffrey Burton Russell, *The Devil: Perceptions of Evil from Antiquity to Primitive Christianity* (Cornell, 1977), pp. 169–70. Jung envisaged the duality as presaged in the nature of deity: 'Yahweh . . . is everything in its totality; therefore, among other things, he is total justice, and also its total opposite' (*Psychology and Religion: West and East*, p. 372) – a concept in accordance with scriptural authority (H. W. F. Saggs, op. cit., pp. 105–13; Russell, op. cit., p. 251).

72 Guthrie, op. cit., pp. 248–51; Buxton, op. cit., p. 388. The essence of Gnosticism is the struggle to reverse 'le péché d'une entité divine,

péché qui établit l'existence de ce monde et de l'homme,' (Ugo Bianchi, 'Perspectives de la récherche sur les origins du gnosticisme', *The Origins of Gnosticism* (Leiden, 1967), p. 7; cf. idem, 'Péché originel et péché "antecédent"', *Revue de l'histoire des religions* (Paris, 1960), clxx, pp. 117–26; idem; 'L'orphisme a existé', *Mélanges d'histoire offerts a Henri-Charles Puech* (Paris, 1974), p. 136; cf. Bleeker, *The Sacred Bridge*, pp. 138–40. The dualist myth forms a strikingly recurrent theme in Rider Haggard's novels, notably *Nada the Lily* and *Eric Brighteyes*.

73 Ugo Bianchi, 'Seth, Osiris et l'ethnographie', *Revue de l'histoire des religions* (1971), clxxi, pp. 119–27; H. H. Rowley, *The Old Testament and Modern Study: A Generation of Discovery and Research* (Oxford, 1951), p. 94; Ugo Bianchi, 'Prometheus, der titanische Trickster', *Paideuma, Mitteilungen zur Kulturkunde* (1961), vii, pp. 414–37; H. R. Ellis Davidson, *Scandinavian Mythology* (London, 1982), pp. 104–5 (Kirk, op. cit., p. 207, notes Loki's likeness to Prometheus. His homosexuality, slaying of Baldur, etc., also bring him close to Seth); Máire MacNeill, *The Festival of Lughnasa: A Study of the Survival of the Celtic Festival of the Beginning of Harvest* (Oxford, 1962), p. 429; Ugo Bianchi, 'Der demiurgische Trickster und die Religionsethnologie', *Paideuma*, vii, pp. 335–44.

74 Cf. Olof Pettersson, 'The Spirit of the Woods: Outlines of a Study of the Ideas about Forest Guardians in African Mythology and Folklore', in Åke Hultkrantz (ed.), *The Supernatural Owners of Nature*, pp. 101–11; Walter Krickeberg *et al.*, *Pre-Columbian American Religions* (London, 1968), pp. 258–69. Seth's connection with the desert and its denizens is clear (*Revue de l'histoire des religions*, clxxix, pp. 124–25; J. Gwyn Griffiths, *The Conflict of Horus and Seth from Egyptian and Classical Sources* (Liverpool, 1960), pp. 71, 98, 145. Loki was father of wolves (Turville-Petre, op. cit., p. 130), and Hermes was appointed Lord of Beasts by Zeus (Evelyn-White, op. cit., p. 404).

75 Radin, op. cit., pp. 196, 203, 211.

76 Buxton, op. cit., pp. 23–26.

77 Lienhardt, op. cit., pp. 171–206.

78 Evelyn-White, op. cit., p. 116; Apollodorus (ed. Frazer), i, p. 52. The shaft mentioned by Hesiod has also been interpreted as a post or pillar to which the god was bound, 'perhaps originally one of the pillars of heaven' (Martin Hengel, *Crucifixion: In the ancient world and the folly of the message of the cross* (Philadelphia, 1977), p. 11).

79 Sir James George Frazer, *Myths of the Origin of Fire* (London, 1930), pp. 128–29; cf. the parallel story on pp. 127–28.

80 Cf. Bergounioux and Gertz, op. cit., pp. 133–34; Radin, op. cit., p. 166; Paulson, Hultkrantz and Jettmar, op. cit., pp. 359–60.

81 Gösta Kock's attempt to reduce the *Heilbringer* to the status of a 'mere' 'supreme master of the animals', and to deny his heavenly mission, appears misguided ('A Few Reflections Concerning the *Heilbringer*

and the Guardian of the Animals'; *The Supernatural Owners of Nature*, pp. 65–71). Apart from the evidence cited in this chapter indicating the contrary, there is no doubt that the rôles of Saviour and Guardian of Beasts overlapped (notably in the Trickster-figure), and Christ and Orpheus 'parallel the archetype of the man of nature' in the form of harmoniser of the natural order and Good Shepherd (cf. Jung, *Man and his Symbols*, pp. 143–45).

82 So Aeschylus, quoted by J. D. P. Bolton, *Aristeas of Proconnesus* (Oxford, 1962), p. 49. Ararat was the Centre from which the world expanded in the Noachian story of the Flood.

83 Jung, *The Structure and Dynamics of the Psyche*, p. 42. (Cf. the spear of Pepi, ground when he 'was between the thighs of Khent-Merti' (E. A. Wallis Budge, *Osiris and the Egyptian Resurrection* (London, 1911), ii, p. 326).) Leroi-Gourhan, op. cit., plate 74. For the spear as emblem of lightning and emanation of the deity, cf. Cook, op. cit., ii, pp. 704–12; and for its significance in Greece as *axis mundi* and 'way up' and 'way down' between earth and heaven, cf. E. A. S. Butterworth's brilliant study, *The Tree at the Navel of the Earth* (Berlin, 1970), pp. 62, 117, 119.

84 Robert Hertz, *Death and The Right Hand* (Aberdeen, 1960), pp. 79–81.

85 Cf. W. J. Gruffydd, *Math vab Mathonwy* (Cardiff, 1928), pp. 366–75; Jung, *Psychology and Religion: West and East*, p. 406.

86 'The wilderness was the scene of John's ministry, but for Jesus it was the scene of temptation, not ministry. For his ministry he turned his back on the wilderness . . . and proclaimed the good news of the kingdom of God in the populous and fertile region of Galilee' (F. F. Bruce, 'The Date and Character of Mark', in Ernst Bammel and C. F. D. Moule (ed.), *Jesus and the Politics of His Day* (Cambridge, 1984), p. 74). 'Again, the devil taketh him up into an exceeding high mountain, and showeth him all the kingdoms of the world, and the glory of them'. My friend Michael Scott points out that the implication of this verse is surely that Jesus has ascended the World Mountain, from which alone would He have been enabled to survey the world in its entirety.

87 Radin, op. cit., p. 189; Jung, *Man and his Symbols*, p. 113. Kurt Rudolph, *Gnosis: the Nature and History of an Ancient Religion* (Edinburgh, 1983), pp. 165, 168, 170.

88 Jung, *Psychology and Religion: West and East*, pp. 400–409; cf. Berdyaev, *The Meaning of History*, pp. 33–38; idem, *The Destiny of Man*, pp. 25–26, 33–34; A. R. Peacocke, *Creation and the World of Science* (Oxford, 1979), pp. 212–13, 306.

89 'Of course there are some writings so clear in their integrity, and so transparent in certain respects, that within their proper realm they could almost be described as carrying their own self-ratification with them; and I think that the Gospels, when construed for certain essential

purposes, must be regarded as belonging to this class.' (Herbert Butterfield, *Christianity and History* (London, 1949), pp. 124–25). Cf. A. E. Harvey's masterly *Jesus and the Constraints of History* (London, 1982).

90 *Psychology and Religion: West and East*, p. 409. Thus Professor Carrasco suggests that the famous encounter between Moctezuma and Cortes in 1519 partook of the nature of what he terms 'mythic drama' (Carrasco, op. cit., pp. 191–204). In the Middle Ages, 'The collective memory of events that have really taken place is transformed, as time goes by, into myth, depriving these events of their individual features and retaining only those which fit into the model imposed by the myth; events are reduced to categories, and individuals to archetypes'. In turn, 'Re-enactment of the myth "cut off" mundane time and reinstated mythological time' (A. J. Gurevich, *Categories of Medieval Culture* (London, 1985), pp. 98–99).

91 An abstract conception of sovereignty as much as political reality. Cf. the song *Vnbeinyaeth Prydein* in the Laws of Hywel Dda (Melville Richards (ed.), *Cyfreithiau Hywel Dda: O Lawsygrif Coleg yr Iesu Rhydychen LVII* (Cardiff, 1957), p. 15), and the discussion by Brynley F. Roberts, 'Geoffrey of Monmouth and Welsh Historical Tradition', *Nottingham Mediaeval Studies* (Nottingham, 1976), xx, pp. 31–33.

92 MacCana, op. cit., pp. 27–29. Cf. also the Greek goddess Ananke, whose 'arms extended throughout the universe and touching its extremities', and whose spindle turning in her lap is the cosmic axis (West, op. cit., pp. 194–97); Otto J. Brendel, *Symbolism of the Shere: A Contribution to the History of Earlier Greek Philosophy* (Leiden, 1977), pp. 50–69.

93 Cf. Mary Douglas, *Purity and Danger: An analysis of concepts of pollution and taboo* (London, 1966), pp. 94–95; J. Loth, *Contributions à l'étude des Romans de la Table Ronde* (Paris, 1912), pp. 57–58).

94 Rachel Bromwich (ed.), *Trioedd Ynys Prydein: The Welsh Triads* (Cardiff, 1961), p. 474; 2nd edition, p. 560.

95 C. G. Jung, *Psychology and Alchemy* (London, 1968), pp. 333–39. 'The sea is the symbol of the collective unconscious, because unfathomed depths lie concealed beneath its reflecting surface' (ibid., pp. 48–49).

96 U. Cassuto, *The Goddess Anath: Canaanite Epics of the Patriarchal Age* (Jerusalem, 1971), pp. 71–75; John Day, *God's conflict with the dragon and the sea: Echoes of a Canaanite myth in the Old Testament* (Cambridge, 1985), pp. 21–27. The words for 'death' and 'sea' share a common Indo-European root and similarity of concept (A. Smythe Palmer, *Babylonian Influence on the Bible and Popular Beliefs: "Tehom and Tiamat," "Hades and Satan."* (London, 1897), pp. 41–48).

Appendix

1 Thomas Stephens, *The Literature of the Kymry* (London, 1876), pp. 224–25; Edward Anwyl, *Celtic Religion in Pre-Christian Times* (London, 1906), p. 61.

2 Ifor Williams, 'Gwyllon, Geilt, Ŵyll', *The Bulletin of the Board of Celtic Studies* (Cardiff, 1924), i, pp. 228–34; J. Lloyd-Jones, *Geirfa Barddoniaeth Gynnar Gymraeg* (Cardiff, 1931–63), pp. 738–39.

3 A. O. H. Jarman, 'Hwimleian, Chwibleian', *The Bulletin of the Board of Celtic Studies* (1955), xvi, pp. 71–76; idem, 'A Note on the Possible Welsh Derivation of *Viviane*', *Gallica: Essays presented to J. Heywood Thomas by colleagues, pupils and friends* (Cardiff, 1969), pp. 1–12.

4 *The Bulletin of the Board of Celtic Studies*, xvi, p. 73.

5 J. Gwenogvryn Evans (ed.), *The Black Book of Carmarthen* (Pwllheli, 1906), p. 51.

6 Did the 140 go mad, take themselves off to the *Coed Celyddon*, and promptly die *en masse*? If they died naturally, at irregular intervals years later, what is the point of asserting that they 'perished' in the context of the poem? According to the *Afallennau* they were still around 30 years later.

7 Kuno Meyer, 'The Irish Mirabilia in the Norse "Speculum Regale"', *Ériu: The Journal of the Irish School of Learning, Dublin* (London, 1908), iv, pp. 11–12.

8 P. L. Henry, *The Early English and Irish Lyric* (London, 1966), pp. 140–44.

9 J. G. O'Keefe (ed.), *Buile Suibhne (The Frenzy of Suibhne) being the Adventures of Suibhne Geilt* (London, 1913), pp. 22–23.

10 Cf. Welsh *gwawd*, 'song, poetry', which is cognate with Latin *vates*, 'prophet, poet' and with Anglo-Saxon *wóth*, 'sound, melody', '*wóth-cræft*', 'art of poetry', and *wódnes*, 'madness' (Sir Ifor Williams, *Lectures on Early Welsh Poetry* (Dublin, 1944), p. 7).

11 Egerton G. B. Phillimore, 'A Fragment from Hengwrt MS. No. 202', *Y Cymmrodor* (London, 1886), vii, p. 154; J. Gwenogvryn Evans (ed.), *The Poetry in the Red Book of Hergest* (Llanbedrog, 1911), pp. 2, 5.

12 *Y Cymmrodor*, vii, p. 117; John J. Parry, 'Celtic Tradition and the Vita Merlini', *The Philological Quarterly* (Iowa, 1925), iv, p. 198.

13 Louise Bäckman and Åke Hultkrantz, *Studies in Lapp Shamanism* (Stockholm, 1978), pp. 42–43; Rafael Karsten, *The Religion of the Samek: Ancient Beliefs and Cults of the Scandinavian and Finnish Lapps* (Leiden, 1955), pp. 58, 85. For the 'mountain virgin', cf. ibid., p. 13.

14 Ibid., pp. 106–7.

Note (cf. note 5, page 329)

It has been suggested that some of the early Welsh shape-shifting (tenth-century?) poetry derives largely from the perverse ingenuity of mediaeval poets attempting 'to enhance the prestige of the traditional bardic order . . . by being deliberately esoteric in style and content . . .'[1] In the case of *Cad Goddeu*, however, one may compare an initiatory ritual undergone by Cyprian of Antioch in the third century A.D. on the slopes of Mount Olympus.

'In this home of the gods he was taught the meaning of musical notes and sounds. He had a vision of tree-trunks and herbs of divine potency. He witnessed the succession of seasons and the difference of days, the changing spirits that caused the former and the opposing influences that determined the latter. He beheld choruses of *daímones* chanting, warring, lying in ambush, deceiving and confounding each other. He saw too the phalanx of each several god and goddess. After sundown he fed on fruits (not meat). And, generally speaking, he was initiated into the decay and birth of herbs, trees, and bodies.'[2]

This initiation, which it has been suggested involved 'a partial training as a seer'[3], reads in part like a paraphrase of *Cad Goddeu*, and suggests that the poem may reflect similar rites – likewise performed on a holy mountain?

[1]Patrick Sims-Williams, 'The Evidence for vernacular Irish literary influence on early mediaeval Welsh literature', in Dorothy Whitelock *et al.* (ed.), *Ireland in Early Mediaeval Europe: Studies in Memory of Kathleen Hughes* (Cambridge, 1982), p. 243.

[2]Arthur Bernard Cook, *Zeus: A Study in Ancient Religion* (Cambridge, 1914–40), i, pp. 110–111. For the belief that Zeus created men from trees, and the siting of his cult in an oak-grove, cf. ibid., pp. 364–65; iii, p. 481.

[3]John Ferguson, *The Religions of the Roman Empire* (London, 1970), pp. 180–81.

Index

ANATOLY MARCHENKO

MY TESTIMONY

'This will remain an outstanding document of the Soviet human rights movement'

The Guardian

Anatoly Marchenko died on 10th September 1986 at the age of forty-eight, having spent most of his adult life in jails and labour camps. His testimony was smuggled to the West and first published in 1969. It is the harrowing story of the life of a man whose death removed one of the last outstanding figures of the Soviet dissident movement.

'An extraordinarily important book . . . Perhaps not since Dostoyevsky's HOUSE OF THE DEAD has there been such a totally realistic, detailed, factual and yet profoundly compassionate and human account of Russian prison and camp life . . . MY TESTIMONY is a searchlight cutting through the murk of the real Russia'

Daily Telegraph

'Marchenko has in common with Solzhenitsyn a trait of dropping telling details in a deadpan way . . . His testimony is a stark, impressive work . . . He has told the truth and sacrificed himself for that truth'

Sunday Telegraph

BERNARD LEVIN

HANNIBAL'S FOOTSTEPS

In the winter of 218 BC, Hannibal marched to war across the Alps with 60,000 infantry, 9,000 cavalry and 37 elephants. His journey 'captured the imagination of the world'.

2,000 years later, Bernard Levin retraces his hero's steps. With great reluctance he abandoned the idea of taking elephants. The story of his travels is a marvellous blend of history, travel, anecdote and personal philosophy.

'The benign, inquiring spirit of ENTHUSIASMS is still present in HANNIBAL'S FOOTSTEPS, still enjoying and seeking something "beyond the next mountain"'
Bel Mooney in the Listener

'Who could be a more amusing or provocative cicerone on a journey from the Rhône across the Alps towards Turin, following Hannibal's legendary elephantine dash of 218 BC into Italy?'
Peter Jones in The Times

'He had a ball, and so will the reader'
Daily Express

sceptre

A. ALVAREZ

OFFSHORE

Since 1969, when oil was first struck in the North Sea, Britain has become one of the world's major oil producers. We now take for granted the science fiction high technology which allows men to work in some of the most brutal conditions on earth, but how the treasure is extracted from far beneath the sea bed remains a mystery. Al Alvarez travelled offshore and talked to divers, helicopter pilots, oil engineers, crane drivers and roustabouts, geologists, administrators and business-men. His evocative account of life on the stormy 61st parallel paints a unique picture of a brave new world and the men who work there.

'Exciting as well as informative'

The Observer

'Alvarez' sturdy enthusiasm is to be prized'

The Sunday Times

'OFFSHORE reads spot on as a true chronicle of one of the monumental endeavours of our times'

Melvyn Bragg in Punch

'Alvarez captures the sensations and rhythms of North Sea life . . . his strength is that he can build up a rapport with men such as these, penetrate the laid-back image and catch the emotions behind the mask'

The Scotsman

Current and forthcoming titles from Sceptre

A. ALVAREZ

OFFSHORE

ANATOLY MARCHENKO

MY TESTIMONY

BERNARD LEVIN

**IN THESE TIMES
ENTHUSIASMS
CONDUCTED TOUR
HANNIBAL'S FOOTSTEPS**

BOOKS OF DISTINCTION